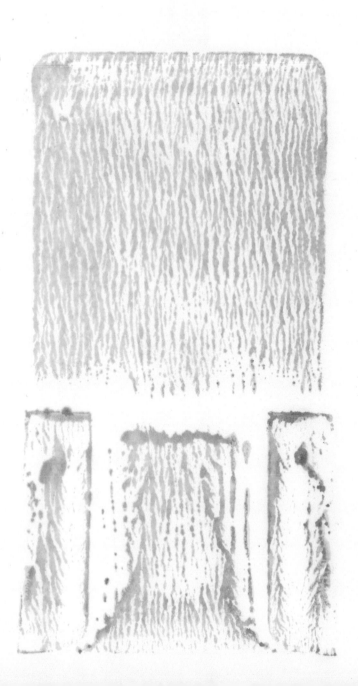

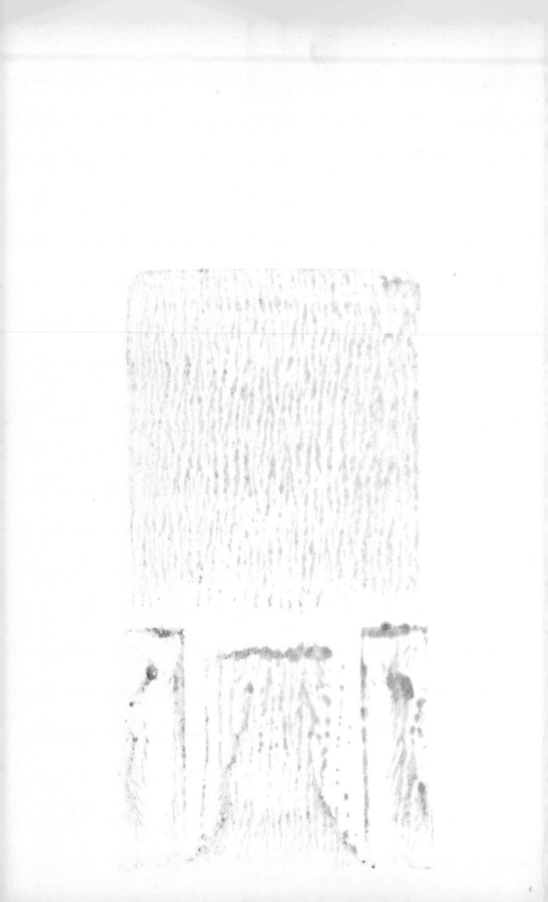

YALE STUDIES IN ENGLISH

Benjamin Christie Nangle, Editor

VOLUME 158

SIDNEY'S ARCADIA

A Map of Arcadia:
Sidney's Romance in Its Tradition
by Walter R. Davis

The Old Arcadia
by Richard A. Lanham

New Haven and London, Yale University Press
1965

Library of Congress catalog card number: 65-11184

Published with assistance from
the Kingsley Trust Association Publication Fund
established by the Scroll and Key Society
of Yale College.

Contents

A MAP OF ARCADIA: Sidney's Romance in Its Tradition

by Walter R. Davis

FOR YOLANDA

Acknowledgments

This book began as a dissertation submitted to the faculty of Yale University for the degree of Doctor of Philosophy, and, I am sure, bears more traces of its origin than I can hope to obliterate. An early draft of Chapter 5 appeared in *Studies in Philology* 57; to the editors of that journal my thanks for permission to use parts of it are due.

Foremost among the debts I have incurred during its composition is the one I owe to Louis L. Martz for arousing my enthusiasm for pastoral in the first place, for guiding the dissertation with wisdom and great patience, and for sustaining me with his friendship both during its composition and afterwards. To William R. Bowden I owe thanks for several pertinent criticisms in the early stages of writing, and to Ferdinando D. Maurino for help with the Italian. To Raphael Alan Pollock I owe thanks for threatening to read my manuscript at several points, thereby frightening me into revision. Finally, I wish to thank the editors of Yale Studies in English for their agonizing care of this book, and especially Davis P. Harding for his painstaking criticism and his moderately successful attempts to save me from many blunders.

I am grateful to the following for permission to reprint copyrighted material: Basil Blackwell and Mott, Ltd., publishers of M. J. Tooley's translation of Bodin's *Six Books of the Commonwealth*; the University of Missouri Press, publishers of Sears Jayne's translation of *Marsilio Ficino's Commentary on Plato's Symposium*; and Oxford University Press, publishers of F. M. Cornford's translation of Plato's *Republic*.

W. R. D.

Notre Dame, Indiana
March 1965

Introduction

This is a study of the plot of Sir Philip Sidney's *Arcadia*.

Such a study faces many difficulties, not the least of which is Sidney's demand that the gallant reader stalk over almost five hundred folio pages in search of plot. But there is a special difficulty facing plot study of this book, above and beyond that of other long and involved books, and it must be dealt with in some fashion before one even starts; that is the uncertain state of the text. The book we have received from the sixteenth century is the product of one major revision and one piece of drastic editorial surgery. The reader therefore feels, at some moments, that he is reading several *Arcadias* at one time—and there are, in fact, three recognized separate *Arcadias*. There is the Old *Arcadia*, a first draft written between 1577 and 1580 which, according to the recent census by William A. Ringler in his definitive edition of Sidney's poems, exists in nine manuscript copies;[1] one of them,

---

1. *The Poems of Sir Philip Sidney* (Oxford, 1962), bibliography, pp. 525–29. The MS copies are: Jesus College, Queen's College, Davies, Phillips, Clifford, Ashburnham, St. John's, Bodleian, and Helmington (this last discovered while Ringler's edition was in proof; see his Preface, p. x); a tenth MS, the Lee, contains poems only.

the Clifford MS, was printed by Albert Feuillerat in 1926 as volume 4 of Sidney's works, and a critical edition collating them all is forthcoming from Miss Jean Robertson. Then there is the New *Arcadia*, an elaborate but incomplete revision of the first two-and-one-half books made by Sidney around 1584, printed in quarto by William Ponsonbie in 1590, and reprinted by Feuillerat in 1912.[2] Finally we have the *Arcadia*, consisting of the revision together with the last three books of the unrevised version, published in 1593 in folio under the direction of the Countess of Pembroke, and reprinted thirteen times within a century after that date.

The Old *Arcadia* is a relatively short and simple book. Its uncluttered plot begins *ab ovo* and proceeds, in orderly fashion, through the phases of a five-act Renaissance drama. What incidental episodes exist are relegated to the four "Eclogues" or pastoral interludes that separate each of the five "Bookes or Actes." The style, like the plot, is patterned but sparsely ornamented.

The nature of Sidney's revision in the New *Arcadia* can best be described as elaboration, a process that took place on many levels: elaboration in characterization,[3] in the presentation of ideas,[4] in style,[5] but most notably in plot. Sidney changed his plot proper very little; the only alterations of note are the new scene that begins the book, the meeting of Pyrocles and Amphialus at the riverside in Book II, and Musidorus' fall from favor at the beginning of Book III. He did, however, change his manner of presenting it considerably by reducing the importance of the narrator, by beginning *in medias res*, and by using flashbacks. And he made really sizable additions, which doubled the bulk of the

2. As Volume 1 of *The Complete Works of Sir Philip Sidney* (4 vols. Cambridge, 1912–26).

3. See R. W. Zandvoort, *Sidney's Arcadia: A Comparison between the Two Versions* (Amsterdam, 1929), ch. 2; Zandvoort praises especially Sidney's subtler handling of Pamela and Philoclea.

4. *Ibid.*, ch. 3.

5. *Ibid.*, ch. 4. See also Mario Praz, "Sidney's Original Arcadia," *London Mercury*, 15 (1927), 511: "Almost every sentence of the first draft has been subjected to a process of stucco decoration."

book and changed its character completely, in the form of thirteen episodes not integral to the plot. One of them is the captivity episode of Book III (itself longer than the original Book III), a complex of moral temptation, tragedy, and medieval siege. To Book I Sidney added the amorous episodes of Argalus and Parthenia, Amphialus and Helen, and Phalantus' tourney. And he wove nine short stories derived from the heroes' pre-Arcadian exploits into the fabric of Book II. The most striking effect of all these additions is, of course, complication; a simple romance became a bulky work that "is at once a romance and a treatise." [6] It also became a more serious work, for the additional episodes, especially the captivity episode's "supreme test of character," [7] shifted the emphasis from the standard conflict between love and friendship to matters of love, politics, ethics, and especially religion. Certainly Fulke Greville's assertion that the revised version was "fitter to be printed than the first" seems just,[8] if we accept his statement of Sidney's intentions, for it is the New *Arcadia* that offers "morall Images, and Examples, (as directing threds) to guide every man through the confused *Labyrinth* of his own desires, and life." [9]

The *Arcadia* that appeared in folio in 1593 carried this prefatory claim:

> The disfigured face, gentle Reader, wherewith this worke not long since appeared to the common view, moved that noble Lady, to whose Honour consecrated, to whose protection it was committed, to take in hand the wiping away those spottes wherewith the beauties therof were unworthely blemished. But as often in repairing a ruinous house, the mending of some olde part occasioneth the making of some new: so here her honourable labour begonne in correcting the faults, ended in supplying the defectes; by the view of what was ill done guided to the consideration of what was not done . . . as much as was intended,

6. Zandvoort, p. 120.

7. E. M. W. Tillyard, *The English Epic and Its Background* (London, 1954), p. 298.

8. Letter to Sir Francis Walsingham, quoted by Zandvoort, p. 2.

9. *The Life of the Renowned Sir Philip Sidney*, ed. Nowell Smith (Oxford, 1907), p. 223.

3

the conclusion, not the perfection of *Arcadia:* and that no further then the Authours own writings, or knowen determinations
could direct.

This is a composite text, consisting of the New *Arcadia* with some
slight revisions (chiefly in the arrangements of the Eclogues)
and, after a gap, the last three books of the Old *Arcadia.* The
latter was altered, whether by Sidney's own hand or another's,
most notably by a paragraph of transition at the beginning, the
omission of Musidorus' attempted rape, and a consequent change
from condemnation to irony in the opening sentence of Book IV.[1]
No attempt to close the gap between the two halves was made
until the fifth edition in 1621, which contained a brief and satisfactory link supplied by Sir William Alexander.

We have no satisfactory text for the critic or the literary
historian to examine, but only a first draft, a fragmentary revision,
and an awkward composite. But it seems to me that the only
sensible response to this problem is to make a choice with some
slight boldness and considerable resignation. It is true that the gap
in the middle of the 1593 folio makes it an imperfect text; and we
can only offer conjectures about the extent to which it actually
conforms to Sidney's "knowen determinations" rather than his
sister's or another's. Nevertheless, it is this version of Sidney's
book that I have chosen for detailed study, for it is as complete
a version of Sidney's masterpiece as exists in our imperfect world,
"the conclusion, not the perfection of *Arcadia.*" And, as C. S.
Lewis has asserted, it is the version that most concerns the literary
historian:

> To him 'the *Arcadia*' must mean the composite text of 1593:
> it, and it alone, is the book which lived; Shakespeare's book,
> Charles I's book, Milton's book, Lamb's book, our own book
> long before we heard of textual criticism. If the recovery of the
> cancelled version is to prevent our looking steadily at the text
> which really affected the English mind, it will have been a
> disaster.[2]

1. For other minor alterations see Zandvoort, pp. 27–40. Ringler (p. 378) argues
that Sidney himself was responsible for the major revisions.
2. *English Literature in the Sixteenth Century, Excluding Drama* (Oxford,
1954), p. 333.

Introduction

At first glance, the composite *Arcadia* seems a morass of incidents and characters without plan or meaning (especially if we are unable to shake from our minds the expectation of chaos which our recently acquired uncertainties about the text produce). A second and steady look, however, reveals an incredible sense of order in this book, not merely a perceptible narrative line, but a network of parallel and contrasting scenes and actions, of intricate thematic analogues, of systems of thought presented and modified, as well.

The lines of plot seem to have far less to do with epic than with the tradition from which *Arcadia* emerged, pastoral romance. This realization has led me to entertain severe doubts about the current assumption that *Arcadia* is "an epic poem in prose,"[3] and instead to entertain the possibility that it is only a very highly developed pastoral romance—this in spite of the great apparent differences between its characters, atmosphere, and tone and those of the best known pastoral works (though we must take into account some of the unusual Renaissance developments in the romance, such as the Heliodoran elements in *Diana enamorada* or the Platonic in *Astrée*). Therefore I have attempted to place it in a pastoral context in order to see how much light this tradition (instead of the epic) can shed on its meaning and true nature.

I might liken the task of analyzing *Arcadia* to a geographer's task in describing a country, first placing it in relation to the surrounding terrain, then indicating its boundaries, pointing out its main topographical features, and finally filling in the details. In constructing my own verbal map of Sidney's "speaking picture," I shall begin with a sketch of the pastoral romances before Sidney, and then show briefly the main debts and resemblances of Sidney's work to them. In my discussion of *Arcadia* itself, I shall start with a definition of its main plot, and then proceed to the details of its major pastoral subplot and all of the minor chivalric episodes, ending with a consideration of the plot as viewed

---

3. See especially Edwin Greenlaw, "Sidney's *Arcadia* as an Example of Elizabethan Allegory," *Kittredge Anniversary Papers* (Boston, 1913), pp. 327–37; Kenneth Orne Myrick, *Sir Philip Sidney as a Literary Craftsman*, Harvard Studies in English, 14 (Cambridge, 1935), ch. IV; and Tillyard, *The English Epic and Its Background*, ch. 10.

5

in the large political context indicated here and there in its course. Finally, I shall attempt in my conclusion to prove that *Arcadia* exploits the themes and techniques of pastoral romance more fully than any other work of the sixteenth century.

That some such division of the task corresponds to the perceptions of Sidney's contemporaries is attested by Gabriel Harvey, who indicated the main points of interest in the landscape thus:

> Will you needes have a written Pallace of Pleasure, or rather a printed Court of Honour? Read the Countesse of Pembrookes Arcadia, a gallant Legendary, full of pleasurable accidents and proffitable discourses; for three thinges especially very notable— for amorous Courting (he was young in yeeres), for sage counselling (he was ripe in judgement), and for valorous fighting (his soveraine profession was Armes); and delightfull pastime by way of Pastorall exercises may passe for the fourth. He that will Loove, let him learne to loove of him that will teach him to Live.[4]

4. *Pierce's Supererogation* in G. Gregory Smith, *Elizabethan Critical Essays* (2 vols. Oxford, 1904), 2, 263.

1. The Growth and Structure of Pastoral Romance

"SELECTED POEMS"

When Jacopo Sannazaro set out to write his *Arcadia* at the beginning of the sixteenth century (and thus to "create" the Renaissance pastoral romance, as he, with his intense consciousness of innovation, probably felt), his intention was to recreate the world of the classical pastoral eclogue in the vulgar tongue. But, because he chose a form of alternate verse and prose, he committed himself to some semblance of plot: something had to "happen" to Syncero. What happened was a tale of unhappy love: a lover's exile from his lady, his wanderings, her eventual death and transfiguration, and the subsequent change wrought on his life by her death. This plot was not at all classical, but rather resembled the great medieval tragedies of love and death—Tristan, Lancelot, and more especially the spiritualization of this action in Dante's *La Vita Nuova* or the events beneath the lyric moments of Petrarch's *Rime*. Thus the pastoral romance started by combining rather curiously the setting and tone of Greek and Latin pastoral with an action that was basically medieval.

The peculiar structure of the pastoral romances is the outgrowth of this blending of two disparate kinds of literature. Though the combination of medieval romance and classical eclogue is a strange amalgam, it is entirely typical of the Renaissance, and indeed the two kinds had several elements in common that pointed to their eventual union.

One such element is their use of setting. Romance dealt in the improbable—unlike epic or tragedy—and the most common way of making the reader accept the improbabilities was to create an exotic setting for the plot where, one might think, anything could happen. Therefore the Greek romances take place in Asia Minor or Egypt, the home of magic; Apuleius is at pains to stress the fact that Lucius' transformation occurs in Thessaly, famous for witchcraft; or, to turn to later romances, the events in Malory take place in the dim past in Camelot, the fantastic adventures of the *Amadis de Gaula* cycle in remote Greece and Asia Minor as well as strange islands. Even when the setting was geographically real, it was deliberately distanced from the familiar by art and wonder. The same interest in setting exhibits itself in the eclogue, for the pastoral tradition is primarily a tradition about a place—concretely localized within the frame of the normal world but also completely abstracted from it—which acts as a sort of laboratory where ideally natural man is anatomized in himself and in his relations to his fellow men and his world.

Arcadia is only the most convincing of never-never lands, and the medieval romance world often approached it when it contained an ideal or free place, like the forest to which Aucassin and Nicolette escaped. Since setting is so important, one of the main topics of romance is the relation between men and their natural environment—the ties between Camelot and the Green Chapel, the lake that gives the sword and takes it back again; usually, by the end of the romance, the hero has established some harmony between himself and the cyclic processes of life on earth. The harmonious vision of man in his world had, of course, always been the chief attraction of the pastoral genre. It is the keynote of Theocritus' First *Idyll*, where the shepherds sit down at peace with the land and Thyrsis' song is described in the same terms as the sounds from the trees and the streams: Thyrsis sings, "Sweet is the whispered music of yonder pinetree by the springs, goatherd, and sweet too thy piping," and the Goatherd replies, "Sweeter, shepherd, falls thy song than yonder stream that tumbles plashing from the rocks" (using a single verb, καταχὲς, to describe the motion of the spring and the music's assault on the ear, and repeating "sweet," αδύ, in reference to the tree, the spring, and the song).[1] Virgil's *Eclogues* define happiness as accord with the land in Arcadia, misery as separation from it. And in *Daphnis and Chloe* the hero and heroine imitate the seasons in two cycles of desire in spring, reaction and suffering in summer, and fulfillment at the harvest. Perhaps it is because both pastoral and romance, in their rather muted concepts of good and evil, define good as concord and evil as discord that the *forms* of both depend so heavily on the harmonious interrelations of separate situations and actions.

The chief link between romance and pastoral is structural. For the Italian critics Pigna, Cinthio, and Minturno, the main difference between epic and romance plot was that the latter was multiple;[2] Tasso further insisted that these multiple plots be interrelated so that one action "has relation to the other, one corresponds to the other," and so forth;[3] and a modern Italian critic has pinpointed that relation as *analogy*. Mario Casella has defined the characteristic structural situation of romance—one common to Boccaccio, Chrétien de Troyes, Ariosto, and, later, Cervantes— as one where several "episodes and stories are bound up together according to some likeness to each other, and according to some likeness—it is never identical—to the central narration."[4] Part I of *Don Quixote* is an excellent example of this procedure, for in it we have several subplots or stories that reflect, from different angles, the central matter of Don Quixote's illusory love for Dulcinea. We can arrange them in a scale from true love to mere madness: from the true love and generous action of The Captive,

1. Trans. A. S. F. Gow, *Theocritus* (2 vols. Cambridge, 1950) *1*, 5.

2. Giambattista Pigna, *I Romanzi* (Venice, 1554), p. 25; G. B. Giraldi Cinthio, *Discorsi dei Romanzi* (Venice, 1554), p. 39; Antonio Minturno, *L'Arte Poetica* (Venice, 1564, ed. of Naples, 1725), p. 27.

3. *Discorsi del Poema Eroica* (1594), in Allan H. Gilbert, *Literary Criticism: Plato to Dryden* (New York, 1940), p. 501.

4. *Cervantes, Il Chisciotte* (2 vols. Florence, 1938), *1*, 89; as trans. and quoted by John Arthos, *On the Poetry of Spenser and the Form of Romances* (London, 1956), p. 191. My discussion of the episodes in *Don Quixote* differs in several respects from Casella's.

to the case of Chrysostome who may be considered either especially faithful or excessively stubborn, to Dorothea the witty and rather indifferent lover, to Cardenio the cowardly or wavering lover whose affection for Lucinda expresses itself chiefly as resentment and jealousy, and finally to Anselmo, the curious impertinent for whom love is merely psychopathic jealousy and insane egotism.

Structural unity by interwoven analogous stories is the heritage of the chivalric tradition, and we find it cropping up in European fiction from the Middle Ages to the seventeenth century: in Chrétien de Troyes, in the prose Arthurian cycle of the thirteenth century, in Malory—where it appears in miniature in the related stories of Gawain, Ywain, and Marhalt, bound in by the cycle of the year—in the refined procedure of the Italian cavalleresque epic, and finally in *Don Quixote*, where it is evoked only to be cast aside for a new idea of fiction. It is not typical of classical Greek and Latin narratives; the earliest example of it is Apuleius' *Metamorphoses*, which stands both at the final stage of the decadence of classical literature and at the threshold of romance literature. Indeed, it is not proper to what we usually think of as narrative, since it is a device of lyric, "the rhythm of association," rather than the Aristotelian "rhythm of continuity" and cause-and-effect relations between actions proper to narrative.[5]

Therefore it is not surprising that a lyrical rather than a narrative analogue to romance structure exists in classical literature— the set of eclogues (*eclogae*, "selected pieces") where several poems are put together, entirely separate from one another but related by parallels or contrasts or a common theme. Take for instance Virgil's *Eclogues*. The unity within the diversity which Servius praised in these poems lies in the common theme of a harmonious relation between men and the universe around them.[6]

5. These terms I owe to Northrop Frye, *Anatomy of Criticism* (Princeton, 1957).

6. See Servius, *In Vergilii Bucolicon Librum Commentarius*, comment on III, 1; in *Servii Grammatici Qui Feruntur In Vergilii Carmina Commentarii*, ed. G. Thilo and H. Hagen (3 vols. Leipzig, 1887) *3*, 29. See also *The Pastoral Poems*, trans. E. V. Rieu (Penguin Books, Harmondsworth, England, 1954), Introduction, pp. 14-15.

At the center, Virgil placed celebrations of the earth's gentle responsiveness to men. Eclogue IV thus prophesies a regeneration of the world in response to the birth of the child; the complementary V shows the death and transfiguration of Daphnis, who thereafter ensures the unity of man with a fruitful land. Eclogue VI is related to IV, for in it Silenus sings not of the regeneration but of the original creation of the earth and man's subsequent relations to it. Eclogue VII starts working out of this center, for it contrasts the happy Corydon, who is pious toward the land and its gods, and the unattractive Thyrsis, who is out of phase with them and thus suffers barrenness and defeat. The ninth and tenth eclogues take us out of the pastoral land and the harmony it brings: in IX we hear of Menalcas' eviction from his beloved land, and in X Gallus imagines a perfect harmony with love and the pastoral land—a vision which he, the exile, cannot turn into fact. These two create a certain symmetry with the eclogues that begin the series, Corydon's brief vision of life with Alexis in the woods close to the gods (a vision which is smashed as Gallus' was) in II, and in I the contrast between Meliboeus evicted into barren lands and Tityrus who remains, happy and fruitful in the *patria*.

In Renaissance eclogues, one might well expect, this kind of unity of the diverse by theme became very elaborate. For instance, beneath the many devices for unity in *The Shepheardes Calender*—such as the continuing presence of Colin Clout, the device of the calendar of successive months, and the patterned alternation of plaintive, moral, and recreative eclogues—we find a single great theme, the humble subordination of man to the created universe. In the plaintive eclogues, it appears as the mirroring of the time of year in the mind of Colin Clout; in the moral eclogues, as the celebration of humility, man's proper stance toward the Creation; and in the recreative, it is the assurance of man's happiness in accord with the continuing health and fertility of the earth. The four "Eclogues" or interludes of Sir Philip Sidney's *Arcadia* (which we shall examine at leisure in Chapter 4) exhibit an even tighter organization of separate songs around a central theme than do Spenser's eclogues. For in each of these are gathered songs expressing different views, courtly and rustic, of a single theme, be it love, marriage, or suffering. There is an especially clear three-part pattern to the first two interludes: each begins by a choric song defining the theme; then, in a second section, a series of intricately related songs by different shepherds opens out that theme; and finally, in the contrasting third section with its classical metrics, the main characters of the book step out to apply the general analysis of the theme to their own affairs. When Sidney enlarged the classical eclogues to make them into pastoral entertainments, he introduced a greater variety of characters in his cast, and of styles and hence tones in his verse, than Virgil had; but he held them all together by a schematic version of Virgil's technique, a theme to which all the parts are related either directly or obliquely.

Some poets went beyond Sidney in this matter. Tentative movements toward a blending of this kind of unity among separate poems with the structure of romance crop up in several sets of Renaissance eclogues into which narrative tendencies have entered. There is, for instance, Pontano's *Lepidina* (1505), which consists of an introductory eclogue followed by seven "pompae" or processions describing scenes from the marriage of the city Naples and the river Sebeto. Or the *Eclogae XII de vita J. Christi* (1485) of Antonio Geraldini, which takes up scenes from the life of Christ in chronological order from the prophecies of his coming (I) through his life on earth to the Crucifixion (VII) and later reappearance at the Last Judgment and the establishment of the New Jerusalem (XI and XII).[7] Especially noteworthy in this connection are the eight *Egloges* of Barnabe Googe (1563). Googe creates a lyrical framework for his pieces by announcing the coming of spring, accompanied by the passions and evils of love, in his first eclogue, and by using the approach of the hot summer months as the occasion for an exhortation to the shep-

---

7. W. Leonard Grant, in "Neo-Latin Biblical Pastorals," *Studies in Philology*, 58 (1961), 25–44, describes two other interesting examples of the narrative set of eclogues: Cornelius Scribonius Grapheus' set of six eclogues, *Panagê* (ca. 1536), celebrating the marriage of Joseph and Mary in imitation of Pontano, and Robertus Obryzius' series of one hundred and fourteen eclogues versifying the Bible, *Eidyllia sacra in utrumque Testamentum* (1587).

herds to leave love for the service of God in the last one; between them, we have several examples of unhappiness in love. But he has blended narrative procedures with the lyric unity by theme and calendar. For one thing, several of the poems are actually stories in verse: V is an adaptation of the tale of Felismena in Montemayor's *Diana*, and VII is a digest of the three related love plots in Book I of the same romance. Moreover, the cases of unhappy love center in two characters who crop up in several different eclogues, the courtly Faustus and the shepherd Dametas. Eclogue V is the story of Faustus' love of Claudia, her death, and his flight; in the next eclogue, we encounter Faustus himself, now become a shepherd and comforted by the rustic Felix. In the second eclogue, the unhappy Dametas, as if in exemplification of the warnings against love in I, makes his complaint against love and dies. At the beginning of the next eclogue, Menalcas and Coridon discuss Dametas, "that Martir died" for love, and then present a comic analogue to his case in the form of an ailing ram defeated in amorous combat, before they go on to other matters. The fourth eclogue picks up Dametas again: Melibeus describes his vision of Dametas risen out of Hell to describe the misfortunes of the lover on earth and the torments that await him in Hell. In Googe's *Egloges*, the characters Faustus and Dametas create a unity by continuity that overlays the usual pastoral unity by assimilation or analogy.

Thus in the sixteenth century we find several tentative movements of two different but related structural procedures—the analogous plotting of the romance and the loose thematic unity of the pastoral—toward each other. The man who first gave the harmonious vision shared by romance and pastoral coherent expression for his age, and who in doing so united the two kinds in the enduring form of pastoral romance, is Jacopo Sannazaro, in his *Arcadia* of 1504.

SANNAZARO: FROM POEM TO PLOT

The most striking technical achievement of Sannazaro in *Arcadia* was the blending of verse and prose elements. He accomplished this in the verbal texture of his book by inserting famous phrases from Petrarch, Boccaccio, Virgil, Ovid, and other poets into the structure of his prose sentences.[8] Furthermore, he assimilated the songs collected in *Arcadia* to the general atmosphere of the book by relating them to characters and scenes described in prose before each song is sung, and to the reactions of the audience afterward. But his greatest achievement was the structural harmony he gave to verse and prose together. When Sannazaro decided to tie his twelve eclogues together by prose links, the most obvious structural procedure was to expand similarities and contrasts between subjects and tones in the poems into a network of similar interrelationships among the characters, situations, and histories of the shepherds who were depicted as singing those eclogues, and hence to assimilate his structure to that of romance. We thus have in *Arcadia* several situations similar in basis but different in particulars.

The main analogous histories in *Arcadia* are Syncero's (the main plot), Charino's, and Clonico's. The tale of Syncero is quickly told in *Prosa* VII. In the ancient city of Naples the boy Syncero fell in love with "a young virgin . . . descended from a lofty line," Philli; during their constant association, he hid his love, choked his affections till he became "more like a shade of death than a living man," and finally fled Naples for Arcadia, hoping to bury his love there. So now he wanders through the land, listening to shepherds, reminded of her by all things. At the end of his story he sings a sestina in which he describes a dream vision of Philli:

> My lady mercifully came to me one night
> In a dream, laughing and beautiful,
> And refreshed my heart as the sun alone
> Over the fields strips the clouds from the earth,
> Saying to me, "Come, leave the gloomy caves
> And gather the little flowers in my fields."

8. Michele Scherillo, ed. (Turin, 1888), p. clvi and notes, passim; also F. M. Warren, *A History of the Novel Previous to the Seventeenth Century* (New York, 1895), p. 220, and "Sannazaro and 'Arcadia,'" *TLS* (Sept. 4, 1930), p. 689.

Although Syncero does not seem to realize it, her words imply that she has died, is transfigured in heaven, and now invites him to join her there. The implication is fulfilled at the end of *Arcadia* when a nymph leads him at dawn into a vast cavern where he hears Barcinio, Summonzio, and Meliseo lamenting Philli's death.

Charino's story is juxtaposed to Syncero's near the center of the book; the connection between them is made clear by Charino's opening statement:

> And to bestow upon your griefs a brighter hope, I assure you that I (who, if not entirely happy, can at least say that I have unburdened myself of part of my bitterness) was in a similar situation and perhaps (save for the voluntary exile which oppresses you so fiercely now) in a more painful situation than you are now or ever were.[9] [132–33]

He too fell in love with a childhood playmate but held himself back till, after a desperate near-declaration beside a woodland pool, he forced himself to flee his home and enter Arcadia. There he was about to throw himself from a cliff when he saw two doves:

> suddenly on the right I saw two white doves appear, and with a joyful bound perch on a leafy oak-tree that stood above me; in a moment they began to exchange a thousand sweet kisses with amorous murmurs. Whence, as a good omen, I took hope of future good fortune. [151–52]

This hope he wishes to convey to Syncero, who had likewise seen his case reflected in doves, though in an opposite manner:

> O how many times do I remember seeing amorous doves come through the solitary woods, kissing with sweet murmurs and seeking their beloved nest—a thing which filled me with envy. [122–23]

The contrast between the similar cases of Syncero and Charino involves not only hope and despair, but tone and atmosphere also. For while Syncero's setting was Quattrocento Naples, Charino's is an indeterminate idyllic place. His beloved is a *pastorella*, not

9. All parenthetical references are to the edition of Michele Scherillo; translations are mine.

15

a high-born young lady, and his sports with her are the rural diversions of woodland walks and bird catching. The two stories are as different as *La Vita Nuova* and *Daphnis and Chloe*.

Syncero's other pastoral double is Clonico, whose tale impinges on Charino's at the end of *Prosa* VIII: he likewise fled an unhappy love and used a pair of doves to dramatize his situation (*Egloga* VIII, 58–63). But Clonico's difference is that he is the victim of a faithless mistress, and his only cure is to have love erased from his consciousness—a task that the magic rites of *Prosa* IX accomplish. The three cases taken together show three possible endings for a love affair, those of the two shepherds—hope and happy fulfillment (Charino) and oblivion (Clonico)—counterpointing the ending of the townsman Syncero's story of despair and faithfulness after death.

Working out from these, we might note several other tangential but pervasive relations between the happenings in Arcadia and Syncero. For one, Arcadia rings with Philli's name sounded by a variety of voices: Sannazaro effectively but quite illogically made her the lady celebrated by the pretentious and silly Montano (*Egloga* II), the Platonist rustics Elenco and Ophelia (*Egloga* IX), and the sage and solemn Meliseo (*Egloga* XII). Syncero reacts strongly when the shepherds remind him of his own case: Galitio (*Egloga* III) recalls his mistress to him, and Selvaggio (*Egloga* X) reminds him of his beloved Naples.

The themes and structure of *Arcadia* provide an even deeper relationship. The book is divided in half, the first half ending with a general lament over the decay of the world (*Egloga* VI), the second with Syncero's discovery of Philli's death and his return to Naples. Furthermore, the halves are analogous. The next-to-last event in each is a funeral lament: Ergasto's lament over the patriarch Androgeo (*Prosa* V and *Egloga* V) and that same shepherd's lament over the matriarch Masillia (*Prosa* XI and *Egloga* XI). Preceding each of these we have a series of love plaints played off against the pastoral landscape: in the first half the tone is set by Selvaggio's, Ergasto's, Montano's, Uranio's, Galitio's, Logisto's, and Elpyno's; in the second half we move into the cases at hand, those of Syncero and his analogues Charino and Clonico. Thus *Arcadia* contains two themes balanced structurally, love and death; they combine at the end in *Egloga* XII and the epilogue *A la sampogna*, where the decay of the world is attributed to the death of the beloved Philli. The appropriateness of the alternation of these two subjects becomes apparent when we reflect that Syncero's two troubles are unhappy love and death. Arcadia thus becomes a projection of Syncero's mind, so that to experience Arcadia is to see his plight in many different mirrors and thus to unite it with the nature of things.

It has frequently been observed that Boccaccio's *Ameto* served as an immediate model for Sannazaro's *Arcadia* in several respects: in its verbal texture, in the alternation of verse and prose, and in general curve of its plot (where the hero first observes several different people, and then receives a revelation that changes his life).[1] *Ameto* is not a pastoral work but a *favola boschereccia:* though it contains two incidental eclogues, its action centers in a mythological Florence with its periphery of the rough Etrurian forests (neither of them resembling the pastoral world), and its chief characters are the hunter Ameto, Nymphs, and the goddess Venus. Its atmosphere and action are thoroughly medieval; it is, in fact, a late medieval romance that approaches the pastoral. It will therefore be instructive for us to compare its construction with that of *Arcadia* in order to see the merging of classical and medieval in Sannazaro's structure.

The main action of *Ameto* begins in springtime when Ameto enters the pious mythological world that gathers in Florence at the Feast of Venus. There, seven Nymphs sit around Ameto in a circle, like seven lenses all focusing at the same place. Each directs her story to Ameto, and each story reflects his. For it is a contest, and he is the judge; what better way to gain his favor than to tell, under various different guises, the story of his love for Lia, and give it a happy ending? All seven stories tell how Venus brings together the Nymph who tells the story and a rude young man,

---

1. See Scherillo, p. cxi: "The whole fabric of the *Arcadia* is rewoven over that of the *Ameto*."

17

and how that young man is refined by the love of the Nymph. This is the technique used in our time by Henry James in *The Awkward Age:*

> I drew on a sheet of paper . . . the neat figure of a circle consisting of a number of small rounds disposed at equal distance about a central object. The central object was my situation, my subject in itself, to which the thing would owe its title, and the small rounds represented so many distinct lamps, as I liked to call them, the function of each of which would be to light with all due intensity one of its aspects. I had divided it . . . into aspects.[2]

Ameto enters imaginatively into each of the stories; quite naturally, he reads himself as the hero of every one of them. And, during each of the hymns that end each tale, he finds himself in love with the teller. But there is a hierarchy in his reactions: after the first story,

> The voices he heard and the fervent loves, the wonderful beauty, and the angelic sound with notes never before heard by him— each by itself, and all together filled Ameto, already exceedingly full of wonder, with more wonder; so much so, that he wished to be Afron . . . and he weighed in his own mind the possibility of loosening from his heart his delight in Lia, so that he might serve Mopsa.　　　　　　　　　　　　　　[54][3]

He has much the same reaction after each story, but his emotions become ever more complex, his passions more heated; after the fifth tale of Agapes, for instance, he wishes to see the Nymph naked at the pool as Apiros did, "wondering within himself, he praises the limbs he had never seen" (104). After the sixth, Fiametta's, he becomes confused and passionate, and wishes he were all the young men at once (121–22). All of his reactions have been lustful, yet at the end of the contest these passions, imaginatively entered into, have civilized him, for Lia says:

> Since he has followed me, I have drawn this man, with my light, out of blindness toward the knowledge of higher things; I made

2. Preface to *The Awkward Age* (New York, 1908), p. xvi.

3. All parenthetical page references are to the *Scrittori d'Italia* edition of Boccaccio's *Opere* (14 vols. to date, Bari, 1918–), 5, ed. Nicola Bruscoli (1940); the translations are mine.

him pursue these things of his own will; and already he seems no longer crude or rough, so good are his intentions, but one can see that he is clever, gentle, and disposed to fine things; for which reason, valuing Venus no less than you do, he thus honors her with sacrifices, as you do—and will do so always.   [137]

But "softening" by imaginative sympathy and love is only one dimension of the change that comes over Ameto at the Feast of Venus. Adolf Gaspary points out that "Jede von den sieben Nymphen . . . hat sich insbesondere dem Dienste einer Göttin gewidmet, und zum Dienste dieser ihren jungen Liebhafter vermittelst ihrer Liebe geführt." [4] The seven goddesses are Pallas, Diana, Pomona, Bellona, Venus, Vesta, and Cybele; they are symbols, respectively, for Prudence, Justice, Temperance, Fortitude, Charity, Hope, and Faith, and the stories the Nymphs tell exemplify these virtues. [5] Ameto, then, is led through the Four Cardinal Virtues and the Three Theological Virtues by the Nymphs, and now stands ready for union with God. The role of the reflectors in *Ameto* is not restricted merely to emphasizing the action or to showing Ameto who he is; they constitute, rather, an educative process, for it is by entering into each of them imaginatively that Ameto refines himself.

The kind of unity we find in Sannazaro's *Arcadia* is the result of a double impulse: one from the thematic unity of the eclogue, one from the allegorical scheme of *Ameto*. A comparison of *Arcadia* with its two models certainly indicates, however, that it owes much more to the eclogue than to Boccaccio. Sannazaro's structure is much looser than Boccaccio's; he relied on fewer and more informal analogues to his central situation, and he did not set them up in schematic relationships around it. Furthermore, Sannazaro's structural unity is not only and not primarily one of plot as Boccaccio's is, but works also by related characters, scenes, topics, and tones; finally, the different parts come together not in a central action but rather in the mere mental state of Syncero. The structure of *Ameto* is formal and clear-cut, as befits a medi-

4. Adolf Gaspary, *Geschichte der Italienischen Literatur* (2 vols. Strassburg, 1888), 2, 18.
5. The ultimate source of this is *Purgatorio* XXXI.

eval allegory; on the other hand, *Arcadia* has the loose but pervasive tonal unity of the eclogue. But Boccaccio's influence shows itself, I think, in the use to which analogous situations are put. In sets of eclogues, it is the reader who perceives parallels or themes; but in *Arcadia*—especially in the latter half when the stories of Syncero, Charino, and Clonico are told—the characters in the romance are the ones who perceive the threads that unite their individual stories, and such perceptions cause sympathy and interactions among them. This was the case with the seven Nymphs and Ameto. The influence of Boccaccio is, then, responsible for pulling analogies into a functional relationship with plot. And as we go through *Arcadia*, we find it growing in plot interest: the first half is a matter of men, scenes, and songs; with *Prosa* VII, we move into related histories and action.

If there is a tendency away from mere tonal unity toward unity among diverse actions in the latter part of Sannazaro's work, we should expect to find it exacerbated in his followers. The bulk of the direct imitations of *Arcadia*—Jacopo di Gennaro's *Pastorale* (1504), Ascanio Botta's *Rurale* (1521), Remy Belleau's *La Bergerie* (1565), Luis Gálvez de Montalvo's *El Pastor de Fílida* (1582), Don Gaspar Mercader's *El Prado de Valencia* (1600), and Don Bernardo de Balbuena's *Siglo de Oro* (1608)—stressed the tonal and semi-autobiographical elements in the romance, and hence concentrated on atmospheric verse weakly linked by prose. But one of the best of them took a better way and imitated a plot motif, the journey of Clonico to the shrine in *Prosa* IX (as did Agnolo Firenzuola in his dramatic scene *Il Sacrificio Pastorale*). Ascanio Centorio's *L'Aura Soave* (Venice, 1556) has considerably more narrative interest than its model; although it does contain a long description of a sacrifice, games, and a singing contest in imitation of *Arcadia*, these appear only as an appendix to a story; and in general the atmospheric and descriptive elements are reduced in order to bring four analogous stories of frustrated love into focus. The main narrative is Lauso's tale of his love for "L'Aura Soave," the wife of a friend (thirty-four years old, and the mother of five children!); when an attempt at suicide and a direct plea to his beloved both failed, he left his city to wander as a shepherd. The shepherd Alanio tells him a contrasting rural and supernatural tale about his friend Ophelte, who was metamorphosed into a fountain by the displeasure of his beloved nymph, Urania. The two other stories, in the latter half of the book, are both urban adventures: Flavio's story of his desertion by the rich burgher's daughter Cinthia, and Fileno's description of the web of deceit by which a confidante parted him from his beloved Calidonia. But Centorio did not stop at creating interrelated plots about a single theme; he went beyond that to interweave two of them into the motif of a journey. When Alanio tells Ophelte's story to Lauso, he is midway in his journey to the grove of Diana at Aricina, the dwelling of the hermit Ismenio, who, he has been told, can prescribe a cure for his friend. Lauso joins him, and at that point the two stories cease to be held together by mere parallelism and mutual sympathy: instead, they run together toward a common goal. Therefore the ceremonies at Ismenio's home weave together prospective solutions for the difficulties of Ophelte, Alanio, and Lauso. If we have not yet reached the point where plots interact, we have at least seen here a situation in which they do something more than reflect one another.

A separate development toward plot occurs in another genre, the heroic romance, where the contact of pastoral interlude with heroic action exerted a narrative pressure on the former, for it became one stage in an over-all plot. When Ariosto, influenced perhaps by the vogue of Sannazaro, led his heroine Angelica into Arcadian France, it was for the purpose of effecting a change in her character: for the proud Angelica, who tries to cure the wounds of Medoro at a shepherd's cottage in Canto XIX, falls victim first to pity, then to love with all its humiliations and pain. Her humbling, his recovery, and the birth and consummation of love between them presents an elemental action that we shall find again and again in the pastoral romances. We find it, too, in the pattern of entrance into Arcady in distress and emergence in harmony common to the pastoral interludes of other chivalric romances—in Feliciano da Silva's *El deceno libro de Amadis, que es el cronica de Don Florisel de Niquea* (1532), Bernadim Ribeiro's *Menina e Moça* (1554),[6] and later in *Gerusalemme Liberata* and Book VI of *The Faerie Queene*.

Both *Orlando Furioso* and *L'Aura Soave* had the effect of pushing the prose pastoral toward a greater emphasis on plot, a plot of a peculiarly curative kind, since the pastoral place in both was made a catalyst where suffering acquired elsewhere was relieved and new relationships were established. The pastoral romance was gravitating toward a plot type exemplified by *The Wizard of Oz*[7] —the multiple journey where characters change by interaction with their companions in new situations caused by an unusual region, and where these changes solidify at a central shrine or magic place. It was Jorge de Montemayor who activated this potential drama in the Italian romances.

MONTEMAYOR: THE DEVELOPMENT OF PLOT

Los siete libros de la Diana of Jorge de Montemayor (1559) shows its debts to *Arcadia* in matters of natural description, verse forms, and some elements of story (the influence of Sannazaro's Clonico episode is especially apparent).[8] But Montemayor obviously delighted in the proliferation and complications of plot as Sannazaro did not, and we may therefore say that, whereas *Arcadia* was a group of poems held together by prose links, *Diana* is a prose fiction with interwoven plots punctuated by occasional poems. In this increased attention to plot we can see the evidence of another influence on *Diana* besides that of the pastoral romances; it is the Greek romance, whose imprint—whether direct or transmitted through the *Amadis de Gaula* cycle—appears, for instance, in the motif of the lovers separated and reunited by a journey and in certain narrative procedures, among them the beginning *in medias*

6. This is a conjectural date; see the edition of José Pessanha (Porto, 1891), p. lxxvii.

7. See Juan Bautista Avalle-Arce, *La novela pastoril española* (Madrid, 1959), p. 71, for a comparison of Montemayor's *Diana* to *The Wizard of Oz*.

8. See *Diana*, ed. Francisco López Estrada (Madrid, 1946), pp. xlviii–l.

res.[9] By these means, Montemayor went beyond Sannazaro in finally effecting the integration of a lyrical or associative structure with the continuous structure of fiction. In the resultant parallel plotting, the *Diana* therefore emphasizes the *interactions* among plots rather than their mere coexistence.

Sannazaro's "reflection" becomes, in Montemayor's book, a set of analogous plots arranged about the central theme of an inadequate return for love—that is to say, infidelity. The primary instance is of course the heroine Felismena's (the source of *Two Gentlemen of Verona*). In the city of "Soldina," Don Felis wooed the highborn Felismena and won her heart; when he had to leave for the court of "Augusta Caesarina," she disguised herself as a man and followed him. There she found that he had jilted her for a city beauty, Celia, who complicated matters by falling in love, not with Don Felis, but with the disguised Felismena, who had increased her torment by becoming Felis' "page." Celia eventually died of unrequited love and Don Felis disappeared.

Felismena, now in the dress of a martial shepherdess, seeks him throughout the real and imagined worlds of Spain. She tells her story to Sireno, Sylvano, and Selvagia in Book II of the *Diana*. These three rustics, whose stories appear in Book I, reflect her case. The shepherdess Selvagia is the victim of a chain of unrequited loves like Felismena's: she loves Alanio, who throws her over for Ismenia; Ismenia however is in love with Montano, but he has eyes only for Selvagia! Montano exhibits one final instance of infidelity when he turns to marry Ismenia, thus leaving Selvagia entirely out in the cold, wandering through the pastoral world grieving over the fickleness of men. The shepherds Sireno and Sylvano are the male counterparts of the two women, for both of them are the victims of the fickle Diana: Sylvano she continually scorned even though he deserved her love; she returned Sireno's love for a while, but later threw him over for the rich old shepherd Delio.

These four unhappy lovers meet a variant of their cases in the person of Belisa, a repentant jilt. And near the end of the book, Felismena meets her fifth analogue in the Portuguese shepherdess

9. See López Estrada, p. lxvi, and Avalle-Arce, p. 78.

Duarda, whose lover Danteo threw her over for Andresa, who has since died.[1] Felismena and Duarda present contrast within extreme similarity just as Syncero and Charino did, Felismena's being a court tale of complex intrigues, Duarda's of simple bourgeois love. Felismena is an ideal of beauty; Duarda, the author candidly admits, is somewhat less than that (152–53).[2] Yet the utmost sympathy exists between them: Felismena says that Duarda's lover (in whom she sees Don Felis) has "truly learned by my ils to complain of thine owne" (156); and the analogy is further emphasized when Felismena's attempt to reunite Duarda and Danteo is interrupted by her own reunion with Don Felis:

> The Shepherdesse having made an ende of her sharpe answer, and
> *Felismena* beginning to arbitrate the matter between them; they
> heard a great noise in the other side of the meadow, like to the
> sound of blowes, and smiting of swordes upon harneies, as if
> some armed men had fought togither. [157]

It is Felis at last, and after Felismena saves him, they go off together.

All of the characters in *Diana* are sensitive to their reflections in other people; they penetrate each other's personalities, and show such penetration by treating other's griefs as their own, as in the following examples:

> When *Selvagia* had made an end of her sorrowfull tale, she began
> to weepe so bitterly, that both the Shepherdes (being a kinde
> of friendly dutie, wherein they had no small experience) began
> also help her with their teares [28]

1. A sixth story, that of Abindaráez, added to the editions after Montemayor's death, has been conclusively proved spurious; see two articles by Henri Mérimée, "El Abencerraje d'après l'*Inventorio* et la *Diana*," *Bulletin Hispanique 21* (1919), 143–66, and "El Abencerrage d'après diverses versions publiées au xvie siècle," *Bulletin Hispanique, 30* (1928), 147–81. Yet it is easy to see why the interpolator added it, for it forms the keystone to the set of tales of infidelity just as "The Franklyn's Tale" does to Chaucer's "marriage group." It is a tale of faith kept on all sides: by a woman who does not forget her lover, by her lover's captor who lets him go to her on parole, by the lovers who keep their word and return, and so forth.

2. Quotations and page references are to the Elizabethan translation of Yong, *Diana of George of Montemayor: Translated out of Spanish into English by Bartholomew Yong of the Middle Temple Gentleman* (London, 1598).

Syrenus thought *Selvagias* song sufficient enough to manifest
his greefe [69]

Whilest the Shepherdesse was telling that which you have heard,
Syrenus, Sylvanus, Selvagia, and faire *Felismena,* and the three
Nymphes coulde not give eare without some secrete teares. [84]

Sometimes, too, they sing linked songs, like those of Selvagia,
Sireno, and Sylvano at the end of Book I, where each picks up a
word from another's song to be the key word of his own song
("to weepe," *llorar;* "rest," *descansaréis;* "lost," *perdida*) in order
to show that they all sing of one common grief. But they show
their awareness of their counterparts best by their actions toward
each other. In *Arcadia,* it was usual to express sympathy for an
unfortunate shepherd, then drop it. Only in two cases did it go
further: when Charino tried to give Syncero hope, and when the
shepherds led Clonico off for a love cure. The *Diana* took its keynote from the Clonico episode: men are bound together by *actions*
here. Thus in Book II we find Sireno, Sylvano, Selvagia, and
Felismena traveling together to the Temple of Diana for a communal solution to their similar problems; when they meet Belisa
in Book III, they all shed copious tears and urge her, too, to join
them in their pilgrimage. This sympathetic action centers in
Felismena; since she is the heroine, her ministrations really tie the
plot together. She saves Sireno, Sylvano, Selvagia, and three
Nymphs from some savages; she sends Arsileo to Belisa; she settles
the dispute between Amarílida and Filemón in a minor episode
and almost does the same for Duarda and Danteo. She comes into
contact with all of the characters in the book, and she is an active
instrument in making each of them happy.

The fact that the characters in *Diana* have an awareness of their
ties to others much more marked than in *Arcadia* has two consequences. First, as we have said, the sympathy between two characters immediately leads to sympathetic actions between them.
Secondly, when a character sees himself in another, he is actually
becoming aware of himself; he is approaching self-knowledge.
The plot of self-knowledge centers in the Temple of Diana, where
the sage Felicia serves as a catalyst, first showing each character

25

who he is, then suggesting ways of working out his problems. Thus in *Diana* the existence of pastoral doubles is one of the prime factors in determining the kind of actions that develop and the general curve of the plot.

With *Diana*, the prose pastoral (aided by the Greek romance) swings fully into the orbit of romance. The prose becomes dominant, the verse being relegated to decoration, and change of fortune by action thus replaces sentiment as the main interest. The plot, as prescribed by the Italian critics, is multiple with one figure predominating: "The romance, they say, has as its object a crowd of knights and ladies and of affairs of war and peace, though in this group one knight is especially taken whom the author is to make glorious above all the others . . . and he takes for description diverse and contrasted lands and the various things that happened in them during all the time occupied by the fabulous story of the matter he sets out to sing," [3] and the minor plots are related to the major one by analogy. It is this scheme of analogous multiple plots that Montemayor bequeathed to his successors. We find it, for instance, in Bartholomé López de Enciso's *Desengaño de Celos* (1586), with its inserted tales of Clarina, Laureno, and Luceria; or in the subplots of Acrisio and Elicio in Juan Arze Solórzeno's *Tragedias de Amor* (1608), as well as in later romances such as Don Gabriel de Corral's *Cintia de Aranjuez* (1629).[4] Or, to turn to major examples, we find such plotting in Cervantes' *Galatea* (1585), where the interwoven stories of the noble Lisandro, of the shepherdess Teolinda, and of Silerio, Rosaura, and others nearly obscure the main action; or finally, D'Urfé's *Astrée* (1607–1628), which contains over thirty stories of the difficulties of love to parallel Celadon's love affair with Astrée.

The only notable development of narrative form, however, occurs not in these works but in the immediate continuation of

3. Antonio Minturno, *L'Arte Poetica*, p. 27; trans. Gilbert, *Literary Criticism*, p. 278; see also my n. 2, p. 9.

4. On these three Spanish romances, see Avalle-Arce, especially pp. 156–57, 177, and 172 respectively.

Diana, Gaspar Gil Polo's romance *Diana enamorada* (1564). Gil Polo, in simplifying Montemayor's plot line, allowed himself only three plots centering in the disintegration of a marriage because of Fortune—Marcelio's story of separation from his fiancée and her family at sea, Diana's own story of her desertion by the disgusted Sireno and her jealous and adulterous husband, and Ismenia's tale of the fickleness and jealousy that made her marriage to Montano collapse. But he bound these analogous plots together in such a way as to create a thematic unit of each of his five books; thus his headnotes to each book take up the previous actions and relate them to a general theme—in I, the co-operation of "lawlesse love" and Fortune in tormenting men (as seen in the cases of Diana and Marcelio); in II, the part of jealousy in misfortune (seen in Diana's tale and Ismenia); in III, the benign counterchanges in Fortune (as Marcelio hears of his beloved, and all approach solutions to their problems at Felicia's temple); and in IV, the happiness of men relieved from mishap. What these headnotes tell us further is that the parallel plots in *Diana enamorada* proceed book by book through the tight five-act plot structure of comedy, from exposition to complication to the turning point in Book III, and to the dénouement of IV and V. Gil Polo's achievement here was high indeed, for he carried the pastoral romance plot to its highest point before Sidney's *Arcadia,* a point where prose pastoral not only reached the firm action and tight interrelations between plots characteristic of the heroic romance at its best, but went beyond that to achieve a classical clarity of outline.

SCENE AND ACTION IN THE PASTORAL ROMANCE

Having described the process by which pastoral romance developed a plot—from selected poems to thematic unity to multiple plot—we must now go on to define just what the plot typical to the genre was. This plot type will be found to be especially dependent on the romantic scene, for, as we have insisted before, the pastoral is primarily a tradition of a peculiar scene. Yet the pastoral is not a descriptive genre; its vision, on the contrary, embraces the state of man in harmony with his environment (as against the epic tradition of man in heroic conflict with it). Therefore, we find in pastoral works both a scene and some means for expressing man's accord with it—in the eclogue, a rather static presentation or evocation of it, in the romance an *action* toward it. Our task here, then, will be to define a common vision as it operates in a scene and in the action implicit in that scene.

Perhaps the finest expression of the pastoral vision—and one which contains the seeds of its later developments [5]—is Virgil's Tenth *Eclogue*, "Gallus." At the beginning of the poem, the townsman Gallus is pictured as having left the world of fact for Arcadia in order to mourn his unhappy love affair. Here, the land weeps with him:

> pinifer illum etiam sola sub rupe iacentem
> Maenalus et gelidi fleverunt saxa Lycaei

(for him, as he lay beneath the solitary rock, even pine-bearing Maenalus and the crags of cold Lycaeus wept).　　　[14–15]

Apollo, Silvanus, and Pan come to offer him comfort, and Pan connects unrequited love with the nature of things:

> nec lacrimis crudelis Amor nec gramina rivis
> nec cytiso saturantur apes nec fronde capellae

(cruel Love is no more sated with tears than the grass with streams or the bees with clover or the goats with leaves). [29–30]

Gallus sings a lament in which he contrasts the snow and ice of the outside world (46–49) to the *mollia prata* (42) of the poet's world; the hardships his mistress will endure in the campaign (she has run off with a soldier) to the sweet life she might have lived with him in Arcadia; the war of the world to the Arcadian hunt. He creates an Arcadian *counterpart* of himself who lives in peace and love:

5. The imprint of "Gallus" upon Sannazaro is especially strong; not only do the experiences of Syncero in Arcadia resemble Gallus' very strongly, but Sannazaro seems implicitly to compare both Syncero and Charino to him by placing a quotation from *Eclogue* X in each of their stories (see *Arcadia*, pp. 132 and 145). See also Francesco Torraca's discussion of the division of motifs from "Gallus" between Charino's and Syncero's tales, in *La Materia dell' Arcadia del Sannazaro* (Castello, 1888), p. 30.

atque utinam ex vobis unus vestrique fuissem
aut custos gregis aut maturae vinitor uvae.
certe sive mihi Phyllis sive esset Amyntas
seu quicumque furor (quid tum, si fuscus Amyntas?
et nigrae violae sunt et vaccinia nigra),
mecum inter salices lenta sub vite iaceret

(and would that I had been one of you, the shepherd of one of
your flocks or the tender of your ripe grapes. Surely then, my
darling, whether it were Phyllis or Amyntas, or whoever it
were—and what if Amyntas is dark? violets are black, and so are
blueberries—would be lying beside me among the willows,
under the pliant vine).   [35–40]

The poem ends in complete despair, for Gallus has described what
he might have become if things were different from what they are.
Three aspects of this poem are notable. First, Gallus imagines a
pastoral double or alter ego for himself, that is, he sees himself as
another, and might (if he wished) examine himself thus. Second,
Gallus is torn apart by love, but imagines a regeneration for himself in the life he might have led as a shepherd, in the person of his
pastoral double. Third, the necessary condition for such a regeneration would be an exchange of life in the great world for life
in Arcadia. These facts tell us that the scene of Arcadia is most
important for its *function* in accomplishing the vision of a man's
complete accord with himself as reflected in a harmony with his
environment.

So it was, too, at the inception of the pastoral tradition. The
received opinion of Theocritus is that he was providing escape
from the turbulent city life of Alexandria by means of realistic
pictures of rustic life in Sicily. That is not true; in fact, his scenes
present a purely artificial backdrop for a trenchant (but not naturalistic) analysis of the mind of essential man in all its complexity.
For one thing, he was scarcely pretending to transcribe actual
rustic songs; his style ranges from the colloquial (as in *Idyll* V)
to the "poetic" and highly colored (as in I and VII), and even
varies within the poem (as in III); his dialect, moreover, was not a
representation of Sicilian Greek, but, as A. S. F. Gow has shown,
"an artificial and arbitrary concoction of the poet's and part of his

convention." [6] The same is true of his settings: though a few of
the *Idylls* have specific settings (VII in Cos, V in Alexandria),
most of them take place in no specific locale and do not even tempt
us to construct one for them, so sketchy are their natural details.
"These idylls," writes Gow, "are not meant to be localized at
all . . . as Theocritus, when asked, 'Where do peasants talk in
such a dialect, or on such themes?' would have replied, 'Why,
nowhere,' and have thought the question foolish, so he would have
returned the same answer to the question, 'Where did Simaetha
and Bucaeus live?' and with the same emotion . . . to tie down
to a precise locality what are after all scenes from fairyland is to
misunderstand the convention the poet is using." [7] If we look at
the actual details of setting given by Theocritus, we shall find that
such specific things as a cave, a road, or a Priapus are few, and that
most often there are but three "props"—a hill, a stream, a tree—
that are arranged and rearranged in various combinations. On the
other hand, the function this setting does actually perform is to
place the characters in a close relation to nature. For instance, the
elements of atmosphere in the first *Idyll* (which we examined
briefly at the beginning of this chapter) stress two factors: that
nature is the norm for man and his arts—thus the song of Thyrsis
"falls" like the waters of the stream, and is as sweet as the wind in
the pines—and that in this natural setting exist the gods who direct
men's lives: "at noontide pipe we may not, for fear of Pan. For
then, of a surety, he is resting wearied from the chase. And he is
quick of temper and bitter wrath sits ever on his nostril."

Theocritus presents us with essential man, very close to the
earth and to the gods, in an artificial atmosphere from which all
the accidental elements of civilization have been excluded. The
action this setting allows him to present is as universal as possible—
the devious and often paradoxical effects of love on the simple
human mind. [8] The analysis is usually quite complete, since it pre-

6. "The Methods of Theocritus and Some Problems in His Poems," *Classical
Quarterly, 24* (1930), 151.

7. Ibid., p. 152; see also Gow's edition of Theocritus, introduction, *1*, xx.

8. See W. F. Jackson Knight's statement in *Roman Vergil* (2d ed. London,
1944), p. 112, that Theocritus made strong emotions "seem especially at home in
beautiful country."

sents conflicting or even self-contradictory motives together in one mind, in intimate combination. Witness the intricate play of *Idyll* IV, where Theocritus first shows us Battus as a cynic who sees nothing in the pastoral world but foolishness, dishonesty, and lechery; then as a self-deluding fool; then as a pitiable lover whose mistress has died and left the world dark for him; finally as a combination of all three. It is no contradiction for a man to be pathetic and a trifle silly at the same time, and Theocritus is especially adept at portraying this combination of foolishness and pathos: he does it again in *Idyll* III and in the two idylls on Polyphemus and Galatea, VI and XI. He often uses paradoxical situations in love to bring out the presence of conflicting emotions in one mind: in II, one of the finest analyses of love before Ovid's *Amores*, the combination of love and hate, of desire for revenge and desire for love, in Simaetha's mind; in VI Polyphemus' cunning refusal of the girl who once scorned his advances; in I, Daphnis' refusal to consummate his love even though he apparently can with ease. It is always the meeting of conflicting emotions that interests Theocritus.

When Virgil wished to give especial value to this imagined world of harmony between men and nature, he did so by introducing contrasts between it and the world in which men actually live, "the world of fact—a world less real than the other . . . yet persistently intrusive none the less," [9] where men order others to be evicted from their farms or to go off on campaigns in the wastes of Germany. The tissue of contrasts between them is Virgil's device for precise definition of the human meaning of his artificial world of the mind: its offer of hope to cure the despair of the real world (in I and IX), its encouragement of humility (VII), its status as the source of human values (VI). The theme of this land is concord; its effect on the minds of men is contained in the promise that, in nature, any pain will be subsumed in the inevitable alternation of pain and joy, that decay will be followed by natural rebirth. Therefore, in the *Eclogues*, we find an insistent action of human regeneration in contact with the earth: the renewal of the earth by means of the new child in IV, the success

9. Rieu's edition of the *Eclogues*, p. 123.

of the despairing lover in VIII, the death and deification of
Daphnis in V, or the revitalization of Tityrus in I.

The scene of *Daphnis and Chloe*, the only surviving classical
pastoral romance, is more complex than Virgil's, for it contains
not two contrasting places but three, a supernatural center and
two surrounding areas. At the center stands the Cave of the
Nymphs which is to play such a large part in the story of Daphnis
and Chloe, from their discovery as infants there to their final
marriage and consummation there. The region around this cave,
which is the scene of most of the action, is the pastoral land—the
tenant farm of Lamon, the fields of his neighbor Dryas and other
shepherds; the life there is simple, the people deliciously naïve and
often rather funny, exhibiting in their actions both good and evil
in simple and direct forms. Beyond these fields lies the great world
of Lesbos and the sea, especially the city of Mytelene, with its
sophisticated young men and courtesans. But the city-world here
is not at all the same as the "real" world represented by Virgil's
Rome; it is, in fact, just as stylized, just as unreal as the pastoral
scene. Most of the characters of the city-world—the dissolute but
good-hearted young master, the loose woman Lycainion, the para-
site Gnatho—seem clearly to have been modeled on the type
characters of New Comedy.

Furthermore, our reception of this world is governed by the
lens of Longus' prologue:

> Once while I was hunting in Lesbos I saw in a grove of the
> Nymphs the fairest sight I have ever seen. It was the painted
> picture of a tale of love. The grove itself was beautiful; it was
> thick with trees, and abounding in flowers, all well-watered
> by a single fountain which brought refreshment to both alike.
> But more delightful still was that picture, both for its consum-
> mate art and for its tale of love. Its fame drew many visitors,
> even from a distance, to supplicate the Nymphs and to view
> the painting. In it were represented women in childbed, and others
> fitting swaddling clothes upon infants. There were sheep nursing
> them and shepherds taking them up; there were young lovers
> pledging faith to one another, an incursion of pirates, an attack

by invaders. All these scenes spoke of love, and as I looked upon and admired them I conceived a strong desire to compose a literary pendant to that painted picture.[1]

The deliberate distancing and the insistence on artifice here show us that the Lesbos we see in this book is not only different from the Lesbos of the author's day, but also merely that distillation of Lesbos drawn from a picture, "a literary pendant." The contrast between the fields and Mytelene, therefore, is not a contrast between two versions of reality—ideal and fact—as it was in Virgil, but rather the contrast between two segments—urban and rustic—of an artificial scene. Longus created a genuine fictional world with several parts, and by so doing he extended the scope of the action considerably; for (since Mytelene can touch the tenant farm in a way that Augustan Rome could never have touched Virgil's "Arcadia") the world outside the pastoral land becomes the main impetus for action inside that land. The several incursions from the outside world—invasion by Tyrian pirates and by the Methymnians, the coming of the young master Dionysophantes—act as "disturbing influences" [2] to force the action of the lovers' growth. And, therefore, nearly every step in the story, especially from Book II on, begins with an incursion from the outer world, proceeds in actions and reactions within the pastoral land, and ends in a consecration at the Cave of the Nymphs.

As the geographical rhythm of the individual incidents, each driving toward the supernatural center of the land, implies, the over-all action of *Daphnis and Chloe* records a coming into harmony with the forces of nature—specifically, the accordance of two children with the force of Eros, Lord of the earth, the animals, and men (through contact with his agents Pan and the Nymphs, the male and female principles of earth),[3] and all that implies about maturity and truth to one's self and nature. Therefore the plot records the growth of the two children toward sexual

1. Translated by Moses Hadas in *Three Greek Romances* (Garden City, N.Y., 1953), p. 17.
2. Ibid., introduction, p. 9.
3. See *Three Greek Romances*, pp. 20–21, 39–41, 50–51.

maturity and true identity, and envelops it in the rhythm of two seasonal cycles separated by a long winter. The first cycle, which fills Books I and II, goes from the inception of desire to a love pledge. There are three periods in this cycle, corresponding to spring, summer, and fall: the first ends with desire firmly implanted in both lovers; the second is a long period of reaction, passion, and frustration; in the third, Daphnis and Chloe grow together and finally pledge troth. Books III and IV contain the second three-part cycle of desire for sexual fulfillment in the spring of the next year, experimentation and experience in summer, and final consummation in marriage at the harvest.

The three masterpieces of classical pastoral, though differing in character as widely as in the five centuries separating their composition, all show a common tendency to assert the *function* of scene in action and therefore to stress the *interactions* of men with the land, whether they are presented as static conditions of human simplicity or actions implying human rebirth. What is notable in a historical view is that, as contrasts between the pastoral land and other places deepen, so too the amount and complexity of the action—different kinds of action in the contrasting places—increases. It is this scheme of contrasting places and contrasting kinds of action, amplified by new scenic and narrative possibilities from romance, chivalric and otherwise, that the Renaissance pastoral romance inherits from classical pastoral. Since the Renaissance romances span one century instead of several—and for our purposes cover only eighty years from Sannazaro's first *Arcadia* in 1504 to Sidney's second *Arcadia* before 1584—their characteristics remain relatively fixed, with less marked divergences among different examples of the genre than in their classical models. We may, in fact, treat the settings of these romances as variants of one setting, their patterns of action as variations on one central pattern determined by that setting.

The heroes of the Renaissance pastoral romances are always *sojourners* in the Arcadian preserve, never native shepherds. This fact, together with the continuing contrast between the pastoral land and other places necessary to exhibit its meaning, makes the settings of the Renaissance pastoral romances always *multiple*.

The pattern formed by the subdivisions of this setting may be graphically if roughly imaged as a center with two concentric circles surrounding it, implying a kind of purification of life proceeding inward: from the gross and turbulently naturalistic outer circle, to the refined pastoral inner circle, and then to the pure center of the world.

The center is always supernatural, usually either a shrine like the Cave of the Nymphs or the dwelling of a magician. It may be the actual dwelling place of the god, who may reveal himself to shepherds there, as in the Florentine pastoral preserve of Venus in Boccaccio's *Ameto* or the valley of the cypresses where Calliope rises to address the shepherds in Book VI of Cervantes' *Galatea*. Or it may be a supernatural center without a god, like the cave, the home of all fertilizing waters, in the center of Sannazaro's *Arcadia*. Or it may be merely the home of a magician or priest who can supplicate the god, like Ismenio's castle in *L'Aura Soave*. The most comprehensive of these centers is the Temple of Diana which draws all forces to it in Montemayor's and Gil Polo's romances; it is the shrine of the goddess, of course, presided over by her priestess, the sage and mysterious Felicia; but it is also the center of Spanish chivalry, for inside its baroque façade stand statutes of The Cid, Fernán Gonzalez, Bernardo del Carpio, and other heroes.

The inner circle surrounding this supernatural center is "Arcady," the pastoral land. It is, as it had always been, a purely artificial concoction derived from literature—a fact that Sannazaro indicated very forcefully by making his descriptive passages a deliberate contexture of references to well known passages in Ovid, Virgil, Petrarch, and others. Even when this land is given an air of actuality by proper names, it turns out to be an artificial heightening of the actual. The setting of *Diana*, for instance, is this: "In the fieldes of the auncient and principall citie of *Leon* in Spaine, lying along the bankes of the river *Ezla*, lived a Shepherdesse called *Diana*"; it is securely fixed, geographically, by the city "Soldina" (Seville) [4] to the south and the Portuguese cities of

4. See López Estrada, ed., *Diana*, p. 96, note.

Lisbon and Coimbra, with "towres Pyramydes, and shining pin-
nacles, reared up to the skies" (152) on the west. Yet, for all
the precision gained by this naming, the reader soon realizes that
Montemayor's world is not rustic Spain but a classical world
transported to the Spanish countryside. The shepherds there are
the shepherds of literary tradition, gentle, adept at song, leisurely,
caring for little more than their flocks and love; all day long they
sit in the shade, piping as if they would never grow old. There
are subhuman Savages there, and classic Nymphs, half-women,
half-goddesses, not to mention Felicia and all the magic in the
implausible Temple at the center of this land. Montemayor's pastoral land is as indeterminate, and therefore as much of an artifice,
as Theocritus', Virgil's, or Sannazaro's.

The main difference between the classical and Renaissance
pastoral lands lies in the way in which each was abstract; for, while
it always remained a fairyland, "Arcady" developed from an
abstract stage without time or place that excluded as much of
actual life as possible, to a place that was the abstract of life and
hence was so inclusive as to approach a microcosm. The Renaissance pastoral world becomes "every place" instead of "no place."
Sannazaro's Arcadia contains an ornate temple (*Prosa* III) as well
as shady glens, epic funeral games (*Prosa* XI) as well as pastoral
sports, and a richly varied cast of shepherds to confront each
other: ordinary rustics, Platonist rustics like Elenco and Ophelia,
silly and pretentious ones like Montano and Uranio, and learned
disguised noblemen like Ergasto, Galitio, and Selvaggio. Montemayor's pastoral circle is even more compendious, for it includes
demi-goddesses and subhuman savages "covered all over with long
and thicke haire" (49) as well as men, the violence of battle as well
as pastoral leisure, knights as well as shepherds, courtly as well as
bourgeois love, art as well as nature.[5] What C. S. Lewis says of
Sidney's pastoral circle is true of Montemayor's (as well as Gil
Polo's and Cervantes') too:

> Sidney by no means commits himself to the claim that his
> Arcadia represents the state of innocence in any strictly Christian

5. Compare the contrasting but equally serious descriptions of the natural
beauty Belisa and the courtly lady Felismena on pp. 71 and 91 respectively.

or Stoical sense. Its woods are greener, its rivers purer, its sky brighter than ours. But its inhabitants are 'ideal' only in the sense that they are either more beautiful or more ugly, more stately or more ridiculous, more vicious or more virtuous, than those whom we meet every day. The world he paints is, in fact, simplified and heightened; because it is the poet's business to feign 'notable images' of virtues and vices.[6]

The reason for the microcosmic bent of Renaissance "Arcadies" is, of course, the nature of the action that is to go on inside them: they are melting pots where different realms of life meet, interact, and illuminate each other.

Since the pastoral circle is microcosmic, it represents a purification of the outer circle of the great world whose elements it abstracts. The outermost circle of the romance setting is the polar opposite of the inner circle: it is urban, complex and sophisticated; it is turbulent, the realm of warfare and death; and it is not a pure artifact, but rather a naturalistically drawn version of the world men really live in. There are, however, two distinct types of outer circles: in romances like Sannazaro's and Belleau's that stress semi-autobiographical and atmospheric elements, the outer world is assumed to be the actual milieu of the author rather than part of a fictional world (as it was in Virgil's *Eclogues*). In *Arcadia* it is the world of Naples where the Sannazaro family lived, of Baja, Vesuvius, and the Sebeto where the author's friends Caracciolo (*Egloga* X), Cariteo, Summonte, and Pontano (*Prosa* XII) live. The function of its contrast with the inner circle is not to contrast ways of life, but to define the nature and appeal of an imagined world—the world of poetry—by means of its differences from reality.

However, in romances which, like *Daphnis and Chloe* and *Ameto*, detached their stories from autobiography to become fully developed fictions, the outer circle is not the "real" world, but the outermost part of a fictional world; it becomes, in fact, a representation of the world of *epic* in direct contrast to that of pastoral. The reason for this is partly the influence of chivalric romances like *Orlando Furioso* and *Menina e Moça* on Montemayor, but may just as likely have developed out of the microcosmic nature

6. *English Literature in the Sixteenth Century*, p. 341.

of the inner circle. Sometimes, as in *Diana*, the heroic world is a highly stylized version of the courtly world of the cities around the pastoral land, separate but not excluded from it; there, the main heroic elements are high love,[7] warfare, and chivalry. But sometimes, too, the outer circle expands to include the vast turbulent scene we usually find in epic, as when Gil Polo introduced characters from over the seas, shipwrecked on the Spanish coast, or when Lope de Vega in his *Arcadia* (1598) or Corral in *Cintia de Aranjuez* (1629) introduced naval combats and pirates into their outer circles.[8]

Whether the outer circles be "real" or fictional, it is obvious that the three parts of the pastoral setting represent a gradual purification toward the center: from the turbulent, heroic, and sometimes "subnatural" world with all its complexities and accidents, to the simple natural world that includes the outer world's elements purified, to the supernatural center where the human and the divine meet.[9]

The action of the pastoral romance is simply the progress of the hero through the various areas of the setting: from the outer circle into the inner circle, hence to the center, and out again. Since each circle of the setting encourages a certain kind of activity, this progress is equivalent to entrance into Arcady in pain and turmoil and re-emergence in harmony with oneself. More particularly, the standard pastoral action consists of these elements in this order: disintegration in the turbulent outer circle, education in the pastoral circle, and rebirth at the sacred center.

> *Disintegration:* the sojourner-hero usually enters the pastoral land from the heroic world under the pressure of some grief or love that has left his mind a set of conflicting emotions he cannot resolve.
>
> *Education:* once there, he learns certain basic truths that show him how to reconcile his conflicts. He usually does this by a process of *analysis*—by seeing his situation reflected in those of other people around him, and then coming face to face with his

7. This love becomes assimilated to epic by the theomachia between Venus and Pallas Athene which preceded Felismena's birth.

8. See Avalle-Arce, *La novela*, p. 172.

9. See the excellent article by Bruce W. Wardropper, "The *Diana* of Montemayor: Revaluation and Interpretation," *Studies in Philology*, 48 (1951), 130.

own divided mind; this process of analysis is the ultimate raison d'être for the analogous and interacting multiple plots of romance.

Reintegration: at the center under the aegis of a god or a magician, he adjusts his conflicts, composes his mind, and leaves for the outer world again.

We can see the workings of this three-part pattern more intimately in the particular cases of the major romances, which may stand for the many versions of it we find both before Sidney and after, in *Pandosto, Rosalynde,* Spenser's Book of Courtesy, and Shakespeare's two great pastorals, *The Winter's Tale* and *The Tempest.*

As we should expect from the lyrical structure of Sannazaro's *Arcadia,* action in the sense of conflict and development seems to be totally absent from it: Syncero merely listens to love tales and elegies, attends the rites of the gods of earth Pan and Pales, takes part in funerals, and finally returns to Naples to find his beloved dead. Yet his fortunes have taken a turn by the end of the book and therefore create a clear contrast with his state at the beginning. In the early part of the book, the mysteries about Syncero keep our attention focused on his mental turmoil; by the melancholy tone of his descriptions and his excessive reactions to love and grief, we know that he is torn apart by unhappiness in love. That he is not what he seems to be, but is really someone disguised as Syncero the foreign shepherd, reinforces our sense of his self-division: he is not really he. At the end of the book he feels that he has changed from what he was, for in the epilogue *A la sampogna* Syncero, standing outside Arcadia, announces himself not only as the usual sadder and wiser man, but as a "coltissimo giovane" (315) and no real shepherd—Jacopo Sannazaro rather than Syncero. He realizes that his sojourn in Arcadia was an instructive masquerade and is now willing to resume his rightful place in society. Surely this is no happy vision of a rebirth; what it does imply is a quelling of the forces in turmoil within him, the close of a chapter in his life made possible by his acceptance of the fact of death. Thus he learns of Philli's death in the cavern that houses the fertilizing waters of the earth (indicating the cyclic recurrence of birth and death), and the lament for Philli is distanced from him and us by being sung by Meliseo and others for whom she becomes a kind of earth goddess in her new life in heaven. This ending assimilates *Arcadia* to one of the primary pastoral themes (exemplified in Virgil's First *Eclogue* or Spenser's "April" eclogue), the subordination of individual human feelings to the great processes of the earth.

We find the catharsis, the necessary step from his inner turmoil at the beginning to his resignation at the end, in his reactions to the several stories and songs that reflect his plight. After almost every lament, Syncero weeps and tries to comfort the singer as the woods resound with his grief; indeed, he often forms part of a mournful chorus of all the shepherds, and he even becomes an active mourner in the funerals of two strangers, Androgeo and Massilia. This sympathy produces a twofold process in Syncero: it draws him out of himself into relations with others, and through them it draws him into a real relation with the world and human life. By the latter I mean to indicate that two facts are made plain to Syncero: that his case is by no means unique, but part of a common human experience, and that his case has its rightful place in the order of the natural world. The total effect of this sympathy is that Syncero's situation is not only analyzed but generalized in Arcadia; he has been educated for his acceptance of death by seeing the commonness of unhappiness in love, the unifying power of such a common suffering, and the necessity of death and decay as part of the unalterable course of the earth.

Therefore, Syncero's experience follows a threefold outline of disintegration, education by analysis, and rebirth. He starts as Jacopo Sannazaro pained by his fruitless love for Phyllida in the real outer world of Naples. He enters the inner circle of Arcadia disguised as the shepherd Syncero, where he undergoes education in the ubiquity of unhappy love and death by listening sympathetically to the love laments of Selvaggio, Ergasto, Montano, Uranio, Galiteo, Logisto, Elpyno, Charino, and Clonico, and to the elegies on Androgeo and Massilia. Led by a vision, Syncero goes to the center, the cave whence fertilizing waters run, to hear of Phyllida's death. And thence, grieving but accepting, he goes back to the outer world to resume his true identity.

That is the action Sannazaro derived from Boccaccio's *Ameto,* where it was, of course, much more explicit because of the allegory, and entirely different in tone. When Ameto, propelled by love of Lia, leaves the rough deep forests of Etruria in spring, he signalizes the change that is occurring in his life by changing his clothes, having "cast off his mean clothing and clothed himself in a more ornate costume" (24). In the inner circle, the mythical world of piety, love, and pastoralism that gathers at Florence, he receives his education. Here we can see an explicit example of the identity of sympathetic entrance into the parallel cases of others, analysis, and education; for (as we saw before) his reactions to the seven stories of the nymphs are really reactions to his own possible refinement, and these reactions are, allegorically, what gain him the four cardinal and three theological virtues. The process is completed at the third place, the shrine of Venus, whose voice comes out of the thunder commanding Ameto's baptism and rebirth in spiritual love. And so "he tore his rough clothes from his back and plunged into the clear fountain" of Venus (143), whence, after his baptism, he receives the new clothes of instruction from the seven nymphs. Now, as he shifts his perceptions from the eyes to the intellect, he despises his *"primitiva vita,"* pledges himself the servant of love, and goes out through the circles into his new life. The various schemes of the three places—forest, Florence, and shrine; rustic skins, better clothes, and rich clothes; the life of survival, the life of sensual love, and the life of intellectual love—all these schemes and more express explicitly the action which Ameto undergoes as he passes from outer circle to center and out again.

Of course, this tale has the pastoral pattern without the pastoral meaning Sannazaro gave to it; the classic situation in the Renaissance romances was not transfiguration but coming into harmony with oneself. And so Syncero, while he acquires knowledge as Ameto does, stresses more the acceptance of his grief by means of this knowledge. Therefore, throughout *Arcadia,* we hear Gallus' strains of melancholy acceptance:

> Tristis at ille: "tamen cantabitis, Arcades," inquit,
> "montibus haec vestris, soli cantare periti

Arcades. o mihi tum quam molliter ossa quiescant,
vestra meos olim si fistula dicat amores"

(But unhappy Gallus said, "Yet you, Arcadians, will sing my
story to your mountains, Arcadians alone skilled in singing. O
how softly would my bones then rest if your pipes would sing
of my love in days to come").

The progeny of Sannazaro exhibit usually a more optimistic
form of the threefold pattern, for harmony is interpreted by them
as success in love or relief from it. Such is its appearance in the
major part of *L'Aura Soave*, where Lauso takes up the disguise of
a shepherd and flees Rome under the pangs of shameful passion,
comes to the other shepherds in the fields outside the city, tells
them his story and receives their sympathy, then hears Alanio's
story of Ophelte's similar experience of the stony-hearted mistress.
Prompted by sympathy, he goes with Alanio to the inner place,
the castle of Ismenio, where ceremonies for the release of both
him and Ophelte are conducted, issuing later in a miraculous
release from his love for "L'Aura Soave" and his return home as
his own man once more.

Gil Polo's *Diana enamorada* is a fuller example of this pattern
since his world is more extensive and his cast larger. Marcelio, disguised as a shepherd, enters the pastoral circle of Ezla from the
great world, where he has suffered shipwreck and the violences of
men and nature, and, worse, separation from his beloved Alcida
and her family. Once inside the pastoral land, he hears Diana and
Ismenia tell how they, like him, suffer separation from their loved
ones, either by jealousy or another's deceit; the three help each
other on their journey to Felicia's Temple of Diana, where they
hope a cure to their problems can be given. Once they reach the
Temple, all three find their loved ones there, and so Felicia unites
Marcelio to Alcida, Ismenia to Montano, and Diana to Sireno. If
there is some tendency here to go beyond mere analysis of the self
through others to reach sympathetic action on the behalf of
others, then it owes its existence to the original *Diana* of Montemayor.

The action in the Temple of Diana in Book IV divides the
Diana in two. Books I–III pose problems, Books V–VII solve

them. Books I–III show a "communal search" [1] for the cure to love's division of the self, while Books V–VII present a set of interwoven individual searches for salvation, in which the bulk of the action devolves upon Felismena. We might further add that the first three books outline the analysis of Felismena's difficulties in her reflectors, while the last three further her education in active virtue. As we discovered in our treatment of the reflectors in *Diana*, the fact that other people suffer the same ills as the heroine is the immediate cause of her helping them; or, to put it another way, analysis of the self immediately produces an education of the self in active virtue. Felismena's education consists in helping others. She alone of all the characters is not cured of her ills by an outside agency; she must somehow *win* happiness for herself. Apparently, in the conferences at the Temple, Felicia tells her how to win it, for upon leaving, "*Felismena* (who had that day put on againe her Shepherdesses weeds)" was "particularly and well advised what to doe" (126). What she actually did, and, it seems most probable, what she was instructed to do, was to find Don Felis and save him, and also to help Arsileo, Filémon, and Duarda —to accomplish her own happiness by helping people in circumstances similar to her own. And these people are of a lower class, shepherds; the noblewoman's services to such, in a class-conscious book like *Diana*, amounts to genuine humility as well as active sympathy. "To see her difficulties in their true perspective she has to live in the country." [2] She sees them, in their true perspective, reflected in the difficulties of these shepherds. And she cures them by stooping to help them.

It is significant that Felismena's disintegration and reintegration are shown largely by changes of clothing. The self-division she is suffering when she enters the world of Ezla is apparent not only from the fact that she is wearing a disguise, but also that this disguise—as a warlike shepherdess—signalizes (as it does in the case of Sidney's Pyrocles) the uncertainty of sex she exhibited as a page beloved of Celia and loving Don Felis. She doffs it only once, at the Temple of Diana: "*Felicia* tolde her . . . that during her

1. Wardropper, pp. 133–34.
2. Ibid., p. 143.

abode in her pallace, she shoulde put off her pastorall habits, untill the time came, when she was to weare them againe" (90). This time is that of her leaving the Temple for the pastoral fields: "thou shalt depart from thine owne house heere, in the same habite that thou camest" (123). In this habit she helps the other shepherds, finally commits her last masculine act in helping Don Felis, and achieves reintegration as her former self along with union with him. Her disguise is symbolic both of her role for the shepherds and of the pastoral life's role for her. And her changes of clothes define very clearly the pattern of her actions in the various scenes.

She starts *in propria persona* in the outer world of courtly Spain as a young noblewoman in love with the unfaithful Don Felis. Disguised humbly as a warlike shepherdess in order to seek out her beloved in the pastoral world of Ezla, Felismena meets and helps Sireno, Sylvano, Selvaggia, and Belisa, all of whose fortunes reflect hers. She goes with them to the supernatural center, the Temple of Diana, where—clothed now in royal robes—she learns how to right her love. She must resume her pastoral disguise and go out into the pastoral circle again to help Belisa and Arsileo, Amarílida and Filemón, Duarda and Danteo, and finally her own Don Felis. At that point he repents, and they marry and return together to the outer world from which they came.

The Renaissance pastoral romance seems as distant in character as in time from Virgil's "Gallus"; yet most of its seeds are there— the change of life a sojourner would experience in Arcadia extended to a plot, Gallus' imagined pastoral double multiplied into reflecting episodes, and so forth. What the pastoral romance in fact did was to implement the pastoral vision of the concord between man and his environment by a plot, an action. This action outlined the change from disharmony to harmony, showed the change as occurring only by a man's sympathetic relation to others, and presented it as a product of changing one place for another, a *natural* place. This is the harmonious vision that pastoral romance brought to Sir Philip Sidney.

2. Sidney and the Pastoral Romance

SOURCES

Sidney's *Arcadia* is only slightly indebted to the earlier pastoral romances for sources, since the raw materials of *Arcadia* are, in fact, as often chivalric as pastoral. But we can make an exception of the Eclogues or pastoral interludes, and we may as well indicate Sidney's debts to the tradition there. The song "Lady reservd by the heav'ns" (in the First Eclogues), a debate on court and country values between the exile and the shepherd, obviously owes its inspiration to Virgil's first *Eclogue*, and imitates its opening in lines 11–14:

> But ô happy be you, which safe from fyry reflection
> Of *Phoebus* violence in shade of sweet *Cyparissus,*
> Or pleasant mirtell, may teach th'unfortunate *Eccho*
> In these woods to resounde the renowmed name of a goddesse.

The lament for Basilius in the Fourth Eclogues, "Since that to death is gone the shepheard hie," is modeled on the traditional pastoral elegy of Moschus for Bion; the main similarities are the refrain, the addresses to Echo and Philomela, the flower passage, and the central comparison of nature's cycle to man's. Though Moschus forms the basis for many Renaissance elegies—notably Alamanni's first Eclogue and *Egloga* XI of Sannazaro's *Arcadia*—

Sidney is closer to the original than to any of the imitations.[1] The dialogue "Come *Dorus,* come" (the First Eclogues) owes much of its material and its intricate versification to the song of Montano and Uranio in Sannazaro's *Egloga* II,[2] as does a later song, "Downe, downe *Melampus,*" in the Second Eclogues.[3] Likewise the dialogue between the lovelorn Dorus and the reasonable shepherd Dicus in the Second Eclogues has many similarities to Sannazaro's *Egloga* VIII. Although it is difficult to fix the source of a sestina, since all tend to employ similar pastoral key words, Sidney's "Ye Gote-heard Gods" seems closer to Sannazaro's *Egloga* IV than to any of the other examples of the form in Centorio, Montemayor, and Gil Polo.[4] Finally, the pastoral epithalamion from the Third Eclogues, while it has the whole tradition stemming from Sappho and Catullus behind it, owes its general outline and its stanzaic structure to the song for Diana and Sireno at the end of Book IV of Gil Polo's romance.[5]

In the narrative parts of Arcadia, however, we can cite with justice little more than three instances of borrowing from the pastoral romance, all of them from *Diana.* The opening scene of Strephon and Klaius on the beach is of course an allusion to the opening dialogue between Sireno and Sylvano; [6] the story of the original Zelmane who disguises herself to follow Pyrocles in Book II is a digest of Felismena's plot; finally, the pretended execution of Pamela and Philoclea in Book III shows some resemblance to the delusions Belisa fell victim to.[7] In addition, Sidney may have developed the briefly mentioned contest of running at the ring and some elements of Phalantus' tourney from Gálvez de Mon-

1. For the parallels with Sannazaro, see Ringler, ed., *The Poems of Sir Philip Sidney*, notes, pp. 419–20.

2. See Hector Genouy, *L' "Arcadia" de Sidney dans ses rapports avec l' "Arcadia" de Sannazaro et la "Diana" de Montemayor* (Montpellier, 1928), p. 119; the debt of Sidney's last page or so to lines 81–100 of *Egloga* II are the most pronounced.

3. See especially lines 37ff. in Sannazaro.

4. Genouy, pp. 178–79.

5. See Ringler, p. 411.

6. See T. P. Harrison, Jr., "A Source of Sidney's *Arcadia*," University of Texas Studies in English, 6 (1926), p. 56.

7. Genouy, pp. 115, 116.

talvo's *El Pastor de Fílida*.[8] For the rest, the sources are either classical or chivalric. The incidental episodes, especially those whose setting is Asia Minor, all exhibit the characteristic themes and melodramatic atmosphere of the Greek romances; and it is quite probable that two of them—the stories of the Paphlagonian king and of Plangus and Andromana—were derived directly from Heliodorus' *Æthiopica*.[9] Isoud in Malory's *Morte D'Arthur* probably suggested Gynecia and her love philtre, while the destructive lovers Tristram and Lancelot may have suggested some elements of the Amphialus story,[1] though his character and political actions are closer to Plato's study of despotic man in *Republic* 570–72; the character and intrigues of Timantus in Book IV certainly come from Plato's concept of the timocratic man (*Republic* 548–49). The gigantic chivalric romance *Amadis de Gaula* supplied the episodes of Helen and Musidorus in Book I, the tale of Pamphilus in Book II, and perhaps some of the details of Pyrocles' imprisonment in Book III.[2]

What is of paramount importance is that the main plot of *Arcadia* came from a chivalric romance. A rapid reading of Book XI of *Amadis de Gaula* should convince anyone that Moody and Zandvoort were correct in assigning the adventures of Agesilan and his cousin Arlanges there as the source of Sidney's plot.[3] Sidney combined two episodes to form his plot: in the first (Chapters 15–21, 33–41, and 52–56), the heroes fall in love, Agesilan with a picture of Diane, Arlanges later with the real Cleofile, and

8. Compare Montalvo, in Marcelino Menédez y Pelayo's *Origines de la Novela* (4 vols. Madrid, 1907–25) 2, 578, and Sidney (1598 edition), p. 117, the imprese of Montalvo's shepherds (pp. 579–81) with those of Sidney's knights (pp. 58–60). Compare also Montalvo's description of his Uranio's costume (p. 579) with those of Sidney's Knight of the Tombe (p. 219) or the Blacke Knight (p. 297) at the siege in Book III.

9. See Samuel Lee Wolff, *The Greek Romances in Elizabethan Prose Fiction*, Columbia University Studies in Comparative Literature (New York, 1912), pp. 312–13.

1. See Marcus Seldon Goldman, *Sir Philip Sidney and the Arcadia*, Illinois Studies in Language and Literature, *17*, no. 1 (Urbana, 1934), pp. 195–99, 203–05.

2. See Zandvoort, *Sidney's Arcadia*, p. 195.

3. William Vaughn Moody, "An Inquiry into the Sources of Sir Philip Sidney's *Arcadia*," MS honors thesis, Harvard University, 1894; Zandvoort summarizes Moody's argument on pp. 194–95.

proceed to the island of Guindaye and Diane's court disguised as the female minstrels "Daraïde" and "Garaye"; in the second, at Galdap (Chapters 83–86), Daraïde is beset by the loves of both King Galinides, who believes he is a woman, and Queen Salderne, who sees beneath his disguise. Sidney combined the episodes of Guindaye and Galdap by having Pyrocles, disguised as the Amazon "Zelmane" (in the Old *Arcadia* it is "Cleophila" after *Amadis*) and drawn to the isolated retreat in Arcadia by Philoclea's picture, love Philoclea and be loved by King Basilius and Queen Gynecia at the same time, while his cousin Musidorus (disguised as the shepherd "Dorus") loves Philoclea's sister Pamela. Sidney split a third scene at Lemnos (Chapters 88–89 of the *Amadis*) between his two heroes: Pyrocles is forgiven and falls asleep beside his beloved as Arlanges did, while Musidorus and Pamela sing songs and carve trees in a grove on their way to the coast (Book III). Garaye's fight with the corsairs (Chapter 57) he transformed into Musidorus' fight with some stray rebels (Book IV). The incident of the war at Galdap (Chapter 86) became the revolt at the end of Book II; a council of war there became the council at the supposed death of Basilius (Book IV).

"Truly I have knowne men, that even with reading *Amadis de gaule*, which God knoweth, wanteth much of a perfect *Poesie*, have found their hearts moved to the exercise of courtesie, liberalitie, and especially courage," wrote Sidney.[4] The effect of his transformation of *Amadis* into main plot of *Arcadia* was precisely to make it a perfect poesy, partly by placing it in a significant pastoral setting and thus endowing it with meaning, partly by surrounding it with reflecting episodes and tightening its structure. By turning the aimless travels of the heroes into the pastoral change of place, he made them significant in the action; and, within the new scene, he made the constantly reiterated amorous self-division of Agesilan the beginning of a full record of change or maturation of personality by love (a record reinforced by parallel plotting).

His greatest achievement in refining raw material was in structure: he gave it pointed unity of place, reduced the time consider-

4. *The Defence of Poesie,* in *Works, 3,* 20.

ably, pulled the various adventures into real relation by causal connections, and reduced the seesaw motion of his source to a series of events rising to a single climax. The sign of his structural achievement is the finished form of *Arcadia* in five books separated from one another by pastoral interludes or "Eclogues," for this division shows how closely *Arcadia* is modeled on the five-act structure of dramatic plot.[5] This fact comes out clearly in the Old *Arcadia*, where the more simple plot and the designation of each division as a "Booke or Acte" make it explicit, but it is true of the final *Arcadia* as well, where, if the episodes sometimes blur the main plot line, they also stress the major phases by thematic unity. Book I therefore contains the exposition; by its end, the heroes have established themselves in the pastoral retreat and begun to make love to their mistresses. Book II, in which the princesses reciprocate the heroes' love and Basilius and Gynecia come to the fore as complicating agents, constitutes the rising action. The complications rise to their highest pitch in Book III, where, however, all of the persons are left on the verge of satisfactory solutions of their desires. Book IV starts the series of reversals, from the minor characters Dametas and Mopsa to the princes and Basilius, while of course Book V brings all matters to dénouement.

The pervasive influence of the pastoral romance on *Arcadia* may be gauged from the fact that Sidney's structural model for reducing the *Amadis* to tight formal units was Gaspar Gil Polo's *Diana enamorada*. Gil Polo, as we know, imposed a clearly articulated structure on the kind of thematic unity he inherited from Montemayor by dividing his book into five acts, each separated from the others by a set of pastoral songs and each beginning with a definition of its progress. Thus while Book I introduces two characters suffering a disintegration of personal relationships, Book II carries them toward a solution of their problems at Felicia's temple; Book III starts the reversal in the reunion of Marcelio with Polydoro and Clenarda, and Book IV completes it

---

5. See Bertram Dobell, "New Light upon Sir Philip Sidney's 'Arcadia,'" *Quarterly Review*, 211 (1909), 81; C. M. Dowlin, *Sir William Davenant's Gondibert* . . . (Philadelphia, 1934), p. 72, n. 108; and Richard H. Perkinson, "The Epic in Five Acts," *Studies in Philology*, 43 (1946), 473. Perkinson rather unconvincingly suggests Chaucer's *Troilus* as the source of Sidney's structure.

when all the characters find their loved ones with Felicia; Book V merely celebrates the dénouement. *Diana enamorada* supplied Sidney not only with the form of his plot line but also with a precedent for binding all the incidental stories in a book or act as the expressions of a single theme (as we shall see at more leisure in Chapter 5); Sidney even adopted Gil Polo's device of summarizing the state of his theme in each book, as for instance at the start of Book IV:

> The almightie wisdome evermore delighting to shewe the world, that by unlikeliest meanes greatest matters may come to conclusion: that humane reason may be the more humbled, and more willingly give place to divine providence . . .   [391] [6]

> The complaints that men do ordinarily attribute to Fortune are verie great, which would not be so many nor so grievous, if they considered well the good that commeth oftentimes by her mutabilities . . . a wise man (how much soever he is touched with her) should not live with affiance in the possession of worldly felicities, nor with despaire in suffering adversities; but should rather moderate himselfe with such wisedome, to entertaine pleasure as a thing not permanent, and griefe and sorrow as things that may have an ende in time.[7]

Our brief survey indicates that Sidney's debt to the pastoral tradition for source material is not very significant. What our account of the formation of *Arcadia* does indicate, however, is the importation of nonpastoral material and its formation into a whole by the techniques of pastoral romance. It is in the matter of meaningful form, therefore, that we shall find the true extent of Sidney's relationship to Sannazaro, Montemayor, and their imitators.

SIDNEY'S MORALIZATION OF PLOT

What *Arcadia* does owe to the earlier pastoral romances is something more general and at the same time much more important than sources. It inherits their vision as embodied in a cer-

6. Quotations and page references throughout this study are taken from the 1598 folio of *Arcadia*. I use this rather than the 1593 edition because it corrects several obvious errors in that text and is more readily available to the reader.
7. Yong's translation, p. 450.

tain scene and a peculiar pattern of action within that scene. The scene is of course the pastoral land, not exactly Edenic but exhibiting good and evil in pure and radical forms; Sidney stressed the abstraction inherent in such a scene by making his land an artificial retreat walled off by Basilius from the rest of the world. The importance of the scene is underlined as in the romances by surrounding it with contrasting lands where warfare and confusion reign, the total effect being that of a many-tiered fictional world. Since the central assumption in the pastoral vision is that scene determines act, that a pure natural environment will produce a harmonious relation of parts in the human soul, then the plot of *Arcadia* becomes defined by the acts of entering and leaving the pastoral retreat—amorous distress forcing one into the retreat, success allowing re-emergence from it. The plot determined by this scenic vision in *Arcadia* falls into the standard pattern of the romance plot (which is itself only the fullest narrative example of love psychologically or analytically considered, the main subject of pastoral since Theocritus): an initial breakdown under love at the borders of the retreat, a prolonged period of analysis of the self in parallel to others in the retreat, education or illumination there, and a final reintegration (in Sidney's case alone, a religious one) followed by a return to the world.

Even a brief résumé of the action of *Arcadia* will show how very basic to it is the pastoral romance narrative pattern. Pyrocles and Musidorus, cast up on the shores of Arcadia out of the turbulent world of Asia Minor, fall in love with the princesses Philoclea and Pamela; bitten by love, they change their names and assume pastoral disguises in order to be allowed to enter the retreat where their mistresses reside. Once there, they gain the love of their mistresses in a series of interviews interlarded with stories of love and turmoil. But their minds are still disrupted by conflicting desires, and a series of interruptions—including a peasant revolt and a full-scale civil war—combined with the importunities of several unwanted lovers only spreads their disorder further. They work out of it by two means: control fostered by a reasoning faculty that has been strengthened by trial; and illumination by their mistresses, producing the liberating recognition of the connection of the self to others and nature under divine Providence. At the end, they achieve harmony of soul just as the outside world enters the pastoral retreat in order to try them and lead them back into the world from which they came.

Any brief treatment of the plot of *Arcadia* does violence to the reader's experience of the book, for its very bulk, diversity of materials, and complexity of form appear as its main characteristics. It is this complicated nature of *Arcadia* which makes it seem at first so unlike its predecessors, and yet it is precisely there that Sidney's real grasp of the implications of pastoral shows through. Four of these complicating elements are worth especial note here: a more complex setting, a much more complicated plot, the importation of nonpastoral matter in considerable bulk, and a preponderance of argumentation. The first two develop trends already existing in the pastoral romance; the last two, which do not, constitute Sidney's essential innovations.

The fictional world of *Arcadia* differs from its predecessors in circumstantiality and range, but the most important difference is in structure. We have characterized the world of pastoral romance as a center and two concentric circles, the inner one pastoral, the outer one its antithesis; *Arcadia* has three of these concentric circles. The innermost circle, the pastoral retreat within Arcadia where Basilius has immured himself and his family, is the usual pastoral place, the purely artificial domain of the natural, amorous, and contemplative. Its center, less clearly focused than Sannazaro's or Montemayor's, is not a shrine but a group of places: two lodges, one for the family Dametas and Pamela (hence the focal point for Musidorus), the other for Basilius, Gynecia, and Philoclea (the focal point for Pyrocles), an arbor where tales of love are told, and a cave where events of lust, death, and judgment occur. The emphasis here is therefore less supernatural than microcosmic. The outermost circle includes most of the classical world, Magna Graecia and Macedonia, the kingdoms of Phrygia, Pontus, Paphlagonia, Lycia, and Iberia in Asia Minor; it is a turbulent and melodramatic world reminiscent of the Greek romances, the domain of pirates, tyrants, giants, and Amazons, the scene of constant civil and international strife. Between these opposed circles lies the state of Arcadia proper, whose condition is a mean between the others, since it is peaceful and agricultural like the retreat, but contains the seeds of civil disruption in Amphialus and the villainous Cecropia and Demagoras. In the pastoral scale of purifications from subnatural to ideally natural, the circle of Arcadia forms a kind of tertium quid, the kind of natural but imperfect state attainable in the world. The scale therefore runs from the subnatural world of tooth and nail, to the ordinary world as we find it, to the natural and idyllic, to a microcosmic center where basic matters of love, lust, and death exist in their utmost purity; the purification here is not metaphysical but abstractive. In terms of action, the middle circle of Arcadia forms a "threshold" world leading from the turmoil of the active life into the peace of the contemplative; it is there that the heroes fall in love with the women who guide them into the retreat. It is apparent that Sidney patterned his three-part setting more elaborately than the other romancers did; and he made this pattern especially explicit by giving his heroes different names, appearances, and roles in each—Pyrocles and Musidorus in the outermost circle, Daiphantus and Palladius in Arcadia, the Amazon Zelmane and the shepherd Dorus in the pastoral retreat.

The plot of Sidney's *Arcadia* is more complicated than that of any pastoral romance (with the possible exception of its only notable successor, *Astrée*). The intrigue is filled with turns, counterturns, and recurring obstacles to fulfillment. Moreover, it is a double plot with twin heroes; this factor does not complicate plot line as much as it might, however, for the two lines are conducted in such close parallel that their effect is one of seeing a single action from two points of view. What really produces confusion in the reader is the series of thirteen incidental episodes let into the narrative at various places. Paramount among them is that gigantic interruption of the amorous intrigue, the captivity episode of Book III. On a much smaller scale are the nine short political tragedies which the princes relate out of their experiences in Book II: the tales of the kings of Phrygia, Pontus, and Paphlagonia, the tales of Erona, Plangus, Pamphilus, Chremes, Andromana, and Plexirtus. Finally, there are the three preliminary episodes of passion in Book I, the stories of Argalus and Parthenia and Amphialus and Helen, and the emblematic tournament of Phalantus.

Sidney imposed a strict decorum in the settings of these stories: the tales of turbulent politics all come out of the princes' past in Asia Minor; the tales of Amphialus and Argalus, which show love flawed by the adversities of the world, occur in the kingdom of Arcadia proper; the pastoral retreat itself is reserved for the main amorous plot and whatever shepherdish doings resemble it. It is only in their number that these episodes make *Arcadia* distinct from previous pastoral romances, where it was not only standard practice but necessary also to have a number of subsidiary plots tangent to the orbit of the main plot. And, as we shall demonstrate in detail in Chapter 5, these episodes conform to romance practice in acting as analogues to the main plot, each showing its events in a different light. But Sidney put these reflecting stories to a use different from Sannazaro and Montemayor: if we remember that most of them are stories that the princes themselves tell, we can see that they do not always present cases that the heroes enter in order to understand themselves, but function rather as exempla. They are directed not only inward to instruct the heroes, but outward to clarify the nature of the action for the readers as well. Thus Sidney's amplification of plot assumes a peculiarly didactic hue.

The incidental episodes are the vehicles of all of the nonpastoral matter that enters *Arcadia*, most of it either political or chivalric. To be sure, the mere presence of chivalric matter in a pastoral romance is not unprecedented; through Montemayor and Gálvez de Montalvo it had become a standard feature of the Spanish pastoral. And Sidney preserved decorum by placing most of it outside the pastoral retreat and pushing it back in time into his heroes' pre-Arcadian adventures. Yet never before had the pastoral romance sustained such a weight of tournaments and battles; and of course it had never before contained even a hint of the vast political intrigues we find in *Arcadia*. However, Sidney's distribution of this narrative material brings it under the control of his pastoral plot, for the chivalric and political events always parallel the action of love in Arcadia. Thus, for instance, while Musidorus experiences the operation of love in Book II he recalls his former active life in Asia Minor. The two heroes often pair off to form active and contemplative attitudes toward the same problem (as their different disguises as female warrior and shepherd imply)—Musidorus fighting for love outside Cecropia's castle while Pyrocles suffers for it within, Musidorus encountering Helen's knights at the same time as Pyrocles muses on the borders of the retreat, Musidorus eloping while Pyrocles exercises restraint—and so forth. In fact, one part of the vast design of *Arcadia* is the network of corresponding actions between the active political and chivalric sphere of life and the contemplative amorous and pastoral sphere, the most comprehensive of them being the conduct of the state of Arcadia in relation to the love plot.

The final innovation to consider here is the great importance given to argumentation and debate of all kinds. "It is significant," C. S. Lewis remarks, "that the whole story moves neither to a martial nor an amorous, but to a forensic climax; the great trial scene almost fills the fifth book." [8] The crisis of the plot occurs in a series of wide-ranging debates between Cecropia and her nieces Pamela and Philoclea in Book III, the final turning point in the debate on Providence between Pyrocles and his mistress in her bedchamber, the personal resolution in a dialogue between the heroes in prison. The very dual nature of the main plot makes it possible for the heroes to generate two different views of a matter which can then clash in dialogue. This argumentative material is quite different from the debates on questions of love we find in earlier romances (though the long dialogue on love and reason translated out of Leone Ebreo in Book IV of *Diana* is exceptional in approaching it); [9] it ranges far beyond that in bulk and subject, embracing as it does problems of love, ethics, political wisdom, theology, and even metaphysics. Its effect, of course, is to exert a consistently exemplary pressure on plot, to reveal the moral implications of every step.

Sidney's major innovations in the pastoral romance tend to one result: explicit scenic pattern, tales designed to show the reader

---

8. *English Literature in the Sixteenth Century*, p. 335.

9. See López Estrada, ed., *Diana*, pp. 194–201; the portion of Leone that Montemayor takes is pp. 57–62 in the translation of F. Friedeberg-Seeley and Jean H. Barnes (London, 1937).

the true nature of events, nonpastoral matter in parallel to pastoral, and extensive discussion all have, cumulatively, the effect of amplifying the main plot far beyond its original scope. The final purpose of this amplification is to show the universal applications, or the philosophical underpinnings, of the plot of pastoral romance established by Montemayor—in a word, to moralize plot.[1] Fulke Greville's assertion of his friend's intentions points to the same qualities we have isolated in the work as it exists: his end, wrote Greville, "was not vanishing pleasure alone, but morall Images, and Examples, (as directing threds) to guide every man through the confused *Labyrinth* of his own desires, and life."[2] Since for Sidney the precept must come only in the concrete example, such a comprehensive ethical aim must issue in copiousness and variety of incident:

> In all these creatures of his making, his intent, and scope was, to turn the barren Philosophy precepts into pregnant Images of life; and in them, first on the Monarch's part, lively to represent the growth, state, and declination of Princes, change of Government, and lawes: vicissitudes of sedition, faction, succession, confederacies, plantations, with all other errors, or alterations in publique affaires. Then again in the subjects case; the state of favor, disfavor, prosperitie, adversity, emulation, quarrell, undertaking, retiring, hospitality, travail, and all other moodes of private fortunes, or misfortunes. In which traverses (I know) his purpose was to limn out such exact pictures, of every posture in the minde, that any man being forced, in the straines of this life, to pass through any straights, or latitudes of good, or ill fortune might (as in a glasse) see how to set a good countenance upon all the discountenances of adversitie, and a stay upon the exorbitant smilings of chance.[3]

1. Several critics have remarked this moral bent as the main trait of *Arcadia;* J. F. Danby, for instance, writes that Sidney "is so consciously the intellectual moralizer of his material that in any case where we might suspect discrepancy, it is wise to bear in mind the possibility that we have missed his plan": *Poets on Fortune's Hill: Studies in Sidney, Shakespeare, Beaumont and Fletcher* (London, 1952), p. 57. Zandvoort calls *Arcadia* "at once a romance and a treatise" (p. 120).
2. *The Life of the Renowned Sir Philip Sidney,* p. 223.
3. Ibid., pp. 15–16.

Though Greville's own political bent makes his account somewhat lopsided, he does underline the two spheres of moral action which run parallel in *Arcadia,* the private and public or the ethical and political. And he does demonstrate that its moral aim dictated the very complexity or comprehensiveness which so strikes every reader of *Arcadia.*

This is the place of Sidney in the history of pastoral romance: while Sannazaro created a thematic unity out of selected poems and Montemayor developed this unity into interwoven plots, Sidney's contribution was the overdevelopment, *the moralization of plot.* It is just this trend that the Spanish romances were following at the time of Sidney's death; incipient in Gil Polo's headnotes on Fortune and virtue, the ethical motive broke into full bloom in Bartolomé López de Enciso's *Disengaño de celos* (1586), with its long inserted tales, its emphasis on humility, and its avowed purpose of stripping the mask of love from the vice of jealousy; [4] it continued in the exemplary novel of Molineo inserted into Bernardo Gonzáles de Bobadilla's *Nimphas y Pastores de Henares* (1587), and came to rest in the formalization of Juan Arze Solórzeno's *Tragedias de Amor* (1608), to which are attached "Alegorías" explaining the plot's ethical points.

While a consideration of *Astrée* is beyond the scope of our study, it might be valuable to point out the elements wherein D'Urfé followed Sidney's lead to bring the genre to its final stage and decay. Its episodic complication is tremendous; there are over thirty stories—in contrast to Sidney's mere thirteen—let into the plot, each related to the main narrative thread by the theme of love's difficulties. Like *Arcadia,* it is as courtly and chivalric as it is pastoral. The two elements start in a rhythmic alternation between the two poles of Lignon with Astrée and other pastoral figures and the Castle of Issoura with Celedon involved in Galathée's world of fifth-century politics, and end intertwined when the hero and heroine become involved in Polémas' siege of Galathée at Marcilly (an episode reminiscent of Tiridates' attack on Erona in *Arcadia*

4. See Avalle-Arce, pp. 155–56; he attributes this author's moral seriousness to the pressure of the Counter Reformation.

II). Of course, the discussions in *Astrée* are endless, but (and here we see the divergence of D'Urfé from Sidney) they involve questions of conduct rather than debates about values; and the rather spineless plot, which hinges on formalities and must be resolved by magic, lacks entirely the large moral scope of *Arcadia*.

This large moral scope can best be seen by analysis, by breaking down the copious action first into the main plot and then into its ramifications in several areas—in the pastoral plot that runs so closely beside it, in the scattered episodes that light it up at several points, and in the public action of which these smaller actions all form parts. To these four divisions correspond the various ingredients Gabriel Harvey found in the book, the amorous, the pastoral, the chivalric, and the political.

3. Amorous Courting

The very explicit and argumentative nature of *Arcadia* simplifies the task of defining its main plot. The action of pastoral romance hinges on a series of scene changes; in Sidney's *Arcadia*, whenever one changes scene one first discusses it, so that its full private and ethical significance is realized. By way of illustration, let us examine the first and last dialogues of the heroes Pyrocles and Musidorus—one pair of episodes among the many related scenes and actions making *Arcadia* the monumental pile that it is. Each of the two dialogues deals with a shift from active to contemplative virtues by means of going from one place into another.

TWO DIALOGUES IN ARCADIA

The first dialogue takes place at the borders of the desert retreat in Arcadia where the Princess Philoclea (with whom Pyrocles has just fallen in love) and the rest of the Arcadian royal family have sequestered themselves. Musidorus finds Pyrocles moping there, and rebukes him for having made a breach in their plans: "since our late comming into this countrie, I have marked in you, I will not say an alteration, but a relenting truly, and a slacking of the

59

maine career, you had so notably begun & almost performed" (30). The breach Pyrocles contemplates will separate their old life of heroic virtue in Asia Minor—inspecting laws and customs, helping the distressed, fighting battles for the right—from the new life of love and its discipline that awaits them inside the Arcadian retreat. Musidorus senses this and therefore tries to draw his cousin from "solitarines, the slie enemy, that doth most separate a man from well doing" (31); but Pyrocles appeals to a higher value for contemplation: "who knowes whether I feede not my minde with higher thoughts? . . . the workings of the mind I find much more infinite, then can be led unto by the eie . . . And in such contemplation, or as I thinke more excellent, I enjoy my solitarinesse; & my solitarines perchance, is the nurse of these contemplations" (31). The split involves subjecting oneself totally to the good of the soul as against acting out the soul's precepts: Musidorus says, "the gods would not have delivered a soule into the body, which hath armes and legges, only instruments of doing, but that it were intended the mind should imploy them; and that the mind should best know his owne good or evill by practise" (32). Furthermore, Pyrocles is breaking with the virtues sponsored by one sphere of existence, the heroic, and taking up those of another, that of love; fortitude, magnanimity, and steadfastness, all means between excess and defect, are proper to the world of action, while in the sphere of contemplation, Pyrocles seems to be groping after a higher virtue like charity.

A theme of *change* plays around Pyrocles here: "such a change was growne in Daiphantus [Pyrocles]," "this great alteration," "the oft changing of his colour," "the change you speake of." And, in order to show that the change involves personality as well as a way of life, Pyrocles' physical appearance is subjected to change: "even the colour and figure of his face began to receive some alteration" (30). That change in him is both caused by and analogous to the shift of scene from the great world of Greece and Asia Minor to the little pastoral retreat in Arcadia. Pyrocles tries to indicate the quality of the shift in values involved by describing the new scene as an emblem of Paradise:

60

Lord (deare cosin, said he) doth not the pleasantnesse of this place carry in it selfe sufficient reward for any time lost in it? Do you not see how all things conspire together to make this countrie a heavenly dwelling? Do you not see the grasse, how in colour they excell the Emeralds, every one striving to passe his fellow, and yet they are all kept of an equall height? And see you not the rest of these beautifull flowers, each of which would require a mans wit to know, & his life to expres? Do not these stately trees seeme to maintaine their florishing old age with the only happinesse of their seat, being clothed with a continual spring, because no beautie here should ever fade? Doth not the aire breath health, which the birds (delightful both to eare and eye) do dayly solemnize with the sweete consent of their voices? Is not every *Eccho* thereof a perfect Musicke? & these fresh & delightfull brookes how slowly they slide away, as loth to leave the company of so many things united in perfection? . . . Certainely, certainely, cosin, it must needs be that some Goddesse inhabiteth this Region, who is the soule of this soyle: for neither is anie lesse then a Goddesse, worthie to be shrined in such a heape of pleasures: nor anie lesse then a Goddesse could have made it so perfect a plotte of the celestiall dwellings.   [31–32]

Like the Garden of Paradise in its eternal fertility and its order of conflicting parts, this place draws the mind to that place of which it is the visible symbol. Such a characterization of the pastoral retreat is a blend of two traditions which we should examine briefly in order to get the full significance of this dialogue. One, which runs from the Middle Ages to the seventeenth century as a result of the commentaries on *The Song of Songs*, characterized the mind of innocent contemplative man as a miniature Garden of Paradise.[1] Its poetic culmination is the last section of the *Purgatorio* where Dante, having perfected himself in the active virtues and thus achieved the intellect's control over the other two parts of his soul, contemplates the Earthly Paradise as an image of his soul (the relation between the breeze, the birds, and the leaves corre-

1. Miss Ruth Wallerstein has traced this line of thought exhaustively in *Studies in Seventeenth-Century Poetic* (Madison, Wis., 1950), pp. 183–277.

sponds to the harmony between his intellectual, animal, and vegetative souls); [2] there he perceives Matelda, who corresponds to
Leah or the active life in his dream, and she leads him to Beatrice,
who corresponds to Rachel, and leads him into love and the contemplative vision. The other tradition, which is classical and crops
up again in the Renaissance, does not stress the similarity of any
garden to Eden, but merely presents it as a fit place for contemplation. Justus Lipsius, in his characterization of such a garden, tones
down any Paradisal suggestions out of respect for its actuality,
and emphasizes instead its function, its operation on "mans wit":

> Lastly, what a sweet odour is there? What percing savour?
> And I wot not what part of the heavenly aire infused from
> above . . . The mind lifteth up and advanceth it self more to
> these high cogitations, when it is at libertie to beholde his owne
> home, heaven. . . . Yea I seem to shake off all thing in mee
> that is humaine, and to be rapt up on high upon the fiery chariot
> of wisdome. . . . I am guarded and fenced against all externall
> things, and setled within my selfe, carelesse of all cares save one,
> which is, that I may bring in subjection this broken and distressed
> mind of mine to RIGHT REASON and GOD, and subdue all
> humaine and earthly things to my MIND. That whensoever
> my fatal day shall come, I may be readie with a good courage
> joyfully to welcome him, and depart this life, not as thrust out
> at the windowes, but as let out at the dore.[3]

The stress on function, though present in Sidney's passage, is sub-
ordinated to the Edenic motif; it comes out more strongly in a
song of Musidorus:

> O sweet woods the delight of solitarinesse!
> O how much I do like your solitarinesse!
> Where mans mind hath a freed consideration
> Of goodnesse to receive lovely direction.
> Where senses do beholde th' order of heav'nly hoste,
> And wise thoughts do behold what the creator is:

2. *Purgatorio* XXVIII, 7–18.

3. *Two Bookes of Constancie*, trans. Sir John Stradling, 1594; in the edition of
Rudolf Kirk (New Brunswick, N.J., 1939), pp. 133–37. See also Erasmus' *Col-
loquium Religiosum*.

Contemplation here holdeth his only seate:
Bounded with no limits, borne with a wing of hope
Clymes even unto the starres.   [233]

It is mainly by the creation of this traditional scenic background, which is both symbolic of the state of mind acquired therein and helpful to the acquiring of that state, that Sidney justified the action we see in the dialogue which occurs there: the transition from the active to the contemplative life.

The last dialogue in Arcadia takes place in the prison cell where the princes, awaiting their trial for the crime of regicide, contemplate death. But the real scene is the world at large, for as Pyrocles and Musidorus explore themselves here, they work out into ever larger contexts, from their individual situation to the nature of the universe. And so they make their prison an allegory of the world and affirm the subjection of human affairs to Divine Providence, or, in Lipsius' terms, the threefold subordination of external to internal affairs, of the lower parts of the soul to the intellect, and of man's life to God's will. They reject the soul's present bondage to the body, "though many times rebelliously resisted, always with this prison darkened," and look forward to the world of light to come, when the soul will be "free of that prison, and returning to the life of all things, where all infinite knowledge is" (445). The shift of scene contemplated in this dialogue is, then, not from an heroic to an amorous and pastoral part of the world, but from this life to the life after death. Pyrocles' radical conceit of death as a "second delivery" from the womb of mother earth into a new childhood indicates that the shift requires a much greater transition in ways of knowing and acting than the first one did.[4]

---

4. The immediate source of the entire prison scene is DuPlessis Mornay; see *A Woorke concerning the Trewnesse of the Christian Religion,* trans. Sidney and Arthur Golding (London, 1587), p. 246: "And therefore wee ought surely to say, that this Mynde or Reason ought not to bee ever in prison. That one day it shall see cleerely, and not by these dimme and clowdie spectacles: That it shall come in place where it shall have the true object of understanding: and that he shall have his life free from these fetters and from all the affections of the body. To be short, that as man is prepared in his mothers wombe to be brought foorth into the world; so is he also after a sort prepared in this body and in this world, to live in another world."

"We shall not see the culours, but lifes of all things that have bene or can be"; they will no longer need to struggle toward an idea of the intelligible world by means of its visual images on earth (such as this pastoral retreat itself is), for "nowe we see through a glasse, darkely: but then face to face." And human effort to know God by the senses and discursive reason will dissolve in love, the soul's union with "that high and heavenly love of the unquencheable light." Memory, perhaps even friendship and human love, will be canceled along with all earthly modes of thought and life, as Musidorus says in a summary statement:

> with the death of bodie and sences (which are not onely the beginning, but dwelling and nourishing of passions, thoughts, and imaginations) they fayling, memorie likewise failes, which riseth onely out of them: & then is there left nothing, but the intellectuall part or intelligence, which voide of all morall vertues, which stande in the meane of perturbations, doth only live in the contemplative vertue, and power of the omnipotent good, the soule of soules, and universall life of this great worke. [444–45][5]

Musidorus defines the "morall vertue" that keeps men on an even keel in this world as the mean between opposing motions of the will; this is of course the Aristotelian definition, a disposition to choose the "mean between two vices, that which depends on excess and that which depends on defect";[6] so, for instance, temperance is the mean between self-indulgence and insensibility. All through *Arcadia*, Pyrocles and Musidorus have had to develop

5. Thus as love is the beginning of the contemplative life, death is the fulfillment of it. Compare Leone Ebreo, *Dialoghi D'Amore*, trans. Friedeberg-Seeley and Barnes, p. 25: "Thus in the moral life virtue is moderation in respect of profit and pleasure; but in the contemplative life it consists in a negative attitude to these. In the moral life all extremes are sinful; in the contemplative only deficiencies are so. . . . our inextinguishable burning love of wisdom and virtue makes godlike our human mind, and transforms our frail body, vessel of corruption as it is, into an instrument of angelic spirituality. . . . the perfection of good lies in an extreme." Leone seems to have the civic and purifying virtues in mind; see our discussion below.

6. *Nicomachean Ethics* 2.6.1107 a.

this sort of virtue, especially in learning to control their passions by reason, in order to avoid the vice of lust. But the tendency to excess or defect will die with the body, and then a totally new kind of virtue will arise, one that depends not on balance or control, but rather on one single power enlarging itself, the intellect stretching out toward union with God. For in heaven all things will gather into the "vitall power" of intelligence, and the intelligence itself will be transformed until, "even growne like to his Creator," it "hath all things, with a spirituall knowledge before it."

Technically, the prospect the two young men face is the shift from the realm of the civic virtues to that of the virtues of the purified mind. The distinction is based on the four levels of virtue suggested by Plotinus and Macrobius, and hence adapted to Christian ethics.[7] Civic or political virtue consists of the control of the passions by reason for the benefit of the self and other men; temperance, for instance, is the act of subduing immodest desires to reason. The cleansing virtues in man removed from the practical life consist in putting away the desires of the body completely and thus purifying the soul from the body; here, temperance is the abstaining from everything that the habits of the body impel the soul to seek. In general, the first two levels of virtues can be identified with the classical and Christian ethical systems respectively; this one can readily see by comparing Aristotle's treatment of temperance as a virtue that keeps the soul complete with Milton's treatment of it as a means of making man Godlike.[8] The last two levels take us out of earthly life completely: the virtues of the purified mind, which seem to be received by illumination from the One, consist in the turning of the soul toward the One; temperance here consists in forgetting earthly longings completely.

7. See Plotinus, *Enneads* 1.2, and Macrobius, *In Somnium Scipionis* 1.8. Frank Kermode treats this scheme all too briefly in "The Cave of Mammon," in *Elizabethan Poetry*, Stratford-upon-Avon Studies, 2 (New York, 1960), pp. 169–72. Kermode tentatively identifies Aquinas' infused virtues with the virtues of the purified mind (see *Summa Theologica*, First Part of the Second Part, qu. 68, art. 1) and quotes discussions of the four levels by Benedict XIV and Torquato Tasso.

8. Compare *Nicomachean Ethics* 3.10–12 (1118 a–1119 b) and *Areopagitica* in *The Student's Milton*, Frank Allen Patterson, ed. (New York, 1930), pp. 737–38.

The final level of exemplary virtues is unattainable by man, since it resides only in the Divine Mind as the pattern or Idea of all the virtues. After defining each of the four cardinal virtues in this hierarchy, Macrobius sums it up thus: "The first type of virtues mitigates the passions, the second puts them away, the third has forgotten them, and to the fourth they are anathema." [9] The three levels of virtues attainable by men are proper to the three spheres of life, the active, contemplative, and posthumous lives.[1] Moreover, they lead to one another, for just as the contemplative life prepares for death by purifying the soul from the body's taint, so too the exercise of active virtue can, under the extreme pressure of temptations, so strengthen the reason that it can put passion aside entirely and live in the circle of the purifying virtues.

The princes imply that they have reached the second level of virtue and affirm their desire for the illuminative virtues of the purified mind; with that affirmation their view of reality opens up, for the transition they contemplate is a transcendence as well. It is appropriate therefore that they end their discourse with a hymn in the form of a sonnet whose very structural procedure is one of transcendence. The octave presents the argument of ordinary moral virtue steadfastly engaged in battle with the base passions:

> Since natures workes be good, and death doth serve
> As natures worke: why should we feare to die?
> Since feare is vaine, but when it may preserve,
> Why should we feare, that which we cannot flie?
>
> Feare is more paine, then is the paine it feares,
> Disarming humane mindes, of native might:
> While each conceite, an ougly figure beares,
> Which were not evill, well vew'd in reasons light.

With the acceptance of "reasons light" and the subordination of all passions to it, the octave is transcended. The sestet replaces

9. Macrobius, *Commentary on the Dream of Scipio*, trans. W. H. Stahl, Records of Civilization, Sources and Studies, 48 (New York, 1952), p. 123.

1. This is Macrobius' addition to Plotinus. See also the quotation from Leone Ebreo, n. 5, above.

persuasive discourse with vision; [2] a flowing description supersedes the style of contrasts, balances, and enchainment by figures of verbal repetition; and the struggles of the moral life fade before the slow opening up of the glorious light of heaven:

> Our owly eyes, which dimm'd with passions be,
> And scarce discerne the dawne of comming day,
> Let them be clearde, and now begin to see,
> Our life is but a step, in dustie way.
> > Then let us hold, the blisse of peacefull mind,
> > Since this we feele, great losse we cannot find.

When taken together, the two dialogues we have examined form halves of a cycle, for the second fulfills the promise of the first. The new scenes the heroes enter in each are implicitly linked, for, as we saw, the desert retreat is an emblem of the Garden of Paradise, and to experience that place is to begin a journey out of this world into the world hereafter and thus to start toward union with God.[3] But one need not work directly from pastoral simplicity to union with the One—indeed, Sidney seems to imply that one cannot do so—for a middle term, as it were, is required to link senses to thoughts, and that mode of linkage is both glorious and troublesome. It is *love* that draws a man from the life of action to the life of contemplation in Arcadia; and it is love, which operates with unusual freedom in the pastoral world, that makes a man know himself to such an extent that he wishes to contemplate pure divinity. There are standard terms for this proc-

2. The idea that a shift from purely verbal to visual expression signalizes the transcendence of discursive thought by contemplative vision is a standard one in the works of the Renaissance Neoplatonists. Its ultimate source is the Platonic insistence that the eyes are the most dignified of the senses; a more immediate source is Plotinus, *Enneads* 5.8.6. See also Ficino's expansion of Plotinus' idea in *Opera Omnia* (Basle, 1576), p. 1768; and E. H. Gombrich's discussion of the matter in "*Icones Symbolicae:* The Visual Image in Neo-Platonic Thought," *Journal of the Warburg and Courtauld Institutes,* 11 (1948). On pages 188–89 of his article, Gombrich quotes a passage from Christoforo Giarda's *Bibliothecae Alexandriae Icones Symbolicae* (Milan, 1626) which shows how the visual symbol takes us out of our body's prison into contemplation of the divine Ideas.

3. Note Milton's and Marvell's later accommodation of the pastoral place to Eden, through which one approaches heaven.

ess (terms, indeed, which we should expect to find in the work of a man who kept *Il Libro del Cortegiano* by him at all times), the terms of Neoplatonic love fixed by Marsilio Ficino and popularized by Baldassare Castiglione. Ficino had made his distinction between Divine Love (in the intelligible world) and Human Love (its reflection in the visible world) hinge in part on the contrast between the related contemplative and active lives; human or active love should lead to the divine or contemplative form. What we have in our two dialogues, then, are the steps onto the first and last rungs of the Platonic ladder: love of a woman ("the soule of this soyle") is a step in this our dusty way to "that hye and heavenly love" of God ("the soule of soules").

And, taken together, the two dialogues outline the action which *Arcadia* imitates: the perfection of the hero through love. Therefore we shall proceed to discuss the entire main plot of *Arcadia* which intervenes between these two dialogues, taking them as points of reference and using the terms of love they suggest. We should not expect to find a direct and complete ascent through the six steps of the Platonic ladder from woman to God; rather, we should hold this in mind as the standard model against which to measure its specific embodiment in fiction. Actually, as we shall see, Sidney used the first and last steps as a frame; within that frame he constructed a radically different picture of the workings of love, an account rather simpler than the Platonic, and much less certain.

We must start with the realization that the book falls into two parts because of the mock ending in Book II where a revolt arises and fails, Philanax arrives with troops to help his king, and, since the prophecy of the oracle at Delphi seems fulfilled, Basilius gives thanks to Apollo and is ready to pack up and go home. The love plot of Pyrocles and Musidorus has reached a point of rest, too, for each of them has gained his immediate goal, a pledge of mutual love from his chosen mistress. But of course the machinations of Cecropia at the beginning of Book III upset the balance and reshuffle the combinations. And the love plot goes on to a new problem: once love has been pledged, what kind of relation, what kind

68

of life, are the lovers to forge for themselves? The ending of Book II thus divides the action of *Arcadia* into two phases: from heroism to love, and from love to perfection.

FROM HEROISM TO LOVE

Contrast between the former lives of the two young princes and the adventures they face in Arcadia plays all through Book I: at the beginning in the contrast between Strephon and Klaius and Musidorus enduring the violence of the sea; then, spatialized, in the pairing of war-torn Laconia and peaceful pastoral Arcadia. It invades the action when Pyrocles helps the helots in Laconia at the same time as Musidorus is enjoying himself in Arcadia, or when Musidorus rather futilely decimates Helen's escort while Pyrocles loiters on the borders of the retreat. The contrast culminates in the first dialogue on heroism and love, which we have discussed, and this dialogue leads directly into a second one when Musidorus finds his cousin in love, having perfected by a "womanish" disguise the changes the first dialogue had promised, and having changed his name significantly from Pyrocles ("fiery-fame," well deserved fame being the highest goal of the active life) to Zelmane ("mad with zeal"). It is this second dialogue—on the nature of love—that marks the transformation of *Arcadia's* plot from an heroic to a love plot. In it, the princes lay the groundwork for the whole book, for they question whether love of a woman is a base passion or a sacred movement of the soul that leads it to Heavenly Love. During the argument Pyrocles takes the commonly accepted position of Ficino and Pico that recognizes three kinds of love, bestial love (or lust), Divine Love, and Human Love (the reflection of the Divine Love in matter); while Musidorus, like Equicola, Betussi, and some of the other simplistic popularizers of Neoplatonism, recognizes only two kinds, honest or heavenly and dishonest or earthly. Musidorus therefore deals with Human Love as the Neoplatonists dealt with *amor ferinus* or mere lust: for him, love is a passion like fear, anger, joy, or sorrow, but worse because it cannot be turned "toward some good by the direction of Reason" (44). Its end is sensual pleasure, and it is accompanied by unquietness, longings, fond comforts, discomforts, jealousies, and rages. It is, indeed, only a fake, a "bastard Love" usurping the name of the true Heavenly Love, "for indeed the name of Love is unworthily applied to so hatefull a humor," a passion "engendred betwixt lust and idlenesse" (44). Bastard love imitates true love even in its workings on the mind:

> hereupon it first gat the name of Love: for indeed the true love hathe that excellent nature in it, that it doth transforme the verie essence of the lover into the thing loved; uniting, and as it were incorporating it with a secret and inward working. And herein do these kind of loves imitate the excellent; for as the love of heaven makes one heavenly, the love of vertue, vertuous, so doth the love of the world make one become worldly, and this effeminate love of a woman, doth so womanize a man.
> [44–45]

It works the same way as true love did in Ficino, but of course it leads in the opposite direction:

> It also often happens that the lover wishes to transform himself into the person of the loved one. This is really quite reasonable, for he wishes and tries to become God instead of man; and who would not exchange humanity for divinity? It also happens that those snared by love alternately lament and rejoice in their love. They lament because they are losing, destroying and ruining themselves; they rejoice because they are transferring themselves into something better.[4]

Pyrocles counters many of his cousin's arguments by showing how Human Love, even if it does show some of the symptoms of lust, resembles Heavenly Love and leads to it. For one thing, Human Love is not an evil passion in itself, but is sometimes accompanied by other passions residing in the imperfect lover; in fact, "Even that heavenly love you speake of, is accompanied in some hearts with hopes, griefes, longings, and dispaires" (46). Moreover, even though Human Love has enjoyment of the be-

4. *Marsilio Ficino's Commentary on Plato's Symposium,* trans. Sears Jayne, University of Missouri Studies, 19 (Columbia, 1944), p. 141.

loved as its end, it has an end beyond that: "I spake of the end to which it is directed; which end ends not, no sooner then the life" (46). In orthodox theory, "Love is nothing else but a certaine coveting to enjoy beautie," [5] the difference between kinds of love being the shift from one kind of beauty as object, through others, to the final heavenly beauty. This theory is reflected in Pyrocles' plan for a trip up the Platonic ladder:

> in that heavenly love, since there are two parts, the one the love it self, th'other the excellencie of the thing loved; I, not able at the first leap to frame both in me, do now (like a diligent workeman) make ready the chiefe instrument, & first part of that great worke, which is love it selfe. [46]

Pyrocles is nearer the truth (as Sidney, after Bembo, must have seen it) than Musidorus, for Heavenly Love cannot arise suddenly out of nothing, but must proceed from the groundwork of Human Love. As Ficino and Bembo said, we must begin with the impressions of the senses, with the shadow of divine beauty in the beloved; and so Pyrocles, "if we love vertue, in whom shall we love it but in a vertuous creature? without your meaning be, I should love this word *Vertue*, where I see it written in a booke" (46). It is indeed proper for Musidorus to point out the dangers, but if one is to perfect oneself one should take the chance. Love is evil or good according as it is left uncontrolled (and thus falls to the sensual madness of lust) or controlled (and thus will lead man from Human Love with its tinge of the senses up "the stayres, by the which a man may ascend to true love" of God). [6] Thus the problem of love that this scene initiates is synecdochic of the whole moral problem of the control of conflicting desires. And the first transformation of the plot here does not veer away from former heroic problems but intensifies them instead, so that now the preservation of the Aristotelian mean between desires is what carries man toward divinity, while departure from that mean drops him to the level of bestiality.

5. *The Book of the Courtier*, trans. Sir Thomas Hoby (London, Everyman's Library, 1928), p. 303.
6. Ibid., p. 307.

Therefore love takes over the plot. We soon encounter a scene
that doubles the one we have just discussed, for in it Pyrocles discovers Musidorus disguised in turn for love of Pamela, and scolds
him:

> Why how now deare cousin (said she) you that were last day
> so high in the pulpit against lovers, are you now become so
> meane an auditor? Remember that love is a passion; and that
> a worthie mans reason must ever have the masterhood. I recant,
> I recant (cried *Musidorus*) and withall falling downe pros-
> trate, O thou celestiall, or infernall spirit of Love, or what other
> heavenly or hellish title thou list to have (for effects of both
> I finde in my selfe) have compassion of me.   [65–66]

The first effects of love are hellish and disturbing rather than ex-
alting, and illustrate the need for control in order both to turn
love toward its higher manifestations and to keep the mind whole
in the "morall vertues, which stand in the meane of perturbations."
For all of the characters suffer from a partial disintegration of personality, or what the princes call "self-division," a state in which
different tendencies to action or parts of the mind oppose each
other instead of co-operating as they would in an integrated personality. The factions in the civil war within the microcosm are
Reason and Passion: Love has so armed the rebel Passion that it
can no longer be kept subject to Reason without great struggle.
Since the problem of control is more difficult than ever before, the
discord within the heroes leaves them barely able to proceed
toward their goals. Pyrocles' remark on his condition is typical of
this phase: "the discord of my thoughts, my Lute, doth ill agree
to the concord of thy strings; therefore be not ashamed to leave
thy maister, since he is not afraid to forsake himselfe" (98). Their
psychological difficulties in part stem from and in part reflect the
tangle of situations that develop early in the plot. Pyrocles, "oppressed with being loved, almost as much, as with loving" (162),
has to fight off his foolish lover Basilius and at the same time temper the shrewd jealousy of his wife Gynecia with her veiled
threats to reveal his disguise. He can reveal his love to Philoclea
only at a point when she has been sent to him in the disgraceful
role of her father's procuress.

Musidorus is not cumbered with loves, but, because of his dis-

hind control and refusal to control. From the first it is apparent
that the sisters' values are grounded in a context somehow lacking
to Cecropia: for instance, Pamela values a purse she embroiders
for its usefulness or place in a hierarchy of goods, whereas to
Cecropia the purse is beautiful and valuable—like Pamela—only
for itself. Thus while the sisters advocate control or moderation of
desires out of consideration for others, Cecropia tempts them to
give rein to desires, to pass all bounds in order to please themselves.
In this, the aunt's lineaments begin to emerge as those of Pride, the
worship of the self, which is fatal to love, for it uses love only for
self-aggrandizement and thus for instance gives the "beloved" no
importance save as a crystal container to keep a woman's beauty
from spilling (251). For the humble princesses, on the other hand,
love is a true joining that demands the subjection of both parties
for their mutual happiness. On the social level, the princesses believe in subjection to parent and ruler while Cecropia, of course, is
tempting them to cast aside parental control, and has previously
goaded her son Amphialus into organizing a rebellion against the
rightful king of Arcadia. The hero believes in controlling his desires because of his love of order and hierarchy; he is humble, and
his humility blossoms into love. The man who has not acquired
control through exercising it does not believe in control, and the
people who before seemed merely pitiable in their subjection to
Passion now appear in a new context as just this side of villainy,
with its "values" of Pride, selfishness, subversion, and hatred.

The big scene between Pamela and Cecropia takes the reader
from the moral to the theological level, from the positions for or
against control to the beliefs behind them. Cecropia begins with an
atheistic attack justifying Pride or moral chaos: "feare . . . was
the first inventer of those conceipts" of religion and hierarchy,
and she would therefore not have Pamela "love Vertue servilly,"
but know her own worth and exercise the power of beauty. Her
peroration reminds the modern reader of Satan's theme in *Paradise
Lost*, "the mind is its own place": "Be wise, and that wisdome shall
be a God unto thee; be contented, and that is thy heaven" (268).
Pamela replies to this solipsistic position with a thorough defense
of the universe as order. The idea of God as harmonizer of the
universe follows from the very nature of the elements, for

there must needes have bene a wisedome which made them concurre: for their natures being absolute contrarie, in nature rather would have sought each others ruine, then have served as well consorted parts to such an unexpressable harmonie. For that contrary thinges should meete to make up a perfection without a force and Wisedome above their powers, is absolutely impossible. [269][8]

If harmony, then God; if God, then a benevolent Providence controlling the world. Pamela goes on to summarize the conflict of beliefs in the two meanings of the word "Nature": by it, the proud man means "a Nature, as we speake of the fire, which goeth upward, it knowes not why," the progeny of chaos and fortune; to the Christian, however, it is the visible sign of God's presence, "a Nature of wisdom, goodnesse, and providence, which knowes what it doth" (269).

While Pamela defends humility, the virtue which she and her sister display most clearly in their trials is one from which humility and many other purifying virtues flow: it is Christian patience, which works out of their belief in God's providential order.[9] Here we must recall the distinction between the political or classical virtues and the cleansing or Christian virtues. To the Stoics, patience meant sufferance, the ability to remain constant under adversity, to sustain wrongs and rebukes without abdicating control of the passions. Justus Lipsius defined it as "A voluntarie sufferance without grudging of all things whatsoever can happen to, or in a man." [1] And Sir Thomas Elyot, who of course treated patience as a political virtue, said of it,

The meane to optaine pacyence is by two things principally. A direct and upryght conscience, and a true and constant opinion

8. See Boethius, *De Consolatione Philosophiae*, III, xii, in the seventeenth-century translation of "I.T." (Loeb Classical Library, London, 1918), p. 287: "This world could never have been compacted of so many divers and contrary parts, unless there were One that doth unite these so different things; and this disagreeing diversity of natures being united would separate and divide this concord, unless there were One that holdeth together that which He united."

9. This section of the discussion is indebted to John F. Danby's *Poets on Fortune's Hill*, especially pp. 46–73, 108–19.

1. *Two Bookes of Constancie*, ed. Rudolf Kirk, p. 79.

in the estimation of goodnes. Whiche seldom commeth onely of nature, excepte it be wonderfull excellent; but by the dilligent studye of very philosophie.[2]

This is basically a Stoic view, as Elyot's examples of the Emperor Antoninus and Zeno Eleates show. But we are obviously in a different realm when we meet John Dowland's examples of patience in Job, David, and the cripple who waited with hope for God's help (see John 5:1–16).[3] Christian patience is founded on firmer ground than the classical virtue, for it proceeds from a sure faith in Providence; its rewards are greater, too, for its exercise cleanses the soul and brings it nearer the image of God, its great exemplar Christ in His Passion. Miles Coverdale defined it as the ability to maintain an active belief in a divine order even when that order is apparently inoperative: "The patience therefore of Christians standeth not in this, that they feel no passion, or be not fearful, heavy, or sorry; but in this, that no cross be so great, as to be able to drive them away from Christ." [4] Coverdale's terms make it clear that Christian patience is the only real source of the strength to control passion completely, for it allows the soul to accept the suffering which purifies. The wicked aunt's rigorous temptation of Pamela, like a fire transmuting the ordinary virtue of endurance into Christian patience, has left the princess whole and pure; as she prays with her mind "full of deep (though patient) thoughts," she asks humbly, "let thine infinite power vouchsafe to limite out some proportion of deliverance unto me, as to thee shall seeme most convenient," and "suffer some beame of thy Majesty so to shine into my mind, that it may stil depend confidently upon thee" (252–53).

Here we have the second transformation of the plot of *Arcadia*. Before the captivity episode, the desideratum for success in love and in integrating the personality was the Aristotelian "morall vertue," a mean between opposing perturbations—Reason's government of the passions in the microcosm, the prince's control of

---

2. *The Boke Named the Governour* (London, Everyman's Library, 1907), p. 234.

3. "Thou mightie God" in *A Pilgrimes Solace* (London, 1612), nos. xiv–xvi.

4. *Fruitful Lessons* . . . , in *Works* (The Parker Society, Cambridge, 1844), p. 261; quoted by Danby, p. 110.

diverse factions in the state by law and order in the body politic. After this point, the Christian ethic takes over: what is needed in order to control oneself is a firm belief in God's control of the universe and the humility to accept the fact that one is, as part of that universe, in the hands of God. Consequent on this transformation of values is a rise in the reader's expectations for the heroes of *Arcadia*, who are planted firmly between two exempla by this episode. On the one hand, there are the two princesses whom bitter trial raised to moral perfection. On the other hand, there is the tragic Amphialus, whose wavering from control made him a prey to passions and evil counselors like Cecropia and Anaxius; partly by their influence, partly by his own weakness, he became the unwitting author of evil deeds, wrecked his character, and ended in suicide. As the captivity episode drew to a close, the princes found themselves closer to the failure of Amphialus than the perfection of the women: Pyrocles (upon whom the bulk of the action devolved) saw a staged execution of Philoclea, succumbed to despair, and tried to brain himself against the wall of his cell.

The rest of *Arcadia* therefore presents a reintegration of the divided mind—or, to be more exact, a partial recovery based on the classical ethical system, its collapse, and a second and sounder recovery based on Christian patience. Upon the return from Cecropia's castle to the retreat, each of the heroes embarks on a rigorous program of Stoic endurance, and tries to govern his actions by the virtues of the divided mind, such as continence. Continence, as contrasted to temperance, allows only a very fragile control over the passions, but that is all they can manage at this point, for true temperance results only from the subjection of the human will to God's.[5] By great labor and self-restraint, Musidorus

5. See *The Book of the Courtier* (Everyman's Library), p. 271; "Continencie may be compared to a Captaine that fighteth manly, and though his enimies bee strong and well appointed, yet giveth he them the overthrow, but for all that not without much ado and danger. But temperance free from all disquieting, is like the Captaine that without resistance overcommeth and raigneth. And having in the mind where she is, not onely aswaged, but cleane quenched the fire of greedy desire, even as a good prince in civil warre dispatcheth the seditious inward enimies, and giveth the scepter and whole rule to reason." See also Leone Ebreo, *Dialoghi D'Amore*, p. 17; both Castiglione and Leone seem to think of continence as the civic virtue of temperance which mitigates desires, and of temperance itself as the cleansing virtue which has obliterated desires.

manages to maneuver his persecutors into traps so that he can escape to Thessalia with Pamela and marry her there. Appropriately, his control shows itself in playing on *their* uncontrolled desires:

> The muddy mind of *Dametas*, he found most easily stirred with covetousnes. The curst mischievous heart of *Miso*, most apt to be tickled with jelousie. . . . But yong mistresse *Mopsa*, who could open her eyes upon nothing, that did not all to bewonder her, he thought curiositie the fittest baite for her.   [341]

Pyrocles' task is the more heroic as the difficulties he faces are greater; his first job is to pacify the lustful Gynecia, a task which calls for tact and great continence, "having in one instant both to resist rage and go beyond wisedome, being to deale with a Ladie that had her wits awake in every thing" (351). He must seem to promise fulfillment of her desires without actually doing so, and after he convinces her he must play the same game of deceit with Basilius. Furthermore, in order to make his show of love to them the more convincing, he must seem to despise Philoclea. Though this behavior hurts Philoclea to the quick, Pyrocles refuses to change his act lest he ruin his plan for their eventual union. Her pain constitutes the greatest temptation his forbearance could be subjected to; it shows supremely his ability to forego present pleasure for future happiness.

But this is all foolishness. It is an ironic fact that Pyrocles, while displaying Stoic endurance, is actually illustrating its weaknesses, for his restraint, which might otherwise be characterized as mere temporizing, is what leads directly to his capture and trial. The very cave scene where he begins his policy of temporizing offers him a realization of how vain it is, and just how close the fragile control over unruly passions is to mere lust. What draws him into the cave in the first place is a set of songs so close to those he has just uttered (the correspondences reach even to common imagery and rime words) [6] that he is sure his mirror image in love lies

6. All of the songs are organized around the cave's imagery of light (symbolic of "reasons light") and dark (symbolizing "passions darke"). Pyrocles' sonnet rimes on the words "light" and "dark" exclusively; Gynecia's first song uses "darke" words for rimes, and her second, "light."

within. Therefore, announcing the resolve that "whatsoever thou be, I will seeke thee out, for thy musike well assures me we are at least hand fellow prentises to one ungracious master" (338), he plunges in. What he finds inside is, of course, Gynecia lying prone on the floor, exhausted, her mind torn asunder by lust. This is the real image of his mind; the thought Pyrocles must face is that he, the hero striving to control his desires, is in the same state as the harried whore,[7] and when he refuses this realization and temporizes with her, it is as if he has declined a real battle with his own lower nature.

The limitations of his and Musidorus' system of ethics immediately become apparent, for neither of them is firmly enough grounded in virtue to resist a moment of lassitude not untinged with lust at the very high point of his triumph. Once Pamela and Musidorus have escaped the confines of the retreat, they relax in a shady grove. There Pamela falls asleep on the grass while Musidorus meditates on her lovely body, her hair, eyelids, cheeks, lips, even her breath; finally, the sight "did so tyrannize over *Musidorus* affects, that he was compelled to put his face as lowe to hers, as he coulde" (351). It is in this posture that the Arcadian rabble, bursting in on him like a sea of uncontrolled passions, find him; his capture leads swiftly to the ruination of his plans. Likewise, after Pyrocles has dispatched his two clogs Basilius and Gynecia and has at last gained a private interview with Philoclea, the scene dissolves in moral ambiguity. At the beginning of the scene, his motives are not clear: has he some plan for flight and subsequent marriage in mind, or does he intend mere lustful pleasure as Basilius

---

7. The disorder in Pyrocles' mind is conveyed to the reader partly in an allusion whereby Pyrocles appears as Actæon, the symbol of the mind in a state of lust (for this symbolism, see Abraham Fraunce, *The Third Part of the Countesse of Pembrokes Yvychurch. Entituled, Amintas Dale* [1592], fol. 43, and Douglas Bush, *Mythology and the Renaissance Tradition in English Poetry* [Minneapolis, 1932], p. 71, n. 11). Compare the description of the cave (337) with Diana's cave in Gargaphie (Ovid, *Metamorphoses* 3, 157–62), and compare the action with Ovid's story passim: the entrance into the cave because of curiosity, his meeting with a mock Diana there, and her attack on him in the manner of Actæon's hounds. I have treated this matter fully in an article "Actæon in Arcadia" in *Studies in English Literature, 2,* No. 1 (1962).

and Gynecia did? His first thoughts seem to hint strongly at the latter:

> up to *Philocleas* chamber dore went *Pyrocles,* rapt from himselfe with the excessive fore-feeling of his (as he assured himselfe) neere comming contentment. What ever paines he had taken, what daungers he had runne into, and especially those sawcie pages of love, doubts, griefes, languishing hopes, and threatning despaires, came all now to his minde, in one ranke to beautifie his expected blisfulnesse, and to serve for a most fit sawce. [367][8]

Once there, Philoclea's very real grief drives him to distraction, and he finally falls into a faint. The scene ends when Pyrocles recovers, carries Philoclea to her bed, and lies down beside her; after some delicious exploring, the two, exhausted by their emotional ordeal and totally forgetting the need for action, fall asleep in each other's arms. This action is sexually innocent enough, but it does illustrate a lassitude far below the level of heroic action and temperance: all of Pyrocles' restraint has led to fainting spells and sleep in a Bower of Blisse.

Pyrocles falls even further, for when he awakes and realizes, in the hard dawn, the reality of his situation, trapped weaponless in a locked room with Philoclea while Dametas cries "adultery" outside, he can think of only one solution. If he commits suicide, it will seem that he tried to rape Philoclea, failed, and died to save face. The solution of suicide is acceptable in an heroic context (one thinks of the honorable deaths of Cato and Antony); Pyrocles is compared to Achilles, and thoughts of the highest magnanimity run in his head: "putting great part of the trust of his well doing in his owne courage so armed. For indeed the confidence in ones selfe is the chiefe nurse of magnanimitie" (404). But in the new context which entered Arcadia with Book III, suicide is only the worst result of the sin of despair (as it was for Spenser's Redcrosse Knight): symbolically, Pyrocles bungles, and the clatter awakens Philoclea his guide.

In the dialogue that follows, Philoclea attempts not only to

8. Certainly the reiteration of the passions accompanying lust according to Musidorus is significant here; see our previous discussion of the second dialogue between the heroes (pp. 69–71).

dissuade her lover from self-murder, but to restore his shaken mind to Christian patience. It is a dialogue between "unshaked magnanimitie," the heroic or even Stoic view, and "innocent guilt-lesnes," the religious view. They first disagree on the nature of the proposed act itself: to Pyrocles it is heroic action, and therefore good, "For to do, requires a whole hart; to suffer falleth easiliest in the broken minds" (408); to the truly religious Philoclea, however, "Whatsoever . . . comes out of dispaire, cannot beare the title of valure" (407). Their disagreement whether acceptance can be an heroic virtue takes us to the theological level of thought. For to the mere secular hero, man has complete control over his own life, free will unlimited; but to the Christian, his control is itself limited by the higher control of Providence:

> That we shoulde be maisters of oure selves, we can shewe at all no title nor claime; since neither we made our selves, nor bought our selves, we can stand upon no other right but his gift, which he must limite as it pleaseth him.

> It is not for us to appoint that mightie Majestie, what time he will help us; the uttermost instant is scope enough for him, to revoke every thing to ones owne desire. And therefore to prejudicate his determination, is but a doubt of goodnesse in him, who is nothing but goodnesse. [409]

Therefore Philoclea exhorts Pyrocles to faith and patience. Although he is by no means fully convinced, he finally yields and elects to face the evils that the world can bring.

It is apparent that Philoclea's arguments here reiterate those used by Pamela in the captivity episode and lead forward to the princes' acceptance of the same values in the final prison scene. As in Book I of *The Faerie Queene*, the partial collapse of unaided virtue in despair has both taught the hero and led to an immediate re-establishment of virtue on a firmer basis—a Christian one. Philoclea has attempted a major job of reconstruction, and the reader sees that it has taken effect rather suddenly. When Musidorus is brought in captive, Pyrocles is shown to have risen to a higher moral height than even before, and to have gone far toward reintegrating the personality whose fissures have just been displayed.

For he immediately shows classical patience again: Sidney calls him a "resolute man" who "having once disgested in his judgement the worst extremity of his own case, and having either quite expelled or at least repelled all passion, which ordinarilie followes an overthrowne fortune," wonders, having already made the conquest of his own mind, "with what patience" Musidorus "brookes his case" (420).

As the final prison scene opens, the princes reaffirm their attainments: "they like men indeede, (fortifying courage with the true Rampier of patience) did so endure, as they did rather appeare governours of necessitie, then servaunts to fortune" (443). They start with this, and as they work out from their own case, they build on this patience the higher edifice of Christian patience which arises from man's sense of himself in the universe: "O blame not the heavens, sweete *Pyrocles*, sayd *Musidorus*, as their course never alters, so is there nothing done by the unreachable ruler of them, but hath an everlasting reason for it" (444). And so, from the depths of despair, they have raised themselves—with the guidance of the ideal women—to a true moral perfection grounded in God, through classical ideas of virtue to the transcendent Christian ethic, through action to contemplation, through Human Love to Heavenly Love; and the scene ends with their radiant expectation of the union of their minds with "that high and heavenly love of the unquencheable light." They do not die; they return, instead, to the active life, but they return purified and perfected as men of heroic virtue, ready whenever their fatal day comes to walk calmly out the door into the sunlight.

LOVE IN THEORY AND IN PRACTICE

This is a sketch of what I take the plot of *Arcadia* to be: the perfection of the hero through love; its inception and goal are the same as in the Neoplatonic model, but its middle is totally different. *Arcadia* is fiction, not a tractate on love, and, like most fiction of the 1570s and 1580s such as *Euphues*, Gascoigne's *F. J.*, and Melbancke's *Philotimus*, it concerns the testing and modification of theory by experience; it is therefore important to notice the chief departures from Plato, the parts of the standard process that Sidney blurred, modified, or omitted entirely. For instance, delight in a woman's beauty, idealization of it, and perception of the moral values behind it occurred simultaneously, but love of a particular woman never extended itself to include all beauty. More importantly, the transfer from moral to religious values became exceedingly difficult in the world of men; it did not result from the process of love itself, but was arranged by direct doctrinal instruction on the part of the virtuous women beloved.[9] It is important too to remember that the lover does not reach mystic union with the One in this life, but can only look forward to it with longing in the life to come; what he *does* gain is faith in a beneficent Providence, so that he can fully love God, knowing that God loves him. Furthermore, the control of reason over appetite is at best sporadic until the end; since events take place in an imperfect world, forces both outside and within the heroes disturb the serenity assumed by theory, and suddenly make the path to Heavenly Love turn into the descent to *amor ferinus*. The princes finally achieve perfection, but before they do they stumble. It is perhaps for this reason that Arcadia ends, not with the magnificent prison scene, but with a turbulent trial where Sidney displays all the real or potential misdeeds of Pyrocles and Musidorus and then allows them to be insulted and condemned but at last forgiven.

9. Thus Sidney approaches Spenser's position in the *Fowre Hymnes*, where heavenly love results from earthly love, though not in an unbroken chain. See William Nelson, *The Poetry of Edmund Spenser* (New York, 1963), p. 99.

4. Pastoral Exercises

STREPHON AND KLAIUS

Arcadia does not open with its heroes Pyrocles and Musidorus, but rather with the two young shepherds Strephon and Klaius, who bear a certain analogical relation to the heroes. The first few pages of the romance outline their situation as they stand at the tip of the Peloponnese lamenting the anniversary of Urania's departure for the island of Cythera. As they mourn, we gradually learn what Urania has meant to them and what effect she has had on their lives; the effect is a familiar one, for it is something of a textbook case, a more complete and explicit example of the operation of Neoplatonic love than the one we examined in the last chapter. For by using Urania as both tutor and loved object, they have climbed a certain way up the Platonic ladder. They started with sights and sounds, "these two senses, which have litle bodily substance in them, and be the ministers of reason":[1]

> the least thing that may be praised in her, is her beautie. Certainly as her eye-lids are more pleasant to behold, then two white kiddes climbing up a faire tree, and browsing on his tendrest branches, and yet are nothing, compared to the day-shining

1. *The Book of the Courtier*, p. 313.

starres contained in them; and as her breath is more sweete then a gentle South-west wind . . . and yet is nothing, compared to the hony flowing speach that breath doth carrie; no more all that our eyes can see of her . . . is to be matched with the flocke of unspeakeable vertues, laid up delightfully in that best builded fold. But in deed as we can better consider the sunnes beautie, by marking how he guildes these waters and mountaines, then by looking upon his owne face, too glorious for oure weake eyes: so it may be our conceits (not able to beare her sun-stayning excellencie) will better way it by her workes upon some meaner subject employed. And alas, who can better witnesse that then we, whose experience is grounded upon feeling? hath not the onely love of her made us (being silly ignorant shepheards) raise up our thoughts above the ordinary levell of the worlde, so as great clearks doe not disdaine our conference? hath not the desire to seeme worthie in her eyes, made us when others were sleeping, to sit viewing the course of heavens? when others were running at base, to runne over learned writings? when other marke their sheep, we to marke our selves? hath not she throwne reason upon our desires, and, as it were given eyes unto *Cupid?* hath in any, but in her, love-fellowship maintained friendship between rivals, & beautie taught the beholders chastitie?   [2–3][2]

Urania's love, eschewing sensual delight, has imposed reason as a restraint upon their desires, and by so doing has raised them above the gain-loving pursuits of their companions to progressively higher goals. The passage outlines, in general terms, a ladder

2. This passage is a tissue of reminiscences of Platonic passages, especially from *The Book of the Courtier*. For the raising of their thoughts, see "[the soul] therefore waxed blinde about earthly matters, is made most quicke of sight about heavenly" (319); on self-knowledge, "the soul . . . turning her to the beholding of her owne substance, as it were raised out of a most deepe sleepe, openeth the eyes that all men have, and few occupie, and seeth in her selfe a shining beame of that light, which is the true image of the Angelike beautie partened with her" (318–19). For the control of reason over desire, see "beautie is good, and consequently the true love of it is most good and holy, and evermore bringeth forth good fruites in the soules of them, that with the bridle of reason restraine the ill disposition of sense" (306). And for love's ability to unite opposites, "Thou with agreement bringest the Elements in one . . . Thou bringest several matters into one, to the unperfect givest perfection, to the unlike likenesse, to enmitie amitie" (321). It is also notable that Klaius characterizes himself in this passage as the philosopher who has just emerged from Plato's cave.

of love. While she was with them they went from the first step, delight in corporeal beauty, to the fourth, delight in the virtues the body images (having assumedly left out the third step, love of all beauty). After she left, they progressed in their own minds to the fifth step, from moral values to metaphysical ones, and traced "the footsteps of God" in the created universe and in their souls, thereby perceiving their essential harmony with the emblematic universe of divine order around them.

While the theoretical outline of their love affair is clear, certain elements in the story mystify us. No reason is ever given for Urania's departure, and yet it seems assumed that she will never return. Of course it is appropriate that the woman leave, once she has started the process of love, so that love can go on to its higher forms. But does that mean that she has died? One sentence seems to imply that: "But woe is me, yonder, yonder, did shee put her foote into the boate, at that instant, as it were dividing her heavenly beautie, betweene the Earth and the Sea." Sidney's background will help us here, for the names "Urania" and "Cythera" were rich in associations for the Renaissance, and an examination of them will extend our awareness of the meaning of Strephon and Klaius and show the importance of their story.

Urania was originally the muse presiding over the planetary motions in the heavens (thus our Urania raised the shepherds to "sit viewing the course of heavens"); [3] hence, because of her associations with the heavens and the One, she became an image of heavenly love in Eryximachus' speech in *Symposium*: "this is the beautiful Love, the Heavenly Love, the Love belonging to the 'Heavenly' Muse Urania; but that of 'Manyhymn' Polymnia is the common one." [4] In Ficino's *Commentary* on *Symposium*,

3. The shift from Urania as muse of the heavens to Urania as muse of divine or mystical poetry was an easy one; thus Dante invoked her before the apocalyptic pageant in *Purgatorio* xxix. Du Bartas seems to have fixed her position as the Christian muse in his *L'Uranie* (1574), and was followed in this by Spenser and Milton.

4. *Symposium* 187 C, trans. W. H. D. Rouse in *Great Dialogues of Plato* (Mentor Books, New York, 1956), p. 84 (I use Rouse's translation because it stresses the importance of the muses' names). The assimilation of the operation of the muses to that of love in Platonic thought by means of their common goal in the heavens

some of the ideas in this speech were fused with the two different myths of the birth of Venus from Pausanias' speech, and combined with Plotinian metaphysics to clarify the contrast between "Aphrodite Ourania" and "Aphrodite Pandemos":

> The first Venus, which is in the Angelic Mind, is said to have been born of Uranus "of no mother," because for the natural philosophers, *mother* means *matter*, and the Angelic Mind is completely foreign to any relationship with corporeal matter.
>
> The second Venus, which is in the World-Soul, was born of Jupiter and Dione: born of Jupiter, that is, of that faculty of the World-Soul which moves the heavens. She it was who created the power which generates these lower forms.[5]

Of course, the place where Aphrodite rose from the sperm of Uranus spread on the sea foam was the island of Cythera, and this island therefore became her first seat in the world. In late medieval literature, Cythera became a kind of shrine of love, where the spirit of Aphrodite Ourania dwelt eternally (this in spite of her later removal to Cyprus, which the Renaissance Neoplatonists may have associated with the second or "Common" Aphrodite).[6] The medieval tradition of Cythera was conveyed to the Renaissance mainly by the *Hypnerotomachia* (1499) attributed to Fran-

---

and the *furor* both inspire has been a continuing one. Franz Cumont finds that the use of the muses as psychopomps on Roman sarcophagi shows that they were considered to draw the human soul in rapture back to its former home: *Recherches sur le symbolisme funeraire des Romains* (Paris, 1942), ch. 4; see also Jean Seznec, "Paul Claudel and the Sarcophagus of the Muses," *Perspectives of Criticism*, ed. Harry Levin, Harvard Studies in Comparative Literature, 20 (Cambridge, Mass., 1950), p. 14. In Sidney's own century, Sir Thomas Elyot defined *Musa* as "that parte of the soule that induceth and moveth a man to serche for knowledge" (*The Boke Named the Governour*, III, xxiii), and Sidney's protegé Abraham Fraunce wrote, "They are called Musae, of the verb μυίω, which is, to teach and instruct a man in those things, that are sacred and holy, divine and mysticall, whereof came the word mysterie" (*Amintas Dale*, p. 33v).

5. *Commentary* on *Symposium* 3.7; trans. Jayne, p. 142.

6. See, for instance, *Le Roman de la Rose*, ll. 15659–98, *The Court of Love* attributed to Chaucer, ll. 48–49 and 69–71 (in both of these, the island of Cythera becomes confused with Mt. Cithæron in Boeotia), the picture of the embarkation of Helen and Cythera attributed to Antonio Vivarini (1415–1480), and Thomas Usk's Island of Venus in *The Testament of Love*, in W. W. Skeat, *Chaucerian and Other Pieces* (Oxford, 1897), p. 16.

cesco Colonna;[7] in that strange work, Cythera, where Venus dwells eternally with Adonis, becomes the goal of Poliphilo's dream journey, where the secrets of love are revealed to him and Polia and where they spend their spiritual lives in love. Likewise, Cythera seems to be the "Island strong," more renowned than Cyprus, seat of the Temple of Venus where Scudamour wins Amoret in Book IV of *The Faerie Queene* [8] as well as the place referred to as the Heaven of Venus in *An Hymne in Honour of Love:*

> a Paradize
> Of all delight, and ioyous happie rest,
> Where they doe feede on Nectar heauenly wize,
> With *Hercules* and *Hebe,* and the rest
> Of *Venus* dearlings, through her bountie blest,
> And lie like Gods in yuorie beds arayd,
> With rose and lillies ouer them displayed.   [ll. 280–86]

The meaning of Cythera to Watteau over a century later was not much different.

Sidney's allusions clarify the delicate aura of symbolism which hangs over the opening pages of *Arcadia.* Urania symbolizes Heavenly Love: her departure for Cythera, "dividing her heavenly beautie, betweene the Earth and the Sea," is imaged in terms appropriate to the arrival of Aphrodite Ourania, the link between heaven and earth, at Cythera. And having come to the shepherds in order to initiate the process of love, she has left for her proper home in the Heaven of Venus, leaving her human lovers bereaved (like mankind) but now strong enough to climb to the higher orders of love by themselves in Arcadia. The position of the story, as well as its symbolic overtones, indicates that it is a kind of general emblem of the possible transformations of the soul that love holds out to all men; and to Pyrocles and Musidorus in particular, it shows what may happen in Arcadia.

---

7. The Elizabethan translation of the first part of the *Hypnerotomachia* by R. D., 1592, is dedicated "To the Thrise Honourable and Ever Lyving Vertues of Syr Phillip Sydney Knight."

8. For analogues in the *Hypnerotomachia* to *The Faerie Queene* IV, x, see Earl B. Fowler, *Spenser and the Courts of Love* (Menasha, Wis., 1921), pp. 35, 54, 61.

But we found in our previous chapter that such a transformation comes to the princes only after the greatest difficulty. What is a calm and sure process for the humble shepherds in Arcadia is a difficult problem for the princes from the great world. Therefore, as E. M. W. Tillyard has noticed,[9] a break in style occurs just after the shepherds have celebrated Urania's effects on them:

> hath not she throwne reason upon our desires, and, as it were given eyes unto *Cupid?* hath in any, but in her, love-fellowship maintained friendship between rivals, & beautie taught the beholders chastitie? He was going on with his praises, but *Strephon* bad him stay, and looke: and so they both perceived a thing which floated drawing nearer and nearer to the banke; but rather by the favourable working of the Sea, then by any self industrie. They doubted a while what it should be; till it was cast up even hard before them: at which time they fully saw that it was a man.   [3]

The formal balance marked by alliteration and word play gives way to a looser unbalanced structure describing the process of discovery directly as it appears to the eye, as we turn our eyes from Strephon and Klaius to Musidorus on a sea strewn with the relics of violent death.

Tillyard characterizes the contrast as one "between the idea of man's 'erected wit' and the pitiful spectacle of what in crude fact man has made of man," but the context of *Arcadia* we have examined shows it to be more than that. It includes, as well, the contrast between the balance and control of the pastoral life—the home of "the contemplative virtue" by means of which love can grow steadily toward union with its developing object—and the realm where men must fight fortune, the elements, and each other, where their struggle to preserve the moral "meane of perturbations" gives love no chance to flower. Furthermore, here pastoral and epic, the two worlds which must achieve some sort of rapprochement in the rest of the romance confront each other. Sidney's allusions help us to realize this dimension of the contrast. The opening of *Arcadia* is a capsule version of the initial episode

9. *The English Epic and Its Background,* p. 303.

of Montemayor's great pastoral romance, the *Diana*. "The hope-
lesse shepheard *Strephon* was come to the sands, which lie against
the Island of Cithera" just as "Downe from the hils of *Leon* came
forgotten *Syrenus*"; each, when he reaches the spot where his
beloved left him, is joined by his "friendly rivall" in love (Klaius
and Sylvano, respectively). And each opens with an apostrophe
to remembrance:

> Remembrance, restlesse Remembrance, which claymes not only
> this dutie of us, but for it will have us forget our selves.   [1]

> Ah Memorie (cruel enemie to my quiet rest) were not thou
> better occupied to make me forget present corsies, then to put
> before mine eyes passed contents?[1]

But the new note struck by the appearance of Musidorus recalls
another work and another genre, the opening of Heliodorus'
Æthiopica, which Sidney, after Scaliger, considered an epic: [2]

> when they came so near as their eies were ful masters of the
> object, they saw a sight ful of piteous strangnesse: a ship, or
> rather the carkas of the ship, or rather some few bones of the
> carkas, hulling there, part broken, part burned, part drowned:
> death having used more than one dart to that destruction. About
> it floted great store of very rich thinges, and many chestes which
> might promise no lesse. And amidst the precious things were a
> number of dead bodies, which likewise did not only testifie both
> elements violence, but that the chief violence was growne of
> humane inhumanity: for their bodies were full of grisly wounds.
>   [4]

> they cast their eyes somewhat neare the shoare: where a shippe,
> tyed with cables to the maine land, lay at road, without sailers,
> and full fraughted, which thing, they who were a farre of might
> easily conjecture: for the burden caused the shippe to drawe
> water within the bourdes of the deck. But on the shore every
> place was ful of men, some quite dead, some halfe dead, some
> whose bodies yet panted, and plainly declared that there had
> ben a battell fought of late.[3]

1. Yong's translation, p. 2.
2. *The Defence of Poesie*, in *Works*, 3, 10.
3. Underdowne's translation of Heliodorus, 1587; ed. W. E. Henley, The
Tudor Translations (London, 1895), p. 9.

Pastoral Exercises

The conjunction of great riches and death, the ship and the bodies, and the use of the viewers to obtain pathos are similar, as are the descriptive processes applied by Sidney to the ship and by Heliodorus to the bodies. By his sudden juxtaposition of different styles and literary traditions in this way, Sidney intensified the contrasts in ways of life which his opening pages were designed to present.

One further aspect of the contrast between hero and shepherd deserves notice, that is, the opposition between life and death which the first clause of the book introduces:

> It was in the time that the earth begins to put on her new apparell against the approch of her lover, and that the Sun running a most even course, becomes an indifferent arbiter betweene the night and the day; when the hopelesse shepheard *Strephon* was come to the sands.

When Musidorus floats into view, the board he holds to "seemed to be but a beere to carrie him a land to his Sepulcher," and, once on the beach, he starts to cast himself back into the waves, "that before being in appearance dead, had yet saved his life, and now comming to his life, shoulde be a cause to procure his death; but they ranne unto him." To land near amorous Arcadia is to come out of the watery realm of death into a new life like that of the year. In the paired descriptions of Lacedæmon and Arcadia that follow the rescue, Sidney presented a spatial summary of our series of contrasts between the heroic, chaotic, and deathly and the pastoral, orderly, and life-giving qualities:

> The country (answered *Claius*) where you were cast a shore, and now are past through, is Laconia, not so poore by the barrennes of the soyle (though in it selfe not passing fertill) as by a civill warre, which being these two yeares within the bowels of that estate, betweene the gentlemen and the peasants (by them named *Helots*) hath in this sorte as it were disfigured the face of nature, and made it so unhospitall as now you have found it: the townes neither of the one side nor the other, willingly opening their gates to strangers, nor strangers willingly entring for feare of being mistaken.
>
> But this countrie (where now you set your foot) is Arcadia: & even harde by is the house of *Kalander* whither we leade you:

this countrie being thus decked with peace, & (the child of peace) good husbandrie. These houses you see so scattered are of men, as we two are, that live upon the commoditie of their sheepe: and therefore in the division of the Arcadian estate are termed shepheards; a happy people, wanting little, because they desire not much. [6]

The pairing of the two nations sets the scene for two simultaneous actions which illustrate once more the contrast between heroic and amatory, for, as we soon find, while Musidorus contemplates fertile Arcadia, Pyrocles experiences the ravages of war in Lacedæmon. Our opening pastoral scene, then, has set in motion a whole series of dichotomies in the plot between the pastoral life, where things accord to an ideal order, and the heroic life in the world, where they do not; and it soon leads, therefore, to the climactic dialogue on love and war. But once the shepherds have brought Musidorus from the bloody sea into the green valleys of Arcadia, they leave; for the main plot has begun.

THE FIRST ECLOGUES AND LOVE

Strephon and Klaius do not appear in *Arcadia* again, but their story follows Pyrocles and Musidorus in the series of songs gathered into four "Eclogues" or pastoral interludes at the end of each book. Near the end of the First Eclogues, Pyrocles expresses curiosity about them and receives in reply a long narrative song from the shepherd Lamon. It is an excellent example of Sidney's pastoral art, for while its style is rustic and its matter popular, it encompasses considerable complexity of attitude, as we can see in the opening lines, which make "plaine" mean both "low" and "miserable" and weigh the courtly audience between hardheartedness and sympathy for such lowness:

> A Shepheards tale no height of stile desires,
> To raise in words what in effect is lowe:
> A plaining songe plaine-singing voice requires,
> For warbling notes from inward chearing flow.
> I then, whose burd'ned breast but thus aspires
> Of shepheards two the seely cause to show,

Pastoral Exercises

> Need not the stately Muses help invoke
> For creeping rimes, which often sighings choke.
> But you, ô you, that thinke not teares to deare
> To spend for harms, although they touch you not:
> And deigne to deeme your neighbors mischiefe neare,
> Although they be of meaner parents got:
> You I invite with easie eares to heare
> The poore-clad truth of loves wrong-ordred lot.
> Who may be glad, be glad you be not such:
> Who share in woe, weygh others have as much.

The narrative starts by describing the life of the shepherds before the advent of Urania as idyllic but inextricably low and earthly as a condition of its serenity:

> Their chearfull minds, till pois'ned was their cheare,
> The honest sports of earthy lodging prove;
> Now for a clod-like Hare in form they peere,
> Now bolt & cudgill Squirrels leape do move.

With the coming of Urania, who is always associated with light, it is as if the sun of heaven has broken through the loam of earth with its rays, as if spirit has penetrated matter. She appears

> One day (ô day, that shin'd to make them darke!)
> While they did ward sun beames with shady bay;

but they cannot shield themselves for long; as she runs to recapture an escaped sparrow, they are captured by "her beames," the refulgence of her body which is really "Love that shin'de in shining maid." The inception of love once established with symbolic overtones, the poem settles down to a lengthy description of a peasant game called "barley-break" (wherein one couple tries to draw others into a circle called "Hell"), a device by which Strephon (who plays the game with Urania) and Klaius (who watches) are wound fully into the net of love. Here the poem asserts its poise. The description is full of robust comic detail, fisticuffs and naïve slyness, and is moreover done realistically, since it refers to Elizabethan rustic customs and the hares at Wilton; but, as so frequently in the poem, an increase in homeliness conceals a sharpening of satire. The following lines, for instance, hint strongly that the gameful spite of the shepherds is only their imitation of the more earnest spite at court:

> The two that in mid place, Hell called were,
> Must strive with waiting foot, and watching eye
> To catch of them, and then to hell to beare,
> That they, as well as they, Hell may supplie:
>   Like some which seeke to salve their blotted name
>   With others blott, till all do tast of shame.

Furthermore, rusticity and sly satire exist side by side with cosmic Neoplatonic allegory here, for during the game Strephon changes partners from Urania to gross Cosma to the delicate little Nous, ending in heated pursuit of the radiant Urania again. The names of these girls suggest that the Plotinian hypostases are involved, and except for the puzzling rejection of *Nous* the game presents a reasonably consistent allegory of the circular operation of love.[4] Thus Strephon, in all his pastoral innocence, mimes out the descent of the soul, its refusal of the created cosmos of matter and of the divine world of Ideas for something higher like union with the One to which Urania or Heavenly Love may lead him. Therefore, we may perhaps associate with our game of barley-break this incongruous passage from Plotinus on the human soul's awakening to love and speedy pursuit of it:

> The soul, receiving into itself an outflow from Thence, is moved and dances wildly and is all stung with longing and becomes love. Before this it is not moved even towards *Nous*, for all its beauty: the beauty of *Nous* is ineffective till it catches a light from the Good, and the soul by itself lies flat and is completely ineffective and is not stirred by the presence of *Nous*. But when a kind of warmth from Thence comes upon it, it gains strength and wakes and is truly winged; and though it is moved with passion for that which lies close by it, yet all the same it rises higher to something greater which it seems to remember. And as

4. By his allegory, Lamon fulfills Kalander's prediction that the shepherds in Arcadia would sometime deal with high matters "under hidden formes" (15). Compare Book II of Bernard Silvestris' *De Mundi Universitate*, where the female figures Noys, Urania, Physis, and Natura come together to create man.

long as there is anything higher than that which is present to it, it naturally goes on upwards, lifted by the Giver of its love. It rises above *Nous*, but cannot go on above the Good, for there is nothing above. If it remains in *Nous* it sees fair and noble things, but has not yet quite grasped what it is seeking.[5]

Strephon and Klaius move into and out of allegory throughout their story for their edification and ours, and after their education in this strange and complex game they see Urania as a symbolic figure like Dante's Beatrice rather than a shepherdess. Thus a vision of Urania interrupts young Strephon's comic lament in order to bind him to the allegorical injunction to leave the earthly for the heavenly:

> Alas! a cloud hath overcast mine eyes:
> And yet I see her shine amid the cloud.
> Alas! of ghosts I heare the gastlie cries:
> Yet there, me seemes, I heare her singing loud.
> This song she singes in most commanding wise:
> Come shepheards boy, let now thy heart be bow'd,
>   To make it selfe to my least looke a slave:
>   Leave sheepe, leave all, I will no piecing have.[6]

He obeys, casts away rams, sheep, and dog, and breaks his pipe: he has now arrived at the point Klaius described earlier, when she made them look to their souls "when other marke their sheepe." After having solemnized his change from shepherd to lover, Strephon turns to find Klaius behind him, Klaius whose sufferings show his own sufferings "in perfect image." It is at this point that Basilius breaks off the song because of the lateness of the hour and

5. *Enneads* 6.7.22, trans. A. H. Armstrong in *Plotinus* (London, 1953), pp. 74–75; I have used this translation instead of MacKenna's because it preserves the Greek names.

6. See Sannazaro, *Arcadia, Egloga* VII:

> Madonna, sua mercè, pur una sera
>   gioiosa e bella assai m'apparve in sonno,
>   e rallegrò il mio cor; sì come il sole
>   suol dopo pioggia disgombrar la terra;
>   dicendo a me—Vien, cògli a le mie piagge
>   qualche fioretto, e lascia gli antri foschi.

Zelmane's wound; but it is a particularly apt place at which to stop, for the song has brought Strephon and Klaius to a point directly parallel to that of the heroes at the end of Book I. There, we remember, the already transformed Pyrocles had come upon Musidorus in the posture of Klaius, for he had just changed from prince to shepherd out of love. After their mutual commiseration the book ended with a fight with the lion and the bear—the incident where Zelmane received the wound that makes Basilius stop the song. Thus the song, while functioning as a lyrical sub-plot to the heroic main plot, draws pastoral eclogue into the realm of the narrative. And the songs around it draw the lines more firmly.

"A Shepheards tale" crowns a series of songs about the nature of love that apply either directly or aslant to the heroes' fortunes in the First Book. The antiphonal song in the "braule" that begins the eclogues sets the theme. The first group of shepherds represents those whose love has been returned, "We love, and have our loves rewarded"; the second, the unhappy lovers, "We love, and are no whit regarded." After exploring their differences, they unite in expressing their common concern:

> *Then all joyning their voyces, and dauncing a faster measure,*
> *they would conclude with some such words:*
>   As without breath no pipe doth move,
>   No musicke kindly without love.

The "braule" establishes in this way both the theme of love and the possibilities of widely divergent fortunes in love. Therefore in the games that follow, the "sport was one of them to provoke another to a more large expressing of his passions." The first is an amoebaean or responsory eclogue between Thyrsis, who takes up the part of the hopeful lover, and the unhappy Dorus, wherein each describes the manner of his falling in love and his hope or despair. Next come the specific cases of the heroes; Dorus explores his feelings about new love in a solo song which concludes:

> Thus, thus, alas! wofull by Nature, unhappie by Fortune,
> But most wretched I am, now Love awakes my desire.

Zelmane follows with a matching song in which she explores the possibilities of hope in her love affairs, and she and Dorus sing a duet in which each expresses obliquely his feelings about love. The theme common to all these songs is love—more particularly, the first effects of love—its beginnings, the immediate reactions of the lover, his ability to express himself, and his hopes and fears for the future.[7]

Yet as the measured insolence of "A Shepheard's tale" toward its courtly audience implies, there is some divergence within the unity of the First Eclogues, for if nobleman and shepherd both suffer under love, they react to it in different ways. Furthermore, the song's explicit characterization of its style as "low" tells us that the differences appear mainly in poetic styles. Distinctions begin to emerge in the first song between Thyrsis and Dorus, for the unhappy shepherd there is also the disguised nobleman. His unhappiness stems from the conflict of love with other values in his mind and from his psychological complexity; therefore the chief thing one notices in the despairing Dorus' style is violent imagery and a tendency to hyperbole, in contrast to the hopeful Thyrsis' calm factualness. The contrast between high and low style at the beginning immediately switches to contrasting conceptions of the mistress and ideas of what love is. For instance, when Dorus invokes the Muses, Thyrsis replies:

> *Muse* hold your peace: but thou my God *Pan* glorifie
> My *Kalas* gifts, who with all good gifts filled is.
> Thy pipe, ô *Pan*, shall help, though I sing sorilie:
> A heape of sweetes she is, where nothing spilled is;
> Who though she be no Bee, yet full of honey is:
> A lillie field, with plough of Rose which tilled is.

7. See Ringler, *The Poems of Sir Philip Sidney*, introduction, p. xxxviii: "One of the most striking things about Sidney's eclogues is their carefully integrated structure. Each of the four groups develops a situation and explores a theme: the first presents the pangs of unrequited love, the second the struggle between reason and passion, the third the ideals of married love, the fourth the sorrows of lovers and the sorrows of death." Ringler's account of the structures of individual Eclogues differs from mine because he is dealing with the arrangement of the Old *Arcadia* rather than that of the 1598 version; for theme and structure in the first two Eclogues of the New *Arcadia* of 1590, see my article, "Thematic Unity in the *New Arcadia*," *Studies in Philology*, 57 (1960), 126–27, 135–36.

And Dorus replies to him:

> Such *Kala* is: but ah my fancies raised be
> In one, whose name to name were high presumption,
> Since vertues all, to make her title, pleased be.
> O happie Gods, which by inward assumption
> Enjoy her soule, in bodies faire possession,
> And keep it joyn'd, fearing your seates consumption.
> How oft with raine of teares skies make confession,
> Their dwellers rapt with sight of her perfection,
> From heav'nly throne to her heav'n use digression?
> Of best things then what world shall yeeld confection
> To liken her? decke yours with your comparison:
> She is her selfe of best things the collection.

The contrast in styles involves homely story as against the sort of involved inner combat between Reason and Passion so familiar to us in *Astrophel and Stella,* factual description of the mistress against involved metaphorical evocation of her, and of course pastoral against celestial imagery. But style is emblematic of theory of love: Kala is a woman, a shepherdess; Pamela is that combination of noble woman and goddess, the Petrarchan mistress. And it is from the fact that as such she seems unattainable that Dorus' love issues in immediate despair in contrast to Thyrsis' hope.

The remarkable fact about this duet is that in it the two divergent views of love coexist harmoniously. The amoebaean form is in large part responsible for their unity at the same time as it expresses a change in relation between the two singers. At the start Thyrsis is defensive and Dorus disdainful, but at the end, as Thyrsis yields the prize, Dorus yields too and calls him his friend. But the two men and styles held together here draw apart after Dorus wins, for he "did so well in answering *Thyrsis,* that everie one desired to heare him sing something alone." It is in his solo, where the lineaments of the high style stand forth clearly, that the split between noble and shepherd becomes apparent:

> Fortune, Nature, Love, long have contended about me,
> Which should most miseries cast on a worme that I am.[8]

Pastoral Exercises

It is a philosophical lyric, a disquisition on the power of Fortune to block a man's desires; of Nature's power above Fortune's to mold a man's character and fate; and of Love's still greater power to overthrow even a Heracleitus. It places man alone in direct contact with the forces governing the universe, which, even in grinding him down, allow him the heroic reward, the dignity of despair. The diction is of course abstract, and the metrical scheme is something new in Arcadia: classical elegiacs.

This song has initiated the second portion of the First Eclogues, where the courtly elements now in Arcadia reveal *their* version of the operation of love. Zelmane rises to cap Dorus' verses with a complaint to Hope in Sapphics, the style again high and abstract, the structure logical and argumentative, hinging as it does on a belief in the immortality of the soul and love's imprint on it:

> Thus not ending, ends the due praise of her praise:
> Fleshly vaile consumes; but a soule hath his life,
> Which is held in love; love it is, that hath joynd
> > Life to this our soule.

It can rise out of the argument of despair only by imaging the lover's love—but not the lover—ringing the praises of the beloved after death. If the impasse is avoided by a witty turn and appeal at the end of this song, it is reasserted in the hexameter duet between Dorus and Zelmane which follows it. That song, an answer to the earlier pastoral dialogue, makes the distinctions between court and country love its explicit subject. By and large, the shepherd has the better life, for even though he is restricted by his humility he has a certain freedom to reveal his love openly, and derives comfort from seeing his "state represented" in his natural environment. This difference Lamon illustrates in "A Shepheards tale," as we have seen, by making his satire underline the split between field and court.

In the songs of the First Eclogues, the divergent views bound together by the common concern of love convey a double irony. On the one hand, the shepherds in their naïveté have no real per-

8. Analogues to the first line occur in Petrarch, sonnets xcix and cli, and Desportes, *Amours*, I, ccv; see Michel Poirer, "Quelques sources des poemes de Sidney," *Etudes Anglaises*, 11 (1958), 150–54.

ception of what is happening to them, or of all that love implies. On the other hand, those who do know find their path strewn with thorns and see only the utmost difficulty in approaching what two of the shepherds in their simplicity have already achieved—the attainment of Heavenly Love and the transformation of the soul. We shall find further ironies developing as the pastoral plot proceeds.

THE SECOND ECLOGUES AND DIVISION

The Second Eclogues continue the First Eclogues, for the theme of this group is the inner divisions of the soul under the extensive sufferings caused by love. It is established at the beginning, as in the First Eclogues, by a device, this one *"a daunce, which they called the skirmish betwixt Reason and Passion,"* between shepherds representing the two elements of the mind. They start in strife for mastery of the soul:

> R. But Reason will, that Reason governe most.
> P. And Passion will, that Passion rule the rost;

they approach in formation, and pretend to shoot at each other, but when they meet it is only to embrace and yield to the power that made them complementary:

> R. Then let us both to heavenlie rules give place,
> P. Which Passions kill, and Reason do deface.

But the second section of the eclogues, which takes us out of the ideological realm into the psychological in laments of shepherds and debates of passion, does not exhibit such easy accords. The first of them is a debate between Dorus, who describes the unmitigated misery of his subjection to love, and the reasonable shepherd Dicus, who finally abandons him as a fool who "Makes Reason lie a slave to servile sense." The case of misery is expanded in the two songs of Strephon and Klaius which follow, their great double sestina and the dizaines of contrarieties in love ("I joy in griefe, and doo detest all joyes"). The original conflict between reasonable shepherd and lovelorn noble shepherd is reasserted in stronger outline by the next song, a debate between the old and foolish Geron, who reflects Dicus' attitude ("suppresse / Those rebell thoughts which are thy slaves but kinde"), and the young and spirited Philisides. Passion wins, and Geron is put down by Mastix (after he has related his quarrel to the original skirmish between Reason and Passion). Philisides' doleful solo introduces a third section, applying the general analysis of Reason and Passion in the first section to the heroes of the main plot. Zelmane sings one song about her tortures in love and another addressed to Reason:

> Reason, tell me thy mind, if here be reason
> In this strange violence, to make resistance.

The eclogues close with a song by Dorus echoing his dialogue with Zelmane in the First Eclogues and reasserting—this time ironically —the simple amorous nature of the pastoral world.

The general similarity of pattern between these eclogues and the First Eclogues is apparent; likewise the common theme of the games expresses the nature of the heroes' adventures in the portion of the plot that precedes them. Book II, we may remember, was the book of suffering: the complicated plans of the noble lovers back-fired and left them with more hindrances than they had had before, and though their love may have been returned, it led only to more problems. Under the weight of such perplexities they felt discord within their souls which left them torn apart, in "self-division." Therefore the theme of the Second Eclogues is the conflict be-tween Reason and Passion in the soul staked out by love, and they thus create an enlarged image of the minds of our heroes.

Here the lyrical subplot of Strephon and Klaius comes into closer relation with the main plot than before. Near the end of the First Eclogues, Dorus asserted the comforting reflection of the shepherd's mind in the landscape; this assumption is sub-jected to ironic revision in the first song of Strephon and Klaius, the magnificent double sestina "Ye Gote-heard Gods." Within this very tight and rich form, Strephon and Klaius disclose the change that has arisen in their lives, a change expressed chiefly in their developing relation to their natural environment and symbolized by the six terms of the sestina. The structure of the poem is therefore one of reversal, which appears in the changed meanings of the six terms; for instance, "valleys" are first "pleasant," then "woeful," then a symbol of affliction, a symbol of lowness and pain, misery, spiritual baseness, and finally complete darkness. Such changes outline the form of the whole, which proceeds by paired stanzas. The first two stanzas invoke six gods of nature; the second pair contrasts the two shepherds to the gods by means of a further contrast between their past life in pleasant relation to their environment and their present life in a world grown dark. The fifth and sixth stanzas draw a conclusion from this experience—their grief has turned nature to something woeful and ugly. Since the seventh and eighth stanzas start anew by taking up the six terms in their original order, they shift the poem into a new gear. Mere change leads into complete reversal, which Strephon and Klaius present in terms of a nightmare vision of the world turned upside down by their grief:

> Me seemes I see the high and statelie mountaines,
> Transforme themselves to low dejected vallies:
> Me seemes I heare in these ill chaunged forrests,
> The Nightingales do learne of Owles their musike:
> Me seemes I feele the comfort of the morning,
> Turn'd to the mortall serene of an evening.

> Me seemes I see a filthie cloudy evening,
> As soone as Sunne begins to clime the mountaines:
> Me seemes I feele a noysome sent, the morning
> When I doo smell the flowers of these vallies:
> Me seemes I heare, when I do heare sweete musike,
> The dreadfull cries of murdred men in forrests.

Because of this dreadful transformation they turn to hatred of the world and themselves. Finally, in the last two stanzas, we perceive the cause of all this change, the decay of nature, their hatred of it, and their pain—the departure of Urania, or Heavenly Love, whose light was both greater than the landscape and, as the link between the material world and the intelligible world, the cause of all fertility in it:

For she, to whome compar'd, the Alps are vallies,
She, whose least word brings from the sphears their musick,
At whose approch the Sunne rose in the evening,
Who where she went bare in her forhead morning,
Is gone, is gone, from these our spoyled forrests,
Turning to desarts our best pastur'de mountaines.

We leave Strephon and Klaius in the waste land, where there is only the memory of her in music to remind them of once pleasant mountains, green forests, and shady valleys.

"Ye Gote-heard Gods" takes the story up at the point where "A Shepheards tale" had left it: now, after they have given up their former life for higher things, the human embodiment of those higher things has abandoned them, thereby leaving earthly life barren and despicable. The irony of Heavenly Love which Strephon and Klaius experienced after Urania's departure constituted a higher form of what Pyrocles and Musidorus feel now, for they too now seek an unattainable mistress, receive no comfort from their environment, and reside on the earth as complete strangers. Once the analogy of the shepherds' past with the present state of the heroes has been established, a second song follows, analyzing the internal disorder resulting from this situation. This is the dizaine "I joy in griefe," a song closely related to the double sestina both in its form and in its theme. For this song takes "Ye Gote-heard Gods" into the microcosm, showing as it does the nightmare world reflected in the conflict within their souls. The conflict is first internalized, then projected outward to end where the sestina had, in the effects of human grief on the soul:

For even the hearbes our hatefull musike stroyes,
And from our burning breath the trees do bend.

But the style is different from that of the sestina and in its difference approximates the noble style. It is abstract and philosophical ("No being now, but sorow I can have") and it presents human suffering as a result of a grand psychomachia of absolutes like Reason, Hope, Despair, Will, and Hate. Strephon and Klaius, by their increased awareness of what was happening to them before in their innocence, have explicitly accepted the lonely heroic view of life and, contingently, the style and concepts of Neoplatonic love:

> Since then my hart did loose his wonted place,
> Infected so with her sweet poysons might,
> That, leaving me for dead, to her it went:
> But ah her flight hath my dead reliques spent.[9]

And, of course, what is more important than the assimilation of their style and concepts to those of the princes, the conflict in their minds reflects directly the disorder of the heroes' minds in Book II. Indeed, at the end of this song, "So well were these waile-full complaints accorded to the passions of all the princelie hearers, while every one made what he heard of another the ballance of his own fortune, that they stood a long while striken in a sad and silent consideration of them."

While Strephon and Klaius move into the emotional orbit of Pyrocles and Musidorus in the Second Eclogues, the rest of the shepherds move further away. As differences in style sharpen into contrasts between the stupid and the spirited, the shepherds rise to direct criticism of the disguised courtiers. It is the fourth song of the eclogues that marks this split, for Geron intends it to be an indirect critique of all the noble lovers, "desirous to set forth what counsels the wisdome of age had laid up in store against such fancies (as he thought) follies of youth, yet so as it might not appear that his words respected them." The eclogue is a variation on the first song between Dicus and Dorus, but the contrasts are now exaggerated, for the bluff, irascible, and dense Geron replaces the friendly and reasonable Dicus, while Dorus' part is assumed by Philisides, a new character considerably more complex than the disguised shepherd. Unlike the first song, this one is not argumentative, for Geron has no understanding of the lover's situation, while Philisides responds to none of his theses but merely grows

---

9. A very common Neoplatonic concept; see e.g. Ficino's *Commentary* on *Symposium* 2.8, trans. Jayne, p. 144: "The soul of a lover does not exist within the man himself, because it does not function in him. If it does not exist in him, it also does not live in him, and he who does not live is dead. Therefore, everyone who loves is dead in himself. But at least he lives in the other person, does he not?"

angry and heaps scorn on him. Thus the song is a mere dramatization of the inability of the two to come into contact, and soon falls from dialogue into long monologues in terza rima. After Geron's long tirade reducing the mistress to a "woman" (with the implication of "quean" that the solitary word often had for Elizabethans),[1] the angry Philisides turns satirist of the satirist Geron. At this point, the speakers generalize their positions as youth and old man, and the song moves into the ancient pastoral motif of the *Conflictus Veris et Hiemis* familiar to us in Spenser's "February" eclogue.[2] As a result, the gap between the two widens and becomes apprehensible as an effect of the eternal conflict of youth, seen as witty and spirited, and age, seen as foolish and life-denying.

Disguised nobleman and real shepherd have no contact throughout the rest of the Second Eclogues. After another shepherd named Mastix intensifies the disgrace of Geron's defeat, the old man calls together his dogs and stalks out of the party. In direct contrast to their rough and tumble, Philisides next signalizes the courtier's triumph over the rustic in classical measures (as Dorus did in the First Eclogues). Significantly, he can find no pastoral partner for his song, and so sings his hexameters to Echo. His song paves the way for the noble characters with their philosophical quantitative songs defining themselves and their situation. As a sign of his lonely nobility each of them is to himself both priest and clerk, as he addresses himself to Echo, his Muse, Reason, or the sweet woods. Dorus' final song summarizes their state, for in praising the pastoral life (to which he pretends to belong) and satirizing the court (to which he actually belongs) he shows their isolation from both their original environment and their new one. The only reason for tolerating such a situation is to enter a mystical union with the Divine through love, and on this hope end the Second Eclogues:

1. Thus the adulterous wife in "A neighbour mine" (Third Eclogues) plays "a womans part" when she goes astray.

2. Alcuin's eighth-century Christian allegory is only the most explicit example of the conflict between youth and age; the motif is deeply rooted in spring festivals, and formed part of the early Roman Fescennine verses. It entered pastoral early and is implied whenever, in an amoebaean eclogue, one of the shepherds is jovial and prosperous, the other crabbed and barren, as in Virgil's *Eclogue* 7.

O sweet woods the delight of solitarinesse!
O how much I do like your solitarinesse!
Where mans mind hath a freed consideration
Of goodnesse to receive lovely direction.
Where senses do beholde th'order of heav'nly hoste,
And wise thoughts do behold what the creator is:
Contemplation here holdeth his only seate:
Bounded with no limits, borne with a wing of hope
Clymes even unto the starres.

THE DIVERSION OF PLOTS

The remaining sets of eclogues stand separate from the plot, since
the main characters are always elsewhere and the king no longer
presides. Furthermore, when Pyrocles and Musidorus drop out of
the eclogues, their pastoral doubles Strephon and Klaius go along
with them. Since these unifying elements are absent, the eclogues
no longer represent discussion of the main plot by both courtier
and shepherd, but rather the shepherd's—the outsider's—commentary, direct or oblique, on the main plot. The result of this
shift in point of view is usually criticism or satire.

The events of the Third Eclogues constitute a direct contrast—
a criticism by contrast—to the main plot in Book III: "I thinke
it shall not be impertinent, to remember a little our shepheards,
while the other greater persons, are either sleeping or otherwise
troubled." The greater persons, we may remember, are all on the
verge of consummation at the end of Book III: Musidorus rests
with Pamela in the glade, about to be captured; Pyrocles lies in a
swoon beside his Philoclea; and both Basilius and Gynecia await
the satisfaction of their lusts in the dark cave. Against these ironic
anticipations, Sidney placed the humble rustic marriage of Thyrsis
(the shepherd matched with Dorus in the First Eclogues) to his
Kala:

Thyrsis not with many painted words nor falsified promises,
had won the consent of his beloved *Kala*, but with a true and

simple making her know he loved her, not forcing himselfe beyond his reach to buy her affection, but giving her such pretie presents, as neither could wearie him with the giving, nor shame her for the taking.

The very first sentence takes a slant look at those who do feign, in their pride, and force themselves beyond their reach, and the implicit contrast between such pastoral humility and courtly pride continues throughout the description of their wooing. All here is nature and humility; Thyrsis' gifts are redolent with the unity of man with the earth—the first strawberries, the spring flowers, wool at shearing time—all simple, natural, orderly, clean and virginal, all in due season of nature.

The songs of the Third Eclogues naturally center on the rustic marriage. The first of them, the epithalamion, brings to the fore the kind of union with natural process implied in the wooing by utilizing the ancient ritual structure of invocation and exorcism—invocation of all the gods of nature, exorcism of the evils resultant from man's turning from nature to civilization. The first stanza displays their kinship with earth and their resulting fertility:

> Let mother earth now decke her selfe in flowers,
> To see her of-spring seeke a good increase,
> Where justest love doth vanquish *Cupids* powers
> And war of thoughts is swallow'd up in peace,
> > Which never may decrease,
> > But like the turtles faire,
> > Live one in two, a well united paire,
> > Which that no chance may staine,
> > O *Himen* long their coupled joyes maintaine.

The rest of the invocation calls on air and water as well as the gods of fructification, and unifies the couple with these elements by comparing them to doves, the elm and the vine, the lily, rivers, herds, rain, and the oak and mistletoe. Then the exorcism (as befits both their pastoral condition and the position of the song next to the main plot) excludes from the feast the elements we saw disturbing the noble heroes, such as strife, greed, jealousy, and especially "peacock pride" and the Cupid of the courts of love, whose presence must not pervert the pure love of Thyrsis and Kala:

> But thou foule *Cupid* syre to lawlesse lust,
> Be thou farre hence with thy empoison'd dart,
> Which though of glittring golde, shall heere take rust,
> Where simple love, which chastnesse doth imparte,
>> Avoides thy hurtfull arte,
>> Not needing charming skill,
>> Such mindes with sweet affections for to fill,
>> Which being pure and plaine,
>> O *Himen* long their coupled joyes maintaine.

Once the positive ideal has established itself in the epithalamion, the eclogues move into its opposite and thus into satire of the main plot.

We enter this satiric mode with the fabliau world of "A neighbour mine," which arises from the theme of jealousy excluded from the bed of Thyrsis and Kala. It is, in fact, an anti-epithalamion, since its plot is the collapse of a marriage, while its characters display a whole assortment of corrupt human emotions. There is the husband so pathologically jealous that he arouses his young wife's desire for the "sweet" he seems to see in adultery. She becomes a subtle whore who seeks her own ruin by extremely intricate shifts: since her desires were aroused by his jealousy in the first place, she uses that same jealousy to make him her go-between. The setting of this grim little comedy directs the satire to specific targets, for it takes place in the countryside near the court, to which any shepherd may be called to perform eclogues before the king. If this place begins to look uncomfortably like Basilius' retreat, the resemblance becomes stronger in the figure of the lover, for he is called "the Courtier":

> Unto his house a jollie shepheard went,
> To whome our prince did beare a great good will,
>> Because in wrestling and in pastorall
>> He farre did passe the rest of shepheards all.

And therefore he a courtier was benamed.

This has the earmarks of a reference to Dorus, and so strengthens the picture the song paints of the court's corrupting influence on pastoral simplicity and its possible disruption of the values of marriage.

"The lad *Philisides*," which follows, also takes its keynote from the epithalamion in style and matter, but it exhibits the impossibility of marriage to the noble swains like Dorus and Philisides, and not its perversion. The fact that its stanzaic structure is modeled on that of the epithalamion only stresses its differences, for each stanza ends with a picture of the earth in decay rather than a prayer to Hymen. He takes up many of the topics of the marriage song—earth, streams, doves, flowers—but shows a complete reversal of the harmonious fertile relation proposed there:

> Earth, brooke, flowr's, pipe, lambe, Dove
> Say all, & I with them,
> Absence is death.

Philisides' next song, "As I my little flocke on *Ister* banke," suggests a link between the innocence of Thyrsis and Kala and the moral decay of "A neighbour mine." By means of a beast fable, he shows how man's own natural power over the vegetative and animal world corrupts him so far that he forgets his ties to them and kills them for his use. This is surely satire not of the court but of mankind as a whole, for it shows that noble pride is only an exaggeration of the insolence common to city and field.[3] But the shepherds do not understand "what he should meane by it," and they immediately interpose a final conciliatory eclogue between Geron, happily married for fifty years, and Histor, one of Kala's disappointed suitors. In its final statement of belief in the general possibility of a number of fine marriages, it assures the disappointed lover of the same happy issue as the successful one, and thus draws together the various versions of the marriage theme. Furthermore,

---

3. Ringler (p. xxxix) justifies the inclusion of this song on other grounds: "The beast fable might on a superficial view appear to break the unity of this group; but a little reflection shows that it is entirely appropriate, for it is concerned with discovering the proper form of sovereignty in the state, just as the other marriage poems are concerned with indicating the proper form of sovereignty in the home."

it reestablishes the concept of marriage as a fruitful union under the auspices of family, commonwealth, and, especially, nature:

> Nature above all things requireth this,
> That we our kind doo labour to maintaine;
> Which drawne-out line doth hold all humaine blisse.

The world must be populated: the utilitarian view of love as corporeal begetting, now established as the norm of the eclogues, replaces the princely view of love as the mystical experience of a birth in the soul. To the minds of the prosaic shepherds left on the scene, such heroic love is lust and its effects, which our heroes take to be the center of life, are mere toys; and it had better come safe into the shores of marriage as soon as possible. Geron reminds us once again of the rift that has occurred as he leaves us with these final words addressed to Histor, and beyond him to the princes:

> Marrie therefore; for marriage will destroy
> Those passions which to youthfull head doo clime,
> Mothers and Nurses of all vaine annoy.

During these eclogues, from the epithalamion to the satires and laments, the picture of man—his nature, fate, and potentialities—has steadily declined to the base minimum of Geron. While this action is entirely separate from the main plot, it is clearly an indirect response to the sad failures Pyrocles and Musidorus exhibited in the Third Book, just as the Eclogues from the First to the Third show man to be ever more miserable in parallel to the heroes' growing misery. The theme of the Fourth and last set of Eclogues, as if to round out the life of man from love to torments to marriage or failure to the end of all, is death. The central event of Book IV, the apparent death of Basilius, draws to itself several other threatened deaths in Arcadia, for the attempted suicide of Pyrocles and Musidorus' battle with the rebels lead indirectly to their capture by the Arcadians and their implication in Basilius' murder; by the end of the book they lie in prison together with Gynecia awaiting trial for regicide: the penalty, death. Basilius' death has also caused civil dissension about the succession among rival factions led by Philanax, Timantus, and others. It is against this background that the shepherds gather to mourn the death of Basilius, and their manner of so doing is a corrective to the nobles who stand bickering over the king's corpse:

> The shepheards finding no place for them in these garboyles, to which their quiet hearts (whose highest ambition was in keeping themselves up in goodnesse) had at all no aptnesse, retired themselves from among the clamorous multitude . . . looking upon the sunnes as then declining race, the poore men sate pensive of their present miseries.

But the death is foreboding of economic distress as well as grievous in itself, and the shepherds are victims as well as critics of civil strife. As Geron envisions it, foreign armies may enter their meadows, perhaps even to master them, and their tender lambs may be slaughtered for forage. The two aspects of their case, their true grief and their impotence, are developed in the three songs of this brief interlude. The first and third, both sestinas, take up the peculiar situation of the powerless subject ground under the weight of events; the main elegy, modeled on the traditional pastoral elegy of Moschus, lays bare the central normative values of pastoral in the relation of man to his natural environment. As the singer takes the measure of man and nature, he develops first their harmony, shown in the sympathy of nature for human death, then their differences, in the contrast between nature's continual cycles of renewal and man's single cycle from birth to final death.

The development of topics in these ceremonial eclogues both establishes a theme which pulls the diverse actions of Book IV into relation and puts the situation at the end of that book into the wider context of the basic human needs. The effect, for once, is not primarily satiric, for shepherd and nobleman are reacting to the same fact, and if the shepherds' reaction is seen to be somewhat more normal and natural than the nobles', the cause is only a function of their impotence. The two positions come to complete resolution later in Book V when the princes in whom power will reside accept a humble and natural view of death (and hence of life) and, moreover, carry it beyond the limits of the pastoral stance:

> Since natures workes be good, and death doth serve
> As natures worke: why should we feare to die?

THE INTERACTION OF PLOTS

In order to gauge the over-all effect of the sporadic pastoral subplot on the main plot, in distinction from its local effects, we must isolate two salient characteristics of its fictional world. First, like Sannazaro's, it is richly traditional; that is, we are always aware of models in the past for present events in it, whether those models be sources, schemes of thought, or literary types like fabliau, beast fable, epithalamion, or pastoral elegy. Such an awareness gives the world of the shepherds a dimension in time, since any present event is seen as the recurrence in a new form of an old event. Second, despite its severe geographical and social limits, it embraces several different kinds of reality. The main plot is conducted wholly on the plane of the Aristotelian "concrete universal" of fiction with particular though typical characters and events; much of the subplot is like this too (for instance, Geron, an old man), but in addition there is the merely particular and historical character like Philisides, the mask of Philip Sidney, and, pre-eminently, the almost totally general Strephon and Klaius, whose lives are suffused by allegory with the eternal light of metaphysical reality. Moreover, these characters hold to a whole spectrum of possible ideas of reality ranging from gentle idealism to the incarnational to the merely natural and materialistic. These two facts show the shepherd's world to be a kind of "ocean" of possibility, where different views of man's nature, concerns, and goals are held in solution. Whenever Pyrocles and Musidorus penetrate it, the particulars of their lives enter the realm of the general, the eternal, and become subject to its judgment. The affairs of the shepherds in Arcadia therefore form an insistent commentary on the main plot by taking up its themes and examining them from various angles typical of human history; as hero and shepherd merge and separate, matters of love and death are shown to be universal but different in divergent walks of life, for instance. Because of this world's nature, the eclogues (whatever their local functions) always exert a normative pressure on the main plot, whether the norm is a high ideal like Heavenly Love which the heroes share or a base fact of life like Geron's, which, though limited and even cynical, yet allows man a considerable degree of happiness. It is notable in this respect that, as Pyrocles and Musidorus work toward central knowledge of themselves through the book, the norms by which they are criticized become progressively less noble and more basic.

The function of the eclogues in *Arcadia* is this: while they divide the plot book by book into themes of love, suffering, marriage, and death, they also generalize the plot and relate this particular action of two Greek princes to the timeless themes of man's life on earth. They draw events into a general thematic unity, and thus provide a framework for all of the incidental episodes Sidney used to amplify his plot.

5. Valorous Fighting

The eclogues represent one polar element of *Arcadia*. The other pole, the chivalric element of which Harvey wrote, is contained in the thirteen incidental episodes which entered Books I, II, and III during Sidney's revision of the Old *Arcadia*. Between these two poles revolve the adventures of Pyrocles and Musidorus, for the one represents the world they leave for love near the beginning of the book and re-enter at the end, while the other represents the world in which they act out their questions of love. While the pastoral subplot presents a steady contrast within muted parallel to the main plot, the sporadic episodes maintain much closer relationships with it. Yet these relationships are quite diverse, for the episodes of war alternately reflect, amplify, moralize, and clarify the main plot.

INDUCTION TO LOVE

The three episodes in Book I are those of Argalus and Parthenia, Amphialus and Helen, and Phalantus' tourney. Both Argalus and Parthenia are characterized by that peculiar moral perfection that consists of holding opposing tendencies in balance in order to achieve the Aristotelian means between prodigality and meanness, bashfulness and shamelessness, buffoonery and boorishness, and rashness and cowardice. Their like virtues pull them together into a single mean, "for likenesse of maners is likely in reason to draw liking with affection" (17). But such a union under the aegis of Reason is soon disturbed by forces of Pride and Passion from outside in the person of a rejected suitor, the proud Demagoras (who loved "no body but him selfe"). He shatters the mirror of perfection by disfiguring Parthenia in revenge, and she flees the country even though Argalus still protests his love: "with a strange encounter of loves affects, and effects, that he by an affection sprong from excessive beautie, should delight in horrible foulnesse; & she, of a vehement desire to have him, should kindly buyld a resolution never to have him" (19). Opposites are now in paradoxical conflict instead of delicate balance. But love triumphs, and Parthenia, with her beauty restored by Queen Helen's physician, returns transformed, almost reborn; she and Argalus marry, and live thereafter as two trees that flourish only in each other's presence.

There are some similarities between the tale of Amphialus and Helen and that of Argalus and Parthenia, besides a plot connection, in that Helen is responsible for Parthenia's cure. Here, too, the protagonists are surrounded with an aura of supreme virtue and beauty, and there is a rejected suitor too, Philoxenus. But he is no villain, rather, the victim of Helen's ungovernable passion: she rejects him for his friend Amphialus, and thereby causes Amphialus to kill Philoxenus, the latter's father to die of a broken heart, and Amphialus to cast away his armor and live in solitary grief over his deeds. Later, Musidorus puts on the discarded armor, is thereupon attacked by Helen's retinue, and slays most of them before matters are straightened out, thus completing a tissue of passions and mistakes, all caused by Helen's initial passion.

Argalus and Parthenia represented perfect mutual love, where love and Reason acted in harmony; Amphialus and Helen represented a twisted, one-sided love where Helen's Passion overthrew her Reason, her lovers, and herself. To these two types of love we might add a third, the rather novel case of Phalantus, or superficial love, where neither partner is really in love. This third episode presents a sardonic view of the usual courtly love affair. When Phalantus filled the air with the conventional hyperbolic talk about his love for Artesia merely because he had nothing better to do, she trapped him into a pledge to maintain her beauty's pre-eminence over that of any other knight's lady. And so now they go from country to country holding tournaments, and winning, too. The contrast of this to the other two episodes is apparent: they were of deadly serious passion, and this is only windy nonsense. Phalantus' talk is to Argalus' and Amphialus' love as his formal tournaments are to their real experience of battle.

The procession accompanying Phalantus and Artesia into Arcadia contains tables picturing the fair women whose courtly defenders have fallen under Phalantus' lance, and in these tables we see a summary of the women in love we met in Book I—Helen and Parthenia—and are to meet in Book II—Andromana, Artaxia, Erona, Baccha, Leucippe, and Zelmane. The tournament itself serves as a ceremonial establishment of the theme of love in *Arcadia*, and emphasizes the difference between the loves we have seen in the past and those of our two heroes. The first seven combats are colorless ceremonial affairs in which Phalantus easily defeats several mere courtly servants while the lover Pyrocles chafes under the restraint of his disguise. Upon this rather meaningless order of events there suddenly bursts genuine feeling: from opposite ends of the field ride the Black Knight (Musidorus) and the Ill Appointed Knight (Pyrocles), who immediately brawl for the priority of defending their ladies; Phalantus enters the free-for-all, and so does a fourth knight, who claims that the Black Knight stole his picture of Pamela. The brawl is settled, Pyrocles receives priority and overthrows Phalantus. The old formal seeming is defeated by a new active love, the farce ends, and Phalantus and Artesia go their separate ways after a round of mutual insult.

The two heroes of the main plot enter each of these episodes rather obliquely, and, while their intervention usually brings about good, it also adds to the confusion: they break up Phalantus' love game; they conquer Demagoras but first fight a bloody battle between themselves disguised; and, in helping Helen, Musidorus causes even further confusion and bloodshed. Instead of being restorers of right, always in command of the situation, they here partake of disorder, and are frequently ineffectual. The confusion they cause is only a reflection of their inner state, for they are struggling to regain their poise here in Book I, caught as it were between their old active lives and the new contemplative lives they hope to embrace. It is clear that once the princes enter the boundaries of Arcadia they encounter a set of circumstances they cannot control, and that as they penetrate further the desert retreat of Basilius within Arcadia, things get even more out of hand. Book I, we remember, is the book of the inception of love; there they first feel it, there they discuss its transforming power in their dialogues. The eclogues had set the theme and had explored the possibilities of happiness and misery as a result. Love has changed Pyrocles and Musidorus so that they can no longer operate as the people they once were—is the change "celestiall, or infernall"?

We are now in a position to explain the rather loose yet telling relationship of episode to main plot in Book I. Each of these episodes shows a pre-eminent man or woman thrown into complete psychological confusion by love just as the heroes of the main plot are. One of them is emblematic (as the "braule" of the eclogues was), one issues in happiness, the other in tragedy. The positions of the episodes are as important as their content, since Sidney introduced each of them between carefully separated steps in the action of the main plot, and juxtaposed each so closely to one of these steps as to suggest either a causal or a direct thematic relationship between plot and episode.

It is just before the wedding of Argalus and Parthenia that Pyrocles sees Philoclea's picture for the first time. Later, at the wedding, he sees Parthenia, and

> marking her, o *Jupiter* (said he speaking to *Palladius*) how happens it, that beautie is onely confined to *Arcadia?* But *Palladius* not greatly attending his speech, some daies were continued in the solemnizing the marriage.   [30]

Musidorus should have attended better, for as Sidney's very next sentence tells us, "such a chaunge was growne in *Daiphantus,*

117

that . . . he would ever get himselfe alone, though almost when he was in company, he was alone, so little attention he gave to any that spake unto him: even the colour and figure of his face began to receive some alteration." We immediately find Pyrocles on the border of the desert retreat, musing on the combined joy and grief of his new experience of love; the first dialogue on the heroic and contemplative lives ensues. And when Pyrocles sneaks away from the hunt, Musidorus makes the obvious association: "he feared, that it might be *Parthenias* excellency, which had broken the bands of a former resolution" (34), and he goes to Mantinea in search of his friend because Parthenia is there. The wedding and the inception of love in the hero's heart are so closely juxtaposed that one is confused with the other in the story. Though there are certain parallels between the episode and the plot, what is striking about their relationship is the feeling that the episode of a happy consummation is a prelude to Pyrocles' love.

After Musidorus has killed several of Helen's servants, and heard her story of passion, he goes on with his search for Pyrocles. He finds him almost immediately (Sidney allowed only one paragraph to intervene between his leaving Helen and his discovery of his friend), and in strange circumstances, disguised as a woman, "With outward force, and inward treason spoilde" (43). Here occurs the second dialogue on the nature of love and its transforming power, and in it we see that Helen's story was proleptic of the state in which Musidorus finds Pyrocles—passion, confusion, transformation.

Sidney made it quite clear that the scene where the disguised Musidorus is discovered is the exact counterpart of the earlier one where he discovered Pyrocles disguised. The songs each lover sings when his friend comes upon him have the same idea and imagery, and certain lines in Musidorus' song echo Pyrocles'; Pyrocles mimics Musidorus' earlier diatribe against love when he discovers his secret (compare 44–45 and 65–66). Between the two scenes comes the interlude of Phalantus' tourney: as soon as Pyrocles returns to the lodge after the second dialogue, news of Phalantus' arrival comes; and Pyrocles' first act after the end of the tourney is to go into the woods where he finds Musidorus as

Dorus. The tournament acts as an interlude which sums up several loves and their effects; and such summary is most apposite to the cases of the friends at this point, in that it shows each man what is happening to himself. Then again, these scenes show the beginnings of two very profound and beautiful unions, but the interlude of Phalantus and Artesia shows only the breakup of a shallow alliance.

The three episodes illustrating three kinds of love (like Syncero's, Charino's, and Clonico's tales in Sannazaro's *Arcadia*) define the nature of the Arcadian retreat the princes enter in Book I and give them a foretaste of the action they are to undergo there. They also serve to mark the stages of the heroes' penetration into the retreat and into love.

DISORDER

The incidental episodes of Book II are quite different from those of the other books. For one thing, they are usually told by the two princes to their mistresses, and acquire therefore a framework lacking in the episodes of I and III. Furthermore, the materials of Books I and III are common, since the siege of Cecropia brings to an end the story of Argalus and Parthenia, and carries further the affair of Amphialus and Helen. But none of the narrated matter of Book II has any such connection with the other books. It stands separate.

The tales of Book II are little moral tragedies: each of them concerns a man whose abuse of a power or principle, whether by denial or overindulgence, brings about the punishment of loss or suffering under that power. This is very neat and ironic: the King of Phrygia's abuse of kingly rights leads to his deposition; Erona's denial of Love's sanctity makes her a slave to passion. There are nine of these little tragedies, centered on the following characters: the King of Phrygia, the King of Pontus, the King of Paphlagonia, Erona, Plangus, Pamphilus (a comic version), Chremes, Andromana, and Plexirtus—all but the last, whose tale remains incomplete, punished by the power they scorned. There is progression in the manner of telling these, since the first three are merely sum-

marized while the rest are given more detailed treatment. Taken as
a whole, these nine little tragedies are like a miniature *Mirrour for
Magistrates*, with a much more sophisticated view of tragedy, but
with as strong, if not as intrusive, a moral emphasis.

The tale of Plangus, Prince of Iberia, and Erona, Queen of
Lycia, is paramount among these episodes; recited at the center of
the book by several different main characters and in considerable
detail, it eventually gives rise to a lecture on the nature of Love
that helps define each character's situation.

The individual stories of the two, and the story of their relationship, tell of crimes against love and the destructive power of
Passion. In causing images of Eros to be defaced, Erona ("one
possessed by Eros") committed an explicit crime against Love.
"Which how terribly he punished . . . quickly after appeared.
For she had not lived a yeare longer, when she was stricken with
most obstinate Love, to a young man but of meane parentage,"
Antiphilus ("anti-Love") (151). Thus the first consequence of
her denial of the Lord of Passion was infliction of a passion which
was not (it is disclosed later) really returned, and which caused a
whole chain of disasters. First, her father, the King of Lycia, died
of a broken heart. Then Tiridates, a bitter rejected suitor who in
a perversion of the idea of Love "wrote . . . the sonets of his
Love in the bloud, and tuned them in the cries of her subjects,"
attacked her, laying waste her entire kingdom until stopped by
Pyrocles and Musidorus. The crime against Love has changed love
to hate and turned it against her. Plangus' crime against love is
implicit: he had seduced Andromana, a commoner's wife, who
later became his father's mistress, then his queen. Once in power,
she banished him from Iberia; she, whom Plangus had first caused
to sin, has become his bitterest enemy. Both Plangus and Erona
awakened evils which, when aroused, wrecked not only their
own fortunes but their countries' as well: Lycia is wasted by war
and Iberia is in the hands of a whore.

These two tales of passion and destruction come together at the
end of Book II. There we are told that Erona had allowed Passion
so to master her Reason as to elevate the base Antiphilus to the
kingship of Lycia. He, conceiving a lust for Artaxia, Tiridates'

sister, had passed a law permitting polygamy. The dissembling Artaxia agreed to a meeting with Antiphilus but captured him and Erona and threw them into prison. Thus we find Erona at the bottom of the wheel of Passion, still loving Antiphilus. And here we find Plangus' final punishment: he is driven by "the power of Love" to love Erona, whose only desire is that Antiphilus be freed. Plangus' attempt to free him fails, Antiphilus is executed for his crimes against Love, and the miserable Plangus now wanders through Greece seeking help in freeing Erona, a woman who does not love him.

The position of the Plangus-Erona tragedy in the center of Book II is important in its relation to the other incidental stories, for several of them come together in it: Plexirtus aids his paramour Artaxia in capturing Erona and Antiphilus; Plangus' mistress Andromana lusts after Pyrocles and Musidorus in a later episode; the incidental fight between Pyrocles and Anaxius evolves from the Tiridates-Erona war.[1]

But, more than this, it is the thematic center of the other tales. It marks the dividing line between two sets of stories, the first told in straightforward manner by Musidorus, the second more elaborately told to Philoclea by Pyrocles. The first set is about civil strife, usually a result of Passion overpowering Reason. The King of Phrygia pays for his fear-inspired cruelty by deposition and death in a "mutinie" led by his erstwhile prisoners. Because the King of Pontus is moved by a compulsive inconstancy to kill Pyrocles' and Musidorus' servants, the princes punish him by conquering his people, putting him to death, and setting up a new order. The *"Paphlagonian* unkinde King" (the source of Gloucester in *Lear*) sets off a whole chain of private and public disasters by his unreasonable treatment of his true son on the advice of his bastard.

The episodes that come after the tale of Plangus and Erona con-

1. Kenneth Orne Myrick, in *Sir Philip Sidney as a Literary Craftsman* (Cambridge, Mass., 1935), pp. 168–69, writes that the narration of the Plangus-Erona tale by three different people "sets the story . . . apart from the occurrences related by Musidorus and Pyrocles. It thus emphasizes certain events which are central in the story of those two heroes. . . . It leads, . . . in short, to the whole train of incidents up to the time when the heroes arrive in Greece."

centrate on the inner workings of passion in a character rather than its effects in deeds (notice that, in the first set, very few of the characters were even given proper names). They all involve lust or passion in high degree. The lusty inconstant Pamphilus ("love-all") makes his life a game of passions, indulges in epic seduction, and is finally paid when he marries a whore. The father of one of Pamphilus' victims, Chremes, "alreadie halfe earth, & yet then most greedie of Earth," likewise becomes a victim of his own sordid passion for money. Andromana ("man-crazy") causes the death of her son and her own suicide by her unbridled passions for Pyrocles and Musidorus. "What she did (being rather with vehemencie of passion, then conduct of reason) made her stumble while she ran, & by her own confusion hinder her own desires" (184). Plexirtus' crimes, committed out of pure reasonless villainy, remain unpunished.

Not only does the tale of Plangus and Erona separate the two types described here, but it also unites in itself the chief elements of both: public disorder caused by private passion. All of the shorter stories reflect one of the two terms of this theme, but only in Plangus and Erona are they combined in equal importance.

The princesses tell the story of Plangus and Erona to a small audience seated in Zelmane's arbor, which, in a manner much like that of "la fuente de los alisos" in Montemayor's *Diana*, has a very special relationship to the topic of love: that is, when a tale or confession of love occurs, it is usually in Zelmane's arbor. Now, between the relating of Erona's fate and of Plangus', there is an interlude where Miso interrupts with a lecture against Love and Mopsa starts a silly medieval tale. Miso's lecture is most appropriate, for the stories of Lycia and Iberia show that Love, usually a beneficent power, becomes destructive when abused. Miso ("hate") recites a poem about Love in which he is described thus:

> A horned head, cloven feet, and thousand eyes,
> Some gazing still, some winking wilie shifts,
> With long large eares, where never rumour dies.
>> His horned head doth seeme the heaven to spight,
>> His cloven foot doth never tread aright.
> Thus halfe a man, with man he dayly haunts,

Cloth'd in the shape which soonest may deceive:
Thus halfe a beast, ech beastly vice he plants,
In those weake hearts that his advice receive.   [155–56]

Part of the humor here is that Miso is mistaking a description of
Pan for one of Eros.[2] But the main point of the joke is in Miso's
description of how she came by the verse she reads: an old crone
once gave her the picture and the poem (which had been bestowed
on the old woman by a painter in return for "a litle pleasure"),
with this advice: "do what thou list with all those fellowes, one
after another; & it reckes not much what they do to thee, so it be
in secret; but upon my charge, never love none of them" (155).
The moral of this interlude is clear: love is what you make it, a
beast to the whore, a god to the gentle.[3] Or, as Pyrocles put it in
conformity with Ficino and the love treatises, Human Love entering by the eyes is innocent; what happens to it depends on the
heart of the lover, for bestial man will reduce it to *amor ferinus* by
the sense of touch, while contemplative man will raise it, in his
mind, to Heavenly Love.[4] The application of this interlude to
Plangus and Erona is clear—Love is not evil in itself, but becomes
a tool for evil when it is abused—and so is its application to the
main plot.

What do the narrated adventures have to do with the events of
the main plot? "Reason" and "Passion" are two terms that echo

2. See Francis Bacon, *The Advancement of Learning*, II, xiii, in *Works*, ed.
J. Spedding, R. L. Ellis, and D. D. Heath (15 vols. Boston, 1860–64), *8*, 444: "The
person of Pan is described by ancient tradition as follows:—horns on his head,
rising to a point and reaching up to heaven; his whole body rough and shaggy;
his beard especially long; his figure biform, the upper part human, the lower
part like a beast and ending in goat's feet"; see also Sannazaro, *Arcadia, Prosa* X
(196): "and on his head he had two horns of a goat, very straight and reaching
toward heaven; . . . his mantle was a copious pelt, starred with white spots."

3. Another point of the interlude seems to be the contrast between old and
new. This appears in the matter (a windy old wives' tale) and manner of Mopsa's
story ("with Dayly Diligence and Grisly Grones," "And so. . . . And so"); and
in the two views of love represented by Miso on the one hand and the heroes on
the other.

4. See Ficino's *Commentary* on *Symposium*, ed. Jayne, p. 193; also, Pico della
Mirandola, *Oratio de Hominis Dignitate*, trans. E. L. Forbes, in *The Renaissance
Philosophy of Man*, ed. Ernst Cassirer et al. (Chicago, 1948), p. 225, and Castig-
lione, *The Book of the Courtier*, p. 304.

and re-echo throughout Book II. The eclogues had staked out "the skirmish betwixt *Reason* and *Passion*" as the theme of the book, thus making explicit connections among its different actions. For Book II presents various instances of the combat between Reason and Passion in the minds of the princes divided by the shock of love; unless Reason subdues Passion and brings it under control, it will unite with the base desires and reduce the hero to a beast. The stories of the kings, Plangus and Erona, Pamphilus, Chremes, Andromana, and Plexirtus tell of people in high place who fought that combat and lost. Taken together, they act as nine little mirrors, each reflecting the present state of the heroes and showing the piteous results of Passion's possible victory. But the episodes also go one step further than the eclogues in defining the case; their subject is not merely how Passion conquers Reason, but how Passion, by conquering Reason, causes public disorder. In this way they go beyond the reflection of plot in order to extend its significance. This fact tells us that the main action has come to encompass more here than it did in Book I, and if we examine the characters who gather around the heroes we shall see how this is so.

The psychological split under which Pyrocles and Musidorus suffer is reflected in the minds of the people who love them—Philoclea, Pamela, Basilius, and Gynecia. In a masterful descriptive passage, Sidney makes clear how Philoclea feels the rebel Passion gather strength, rise, and seemingly destroy the old Philoclea, that nymph of Diana, to leave in her place a new Philoclea, confused, wretched, and ashamed of her change (especially since her love appears to be a Lesbian one). Pamela, too, the most mature and controlled of the royal family, feels a passion she is compelled to hide in pain beneath a cool exterior. While the sisters feel a change in their lives and ensuing confusion, their parents fall far below them into intemperance, the chaos of the mind, and become slaves to desire. Basilius falls into his dotage and runs about the fair fields of Arcadia after his "fair nymph" Pyrocles. Worse, Gynecia ("Woman") gives up a vow as her daughter did—not a vow of virginity, but the marriage vow of chastity—and runs to embrace a shameless adultery. For her passions are strong, and, as a typical woman, she has an "imperfect proportion of reason" (96); passion for Pyrocles therefore splits her asunder and draws her from herself, exhibiting as its immediate results desperation and viciousness accompanied with a shameful realization of what she has become. "Nature gives place; the growing of my daughter seems the decay of my selfe; the blessings of a mother turne to the curses of a competitor" (197).

The passions within the princes' breasts, spreading out like the rays of the sun, have fertilized similar passions in four people. In the latter half of Book II, all of these passions come into the open and start to interact: Basilius, acting out of jealousy and guilt, tries to impede his wife's advances to Pyrocles; she does the same to him and, moreover, begins to fear and hate her daughter Philoclea, who has been forced into the disgraceful office of her father's procuress. The final and most public expression of this passionate uproar in Arcadia occurs at the end of Book II. As Gynecia advances on Pyrocles and Philoclea with "a right conflict betwixt the force of love, and rage of jealousie" (197) burning in her mind, she is met by a real public conflict, for the common people of Arcadia (the many-headed beast of the mind) pour into the retreat in open and violent rebellion against their master.

Private passion causes public disorder in the main plot and, more explicitly, in the incidental tales (where the public dimension dominates the first set, the private the second). Furthermore, the conflict within not only causes the disorder without, but is analogous to it as well. We see this analogy in all the action, especially in the outbreak of the rebellion; and we see it in the verbal texture, too, where the common analogy of Reason as king and Passion as subject pervades the discourse. "If we will be men, the reasonable part of our soule is to have absolute commaundement; against which if any sensuall weaknesse arise, we are to yeeld all our sound forces to the overthrowing of so unnatural a rebellion" (44), "Reason (now growne a servant to passion)" (53), "reason must ever have the masterhood" (65), "disdaines to obey any thing but his passion" (174). We have come full round: the conflict that divides the minds of Pyrocles, Musidorus, Basilius, Gynecia, and Philoclea is mirrored both in the nine little tales that adorn the plot and in the public affairs of Arcadia.

Thus the action of Book II spreads from individual situations out into larger analogous spheres. The episodic narratives clarify the theme and amplify the plot in order to make the book a complete dissertation on its subject.

LOVE AND ORDER

Since all of the major characters (and several of the minor ones as well) are very much involved in the captivity episode, and since it was conceived as one solid block of narrative preceding the rest of the main plot, we must consider it not only as an episode but also as a section of the plot.

There are three strands woven together to make up the episode: the actual siege, the tragedy of Amphialus, and the moral test of Pamela and Philoclea. Basilius' siege consists of a series of nine single combats that rise in a crescendo from the perfect order and courtesy of the first combat to the hatred and lawlessness of the last three. It forms a pattern with the testing of the princesses, since parts of the siege outside alternate with the progressive scenes within the castle, the actions outside representing the public or active world, those inside the private or contemplative; the two heroes are divided between them, Musidorus in the first, Pyrocles in the second. Amphialus, the master of the castle, is the link between these two spheres, for he is the central figure in the heroic action and has another conflict, an amorous one, within his breast.

Once we have fixed the general scheme of the episode, we must inquire into its relevance. We learned that the theme of Book III, as it was established by the Third Eclogues, is marriage. The eclogues presented a description of the solemn and simple wedding of Thyrsis and Kala in ironic contrast to the various wrong or twisted consummations at the end of Book III: the expected fulfillment of lust in the cave, and the perilous positions of Musidorus in the glade and Pyrocles in the bedchamber, both about to fall into lust instead of ascending to spiritual love. The first scene of the main plot after the return from Cecropia's castle asserts the theme of consummation immediately, for there in the cave which is to become the center of lust, Gynecia demands sexual fulfillment from Pyrocles; and their scene counterpoints Musidorus' plans and elopement with Pamela. What does the preceding captivity episode have to do with this theme of marriage? Let us turn, for an answer, to a brief re-examination of the debates that form the first great strand of this episode.

These moral and theological discussions first arose from the question of marriage. In her very first appeal to Philoclea, Cecropia attempted to arouse the girl's self-love and pride as motives for a marriage to her son, a scheme conceived as the protection and perpetuation of the self. Thus sinful appeals were woven into the fabric of the practical argument for a lawless and narcissistic marriage. When Cecropia turns from Philoclea to try Pamela, she finds her on her knees like an emblem of Devotion with the hand of Zeal clasping the hand of Humility, and it is here that the argument becomes explicitly theological. But the specific theme of religion does not turn away from the general theme of love, for devotion has subsumed constancy in love: Pamela's prayer to God had ended, "And ô most gracious Lord (sayd she) what ever become of me, preserve the vertuous *Musidorus*" (253). Therefore in the big scene between Pamela and Cecropia we work out in orderly fashion from the initial practical question of marriage to theoretical questions of autonomy and the nature of the universe.

The debates arose from marriage, and in marriage they end. For the values which Pamela develops by combining various attributes are those values necessary to a true marriage under God. Thus a firm belief in God and His divine order is necessary for humility, and humility is the prerequisite for the mutual self-sacrifice and control of desires that constitutes Christian love. Its opposite, pride, leads through an exaltation of the self to that tendency to loose all desires, and use others to help accomplish them, which can be accurately classified only as hatred of others. What Pamela does here is to lay bare the implications behind the spiritual maturity which alone justifies the bond of marriage.

Furthermore, she draws her argument for the necessity for God from a situation that has its obvious parallel in human marriage. We can understand this fact better if we quote her argument again and place beside it two passages from the pastoral epithalamion at the end of Book III:

> there must needes have bene a wisedome which made them [the elements] concurre: for their natures being absolute contrarie, in nature rather would have sought each others ruin, then have served as well consorted parts to such an unexpressable harmonie.
>
> [269]

> But like the turtles faire,
> Live one in two, a well united paire.

> Let one time (but long first) close up their daies,
>   One grave their bodies seaze:
>   And like two rivers sweete,
>   When they though divers do together meete:
>   One streame both streames containe,
>   O *Himen* long their coupled joyes maintaine. [375]

Marriage and the creation of progeny under God's Nature of wisdom and Providence is an earthly analogue to the creation which set up that Nature.[5] There is a third analogue too: the father uniting the elements of the family is like God uniting the elements of earth, and without the sanction of his authority she will not marry.[6] "Resolutely I say unto you, that he must get my parents consent, and then he shall know further of my mind; for, without that, I know I should offend God" (267). In the tortures that follow—the whippings and the mental torments—the sisters, suffering patiently with God and their lovers in their minds, show

5. A very common Neoplatonic analogy; the best known examples of it are in *The Book of the Courtier*, p. 321, and Spenser's *An Hymne in Honour of Love*, ll. 78–91.

6. See Jean Bodin, *Six Books of the Commonwealth*, abridged and translated by M. J. Tooley (Oxford, n.d.), p. 10: "The commandment that He had given the husband to rule over his wife has a double significance, first in the literal sense of marital authority, and second in the moral sense of the soul over the body, and the reason over concupiscence."

both the general moral stature necessary to a true marriage and a particular loyalty to their chosen mates.

The combats outside the castle counterpoint the scenes of debate within it. To Cecropia's mild first scenes with the sisters corresponds the first general melee, which causes only two accidental deaths; then a series of full-dress single combats between Amphialus and various opponents answers Cecropia's big scene with Pamela. The first opponent is the suave and gentle Phalantus, who after a ceremonial tilt grants Amphialus the palm of victory, shakes hands, and leaves; thereupon, after a brief glimpse inside the castle, Amphialus unhorses five nameless knights in rapid succession. But the sixth opponent is the renowned Argalus, and upon his death the tone of the episode changes markedly, for this death took nobility and love along with it. Thereafter, Amphialus' spirit flags under the pressure of guilt, and he and the other combatants all represent some form of death in their trappings. This tragic tone continues to the end, through a pathetically easy victory over "The Knight of the Tombe" to a bloody draw with "The Forsaken Knight" which makes the whole field dissolve in violence, disorder, and death. The following scenes within the castle answer the growing violence and somberness outside, for it is there that the princesses suffer from the physical violence of whipping, the mental tortures of mock executions, and the perils of rape. Herein the princesses suffer for love and prove their worthiness, but what do the battle scenes have to do with our theme of marriage?

The "Knight of the Tombe" is Parthenia; thus two of the three climactic combats—hers and Argalus'—represent the ultimate sacrifice of love. The perfect lovers of Book I, as they appear here, offer a concrete example of the heroic marriage which the scenes within the castle are defining. In the first scene between them, we see the mutual self-sacrifice, loving hierarchy, humility, and seamless harmony of the diverse by which Pamela had characterized the love of true marriage:

A happy couple, he joying in her, she joying in her selfe, but in her selfe, because shee enjoyed him: both encreased their riches

129

by giving to each other; each making one life double, because they made a double life one; where desire never wanted satisfaction, nor satisfaction ever bred sacietie; he ruling, because she would obey: or rather because she would obey, she therein ruling.   [276]

Furthermore, it is part of the ideality of this love that it not only yield to, but enforce, claims higher than its own; for when Basilius orders Argalus to leave Parthenia for the siege, "true Love made obedience stande up against all other passions" in both of them. Their mutual love is so complete that, as Parthenia says at her husband's departure, "*Parthenia* shall smart in your paine, & your blood must be bled by *Parthenia*." [7] This statement becomes ironically true in this book of ultimates, for as Argalus dies she cries in fulfillment of what has come to be a prophecy, "O *Parthenia*, no more *Parthenia*" (280).

Argalus and Parthenia exemplify the ideal heroic marriage; but such a marriage is modified, by the context of the bloody heroic world, to tragedy. All the conceits expressing mutual interdependence turn into ironic actuality here outside the castle. As Argalus dies, "seeing her, in whom (even dying) he lived," he is said to live on in her as the three brothers in Spenser's Book of Friendship did, "for his last breath was delivered into her mouth" (280). Instead of adding Argalus' life thread to her own, however, she elects to complete their mutuality by becoming his tomb; she reappears disguised as "The Knight of the Tombe," her armor in the shape of a gaping sepulchre, to fulfill her destiny at the hands of her husband's killer. Therefore their epitaph announces a theme both metaphorical and actual, a theme that will be recalled in the

---

7. For a very literal physiological theory behind this common metaphor, see Ficino's *Commentary* on *Symposium* 7.4, trans. Jayne, p. 223: "Phaedrus sends into the eyes of Lysias the sparks of his own eyes, and with the sparks sends along a spirit. The light of Phaedrus is easily joined by the light of Lysias, and the spirit also easily joins his spirit. The vapor of this sort springing from the heart of Phaedrus immediately seeks the heart of Lysias. By the hardness of the heart it is made denser and returns to its former state, as the blood of Phaedrus, so that the blood of Phaedrus is now in the heart of Lysias, a truly remarkable phenomenon." See also *Astrophel and Stella*, xciii.

marriage of Thyrsis and Kala, to whom they form an heroic and tragic counterpart:

> His being was in her alone:
> And he not being, she was none.   [294]

While we see Pamela and Philoclea in training for union under love inside, outside we see the dissolution of life but also the continuation of union after death. Argalus and Parthenia are related to the princesses as past is to future, or as practice (emphasizing the political connections of love and the modifications of the flesh on the life of the spirit) is to theory (emphasizing the religious and eternal bases of love). Their tragedy does not invalidate Pamela's expectations; rather, it shows that marriage may be both more unhappy and more glorious than she anticipates. In this way the lovers whose marriage formed the happy prologue to the experience of love in Book I complete their life as a noble and tragic exemplum to the other lovers.

From the future and the past, we now come to the present case of our heroes as reflected in Amphialus. For Amphialus' last opponent is "The Forsaken Knight," Musidorus, who seems almost to be his double. Not only do their armors match—the one in black rags, the other black with ravens and snakes—but Amphialus takes the title of "Forsaken Knight" on himself, such is their "aliance of passions," and accepts Musidorus' accusations as if they came from his own conscience. In this most laborious battle of all, neither wins, and they both lie on the ground near death as around them the passions of war break loose from all rules of chivalry. Since Musidorus and Amphialus are paired so closely here, we must explore in detail the case of the latter, whose tragedy forms the third thread of the captivity episode.

"Amphialus" means "between two seas," and this name is emblematic of his spiritual vacillation; without a clear sense of right, he becomes a pipe for others to play on. When his mother tells him that she has captured Philoclea, he knows that the right thing to do is to return her to her father immediately, for "if *Philoclea* be displeased, how can I be pleased?" (243). Yet he cannot let her go, for "I would not for my life constraine presence, but rather would I die then consent to absence." His first thought assumes that a lover's happiness depends on that of the beloved; his second hides the idea that he can perhaps be happy while she is not; the first characterizes humility, the second, pride. He himself defines his case most clearly upon his first appearance to Philoclea in the castle by wearing a jeweled collar of interchanging pieces, one of diamonds and pearls that "seemed like a shining ice, and the other piece being of Rubies, and Opalles, had a fierie glistring, which he thought pictured the two passions of Feare & Desire, wherein he was enchained" (243). This is a special case of the rebel Passion paralyzing Reason: because he cannot establish order by subjecting desire to fear or reverence, Amphialus remains to the end a self divided and makes of his life "a pitifull spectacle, where the conquest was the conquerours overthrow, and selfe-ruine the onely triumph of a battaile, fought betweene him, and himselfe" (320). Therefore in his fights with Argalus, Parthenia, and Musidorus he feels that he is fighting himself and mourns the fallen as if they were in fact himself. The cause of his internal disorder is egotism, which, as Myrick says, "is revealed in Amphialus from the time when we first hear of his having slain his foster brother Philoxenus." [8] Therefore he can allow his self-esteem to master friendship, his desire to impress Philoclea to overcome concern for his allies, his passion to possess her to obscure the knowledge that he is harming her. Cecropia's speeches showed that selfishness presupposed a view of life as purposeless and chaotic; here in Amphialus we see a complementary theme, that selfishness produces disorder since it forbids a patient submission of the self to love and the divine order.

Therefore it is characteristic that Amphialus' self-division always makes him the author of violent deeds that he by no means intended to commit: the murder of his friend while he was trying to save him, the killing of Agenor in the siege while he tried merely to dismount him, the unwilled slaying first of Argalus, then of Parthenia. Back at the castle, he learns of all the tortures, both

8. *Sir Philip Sidney*, p. 352.

mental and physical, to which Cecropia has subjected the princesses—deeds done merely because he did nothing to prevent them. But even his attempt to right a wrong leads to another wrong when his mother jumps to her death out of fear of his revenge. Finally, he sums up his unwilled evil deeds:

> thou hast lived to beare armes against thy rightful Prince, thine own uncle: thou hast lived to bee accounted & justly accounted a traitor . . . thou hast lived to bee the death of her, that gave thee life. But ah wretched *Amphialus*, thou hast lived for thy sake, and by thy authoritie, to have *Philoclea* tormented; [320]

and he stabs himself with Philoclea's knives, which he had once carried as a favor in battle.

It is further symbolic of the state of self-division that he, a good man, is served by evil ministers—Artesia, Clinias, Cecropia, and Anaxius and his brothers—who assume command increasingly as he falls. At first Cecropia attacks the princesses only with arguments and keeps him informed of her progress; later she takes over the castle and keeps him in ignorance. Amphialus' combat with the helpless Parthenia is signalized by the arrival of aid for him in the person of Anaxius, a brave man of "partes worthie praise, if they had not beene guided by pride, and followed by unjustice" (287–88), who almost seems to be Amphialus' evil double, since he possesses many of his traits exaggerated to evil ones. He is indeed the sort of person Amphialus might have become were it not for some vestiges of self-control proceeding from love. Anaxius takes Amphialus' place as master of the castle, and he and his brothers replace him as unwanted suitors of the princesses, substituting attempted rape for subjection.

Amphialus' tragedy moves in contrary motion to the great moral victory of the princesses. Since his selfishness taints his magnanimity, he is eaten up by passion and disorder, control always slips from his hands, and he is finally wrecked altogether. The princesses exercise the control over desire that issues from patience, and so love and order can triumph in them. Therefore, Pamela's and Philoclea's final feats of heroic endurance are juxtaposed in the book to Amphialus' final recognition and mortal wound. We can also see how these contrasting actions result from the previous books. Whereas Book I presented us with love and the changes it brings, Book II explored those changes further in terms of the self-division resulting from the war of Passion against Reason. Book III then presents two possible conclusions to that war: if Passion remains uncontrolled, self-division will spread and end in defeat for the self and tragedy; if Reason grows stronger and subordinates Passion again, the self will emerge victorious and whole. The latter possibility is open only to the man who has grounded his virtue firmly in the bedrock of Christian patience.

Such spiritual wholeness is the only possible basis for the true marriage of minds. The captivity episode acts as a preparative for the final union in showing us this and in placing Pyrocles and Musidorus between the exempla of what to avoid in Amphialus and what to seek in their beloved mistresses. In the episode itself they stand closer to the negative example than to the positive, in basically the same state of self-division that they suffered in Book II; near the end of the episode, we find Musidorus, who showed such strong resemblances to the impatient Amphialus, lying immobilized on the field of magnanimity while Pyrocles lies on the floor of the prison of patience, an attempted suicide. The inner harmony of Pamela and Philoclea is left for them to seek in the rest of *Arcadia*. They first struggle to attain true union without its necessary preparation in the soul, and fail; but then, we remember, their very failure helps them to educate and then raise up their souls, and they do so just before the approach of death.

In this book, the episodes amplify and extend the main plot more fully than in any other. The eclogues set up the theme of marriage; the main plot presents various examples of the union of a man and a woman, whether loving or lustful, sanctified or adulterous. But the episodes delve beneath the action to show its basic assumptions, and give us examples of love as order based on humility—whether it be the simple humility of Pamela and Philoclea or the self-sacrifice or Argalus and Parthenia—and of selfishness and disorder in Cecropia and her tragic son Amphialus. Book III also exhibits a complete bond between episode and plot and thus represents the final point in Sidney's increasingly tight control over his narrative material. Before, we have had cases of love forming a prelude to the action or of several unrelated tales in a close relationship with the main plot, but here we have the final fusion whereby the episodes not only amplify the moral significance of the main plot but become part of it. Furthermore, the episodes have extended the main plot by relating it to ever wider contexts. For while Book I surrounded the heroes with images of private persons in love and Book II related private passion to public disorder by means of its episodes, Book III related both private and public realms to ultimate theological concepts while it pulled episode, plot, and theory into a unit. There are no incidental episodes in Books IV and V, but there the horizon has broadened to include the whole great world of Greece and the political impact of the heroes, who for the first time become significant as princes. We shall complete our map of Arcadia by examining its political element in the chapter which follows.

6. Sage Counseling

JUSTICE IN THE STATE AND IN THE SOUL

The political element of *Arcadia* is particularly marked in Books IV and V, which depict the effects of the princes' private actions on the state, and the state's consequent punishment of them; but all through *Arcadia* the body politic parallels the microcosm, and we must remember that reasons of state motivate the initial situation of the Arcadian exile and the central actions of the captivity episode as well. We have it on the testimony of Fulke Greville that these elements in the romance were the paramount ones for Sidney, who, he says, intended in it

> to turn the barren Philosophy precepts into pregnant Images of life; and in them, first on the Monarch's part, lively to represent the growth, state, and declination of Princes, change of Government, and lawes: vicissitudes of sedition, faction, succession, confederacies, plantations, with all other errors, or alterations in publique affaires. Then again in the subjects case; the state of favor, disfavor, prosperitie, adversity, emulation, quarrell, undertaking, retiring, hospitality, travail, and all other moodes of private fortunes, or misfortunes.[1]

The political dimension of *Arcadia*, far from restricting Sidney to the superficial public actions of men, actually gathers up all of the

1. *The Life of the Renowned Sir Philip Sidney*, pp. 15–16.

136

private developments we have traced and projects them onto a large screen; for politics to the orthodox Renaissance theorists was merely the most spacious field for the exercise of moral virtues. It was for this reason, as well as for practical purposes, that Sidney's mentor Hubert Languet advised his pupil, "Next to the knowledge of the way of salvation, which is the most essential thing of all, and which we learn from the sacred scriptures, next to this, I believe nothing will be of greater use to you than to study that branch of moral philosophy which treats of justice and injustice," and Sidney himself wrote that virtue "extends it selfe out of the limits of a mans owne little world, to the government of families, and mainteining of publike societies." [2] To be sure, the private and public realms of life were kept distinct, but they were also firmly related by cause and effect and particularly by analogy. The prevalence of such analogy may be made clear by inspecting a single continuing scheme of thought in politics and its extension into other realms of thought. Its source is Plato's *Republic*, which Greville's mention of the organic cycles of growth and decay recalls [3] and which, as we shall see, supplied the philosophical precepts that Sidney turned into "Images of life."

"Republic" is really something of a misnomer, for, as Socrates kept insisting, the subject of the dialogue is justice in the soul as it is shown by analogy in the state. Therefore the ideological center of the book is Plato's division of the soul into three parts (439): the rational part or intellect, the spirited element, and the irrational appetite, which seeks pleasure and the replenishment of wants. In the intellect resides Prudence or Wisdom, in the spirited part Courage; and Temperance resides in the whole, but especially in control of the appetite (427–31). From this basis Plato worked out a theory of the types of men (580–81): the contemplative lover of knowledge (*philosophon*) who is governed by intellect, the ambitious man or lover of power and

---

2. *The Correspondence of Sir Philip Sidney and Hubert Languet*, ed. S. A. Pears (London, 1845), p. 26; Sidney, *Defence*, in *Works*, 3, 12. Sidney wrote, in reply to Languet's letter, that he had taken up Aristotle's *Politics*; but it was Plato rather than Aristotle who formed the political basis of *Arcadia*.

3. See *Republic* 546.

victory (*philotimon*) in whom the spirited element predominates, and the lover of gain, both monetary and sensual, in the power of the base desires. On this division hinges the analogy of soul and state, for the philosophon is to be the deliberative or governing power of the ideal state (Rulers), the philotimon the executive (Auxiliaries), and the lover of gain in the productive or artisan class. And when that state declined in the course of events, it would fall from a monarchy to a timocracy ruled by the philotimons to an oligarchy under the lovers of gain before it fell into democracy and subsequent tyranny (544–55). The possible analogies of this three-part division of the soul obviously fascinated Plato (as it did Apuleius, who based his *De Platone et eius Dogmate* on it): historically, for instance, the intellect, spirit, and desires represented the Ages of Gold, Silver, and Brass or Iron respectively (415); geographically, intellect dominated Greece, spirit dominated Thrace, Scythia, and the north, and appetite dominated Phoenicia, Egypt, and Asia (435).

The purpose of this tripartite division is to build a context in human affairs for the famous definition of justice as concord: in the state, the Ruler defining goals and the military Auxiliaries obeying him and controlling the supporting masses; in the soul, the reason ruling and the spirited part suppressing desires and working for the good defined by reason. It is this magnificent concept that pervades Western political thought (even though Aristotle's diagram of the soul soon overshadowed Plato's), especially in the Christian revision of it known as "original" or "natural" justice, the state that characterized man's soul before the Fall. St. Thomas Aquinas defined it this way:

> Human nature was so established when it was first brought into being that the lower parts were perfectly subject to the soul [*rationi*, the reason], the reason to God, and the body to the soul, God supplying by grace that which nature lacked for the purpose. Now this boon, which some call original justice, was bestowed on the first man in such wise that he was to transmit it together with human nature to his posterity. But when the first man sinned, his reason rebelled against God, and the con-

sequence was that his lower parts ceased to be perfectly subject to reason, and his body to his soul.[4]

In the sixteenth century—and in Sidney's own intellectual circle —this concept of natural justice became paramount as the center of a theological and political controversy; for while Calvin and his followers denied that totally corrupt man could ever regain his original just state, the more liberal Protestants, including Sidney's friends François Hotman and Hubert Languet,[5] assumed that one could regain it by intensive control of the heavenly part within the microcosm. Thus Jean Bodin in his *Res Publica* could insist that the sovereign attain it:

> We understand by natural liberty the right under God to be subject to no man living and amenable only to those commands which are self-imposed, that is to say the commands of right reason conformable to the will of God. The first of all commandments was the commandment to subordinate animal appetite to reason, for before a man can govern others he must learn to govern himself, surrendering to reason the power of direction, and schooling the appetites to obedience. In this way each man will achieve that which truly pertains to his nature, which is the original and purest form of justice.[6]

The keynote here as elsewhere is the government of the passions by reason that constitutes moral virtue; the argument is that if

4. *Summa Contra Gentiles*, IV, 52; quoted in Charles S. Singleton's *Dante Studies 2: Journey to Beatrice* (Cambridge, Mass., 1958), pp. 237-38; I am much indebted to Chapter 13 of this book for information on medieval concepts of justice.

5. See M. J. Tooley's introduction to his translation of Bodin, *Six Books of the Commonwealth*, p. xx: "In the second half of the sixteenth century the old conception of the primitive state of innocence was undergoing important modification. The liberty that men enjoyed in that primitive natural society was assumed not to have been lost—as Calvin thought it had been lost—but to be inalienable, and its preservation the foundation of all legitimate political authority." Tooley cites Hotman's *Franco-Gallia* (1573) and Languet's *Vindiciae contra tyrannos* (1579) as expressing this view; see, for instance, the anonymous English translation of the *Vindiciae* (1689), p. 14: "Man is composed of Body and Soul, God hath formed the Body and infused the Soul into him, to him only then may be attributed, and appropriated the commands over the Body and Soul of man."

6. *Res publica* 1.2, in Tooley's translation, p. 10.

man can achieve it by his own efforts, his work will be answered by the grace given Adam. Du Plessis Mornay (whose view of the matter we may identify with Sidney's with some justification, since Sidney translated his magnum opus) outlined a procedure for working back into the Edenic state on this assumption. First one must withdraw into the contemplative life:

> Then let us say, that as it had bin a happy case for us, to have continued still in our first state: so is it now for us to returne thither againe; that is to say, to be set againe in Gods favour, that we may one day see his face yet againe. And because this blessednes cannot be brought to perfection in this life so full of wretchednes: we must dispose our lyfe in this world, not to live still in this world, but to dye in respect of these dead things, and to live unto God.[7]

Then, since (as Sir William Temple later said) [8] the contemplative life is the only one that subdues the passions rather than diverting them, one must establish control in the soul in expectation of complete union with God after death:

> Now then, let us examine Wisdom. It is the beholding of God and of things belonging to God. This requireth a man to lift up himselfe above the world, and above himselfe; I meane that a man should retyre from all outward things into his owne soule, the Soule unto her Mynd, and the Mynd unto God.[9]

It was in this way that Plato's definition of justice as harmony of soul became not only a continuing tradition but a pressing interest to political thinkers of the sixteenth century.

Since the concept remained so fertile, we find too that Plato's analogies maintained a continual hold on works of political theory, even when they purported to be empirical rather than abstract and schematic in origin. Thus for instance Bodin presents the following theory as if it were a generalization drawn from his own observation:

7. Mornay, *A Woorke concerning the Trewnesse of the Christian Religion*, p. 328.
8. "Upon the Gardens of Epicurus; Or of Gardening in the Year 1685," in *Miscellanea* (1692); see *Complete Works* (4 vols. London, 1819), 3, 206.
9. Mornay, p. 335; see also p. 336.

There are three principal parts of the soul in a man, that is to say the speculative reason, the practical reason, and the factive imagination. Similarly in the commonwealth priests and philosophers are concerned with the exploration of divine and occult science, magistrates and officers with commanding, judging, and providing for the government of the commonwealth, the ordinary subjects with labour and the mechanical arts. The same characteristics are to be observed in the universal commonwealth of the world. God in His miraculous wisdom has so ordered it that the southern races are ordained to search into the most abstruse sciences in order that thereby they might teach the rest. The northern races are ordained to labour and the mechanical arts, and the people of the middle regions to bargain, trade, judge, persuade, command, establish commonwealths, and make laws and ordinances for the other races.[1]

And later he distributes the moral virtues of prudence, courage, and temperance among the three estates of the clergy, the military, and the commons, which (he says in another place) is the equivalent in France of Plato's classification.[2] At the same time, we see the analogies cropping up in love treatises; Ficino, for one, who loved the idea of the three parts and their analogues as much as Plato did, made it the basis for his classification of kinds of love:

Hence, as we said, a triple Love arises, for we are born or reared with an inclination to the contemplative, the practical, or the voluptuous life. If to the contemplative, we are lifted immediately from the sight of bodily form to the contemplation of the spiritual and divine. If to the voluptuous, we descend immediately from the sight to the desire to touch. If to the practical and moral, we remain in the pleasures only of seeing and the social relations.[3]

Leone Ebreo, of course, took over the distinction and elaborated it into a system of correspondences between kinds of love, parts of the soul, parts of the body, and even realms of the universe.[4] Then too, the scheme was assimilated into classical myth and

1. Bodin, trans. Tooley, V, i; p. 154.
2. Ibid., VI, vi (p. 212) and V, v (p. 172) respectively.
3. *Commentary on Symposium* 6.8, trans. Jayne, p. 193.
4. *Dialoghi D'Amore*, pp. 4, 102–05.

story, especially those illustrating the paradoxical freedom of man to make of himself what he would, like Pico's Protean man—the young Hercules at the crossroads of pleasure and heroic virtue, for instance, or the dream of Scipio that tries to reconcile the active and contemplative lives while excluding pleasure.[5] Or the Judgment of Paris, which had been interpreted since Fulgentius (and perhaps before) as the choice among the active, contemplative, and amorous lives; [6] Ficino interpreted it in the light of *The Republic* thus:

> That there are three kinds of life, the contemplative, the active, and the pleasurable, no reasonable creature doubts. Whence, it is obvious, men choose three roads to felicity, wisdom, power, and pleasure. We however perceive in the name of wisdom the study of the liberal arts and religious contemplation. Under the name of power we can understand authority in civil and military rule, pecuniary affluence, and splendor of glory, and the active or busy virtue. We should no doubt put the pleasures of the five senses and the avoidance of labors and cares under the classification of pleasure. Therefore the poets named the first Minerva, the second Juno, and the third Venus. Once the three approached Paris . . .[7]

This is the symbolism of the myth as it appears in such diverse works as G. B. Nenna's *A Treatise of Nobility*, George Peele's *The Arraignment of Paris*, Richard Barnfield's *Cynthia*, and, of course, the emblem books.[8]

As its place in myth shows, Plato's sovereign idea of justice as harmony in the state and in the related soul possessed considerable potential in the Renaissance as an analogue of human experience, a way of seeing success and failure in life. Therefore, it often forms the structural skeleton of fictional plots. We shall examine

5. Cicero, *De re publica* 6.9, and Macrobius, *In Somnum Scipionis* 2.17.
6. Fulgentius, *Mythologiae* 2.1; Plato's *Philebus* begins as a debate whether Wisdom or Pleasure (represented by Aphrodite) is the highest good for man.
7. *Epistolarum Liber* X, *Opera* (Basle, 1576), pp. 919–20; see also the treatise *Expositio de triplici vita et fine triplici* in *Supplementum Ficinianum*, ed. P. O. Kristeller (2 vols. Florence, 1937), *1*, 80–86.
8. For a list of treatments of this myth in Elizabethan literature, see Hallett Smith, *Elizabethan Poetry: A Study of Conventions, Meaning, and Expression* (Cambridge, Mass., 1952), pp. 4–8.

four of these plots briefly to see the various possibilities in its handling, before we see how Sidney used it. First, the story of Felismena in *Diana*. Her whole story occurs within the framework of the Judgment of Paris established before her birth; her mother's quarrel with Paris' decision was punished by the divine decree that her daughter would be doomed to misfortune in love under Venus and good fortune in battle under Athene. Her actual life works out according to this scheme, but paradoxically so: disappointed in love, she disguises herself as a warrior and fights her way to Felicia's temple of contemplation, whence she issues whole to accomplish her goal in love by saving the beloved Don Felis in battle. Her life thus follows a curve from unjust conflict of parts of the soul to purification to final just co-operation of parts. Brian Melbancke's *Philotimus, The Warre betwixt Nature and Fortune* (1583) handles the scheme of state and soul in a more external fashion. Of course the name of the hero, Philotimus, foreshadows the end of the story, for he is destined to be the lover of honor, the Auxiliary in the state. Nevertheless, at the start his father presents to him the myth of the Judgment of Paris as an image of the choices which lie before him in the pilgrimage of life. He first tries the way of wisdom at the university, but his life there soon breaks up and in Venice he enters the life of Venus full tilt. There he undergoes prolonged suffering from the deceit of friends and the cunning of women, and at last flees, destitute, to wander as a vagabond through Greece. It is there, after a temptation to turn pirate, that he realizes how he has defaced his own image when he sees himself as a beast, just as Io had suddenly seen her bovine reflection in the pool. Thereupon he enters an archetypal pastoral valley, where the old shepherd Laurus comforts him, tells him his own life story of disappointment in the active and amorous lives, and offers to share his contemplative life with him (the episode is a miniature pastoral romance). But Philotimus is destined for other things; so, on a morning, he clothes himself in green, supplicates a great lord who is hunting nearby, and settles in life as the retainer, the auxiliary of the philosopher-prince (whom, if we take the tale as autobiographical, we may identify with the Earl of Arundel).

The Platonic scheme had an even more direct influence on the other two works to be considered. The plot of Gascoigne's entertainment at Woodstock in 1575 concerns the hermit Hemites, who, having been struck blind by Venus for dividing his allegiance between learning and love, has his sight restored when "att one tyme and in one place . . . two of the most valyaunt knightes shall fighte, two of the most constant lovers shall meete, & the most vertuous lady in the world shalbe theare to looke on," [9] that is, when the soul re-achieves harmony, with the sensual and spirited elements at their highest pitch and under the control of Elizabeth, the Lady Reason and the Philosopher-Queen.

A similar allegorical alignment of the soul and the state occurs in Torquato Tasso's *Gerusalemme Liberata*. When Tasso came to moralize his plot, he revealed the full and explicit Platonic scheme beneath it, for he wrote:

> The army compounded of divers princes, and of other Christian soldiers, signifieth Man, compounded of soul and body, and of a soul not simple, but divided into many and diverse powers. . . . Godfrey, which of all the assembly is chosen chieftan, stands for Understanding. . . . Rinaldo, Tancredi, and the other princes are in lieu of the other powers of the Soul, and the Body here becomes notified by the soldiers less noble.[1]

Later he expands on this statement to identify Rinaldo as "The Ireful Virtue . . . which amongst all the powers of the mind, is less estranged from the nobility of the soul, insomuch that Plato, doubting, seeketh whether it be different from reason or no," [2] and goes on to propose a relation between the two powers almost word for word from *The Republic*:

> And such it [the ireful virtue] is in the mind, as the chieftain in an assembly of soldiers; for as of these the office is to obey their princes, which do give directions and commandments to fight against their enemies; so it is the duty of the ireful, warlike, and sovereign part of the mind, to be armed with reason against con-

9. Gascoigne, *Works*, ed. J. W. Cunliffe (2 vols. Cambridge, 1910), 2, 483.

1. *Jerusalem Delivered*, trans. Edward Fairfax, ed. Henry Morley (London, 1890), p. 438.

2. Ibid., p. 440.

cupiscence, and with that vehemency and fierceness which is proper unto it, to resist and drive away whatsoever impediment to felicity. But when it doth not obey reason, but suffers itself to be carried of her own violence, it falleth out, that it fighteth not against concupiscence but by concupiscence, like a dog that biteth, not the thieves, but the cattle committed to his keeping.[3]

Although Tasso does not say so, Tancredi probably represents the third part of the soul, for, as he says, love disjoins Tancredi from Godfey in the same manner as honorable disdain does Rinaldo. In these terms, the plot traces literally and politically the attempt of men to reach civil happiness, their failure because of political dissension, their eventual reunion by priestly advice, and their consequent success; allegorically and privately, it shows how the soul fails to attain earthly felicity because it is divided within itself, how it comes together into the order of natural justice by supernatural aid, and how, whole again, it attains its earthly good and looks toward heaven.

These four fictions exhibit a common tendency to treat a standard plot idea as the disintegration and reintegration of parts of the soul projected into various analogical planes. The plots of *Diana* and *Philotimus* were constructed on the analogy between the parts of the soul and the kinds of men, where the hero achieves justice in his soul by developing from a low to a higher kind of man; in *Gerusalemme Liberata* and Gascoigne's entertainment, the analogy used is that between the parts of the soul and the castes in the state, where the achievement of justice in the soul is mirrored in the political recombination of men.

Thus in the political dimension one can catch up and reinterpret the spiritual development of the hero. In Sidney's *Arcadia* this scheme shows itself chiefly as a continual parallel between the history of the heroes and the history of Arcadia, which is defined most simply as the loss and regaining of justice in both realms. Since we have examined the former in previous chapters, it is the latter that demands our attention here; after we have considered it, we shall show how it presents the adventures of Pyrocles and

3. Ibid., p. 441; cf. *Republic* 588–90.

Musidorus in a new light—the brightest of the lights Sidney directed on them by his accretion of new actions and consequent new points of view.

THE STATE

Political precepts out of Plato's *Republic* are scattered through the incidental episodes of *Arcadia*. For instance, Pyrocles and Musidorus learn of the dangers of the honor-loving man to his state and his own soul from the Pontine giants, whose ireful virtue, when directed by the monarch, "was a serviceable power of the mind to do publike good; so now unbrideled, and blind judge of it selfe, it made wickednesse violent" (133). In Laconia they see the evils of democracy and its image in the desire-ridden democratic man Demagoras (as later, following the declinations of states, they observe despotic man in Amphialus and timocratic man in Timantus). The kingdoms they inspect in Asia Minor all present examples of the different kinds of tyranny, tyranny being defined as the rule of a man whose soul is enslaved by his desires. A different passion therefore rules each king there—the king of Pontus, for example, is "a Tyrant also, not through suspision, greedinesse, or revengefulnesse, as he of *Phrygia*, but (as I may terme it) of a wanton cruelty" caused by envy (131)—and makes him the most miserable of men, as Plato predicted:

> And just as a state enslaved to a tyrant cannot do what it really wishes, so neither can a soul under a similar tyranny do what it wishes as a whole. Goaded on against its will by the sting of desire, it will be filled with confusion and remorse. Like the corresponding state, it must always be poverty-stricken, unsatisfied, and haunted by fear. Nowhere else will there be so much lamentation, groaning, and anguish as in a country under a despotism, and in a soul maddened by the tyranny of passion and lust.[4]

But the two states which Pyrocles and Musidorus observe closely and which together define Sidney's doctrine of the growth and

---

4. *Republic* 577; the translation used throughout is that of F. M. Cornford (London, 1941).

decline of the ideal state in *Arcadia* are Macedon, a reclaimed oligarchy, and Arcadia, a declining monarchy. The situations in these two states are themselves caused by the characters of their leaders, Euarchus ("good ruler") and Basilius ("duke" or "the ordinary king").

Euarchus is the positive ideal, the philosopher-king whose actions are such that "I might as easily sette downe the whole Arte of government, as to laie before your eyes the picture of his proceedings" (122). When Euarchus came to the throne of Macedon, he found the state

> so disjoynted even in the noblest & strongest lims of government, that the name of a King was growne even odious to the people, his authoritie having bin abused by those great Lords, and litle kings: who in those betweene times of raigning (by unjust favouring those that were partially theirs, and oppressing them that would defend their libertie against them) had brought in (by a more felt then seen maner of proceeding) the worst kind of *Oligarchie;* that is, when men are governed in deede by a few, and yet are not taught to know what those fewe be, to whom they should obey. [121]

Oligarchic Macedon is a place where "vertue it selfe [is] almost forgotten," for, as Plato had predicted, "the more they value money . . . the less they care for virtue." [5] From this central greed proceeded "grievous taxations," laws whose main purpose was to catch fines, the selling of offices and the neglect of public defense, producing constant innovations and division of the nation into factions among the great men, while the commons supported one or the other according to their interest. "Such a state," Plato said, "must lose its unity and become two, one of the poor, the other of the rich, living together and always plotting against each other." [6] The main task in such a state was to establish a center of authority by which to draw the scattered limbs into the orderly working which is justice. This Euarchus did at first by exercising great severity toward the subverters of his state, meting out punishments without regard of persons; after reducing Macedon to

5. *Republic* 550.
6. *Republic* 551.

order, however, he changed his tactics and won the love of his people:

> But then shined foorth in deede all love among them, when an awfull feare, ingendred by justice, did make that love most lovely: his first and principall care being to appeare unto his people, such as he would have them be, and to be such as he appeared; making his life the example of his lawes, and his lawes as it were, his axioms arising out of his deedes.   [122]

It is notable that he conceived of his person in the settled state as an example to his people, his rule as a moral education of the commonwealth. As Plato said, the function of the good kings was to mold the state in conformity with an ideal, "when they have seen the Good itself, take it as a pattern for the right ordering of the state and of the individual, themselves included." [7] The king must be a philosopher in order to do this. Therefore, since after the birth of Christ "philosopher" meant "true philosopher" or Christian, it is not surprising that we should find Euarchus' principles strikingly similar to those recommended in such handbooks as Erasmus' *The Education of a Christian Prince*. "A good, wise, and upright prince is nothing else than a sort of living law," wrote Erasmus,[8] and the prime Christian element of that law is love, for "Those who look out for their people only in so far as it redounds to their personal advantage, hold their subjects in the same status as the average man considers his horse or ass";[9] so Euarchus "desdaining, that they that have charge of beastes, should love their charge, and care for them; and that he that was to governe the most excellent creature, should not love so noble a charge" (122). Love is not only God's commandment, but is the key to harmony or justice in a state where the king is not separate from his people but part of them, for Euarchus "wisely acknowledging, that he with his people made all but one politike bodie, wheerof himselfe was the head; even so cared for them, as he would for his owne limmes"; that was Erasmus' point when he wrote:

7. *Republic* 540.
8. *The Education of a Christian Prince*, trans. Lester K. Born, Records of Civilization, 27 (New York, 1936), p. 221.
9. Ibid., p. 161.

He should consider his kingdom as a great body of which he is the most outstanding member and remember that they who have entrusted all their fortunes and their very safety to the good faith of one man are deserving of consideration. . . . the prince will see to it that he is loved by his subjects in return, but in such a way that his authority is no less strong among them. . . . let him love, who would be loved, so that he may attach his subjects to him as God has won the peoples of the world to Himself by His Goodness.[1]

That was the result Euarchus obtained when "by force he tooke nothing, by their love he had all."

It is only natural that the public beneficence of Euarchus flowed from the ethical quality of his mind, for "if for any thing he loved greatnesse, it was, because therein he might exercise his goodnesse" (121). His goodness consists in several harmonious or just relations, first between body and mind, for the mind as the fountainhead of the body both gives it its graces and molds it in obedience: "strong of body, and so much the stronger, as he by a well disciplined exercise taught it both to do, and suffer." The mind's tempering of the body is only a reflection of the justice within; in conformity to his subjection to God, Euarchus has limited appetite by intellect, "contenting himself to guide that shippe, wherein the heavens had placed him, [he] shewed no lesse magnanimity in daungerlesse despising, then others in daungerous affecting the multiplying of kingdomes." By these means, his mind has become what Erasmus, Elyot, and others wished it to be, the picture of justice and the nursery of the cardinal virtues: "he was most wise to see what was best, and most just in the perfourming what he saw, & temperate in abstaining from any thing any way contrarie: so think I, no thought can imagine a greater heart to see and contemne danger" (120–21). It is from these values (which we have opportunity to observe even more closely near the end of *Arcadia*) that there proceed the virtuous actions of Euarchus, whose end is to make both the commonwealth and the individual an image of his own just soul; so he, "the man which

---

1. Ibid., pp. 205–06.

they so long had used to maske their owne appetites, should now be the reducer of them into order" (121–22).

Basilius, in direct contrast to Euarchus, is a man whose soul is usurped by the base desires. First, alarm over the loss of material goods and power; then, lust and the crowd of pleasures that come to tempt the soul that has once opened itself to desire. He is self-loving and surrounds himself with flatterers who make his "dukely sophistry to deceyve him self" seem wisdom. At the opening of *Arcadia*, Kalander tells us, fear has moved him to give the government of his commonwealth over to his Auxiliary Philanax so that he can pursue his desires in the rural retreat with its pleasure houses and nightly entertainments. There, as if symbolizing his banishment "from his owne wits" in his soul (11), he appoints as lieutenant a foolish member of the artisan class, "the most arrant doltish clowne" Dametas, who tyrannizes it over the other members of the royal family.

Does that mean that Basilius is really, at bottom, a lover of pleasure who has become ruler by some mistake? Has he always been contemptible? Not at all. We are assured from the start that Basilius is a man of some moral virtue, although the virtues he possesses are those that fit him to rule a docile and peaceful nation rather than a disturbed one: "though he exceed not in the vertues which get admiration; as depth of wisedome, height of courage and largenesse of magnificence, yet is he notable in those whiche stirre affection, as truth of word, meekenesse, curtesie, mercifulnesse, and liberality" (9). What has in fact happened to Basilius is that he lacked the control to prevent another Fall of Man in himself. It all began with vain curiosity, when he sent to the Oracle at Delphi to discover his future—an act betokening some impiety, this, seeking to pry into the gods' "hidden counsel by curiositie" rather than seeking their mercies by prayers (12), though not a serious one. But Basilius fell from distrusting Providence into a foolish attempt to avoid it entirely by giving up all, abandoning control, and fleeing into voluntary exile. His weakness of character caused the original wavering in religious faith which in turn brought about disturbances in the soul and aroused the crowd of desires that now govern him. What Basilius lost was the state of original or natural justice we saw Euarchus preserving with all his might.

The bulk of *Arcadia* records the spread of injustice, first in the king's soul, then in his state. As soon as Pyrocles enters the retreat disguised as an Amazon, Basilius completes his cycle by suffering his body to revolt against his soul in a most ridiculous fashion. For the old king, released from the responsibility of maintaining his place in the cosmic hierarchy, falls into doting love of the young man. Sidney emphasized Basilius' complete reversal of natural hierarchy by comic images of subjection. He who was before master of all below God is now a slave to passion, "a Prince unconquered to become a slave to a stranger" (99); "You only have overthrowne me, & in my bondage consists my glory" (164). And he to whom the kingdom once knelt now bends his withered legs before a man he believes to be a woman, "falling downe upon both his knees, and holding up his hands, as the old governesse of *Danae* is painted, when she suddenly saw the golden showre" (164); the ridicule of him here and in further postures of the bold young blade or the spruce courtier is scathing. Furthermore, his whole sense of values begins to crack when he establishes Zelmane as an earthly goddess or, worse, when he goes so far as to deny altogether the validity of any concept of honor or obedience to moral law in the soul: "Alas, let not certaine imaginative rules, whose truth stands but upon opinion, keepe so wise a mind from gratefulnesse & mercie, whose never fayling lawes nature hath planted in us" (362). Gynecia sums up Basilius' abuses of nature, and the bonds broken therefrom, just before his symbolic death in the dark cave:

> Remember the wrong you have done is not onlie to me, but to your children, whom you had of me: to your countrey, when they shall find they are commaunded by him, that cannot commaund his owne undecent appetites: lastlie, to your selfe, since with these paines you do but build up a house of shame to dwell in. [398]

The disorder spreads from the individual into the family which, as Bodin had demonstrated, was analogous to the soul as well as the body politic, since reason is to passion as the husband is to the wife.[2] Basilius starts the breakup by forcing his younger daughter Philoclea to act as his procuress with Zelmane, an act that not only brings into the open a jealous conflict between the husband and the wife, but also arouses Gynecia's hatred of her own daugher, thus turning "the blessings of a mother" to "the curses of a competitor" (197).

Finally and inevitably, the injustice in the king's soul produces an open outbreak of injustice in the state. "We see the whole world and each part thereof so compacted, that as long as each thing performeth only that work which is natural unto it, it thereby preserveth both other things and also itself," Hooker wrote,[3] and the popular revolt that ends Book II illustrates the converse, the full moral chaos resulting from Basilius' retirement, the result Philanax hinted at when he wrote, "who wil stick to him that abandones himselfe?" The revolt begins appropriately at a celebration of Basilius' birthday; there the commons, their passions enflamed by drink, start to air their complaints about his reign, mixing private grudges with public causes, thence to turn their malice against his person in complete unreasoning disorder, and finally to seize whatever weapons or tools are to hand as instruments of violence. This is a striking picture of the ultimate results of the denial of duty; and, in fact, this milling crowd of butchers, bakers, plowmen, and merchants is only a reflection of a mind like Basilius' torn apart by conflicting desires that sap its strength and doom it to failure. "O weake trust of the many-headed multitude, whom inconstancie only doth guide to wel doing" (203), cries Sidney, for it is none other than Plato's Chimaera of the desires, "a multifarious and many-headed beast, girt round with heads of animals, tame and wild,"[4] which, when fed, threatens to eat up the soul. Therefore, upon erupting into the retreat, "so many as they were, so many almost were their minds, all knit together onely in madnesse. Some cried, Take; some, Kill; some, Save; but even they

2. Bodin, p. 10.
3. *Of the Laws of Ecclesiastical Polity*, I, ix; in the edition of Christopher Morris (new ed. 2 vols. Everyman's Library, London, 1954), *1*, 185.
4. *Republic* 588.

that cried save, ran for company with them that meant to kill. Every one commaunded, none obeyed" (198). They cannot decide why they are revolting, what reforms they want, or even who is to represent them. They finally (and fittingly) slaughter each other.

Political turmoils reflecting the soul grew ever larger in Arcadia —from the eruption of the lion and bear, to the popular rebellion, to climax in full-scale civil war—and subside in near dissolution of the state. As Basilius declines, two figures come to the fore to claim the neglected throne, despotic man and timocratic man, mirrors of the progressive corruption of Arcadia. The civil war is much more purposive than the revolt in that it has a head, the philotimon Amphialus, possessed of the power to unite all factions under his leadership. Amphialus himself, whose tragedy we outlined in the previous chapter, is drawn on the model of Plato's despotic man, the son of a man denied power in the state, tempted by figures of pride like Cecropia and Clinias to seize power:

> Now imagine . . . a young son . . . drawn towards the utter lawlessness which his seducers call perfect freedom, while on the other side his father and friends lend their support to the compromise. When those terrible wizards who would conjure up an absolute ruler in the young man's soul begin to doubt the power of their spells, in the last resort they contrive to engender in him a master passion, to champion the mob of idle appetites which are for dividing among themselves all available plunder—a passion that can only be compared to a great winged drone. Like a swarm buzzing round this creature, the other desires come laden with incense and perfumes, garlands and wine, feeding its growth to the full on the pleasures of a dissolute life, until they have implanted the sting of a longing that cannot be satisfied. Then at last this passion, as leader of the soul, takes madness for the captain of its guard and breaks out in frenzy.[5]

Amphialus threatens to turn Arcadia into an image of his own soul, for, influenced by the perverted intellect of Cecropia, he draws all the multifarious humors to his service:

5. Ibid., 572.

all such, whom either youthfull age, or youthlike minds did fill
with unlimited desires: besides such, whom any discontentment
made hungry of change, or an over-spended want, made want
a civill war: to each (according to the counsell of his mother)
conforming himself after their humors. To his friends, friendli-
nesse; to the ambitious, great expectations; to the displeased,
revenge; to the greedy, spoile.   [245–6]

He can, moreover, organize all of these conflicting desires into a
working whole, even making use of vice for his purposes, just as
the master passion in the tyrant's mind can unite all in a misdirected
enterprise. These are the forces set against the enfeebled reasoning
element of Arcadia. Basilius shows himself to be a wavering leader
here; he is usually irresolute and, when finally faced with the
decision whether to raise the siege or pursue it, chooses the former
course only because of his passion for Zelmane. So weak is he in
the face of this war that he can only sit in his impotence to observe
his kingdom crumbling to ruins around him, his soldiers slaughtered, the most noble souls in the realm wasted. When the dis-
turbance does subside, it is only by the combination of outside
help and the collapse of the confused philotimon himself, who,
having just turned against his proper lord, then realizes what he
has done to himself thereby and destroys himself together with
the corrupted intellect that has directed him in all this.

With the return of the group to private life, Basilius only suffers
further dissolution, for he is offered the most dangerous gift of
all, satisfaction of his lusts. To achieve the base desires is to
strengthen them, to weaken and torture the manlike part of the
soul, and thus to be dead to virtue's claims. Therefore the sum
of all Basilius' acts is the ignorant copulation by night in the cave
of lust, culminating in death by drinking. His death symbolizes
all his acts in life, for, as Euarchus had realized, to retire into
the life of bodily pleasure is to bury oneself alive (437).

This event has an analogous effect on the state, for it is just the
dissolution of Arcadia as a whole, the final act of injustice, that
results. When a monarchy fails, according to Plato's theory, civil
strife results between the best men who try to preserve virtue and
the old ways and lesser men who want to turn the state to their

own selfish ways,[6] "For some there were that cried to have the state altered, and governed no more by a Prince; marie in the alteration, many would have the *Lacedæmonian* government of fewe chosen Senatours; others the *Athenian*, where the peoples voyce held the chiefe authority" (422). Chief among the innovators who oppose Philanax is the selfish and ambitious Timantus, who gradually draws a majority to his faction. His model is, of course, Plato's timocratic man:

> Ambitious for office, he will base his claims, not on any gifts of speech, but on his exploits in war and the soldierly qualities he has acquired through his devotion to athletics and hunting.[7]

So Timantus:

> a man of midle age, but of extreame ambition, as one that had placed his uttermost good in greatnesse. . . . Of commendable wit (if he had not made it a servant to unbrideled desires). . . . Hee had been brought up in souldierie, which he knew how to set out with more then deserved ostentation. Servile (though envious) to his betters: and no lesse tyrannically minded to them he had advantage of.   [422–23]

The form of government that will result if he wins is timocracy, a state in which the ambitious man's love of honor (*timé*) will usurp the rule of reason; as Socrates said, "Thanks to the predominance of the spirited part of our nature" the timocracy "has one most conspicuous feature: ambition and the passion to excell."[8] The peculiar form of tyranny assumed by timocracy is suppression of the lower classes—in other words, complete inequality, complete injustice because there is complete separation between the rulers and the ruled.

The history of the Arcadian commonwealth is a story of the decay and eventual resurgence of justice: its beginning is the inception of injustice in the soul of its lord, its middle the spread of injustice in him and from him into the state, its end the reestablishment of justice first in the state and then in the soul.

6. Ibid., 546.
7. Ibid., 548.
8. Ibid., 547.

Euarchus, the philosopher-king, is the herald of the ending, for his first action on setting foot in Arcadia is to draw its government from the ultimate form of injustice into order, by quelling revolt, arranging a trial, and setting up a procedure for determining the succession (thus preserving the monarchic form of government). Once justice has come to the state again, the way is open to its re-establishment in the soul of the king; and we see the first move-ment of such an act, restoration of the subjection to God which had been cast away, when Basilius arises from his mock death to see the oracle fulfilled in all sorts of ironic ways and therefore to announce a fresh belief that "all had fallen out by the highest providence" and that disturbances in human affairs come from unjust man: "in all these matters his own fault had been the greatest."

Pyrocles and Musidorus were brought up in the monarchy of Euarchus, and conduct their present activities in the Arcadia of Basilius. They have, therefore, two kinds of rulers set before them as examples in a test to see whether their spirited element will join the intellect or the desires.

THE SOUL

When we place Pyrocles and Musidorus in the full political con-text of *Arcadia*, surrounded by the score of actions that illuminate their actions, we see them more objectively than before and we notice that their traits are so general that they almost seem type characters. For it is in this light that the lineaments of the high-spirited lover of honor (the goal proper to young men of the Guardian class) appear in the cousins. They are men of action, quick to respond to situations with spirit and valor even when these are not precisely the qualities that the case calls for; Pyrocles' name even confirms his inclusion in a type, for it combines desire for glory (κλέος) with the fire of spirit (πῦρο) which Sidney at times seems to link with the choleric humor, "all the composition of her [Zelmane's] elements being nothing but fierie" (69). This spirit the young princes must now give over to the intellect, for their destinies demand that they become rulers, the one of Thessalia, the other of Macedon. They must both, in short, become philosopher-kings like Euarchus, and the goal proper to them at maturity will not be glory but wisdom.

It is therefore incumbent on them to strengthen their intellectual souls by contemplation. Before entering Arcadia, they have completed the normal training of the Guardian, first ethical culture and gymnastic (which both strengthened their spiritual powers and made them subserve reason)[9] and second the proof of the virtues gained thereby in exercise of these virtues (133). This exercise involved not only the spirited virtues like courage in battle, but those of the intellect as well, "publicke actions of princely, and (as it were) governing vertue" (132). Thus they are assumed perfect in the active life, just in soul and in act. But that is not enough: if reason is to rule perpetually instead of fitfully, if it is to lead as well as control, they must go beyond the moral virtues to knowledge of the Good that is their source. In other words, even though they now operate with justice in their souls, that state can be preserved only by grounding the soul in religious wisdom and its consequent virtues, by basing the active life anew on the contemplative.

Their Arcadian adventures then form a small but crucial point in the education of the princes. In the normal Platonic system, the period that has just passed would have been a rigorous testing of their worthiness to be trained as Rulers instead of Auxiliaries. It would have been followed by a rigorous training in mathematics, geometry, and finally dialectic to draw the mind from the material world of action to the intelligible world where contemplation of the One would produce that spiritual union with it that constitutes true wisdom or *phronésis*. But, instead, what the princes face as they enter Arcadia is *love*. Theoretically love led to the same goal of union with the One by a direct *education sentimentale* instead of a rational *paideia;* but that was only theory, and the princes wonder whether it is so in fact, or is only a lamentable byway leading from the path of contemplation into lust. The answer, in theory, is that it depends on the man. Obviously, then, the ad-

9. See the brief account of their education, *Arcadia*, pp. 123-24, and compare it with the *paideia* outlined by Plato, *Republic* 521-34.

venture they face in Arcadia combines elements of education with elements of trial or test. It is this fact that accounts for the forensic nature of their activities, especially in the series of debates we examined earlier.

The two spirited young men conduct their test-by-contemplation in parallel with the disgraceful decline of the weak state. First, the old order breaks up, perhaps to be transcended or perhaps merely to decay. In the souls of Pyrocles and Musidorus, the harmony of reason and spirit achieved in Asia Minor collapses, passion strengthened by love in contemplation revolts against the now tyrannical reason, and personalities seem to dissolve. An injustice caused in part by Pyrocles spreads also in the soul of Basilius, who now falls victim to the base sensual desires, and causes injustice in the family and in the state of Arcadia, as the multitude with all its desires enters into open revolt against its king. This revolt actually gives cause for hope, for the order it disturbs is an ignoble one wherein the king ignores the state, and it could result in a change from sloth to real control. But it does not: Basilius merely re-establishes the old unsatisfactory situation while the princes pursue their old ways of operating to produce the series of false solutions recorded at the end of Book II. Therefore, the injustice now apparent within the old orders of things only increases in the form of a civil war and still further eruptions in the soul. While Basilius fully unleashes his lust on Pyrocles, the princes seek to control these disorders, which are only reflections of the unjust rule of passion in their own souls,[1] by the old question-begging means of heroic activity (even though the answer—patience—has been shown us in the magnificent prison scene of Pamela). This time, the old order fails miserably, for the actions of Basilius, Pyrocles, and Musidorus lead directly to disaster and end in darkness as the king lies dead, the princes enchained in an analogous living death of lust and despair. Failure is extremely fortunate, for now, with the unjust structures of the old orders of state and soul in complete collapse, the way lies

---

1. This is shown explicitly in the cave scene, with its complex symbolism of reflection; see our discussion, pp. 78–79.

open to the construction of a new order based on the values achieved in contemplation by Philoclea and Euarchus.

Every test is an education. For the princes, the retreat into contemplation, as experienced here, is primarily destructive—destructive of the facile assurance encouraged by the active life and of its limited account of human possibilities. In other words, it shows them that their efforts can accomplish nothing unless they break and yield to Providence. They do not, it is important to remember, achieve union with God, they only look forward to it; but their appetites are whetted by the enlightenment their mistresses produce in their failing souls.

In this scheme, Book IV represents an awakening both literal and figurative, for all the characters involved arise from sleep to find out what they have really done, and what they should have done. Pyrocles awakens beside Philoclea to find himself a prisoner and to hear, through the window, accusations of rape (a sin which his mind certainly touched on). Basilius awakens at dawn to find out just whom he has been sleeping with. And Musidorus, in a state of sensual lassitude with Pamela sleeping beside him, starts up to repulse an attack by the baser elements of Arcadia. Once awakened, Basilius sees his sins and repents, while Pyrocles receives a long and effective lecture on Providence from Philoclea.

As they awaken, the dreary desert retreat becomes the world again, for elements from the outside burst in: the remnants of the rebels, the nobles of Arcadia led by Philanax, and the Macedon of the heroes' past in the person of Euarchus and his retinue. When the harshness of a dawn reinforced by parts of reality deliberately excluded from a troubled attempt at the contemplative life shatters their web of wishes, the thematic focus of *Arcadia* shifts from love to its effects in the state, from the private to the public; the fictional context changes too, from a romantic world to something nearer the world we know. Therefore, as Pyrocles and Musidorus rise from their dream of passion, they—and we— are faced with two new dominating political figures, the good courtier Philanax, their accuser, and the ideal Prince Euarchus, their judge. Sidney underlined the new view of reality that must be contingent upon the appearance of these two by making them his central intelligences, the one for the latter part of Book IV, the other for the bulk of Book V. In this way the estates of their minds lie open to the observer, for they form together an exemplary hierarchy for the princes to ascend.

Philanax' name ("king-lover") shows him for the very type of the good courtier whose every action is motivated by the good of the commonwealth: "there lives no man, whose excellent witte more simplye imbraseth integritie, besides his unfained love to his maister, wherein never yet any could make question, saving whether he loved *Basilius* or the Prince better" (12). His love shows itself chiefly in direct and fearless advice, even when it goes against the king's will,[2] as in his letters to Basilius on the subject of his discourting; therein, he berates him freely for consulting the oracle in the first place, points out the vanity of his decision, since one cannot avoid the inevitable by change of place, and tries to lead him back to reason by both political and moral persuasions: a prince should keep himself in the eyes of his subjects to prevent any desires for change, he says, and a prince should cultivate virtue instead of fighting shadows, for "wisedome and vertue be the only destinies appointed to man to follow" (12). It is an irony befitting his original advice that Philanax appears in the retreat at the moment when the worst effects of Basilius' decision assert themselves; it is befitting his character and station that his object, once there, is to establish justice by revealing crime, punishing the offenders, and setting up an interim government until Pamela reaches majority.

Yet the man's very love of his king is also his blind spot; it is a passion that can lead his spirit away from the justice he so desires and into deeds of rashness. Chiefly, it infects his judgment for it tempts him to prejudge the guilt of the four lovers in plotting to kill the king. Thus he assumes that Philoclea's innocence is only bluffing, or at best an attempt to hide guilty lust; when he

---

2. See *The Book of the Courtier*, p. 261, where the "ende" or goal of a perfect courtier is to so gain his prince's confidence that "he may breake his minde to him, and alwaies enforme him franckly of the truth of every matter meete for him to understand, without fear or perill to displease him."

first sets eyes upon Pyrocles, immediately "compassion turned to hatefull passion" (411). He is unfair: he mews Pamela up immediately upon her return lest sight of her arouse the populace to sympathy for her, and during the trial he treats the defendants with a scathing sarcasm unbefitting to their estates or to what he knows of their characters. In short, Philanax' view of events is irrational and therefore insufficient, since it warps every action into a sin against the prince, every character save the victim into a whore or a villain; Gynecia sums it up when she accuses him of excess: "It may be truth doth make thee deale untruly; and love of justice frames unjustice in thee" (450). For Philanax is the good courtier, a fit auxiliary rather than a ruler. As he himself admits, the force of "honest passion" is too great in him to allow him a seat beside Euarchus in judgment; rather, he must stand before him as prosecutor. So too Philanax cannot of himself settle the anarchy at Basilius' death; he can only point to the prince who can.

The figure of Euarchus stands supreme over the concluding events of *Arcadia*. Not only is he an ideal, but he is our central intelligence; what we read is what Euarchus sees and what he thinks of it. By channeling events into this man's view of them, Sidney both objectified the final scenes and opened out the just mind of Euarchus, showing fully his inner workings in order to involve us directly in the values for which he stands. As his function is to harmonize the public disorders of Arcadia (and of the book), so the diverse facts of *Arcadia* draw together into the harmony of his single point of view; and his mind, as it lies open to us, *is* a harmony. Thus at his first actual appearance Euarchus is discovered in an emblematic posture of humility which amply shows how fitting a teacher he is of the omnipotence of Providence and the justice of a man's submission to it, "taking his rest under a tree, with no more affected pompes, then as a man that knew, howsoever he was exalted, the beginning and end of his body was earth" (437).[3] What we see in his mind is, of course, control

3. The scene briefly recalls Adam in order to stress Euarchus' refusal of Adam's pride; thus he *rests* under the tree and calmly accepts the tragedy of postlapsarian life.

obviously grounded in religious belief (since he knows that "it is not possible to governe either himselfe or others well, without the help of God"),[4] control of himself as king under God, control of his person by an instinctive limitation of the desires in the lower parts of the soul. Furthermore, he rigidly directs his virtue to use, for "the treasure of those inward giftes he had, were bestowed by the heavens upon him, to be beneficiall and not idle" (438), and must pour out into the active life, since "doing good" is "the onely happie action of mans life" (437). As his position under the tree implies—willingly humble before God, in control of his soul, and holding his body bound to the precepts of the soul in virtuous action—Euarchus is Bodin's ideal prince who has recovered in himself some of the original justice Adam lost. Therefore it is this dominating image of the mind of Euarchus that redefines, once again, life in this world as the use of what wisdom contemplation produces for effecting good in the governing of peoples. The mind of Euarchus both filters the concluding events of *Arcadia* and sets the standards by which to judge them.

Under the aegis of this man, the "orderer of the present disorders" (440), justice comes to the state and to the soul, the one by his direct intervention, the other merely concomitantly in the pattern of the action. His first accomplishment after being chosen guide of Arcadia is to reunite the parts of the commonwealth, suppressing faction with the aid of Philanax. Once the state has become whole again, it can act, so that his next step is to purge its bad elements in that ritual of justice, the trial, after which the final step will be to ensure the permanence of justice by establishing an hereditary ruler.

Order re-established in the state, we turn to see the same thing happening in the soul during the prison scene just before the trial. We have discussed this scene before, but we now examine two new and important aspects of it. First, what the princes have achieved is the natural justice Euarchus symbolizes. The way was paved by Philoclea in the bedchamber, where Pyrocles finally accepted Providence and thereupon acquired patience, the key to

4. *The Book of the Courtier*, p. 285; see also Erasmus, p. 189.

the virtues that purify the soul. In their dialogue and hymn, the princes show that they have accomplished in their lives the triple subjection they believe in, as they entrust their lives to God, the subordinate parts to reason within the soul, and their bodies to their souls. Then like the Christians under Godfrey made whole in "the state of natural justice and heavenly obedience," they turn to "the contemplation of the eternal blessedness of the other most happy and immortal life." [5] The exercise of the cleansing virtues we saw earlier has as its end the re-establishment of natural justice in the hero; and it looks forward to the soul's reception of illumination in the third sphere of virtues after death. [6]

A second point to notice is that, by completing the action of his romance in the attainment of natural justice in Arcadia, Sidney revealed his ultimate grasp of the philosophical implications of pastoral. For the justice is "natural" because it pertains to the innocent state of nature, "original" because Adam had it and lost it in the Garden of Eden. Therefore, since its association with Eden early in its career, the natural world of the pastoral field or garden became a place which offered men the re-attainment of natural justice by an intensive experience of the humility that washes away the pride developed in his own self-made landscape. [7] The same thing was implied in a passage on gardens by Justus Lipsius quoted earlier:

Yea I seem to shake off all thing in mee that is humaine, and to be rapt up on high upon the fiery chariot of wisdome. . . . I am guarded and fenced against all externall things, and setled within

5. Tasso, pp. 442–43.
6. Plotinus places the re-attainment of original justice later, after the soul's reception of the virtues of the purified mind: "at this height, the man is the very being that came from the Supreme. The primal excellence restored, the essential man is There: entering this sphere, he has associated himself with the reasoning phase of his nature and this he will lead up into likeness with his highest self, as far as earthly mind is capable, so that if possible it shall never be inclined to, and at the least never adopt, any course displeasing to its over-lord" (*Enneads* 1.2.6).
7. See Singleton, p. 224: "Thus if due atonement is ever to be made by man for such a sin, it is required that man, by his own powers, descend as low in humility as he had aspired to rise in pride." The concept, outlined by Mornay, seems to be one of working backward through states the opposite of those which brought about the fall; thus the movement from city to shrine in the romance.

my selfe, carelesse of all cares save one, which is, that I may bring in subjection this broken and distressed mind of mine to RIGHT REASON and GOD, and subdue all humaine and earthly things to my MIND. That whensoever my fatal day shall come, I may be readie with a good courage joyfully to welcome him, and depart this life, not as thrust out at the windowes, but as let out at the dore.

What the prison scene shows is how Pyrocles and Musidorus have been recompensed for the losses in their period of trial and suffering: how love broke down the pattern of civic virtue only to open up the cleansing virtues, how the collapse of Platonic justice in their souls led to the higher form of original justice under God. It is in this regaining of justice on a higher level that the princes, by their own willed acts of virtue, fulfill the pattern they had sensed upon entering the garden where all the diverse came together in harmony, in "so perfect a plotte of the celestiall dwellings."

JUSTICE

Once this movement in the soul has come to completion, the state confronts the soul in a trial of the nature and worth of its experience. The trial scene which ends *Arcadia* is the ultimate expression of political justice newly attained; it is the ceremonial muster of the unified state operating in conformity with its own laws, enacted before Euarchus as judge (with the body of the unworthy king before him) with Philanax below him as presenter and the populace of Arcadia looking on. From its very nature as a final act of order proceeds its main function in the book, which is to redefine and see the elements of pattern in the scattered events which have occurred since the princes penetrated the retreat. It asks, in effect, "What has all this been about?"

The answer arises from three different versions of the plot of *Arcadia;* since they are three different types of stories, they call up questions of what kind of statement fiction makes, and they do

so at the close of Sidney's own fiction.[8] The first version, Philanax', is as neat as any treatise; it can be so neat, of course, only
because its single-minded historiographer possesses just a few facts
on which to hang his consistent fabric. It is pure fabrication, a
story designed to illustrate (rather than test) a preconceived
moral, and Philanax himself seems to half-recognize this fact
when he calls it a "shorte and simple story" or "this tradgedy,"
or when he attempts to exorcise disbelief, lest his auditors will
rather imagine they hear "some tragedy invented of the extremitie
of wickednesse, then a just recitall of a wickednes indeed committed" (453). In this story, the events in Arcadia are connected
from beginning to end by one clear purpose, that being Pyrocles'
regicidal plot; Pyrocles' original disguise was meant to beguile
Basilius, Gynecia's work in the cave was part of the murder plot,
and even the ravishment of Philoclea was part of a plan to cover
usurpation by marriage. The portrait of Pyrocles that emerges
from this "shorte and simple story" is that of a monster, a Machi-
avellian shape-shifter "from all humanitie . . . transformed,"
who "from a man grew a woman, from a woman a ravisher of
women, thence a prisoner, and now a Prince" (453).

To this didactic tale the more realistic version of Pyrocles suc-
ceeds; he possesses more facts, but his story is at best a mixture of
fact and lie (since he omits Philoclea's love for him in order to
protect her, and thus accuses himself of lust). This kind of story
approaches the complexities and confusions of life as we know it,
but the price we have to pay is that moral judgment is completely
baffled. Pyrocles' version finds no simple order in events: for him,
the plot was composed of starts, mistakes, failures, and new starts
—a tangled skein of purpose and accident. The disorder is quite
proper to it, for its motive power was not politics but love, baffling
love, "a passion farre more easely reprehended, then refrayned."

8. The whole problem of ideas of fiction in *Arcadia* deserves study. Book
II would seem especially deserving of close scrutiny because of its explicit
critique of medieval romance, its contrasting kinds of story before and after the
Plangus-Erona episode, and its insistent shifting of narrative points of view. See
above, pp. 122–23 and note 3.

The third version of the plot, that of Musidorus, presents us with a view of events that avoids both a theoretical singleness of scheme and the welter of unexamined experience, and in doing so offers us a brief experience of life seen *sub specie fictionis* as incomplete pattern. He suppresses none of the facts as Pyrocles did, but he does select; he moves away from the vexed problems of purposiveness in the plot to focus on its effects in a judicious attempt to balance its ambiguities. Therefore, he readily admits faults but pleads extenuating circumstances in the "just excuses of loves force" (which, unlike Pyrocles, he sees to be virtuous) and in the good results of their actions: the preservation of the royal family in the attack of the beasts, in the Amphialan war, and in the peasant rebellion. "Our doing," therefore, he says, "in the extreamest interpretation is but a humane error" (463). This is a view we can rest content with, for it reflects what we have seen of the modified Platonic operation of love in the action of *Arcadia.*

The three interpretations present the plot of *Arcadia* in an increasingly favorable light; their effect is to purge any unsympathetic feelings we may have acquired toward the actions. The trial therefore operates as a sort of ritual catharsis under the rational control of Euarchus' law and order; it takes up every possible fault the heroes could have committed, examines each, and eventually exonerates them of it, so that at the end Euarchus can condemn them only for ravishment, and that, he insists (464), by law and not by philosophy or reason. As truth emerges, it comes clothed in brighter and brighter lights. When all identities are revealed, we behold a high and noble tragedy between the father who loves justice more than he loves his son, Musidorus who loves Pyrocles more than his own life, and Pyrocles who, constant to his "resolution of well suffering all accidents" in patience (469), kneels humbly before his father to beg for his friend's life. The audience before whom this is acted direct our feelings too: the good Sympathus moved by "a kindely compassion," Kalander who assimilates his every emotion to Musidorus', and finally even Philanax, who reverses his opinion near the end: "Even *Philanax* owne revengefull heart was mollified. . . . And withall the fame of *Pyrocles* and *Musidorus*, greatly drew him to a compassionate conceit, and had already unclothed his face of all shew of malice" (467).

The purgation is completed when Basilius suddenly arises from his supposed death to release Pyrocles and Musidorus from the sentence of death into the new life of love, marriage, and increase that was prefigured in the opening sentence of *Arcadia*.

7. Arcadia as a Pastoral Romance

Sidney's book is entitled *The Countesse of Pembrokes Arcadia*, and it begins with a dialogue between two shepherds on the nature of love in the pastoral life, a dialogue which alludes to the opening of Montemayor's *Diana*. *Arcadia* has a pastoral setting, the enclosed retreat; the setting moreover follows romance practice by inducing contrast between pastoral and heroic in a set of "circles." It is full of shepherds of all sorts: rustics, courtly shepherds, and disguised noblemen. Its plot is amorous and follows the romance pattern of disintegration, analysis, education, and reintegration in rhythm with the circles of the setting; and it uses subsidiary plots throughout to illuminate the main plot as Sannazaro and Montemayor did. If, on the other hand, *Arcadia* contains many elements that seem to us totally unlike other pastoral romances, we may do well to remember that this most hospitable of genres had opened its arms to epic games, dream vision, mystic love story, Platonic dialogue, autobiography, patriotic celebrations, courtly compliment, Ovidian myth, Greek romantic melodrama, tournaments, warfare, satire, theology, and sea fights before it ever reached Sidney's hands.

While the combination of typical and untypical qualities in this work has suggested to many modern scholars that Sidney started out to write a pastoral romance but finished with an epic on his hands, it seems equally valid to explore the hypothesis that *Arcadia* is not an epic poem in prose at all, but merely a highly developed pastoral romance—and one that pushed the genre to its limits.

One of the least typical qualities of *Arcadia* is that which we have labeled "moralization of plot." By means of narrative accretions and discussions, Sidney both generalized and extended the old narrative pattern; he made the pastoral change of turbulence for peace into a direct contrast between the active and contemplative lives, the operation of love into a modified Platonic scheme, the upsurge of humility into a renewed submission to Providence, and the reintegration of the personality into the regaining of natural justice. The change in focus was mainly from the emotional to the intellectual, and hence from the implied to the explicit. In the old romances, the emphasis being tonal, the plot recorded a change in point of view (such as the acceptance of grief) or a change in fortune, producing joy instead of grief; but, Sidney's emphasis being moral, his plot became the record of a change in the soul brought about by instruction and will. And so, instead of mere reintegration and happiness at the end of his book, we have the attainment of moral perfection by a higher integration of the soul.

The kind of seriousness—or earnestness—that we find imparted to pastoral romance by *Arcadia* is nothing more than what we should naturally expect from the pen of a man of whom Greville said:

> though I lived with him, and knew him from a child, yet I never knew him other than a man: with such staiednesse of mind, lovely, and familiar gravity, as carried grace, and reverence above greater years. His talk ever of knowledge, and his very play tending to enrich his mind.[1]

This seriousness is a salient quality of his other works, though there it is ameliorated by a *sprezzatura* totally absent from *Arcadia*. Just how high are Sidney's claims for poetry in the *Defence of Poesie*, few critics have yet realized; this is not the place to examine

1. Greville, *Life*, p. 6.

them, but we can at least note that they include giving flesh to Ideas of the good, turning literary examples into "verteous action," and hence the perfection of man by bestowing "a Cyrus upon the world to make many Cyruses." While *Astrophel and Stella* could scarcely be claimed as a morally earnest work, it is notable that its main innovation in the sonnet tradition was to take the focus away from the mistress and the progress of love, into the mind of the lover himself, there to explore the conflict of amorous and ethical values.

Sidney himself might have termed his book a treatise rather than a story, in keeping with the letter to his brother Robert on the writing of history:

> a story [history] is either to be considered as a storie, or as a treatise which besides that addeth many thinges for profite and ornament; as a story, he is nothing but a narration of thinges done, with the beginnings, cawses, and appendences thereof, in that kinde your method must be to have *seriem temporum* very exactlie. . . . In that kinde [treatise] yow have principally to note the examples of vertue or vice, with their good or evell successes, the establishments or ruines of greate Estates, with the cawses, the tyme and circumstances of the lawes they write of, the entrings, and endings of warrs, and therein the strategems against the enimy, and the discipline upon the soldiour, and thus much as a very Historiographer.[2]

The stress here is on completeness, copiousness; it is important to realize that the moral force of *Arcadia* comes not from long moralizing speeches and tedious digressions, but from the kind of fullness of detail one finds in a treatise. It comes, in fact, from the thematic density whereby narrative accretions reinforce and expand points made by the main story.

Since we have treated *Arcadia* in a series of narrative "layers," it might be well to draw them together briefly in order to show how each layer adds to the moral effect of the whole in different

---

2. *Works, 3*, 130–31. The Phillips MS of the Old *Arcadia* bears the title: "A treatis made by Sir Philip Sydney, Knyght, of certeyn accidents in Arcadia"; see Zandvoort, pp. 8, 120.

ways. Stripped to its bare essentials, the plot of the romance is a record of love in Arcadia. The wealth of discussion surrounding the action extends its scope by taking it out of the specific; it shows how the problems encountered in Arcadia are representative of larger problems—of the struggle between different ways of life, of the paradoxical nature of love, of Providence, patience, and the cleansing virtues that keep the soul integrated, of the eventual end of man, and so forth. The pastoral subplot does not expand plot but rather underlines its peculiar quality by a muted contrast; for the shepherds face love, internal disorder, marriage, and death in parallel to the young princes in order to show how different life is in the achieved state of natural justice toward which they, the princes, strive. That love is more difficult in the world of action than in nature, that the state of self-division cannot be suffered so patiently nor assuaged so easily, that the problem of marriage is complicated by lust, that death is more difficult to face—all of these realizations that the pastoral games force on us underline the fact that the problems of the two young men are typical of the fallen state of man. The chivalric subplots, which reinforce the major problems rather than adding to their number, also bring out this factor by an opposite kind of contrast. They all occur in a bad world, and therefore present concrete examples of the dangers the heroes face—of love's disruption of the virtuous active life, of passion erupting to destroy the soul and the state, of the results of failure in belief and in control. Finally, the large design of Arcadian decline and readjustment expands the action: it shows that the state suffers the same essential dangers and strives toward the same kind of goal as the individual soul does, that the justice needed by the soul is necessary to the state too, and that the soul of the ruler needs justice not only for its own happiness but for the good of the state as well.

Contrast, reinforcement, expansion; each narrative layer deepens the moral force of plot. We have called *Arcadia's* plot a moralized one. But so great is the thematic density of this book, "at once a romance and a treatise," that it is fair to say that Sidney used the pastoral romance as a vehicle for exploring problems of moral philosophy. The problems acted out on the stage of *Arcadia* can be reduced to two related questions, each involving an evaluation of the experience the young princes undergo: the question of the active versus the contemplative life, and the problem of love's relation to virtue. Though answers to these problems arise in the course of *Arcadia*, they are only tentative, for what is salient in this book is, in keeping with the fictional mode of the 1580's and Sidney's own skeptical cast of mind, the fictional critique of standard answers to important questions about living.

The first problem to arise in Arcadia concerns the adjustment of the claims of the active and the contemplative lives. Should a man choose Pallas Athene or Juno? Does the pursuit of contemplative wisdom necessitate complete abandonment of the world (the price Lipsius seemed ready to pay)? Must there, in fact, be a choice, or is there possible a harmony of soul which can embrace both? And, more pointedly, might it not be that contemplative separation from the disciplined life of action unstrings the mental sinews and releases impulses best kept under strict control? This is the first question the heroes discuss, and with good cause, for the contemplative life they go on to lead in the retreat holds little besides disorder, mental tension, pain, and humiliation for them. Freedom from normal restraint certainly brings out the worst in Basilius and Gynecia, in tempting them to indulge passions inconceivable in the public life at court; and the sense of alienation produced in the young men by contemplation is so great that it paralyzes them completely for a while (as if they are in a state of shock caused by seeing The House of Holiness metamorphosed into The Cave of Despair). Perhaps the state of mind conventionally characterized as dying "in respect of those dead things" of the world in order "to live unto God" is actually what Euarchus says it is, the "burying" of oneself alive to avoid "doing good, the onely happie action of mans life" (437).

By asking these questions, Sidney entered one of the major ethical debates of the sixteenth century, for the pull of the two lives formed one of the many tensions that Sidney felt characterized his century: "in your letters I fancy I see a picture of the age in which we live: an age that resembles a bow too long bent, it must be unstrung or it will break."[3] Essentially, discussion of the virtue of wisdom resolved itself into a conflict between those like Luther, Bovillus, Lefèvre d'Étaples, and the Neoplatonists, who considered it a body of knowledge, a contemplative virtue, and humanists like Erasmus, Vives, Le Caron, and Cardan, who thought of it as active, as the perfection of the will by ethical precepts.[4] Especially as sharpened by the Tudor conflict between politics and religion, this problem was bequeathed to Sidney by the previous generation, as *A Dialogue between Pole and Lupset* and the works, life, and death of Thomas More amply testify.

Sidney's position, though it stresses the need for active virtue, indicates a modus vivendi between the two ways of life rather than a rejection of one for the other. His answer is in fact the classical answer: Plato's answer (that the philosopher-king must attain a vision of the Good in order to mold his kingdom actively toward perfection), Macrobius' answer (that he is doubly blessed who, like Scipio, combines the political virtues with the cleansing virtues), Aristotle's answer, and Lupset's answer:

> he [Aristotle] teacheth and showeth most manifestly the perfection of man to stand jointly in both, and nother in the bare contemplation and knowledge of things separate from all business of the world, nother in the administration of the common weal, without any further regard and direction thereof: for of them, after his sentence, the one is the end of the other.[5]

Contemplation is not the death of action; rather, it is what animates action and harnesses it in the drive toward perfection. Contemplation, in fact, forms the capstone in the education of the Christian Prince, for it makes his soul complete under the governance of God. That is what the ending of the book tells us. But how is the prince to reach that goal when he finds that the con-

---

3. *Correspondence*, ed. Pears, p. 36.
4. That is the picture which emerges from Eugene F. Rice, Jr., *The Renaissance Idea of Wisdom*, Harvard Historical Monographs, 37 (Cambridge, Mass., 1958).
5. Thomas Starkey, *A Dialogue between Reginald Pole and Thomas Lupset*, ed. Kathleen M. Burton (London, 1948), p. 24.

templative life is definitely not a serene retirement, but instead a series of humiliations, disorders, and temptations for desire to drown the soul? Sidney's answer makes use of the very failure which his realistic view of contemplative experience insisted upon. For failure becomes the necessary condition for submission to Providence; the hero must be released from all external controls or pressures in order to act out all tendencies to lust, lassitude, deceit, and despair and so come to know his own weaknesses, to trust God to repair them, and hence to purify himself of them. And the initial disintegration—the breakdown of set ways and poses—is necessary, too, to make way for the final reintegration on the plane of human perfection.[6] Here we come to Sidney's second question, for it is love that produces failure in his romance.

Is love of a woman a virtue or a vice? an aid to perfection or a danger that destroys the soul? Granting the necessity, even the superiority of the contemplative over the active life, does human love really lead to contemplation, to union with the One by way of the virtues, as Ficino, Pico, and Castiglione said? Here the Sidney of *Astrophel and Stella* faces us with an answer that is frankly skeptical as we have seen: though the Platonic ladder is worthy of respect as a concept, and could even be real if the world were the Edenic place Strephon and Klaius inhabit, all is not so golden in our world. Love in *Arcadia* is best characterized by the prophecy Musidorus reports, that "love was threatned, & promised to him, & so to his cousin, as both the tempest & haven of their best yeares" (123). Sidney's compendious treatment of love in *Arcadia* is all the more impressive for the fully truthful and therefore complex attitude he takes toward it.

Sidney's dual attitude toward love is part and parcel of the over-all tone of the work: if it is an exaggeration to say that

6. A good analogue to this action is Book VI of *The Faerie Queene*, where Calidore must leave the world of action for a valley of contemplation, wherein he must undergo humiliation of a mild sort, and have his assumptions shaken thereby, in order to achieve the love of a woman and to realize how the heavenly graces are incorporated in her. Then, once perfected by a vision of the full importance and spiritual ramifications of the virtue he defended in the world, he may act out Christ's harrowing of Hell and achieve his quest in the world of active virtue.

Arcadia *as a Pastoral Romance*

Arcadia is as much a rejection of the experience it records as a celebration of it, yet we can say that its attitude is at least ambiguous. Consider the nature of the pastoral retreat. Like all of the inner circles of romance, it contains elements of good and evil (here defined as justice and lust) in an especially pure form. But its center does not propose a refuge from evil in the form of a shrine linking the natural to the supernatural; rather, it is microcosmic, forcing us back into the nature of man. The cave, which brings into focus the crucial actions (including the interview with Gynecia, the death of Basilius, and the trial), is the center of the retreat's exploration of man in his relation to reality; for expectation and result, appearance and reality, are there confounded—all as a result of human actions, which use the deceit of religious retreat to cover lust, make expected friendship turn into a sexual attack, and turn sensual satisfaction into death. In this way the cave acts as a dark glass reflecting the nature of man as ambivalent.

Therefore, the events for which this cave forms a focus are degrading and even shameful as well as instructive and humiliating. This is true not only for Basilius and his passionate queen, whom the freedom of pastoral life undoes, but also for those on the way to perfection, as we have seen.

Yet for all this it would be ridiculous to maintain that Sidney thought of his plot as a regrettable incident. The result of the incident, after all, is perfection: the princes can win their princesses only after they achieve the original justice proper to the supreme Christian hero. Surely their faults were small, the faults of the inexperienced rather than the sins of the corrupted will; if they have indulged their desires further than was prudent, it was done only in order to learn to control those desires, to become better men than they were while they kept them strictly leashed. As we have said, disintegration occurs only to force reintegration on a higher moral plane, as proper to *Arcadia's* key concept of *trial*, in which one must explore his faults to the full, then suffer willingly the evils resulting from these faults in order to become pure of soul. And it is love, with its dual nature, that supplies the elements of contemplative trial—the emotion is the motive power driving the lover toward his moral goal, the beloved is his guidepost, the failures and temptations along the way are the fires that burn away impurities.

Tradition has it that *Arcadia* owes its inception to its author's enforced retirement to Wilton in 1580. Whether or not this is true, *Arcadia* does present the same ambiguous feelings with which Sidney himself embraced the life of retirement, for he wrote to Languet earlier:

> And the use of the pen, as you may perceive, has plainly fallen from me; and my mind itself, if it was ever active in any thing, is now beginning, by reason of my indolent ease, imperceptibly to lose its strength, and to relax without any reluctance. For to what purpose should our thoughts be directed to various kinds of knowledge, unless room be afforded for putting it into practice? . . . *But the mind itself, you will say, that particle of the divine mind, is cultivated in this manner.* This indeed, if we allow it to be the case, is a very great advantage: but let us see whether we are not giving a beautiful but false appearance to our splendid errors. *For while the mind is thus, as it were drawn out of itself, it cannot turn its powers inward for thorough self-examination;* to which employment no labor that men can undertake, is any way to be compared.[7]

In this letter Sidney attributes to Languet the standard Stoic-Platonist view of retirement represented by his friend Lipsius, and pits against it the Calvinistic insistence on self-examination, "the knowledge of a mans selfe, in the Ethike and Politique consideration, with the end of well doing, and not of well knowing onely," which he proclaimed in the *Defence* to be "the highest end of the mistresse knowledge."[8] That is the problem *Arcadia* faces: the problem of moral improvement in the divided hero whose soul is rapt from his proper self in amorous contemplation. Sidney's response was to re-evaluate the nature of contemplative experience entirely, asserting that *contemplation was not merely a retreat, but a trial of the soul as well.* Though the place and the life there induced rest, a hero's soul was jarred by this unaccustomed rest to examine and thus to know itself. And, as we have seen, the ambigu-

7. Letter of March 1, 1578, in *Correspondence*, ed. Pears, p. 143. Italics mine.
8. See *Works*, 3, 11.

ous nature of love was essential to Sidney's solution because it transformed the serene pastoral life into a trial by puzzling the will. If that were not enough, Sidney supplied guides to self-examination in the ethical sphere in Pamela and Philoclea, as well as accusers of the self in the political sphere in the persons of Philanax and Euarchus.

If the concept of trial is Sidney's intellectual solution of the difficulties inherent in love and contemplation, then the emotional resolution occurs in the series of tonal adjustments we found in the last two books of his romance. Such an adjustment of the attitudes of praise and blame is achieved through two changes in point of view, for the action that has heretofore been conducted in the hermetically sealed retreat ends in the eyes of the world at large, and the exclusive viewpoint of the two young men yields in the end to the older eyes of two hostile observers. Both Philanax and Euarchus disapprove of the pastoral retreat and what occurs there, the one passionately, for political reasons, the other judiciously, for moral reasons. For both of them, unrestricted love is pure danger, contemplative withdrawal a kind of burial of the soul. But their views are not final; they are only part of Sidney's strategy first to generate antithetical attitudes and then to reach a synthesis by their interaction. In the formal trial the young men gradually convince everyone of the falseness of Philanax' arguments and force Euarchus to recognize the gap between formal judgment and true justice. It is in the dialectic of the trial that the opposed attitudes merge into a true evaluation of the Arcadian experience.

The complex tone of *Arcadia* is a good indication of its rather paradoxical relation to the older pastoral romances. It takes up all their issues and complicates them extensively, and this complication is of great value: it both activizes the latent meanings in the genre and subjects them to a long serious criticism. The first of Sidney's two transforming operations was to make the action of pastoral romance explicit. He saw that the series of tonal contrasts between pastoral life and life in the world could be subsumed in the conflict between active and contemplative values, their original tension, and the final completion of one by the other.

Furthermore, he saw that the values of the contemplative pastoral life—humility and harmony—were the very reverse of those that man had embraced to his ruin, and that the pastoral place—like Eden—was the fit and necessary place for his partial regaining of what he had lost, that is, natural justice. This was the action of Dante's *Purgatorio*, where the re-establishment of justice in the pilgrim's soul was signalized by his crossing into the harmonious Earthly Paradise—an action rather feebly conveyed from Dante to Sannazaro by Boccaccio's *Ameto* and rediscovered by Sidney. After all, what had the pastoral romance—with all its vagueness and naïve optimism—been about if not this very regaining of original justice by a purifying contemplation in the humble and unspoiled natural world? Sidney saw the moral pattern of injustice and new justice in the plot of disintegration, analysis, and reintegration, and restored it.

Sidney's second operation was to qualify the optimism of pastoral romance in order to bring its vision closer to observed human reality. Tillyard is right in contending that the introduction of Cecropia gives *Arcadia* "a new and different kind of seriousness" and turns it "into a different kind of novel, one dealing principally with the ultimate problems of man's destiny" by showing real evil in her and thus causing trials and martyrdom.[9] But *Arcadia* is unique among romances not only because Sidney takes cognizance of evil—and in a scale of evil ranging from Cecropia and Anaxius through the tragic Amphialus torn between love and selfishness down to the merely passionate Gynecia—but because he makes us understand it fully in human and serious terms. Evil here is not so trivial as in the faithless lover of the older romances, nor so melodramatic as in the evil enchanter or the savage; it is rather the motion of the perverted will toward the self, to the harm of the self and others. Just as evil appears here in psychological terms as *cupiditas*, so too is good a willing act of submission, *charitas;* and good is very difficult to achieve. We have made much of the fact that the center of *Arcadia*'s world is a cave exemplifying the ambiguity of reality and man's soul rather than the usual temple or

9. Tillyard, p. 298.

shrine. This is the key to Sidney's vision of life. His plot is conducted entirely on the human level; the resolution comes about not by grace or magic or even prophecy, but by a willed action of the soul.

Just as *Arcadia* lacks the overriding supernatural orientation of a Sannazaro, so too does it exhibit the ambivalence rather than the innocence of the human condition. This tenor of Sidney's romance sets it apart from all previous ones. Innocence is a state that one achieves rather than inherits, and the state of original justice which the romance posited implicitly for its end can be reached only through trial. Sidney's microcosmic pastoral retreat has more astringency than its models, for it contains temptations as well as guideposts; his action is more realistic, for he knew that purification comes about by suffering, not by some tender-hearted mortal gift. As that other great English humanist, Platonist, and Calvinist, Milton, wrote, "Assuredly we bring not innocence into the world, we bring impurity much rather; that which purifies us is trial, and trial is by what is contrary."

The Old Arcadia

by Richard A. Lanham

FOR PALMER AND CAROL

Acknowledgments

Few literary epitaphs have been more cruel—or more persistently correct—than Mrs. Barbauld's laconic remark that Sidney's *Arcadia* was a volume which "all have heard of . . . some few possess, but that nobody reads." This hollow notoriety is too bad. For it is not only the scholar's reluctance to let older literature die a natural death which prompts those who know Sidney's delightful story to wish it a larger audience than it now possesses. It has been undervalued and misunderstood. Past generations have invariably put on the tinted glasses of the Sidney legend before beginning to read. They have read a form of the romance which is the product not of Sidney's firm and precise architectonic skill but of his sister's and his friends' unavoidable makeshift. Taken together, these two unhappy accidents have created a wider range of disagreement and misunderstanding than has afflicted any other major Elizabethan work. I try, by polemically widening this range, finally to narrow it.

I would like to thank the General Editor of the Yale Studies in English, Benjamin C. Nangle, for much good counsel; and to acknowledge a long-standing intellectual debt to my teacher in the Renaissance, and the supervisor of the Yale doctoral dissertation out of which this essay grew, Davis P. Harding.

Acknowledgment is made to the publishers for permission to quote from the following works: *The Poems of Sir Philip Sidney*, ed. William A. Ringler, Oxford University Press; C. S. Lewis, *English Literature in the Sixteenth Century: Excluding Drama*, Oxford University Press; Aristotle's *Rhetorica*, trans. W. Rhys Roberts, Oxford University Press; *The Prose Works of Sir Philip Sidney*, ed. Albert Feuillerat, Cambridge University Press. I would also like to thank Mr. Peter M. Miller, Jr., and Mr. Paul J. Cooke for permission to quote from their unpublished doctoral dissertations.

R.A.L.

Hanover, N.H.
March 1965.

". . . doe not his Arcadian Romances
live after him, admired by oure foure-
eyed Criticks?"

FULKE GREVILLE, *Life of Sidney*

1. Texts

The textual history of Sidney's two versions of *Arcadia* has been told and retold so frequently in recent years [1] that only a brief résumé of it need be repeated here. No one knows precisely when Sidney began the original *Arcadia*, how much time was occupied in the writing of it, or when it was finished. According to Edmund Molyneux, at one time secretary to Sidney's father, Sidney began it "at his vacant and spare times of leisure" after returning from his German embassy in June of 1577.[2] He wrote it for his sister Mary, who had become the Countess of Pembroke during his Continental absence, and dedicated it to her. It appears to have been composed in broken times. Sidney himself, in the famous dedicatory letter which he prefixed to the first version of the ro-

1. See the relevant sections in the following works: F.S.Boas, *Sir Philip Sidney: Representative Elizabethan* (London, 1955); Marcus S. Goldman, *Sir Philip Sidney and the Arcadia*, reprinted from University of Illinois Studies in Language and Literature, 17, Nos. 1–2 (Urbana, 1934); Kenneth Orne Myrick, *Sir Philip Sidney as a Literary Craftsman*, Harvard Studies in English, 14 (Cambridge, Mass., 1935); William A. Ringler, Jr., ed., *The Poems of Sir Philip Sidney* (Oxford, 1962); R. W. Zandvoort, *Sidney's Arcadia: A Comparison between the Two Versions* (Amsterdam, 1929).
2. Quoted in Boas, p. 58.

mance, describes to his sister the circumstances of its birth: "Your deare selfe can best witnes the maner, being done in loose sheetes of paper, most of it in your presence, the rest, by sheetes, sent unto you, as fast as they were done." [3] This modest disclaimer has often been dismissed as the polite self-depreciation of the gentleman amateur, but Sidney's latest, and best, editor sees no reason to question it, so long as one remembers that he kept a copy for himself (one which he subsequently revised "on at least five different occasions" [4]). Sidney clearly spent enough time in his sister's company, both at her country house at Wilton and in London, to make his description plausible.

Sidney would seem to have finished the first version of the romance by 1581 at the latest, for in that year Thomas Howell (in his volume of poetry *Devices*) mentions the *Arcadia* and chides Sidney for too long having kept it from circulation. On the basis of this terminal date, 1580 has become the accepted date of completion. It is a conjectural date. But the supporting evidence is substantial. Sidney was rusticated at Wilton from March to August of that year and his famous restless energy may well have found a fictional outlet. The title of the Phillips manuscript of the Old *Arcadia* reads: "A treatis made by Sir Phillip Sydney, Knyght, of certeyn accidents in Arcadia, made in the yeer 1580 and emparted to some few of his frends in his lyfe tyme and to more sence his unfortunat deceasse." [5] In October of 1580 Sidney wrote to his brother, promising to send his "toyful booke" by February; if this book was the original *Arcadia*, then Sidney did not finish at least until the close of 1580, and possibly later. Unfortunately we do not know how much, if any, of the toyful booke he sent by the following February, or even certainly that the original *Arcadia* was the "toyful booke."

Until very recently a student of the *Arcadia* could only con-

3. *The Prose Works of Sir Philip Sidney*, ed. Albert Feuillerat (2d printing, 4 vols. Cambridge, 1962), *1, 3*, hereafter cited as *Works*. The pagination of this printing is the same as that of the first printing for *1* and *4*, and for the early part of *3*, including the *Defence of Poesie*.

4. Ringler, p. 366.

5. *Works, 4*, viii, n. 1.

jecture when Sidney began the thorough revision which was to become the fragment of the New *Arcadia*. Today, thanks to the illuminating and extremely painstaking researches of Professor William A. Ringler, Jr.,[6] one is free to think with some confidence of 1584 as the date when Sidney began his radical revisions. Well into the third book, he laid down his pen in mid-sentence, never again—so far as we know—to take it up. We know neither when he stopped nor why. It has been commonly assumed that death cut short his labors. Thus the editor of the 1613 folio wrote: "Thus far the worthy Author has revised or inlarged that first written Arcadia of his . . . having a purpose likewise to have new or-dered, augmented, and concluded the rest, had he not bene pre-vented by untymely death." [7]

The eight surviving manuscripts of the original version,[8] and the evidence of at least five more now lost, indicate some manu-script circulation, though if we believe Molyneux ("a special dear friend he should be that could once obtain a copy of it" [9]) the demand outstripped the supply. The work was never printed in Sidney's lifetime. When his friend Fulke Greville learned that its publication was contemplated, he took steps to have the revised fragment used in its stead. Ponsonby, who had called the possible publication of the original version to Greville's attention, issued in 1590 the revised fragment in quarto. A folio followed in 1593. This edition added to the revised fragment a conclusion consisting of the last three books of the original as edited—some have said bowdlerized—by either the Countess of Pembroke or someone writing in co-operation with her. The extent of her knowledge of Sidney's intentions in the unfinished New *Arcadia* is still a matter of dispute. The manuscripts of the original version gradually dropped from circulation and memory, and the *Arcadia* of literary history has been the composite 1593 folio—or was until 1907,

6. Ringler, pp. 364–70.
7. *Works*, 2, 218.
8. A ninth preserves the poems only. The only complete description is given in Ringler's bibliography, pp. 525 ff. See also pp. lx, 364–82.
9. Boas, pp. 57–58.

when Bertram Dobell, a London bookseller, acquired two manuscripts of the original version. In the following year he discovered and purchased a third, and five others have subsequently turned up. The manuscripts show no fundamental differences but a great many minor discrepancies.

The discovery of the original version prompted Dobell and others to speculate further about the dates of composition. "From the juvenility of style and tone of the 'Arcadia,'" wrote Dobell in the article announcing his discovery, "I am inclined to think it was commenced at an earlier date than is usually supposed—perhaps even as early as 1578, though it was probably not finished before 1580."[1] S. L. Wolff, thinking one year too short a time to prompt Howell's complaint, "all to long thou hidste so perfite work," pushed the date back a year or two.[2] But without further evidence, it seems impossible to be certain which dates are correct. An exact dating would be valuable. For example, it would be helpful to know how much, if any, of the original *Arcadia* Sidney had written, or even planned, before Lyly had published *Euphues*. Still more convenient would be some indication of whether any part of the romance, either the last book perhaps or episodes in earlier books, might conceivably have been written after Sidney learned of the negotiations for the marriage of Penelope Devereux to Lord Rich.[3] A knowledge of whether the *Arcadia* was composed substantially at one burst of speed would be significant indeed. An answer to this question would take us far in the study of Sidney's stylistic development, a process at the heart of any comparison of the first version with the second. The chronology of the *Arcadia* is extremely important when one compares it to *Astrophil and Stella* on the one hand and the *Defence of Poesie* on the other. In the absence of any firmer knowledge of this chronology, we can only attempt to be aware always of the limitations our ignorance places upon us.

1. "New Light on Sidney's 'Arcadia,'" *Quarterly Review, 211* (July 1909), 74–100, 82.
2. *The Greek Romances in Elizabethan Prose Fiction* (New York, 1912), p. 344.
3. The negotiations began in early March 1581.

The discovery of the manuscripts of the early version, though it did not clarify dates of composition, did at least set straight the question of the various texts and versions. Briefly, then, we have: (1) an Old *Arcadia* complete in five books with eclogues; (2) a revised fragment, the New *Arcadia*, consisting of two books and a long part of a third, with eclogues (and verse amongst the prose) supplied from the original version by a copyist; and (3) the *Arcadia*, the composite folio of 1593 complete with eclogues— not, of course, of Sidney's own arrangement—which is *the* document of literary history from roughly its publication until the discovery of the original version.[4]

Before the original was known, it was an understandable mistake to half hope and half feel that Sidney's main purpose had somehow emerged intact from the unfortunate circumstances surrounding the publication of the 1593 folio. After Dobell's discovery, however, it should have been clear that this was a vain hope. The differences between the two versions, though not yet completely clear, were sufficiently extensive to render the Old an unreliable guide to what was to have happened in the New. The common assumption that the 1593 folio, flawed though it might be, was a complete artistic whole, could no longer be made. The only "complete" version, as the word is customarily defined, was the original version. The New *Arcadia* was what it is today, a fragment. And the composite *Arcadia* was not one fragment but two, part New and part Old. Implicit in Sidney's very decision to revise is the dissatisfaction he would have felt with the composite form in which his romance has offered itself to later times. For he would not have embarked on a drastic revision of what is, after all, a sufficiently long romance in its original form, into a form which was even longer (and which promised to be vast), had he not envisioned the new version as work of a fundamentally different order. The change in intent (a discussion of the nature and direction of the change must be put off until we examine the Old *Arcadia* in more detail) should be sufficient evidence that the last three books of the Old could not and should not

4. I follow here the nomenclature first employed by Wolff (*The Greek Romances*, pp. 345–46), which has become the accepted usage.

be glued on to the New. However intimate the Countess of Pembroke may have been with Sidney's final intentions [5] she could not continue the revision as he would have.

The composite version has been defended by no less eminent a scholar that the late C. S. Lewis. He writes:

> But these questions [the differences between the *Old* and the *New*], however interesting to the student of Sidney, do not much concern the literary historian. To him 'the Arcadia' must mean the composite text of 1593: it, and it alone, is the book which lived; Shakespeare's book, Charles I's book, Milton's book, Lamb's book, our own book long before we heard of textual criticism. If the recovery of the cancelled version is to prevent our looking steadily at the text which really affected the English mind, it will have been a disaster. [6]

One or two misunderstandings here need clarification. First, we do not know that the first version was "cancelled" in the sense Lewis implies. There is no evidence that Sidney attempted to call in the manuscripts and replace them by a more polished version which death prevented his completing. Not Sidney, but Greville, after Sidney was dead, decided that the revised fragment should be printed instead of the complete first version. We have not a shred of evidence as to which Sidney would have chosen to see the light of printed day, except the dying wish Greville records. This request, the conventional one for a man facing imminent death, was that the whole profane romance be destroyed. We can believe Greville if we choose; we can even accept this dying plea as a considered judgment; but it is hard to infer plausibly from it that Sidney would have preferred either the fragment of the New or the composite *Arcadia* to the Old. Lewis' argument depends, of course, on the natural assumption that what a man revises he will think better. Such an assumption in this case rests on the further assumption that death, and not Sidney, broke off the revision. There is no evidence for this.

5. Ringler by an ingenious chain of reasoning has shown that her knowledge of his intentions was greater than many had hitherto credited. See pp. 375 ff.

6. *English Literature of the Sixteenth Century; excluding Drama* (Oxford, 1954), p. 333.

Lewis' fear that attention to the original may distort our view of the composite folio of 1593 seems wholly gratuitous. We ought to remember that the last three books of the composite version, with the Countess of Pembroke's emendations of course, *are* the original version; when we examine the original we examine at least part of the 1593 folio, and vice versa. More generally, it is hard to see how examination of the original could fail to illuminate Sidney's intention in his revision (a legitimate concern for the literary historian) and still more difficult to imagine anyone's admitting the original version as a document of literary history for the 300-year period when it was lost. The area of confusion which scholars should avoid is the one that Lewis goes on to invade: the discussion of the composite *Arcadia* as representing in its present form Sidney's plan or purpose. To use the composite *Arcadia* in discussions of the romance's subsequent influence is one thing. To probe in it for Sidney's primary intention, his reflection of the spirit of the age, is quite another, and a method bound to be misleading since it treats as a single work parts of what are, as they have come down to us, two different romances. The differences between them, of interest both to critics and to literary historians, Lewis' assumptions about the Old *Arcadia* force him to ignore.

Awkward as the situation may be, the modern student of Sidney cannot escape it by ascribing to the composite version an authority that no amount of historical acceptance can confer. We shall never know how Sidney would have finished the New *Arcadia*. By comparing the complete and the incomplete, one can guess. But even the fragile results to be gained from this procedure have most often been sacrificed, for the comparisons between the two have been from the beginning invidious. Dobell not surprisingly felt that the version he had discovered was markedly superior to the revision: "It is to be regretted, I think, that Sir Philip did not leave his work in its original state, since in that form it is much better as a work of art, and very much easier to read than it is in the revised version. . . . It [the Old] is in fact a well constructed and well digested romance, as capable of interesting the modern novel-reader as most stories of the day." [7] Mario Praz

7. "New Light," pp. 81–82, 89.

in an article in the *London Mercury* agreed that "as a whole and in details, it is really superior to its successor. . . . In the old version he depicts life, in the new one he gives us a barren casuistry." [8] F. S. Boas, too, has expressed a qualified preference for the Old, because it seems to possess greater dramatic unity.[9] By and large, though, the best students of Sidney have preferred the New, unfinished as it is. Albert Feuillerat writes in the preface to his edition of the Old *Arcadia:* "This first form of Sidney's celebrated romance is certainly inferior in literary value to the revised form published in 1590. . . . It is at best the immature work of a young man of great promise who is trying his hand at romance writing." [1] R. W. Zandvoort agrees with this appraisal: "It is evident that the original draft stands to the revision as a first sketch to a finished composition." He feels the new demonstrably superior to the old, though he does paradoxically "admit, without prevarication, that it [the Old *Arcadia*] does present a simpler, more coherent story, and that it fully deserves to be appreciated on its own merits, apart from any comparison with the later form. Viewed as a whole, its effect is more satisfying than that of the unfinished and complex fabric of the New *Arcadia*." [2] Kenneth O. Myrick, putting both feet on the same side of the fence, calls the new "a far more impressive work." [3] Other critics have adopted this view.[4] Common to all is the assumption (not always stated) that the Old is simply a rough draft of the New.[5]

Such comparisons teach us little; neither version should be

---

8. "Sidney's Original Arcadia" (March 1927), pp. 507–14, 509–10.
9. *Sir Philip Sidney*, p. 119.
1. *Works, 4*, v–vi.
2. *Sidney's Arcadia*, pp. 102, 118.
3. *Sidney as Literary Craftsman*, p. 190.
4. Marcus S. Goldman, for example, describes it as "the real *Arcadia*, the revision by which, despite its incompleteness, our opinion of Sidney's purpose must be formed" (*Sidney and the Arcadia*, p. 158). Kenneth Muir ("Sir Philip Sidney," *Writers and Their Work*, No. 120, p. 15) and Albert W. Osborn (*Sir Philip Sidney en France* [Paris, 1932], p. 74) point out especially the superior style of the New *Arcadia*.
5. Myrick writes, in another connection "lessons are numerous. . . . In the first draft, however, they are to be found in theoretical discussions no less than in the deeds of the characters" (*Sidney as Literary Craftsman*, p. 296).

measured against the other. A more promising procedure, it seems to me, would be to consider the Old *Arcadia* as an independent, coherent work, to describe as accurately as may be its method and purpose. The Old merits a fresh look, for it has the great advantage of being an artistic whole. It was not, one should hardly need emphasize, written as a "rough draft." We can assess Sidney's intention with some confidence, as we cannot with the New or the composite version. Then, after such an assessment, we can if we wish examine the New to see, by comparison with the Old, what Sidney intended in the revision. But the comparison will hardly tell us much if we do not take the trouble to read the original version closely. For Tucker Brooke was surely right when he wrote: "It will be better to speak of this admirable story [the Old *Arcadia*] separately, for nothing but confusion has ever resulted from the attempt to criticize it in conjunction with the unfinished enlargement that Sidney later undertook." [6]

Even considered separately, the Old *Arcadia* has generated sufficient confusion. No two readers can agree on just what Sidney's long prose work is or does. Literary opinion has been as various as Polonius' outburst on mixed genres. Ostensibly, at least, the piece seems to have all the attributes of a pastoral. Francis Meres, for example, wrote in *Palladis Tamia:*

> As Theocrites in Greek, Virgil and Mantuan in Latine, Sanazar in Italian, and the Authour of *Amintae Gaudia* and *Walsingham's Meliboeus* are the best for Pastorall: so amongst us the best in this kind are Sir Philip Sidney.[7]

But this is hardly a satisfying classification. Tucker Brooke described it as "a love trifle for the amusement of the fair and worthy ladies who are in the beginning being constantly invoked," but it

6. "The Renaissance," in Albert C. Baugh et al., *A Literary History of England* (New York, 1948), p. 474.

7. *Elizabethan Critical Essays*, ed. G. Gregory Smith (2 vols. London, 1904), 2, 321. Puttenham, too, classifies Sidney as a pastoral poet: "For Eglogue and pastorall Poesie, Sir *Philip Sydney* and Maister *Challenner*, and that other Gentleman who wrate the late shepheardes Callender" (*Elizabethan Critical Essays*, 2, 65). To which version either refers it seems impossible to tell certainly. Puttenham wrote before either printed edition, Meres after both.

was a trifle "executed in a very masculine spirit." [8] M. S. Goldman, on the other hand, called it "a pastoral of heroic accent and purpose." "In the original version," he wrote, "the pastoral decoration is not, perhaps, in just proportion, and tends, therefore, to obscure in some measure the heroic intent. But the intent, for all that, is there: heroic incident, didactic tone, and steady strenuousness of attitude reveal it at every turn." [9] For Myrick it is simply a "pastoral romance." [1] This adequate workaday phrase is not necessarily invalidated by the most recent description: "The *Old Arcadia* is a tragi-comedy in five acts, with a serious double plot . . . combined with a comic underplot." [2] Whether the term tragicomedy was used or not, most students of the romance have sensed in it a fundamental ambivalence in attitude. The emphasis has been on the serious or on the comic elements as it suited a particular conception of Sidney or of a larger pattern of his work.

Conjecture about the Old *Arcadia*'s fundamental purpose has been equally wide-ranging. Sidney's friend and biographer, Fulke Greville, thought the *Arcadia* in both its versions primarily serious political allegory.[3] E. M. W. Tillyard considered ethics, not politics, its central concern.[4] For another modern scholar, P. J. Cooke, light-hearted frivolity was its guiding spirit.[5] Against this, we may contrast Ringler's assertion that "The *Arcadia*, in both its old and new forms, is the most important original work of English prose fiction produced before the eighteenth century." [6]

Such diverse opinion would hardly lead one to suspect that Sidney himself had seen fit to confide to posterity what he was about. The famous introductory letter to his sister, though often prefaced to the New *Arcadia*, clearly (since it implies the work is complete) refers to the Old.[7] Familiar as it is, I reproduce it here as

8. *A Literary History*, p. 475.
9. *Sidney and the Arcadia*, pp. 157–58.
1. *Sidney as Literary Craftsman*, p. 194.
2. Ringler, p. xxxvii.
3. *Life of Sir Philip Sidney* etc., ed. Nowell Smith (Oxford, 1907), pp. 14–15.
4. *The English Epic* (New York, 1954), p. 296.
5. "The Spanish Romances in Sir Philip Sidney's *Arcadia*," abstract of unpublished dissertation (University of Illinois, 1939), p. 12.
6. Page xxxvi.
7. Dobell, Feuillerat, Myrick, Ringler all agree on this.

the only authentic—though difficult to interpret—evidence of Sidney's conception of the work:

Here now have you (most deare, and most worthy to be most deare Lady) this idle worke of mine: which I fear (like the Spiders webbe) will be thought fitter to be swept away, then worn to any other purpose. For my part, in very trueth (as the cruell fathers among the Greekes, were woont to doo to the babes they would not foster) I could well find in my harte, to cast out in some desert of forgetfulnes this child, which I am loath to father. But you desired me to doo it, and your desire, to my hart is an absolute commandement. Now, it is done onelie for you, onely to you: if you keepe it to your selfe, or to such friendes, who will weigh errors in the ballaunce of good will, I hope, for the fathers sake, it will be pardoned, perchance made much of, though in it selfe it have deformities. For indeede, for severer eyes it is not, being but a trifle, and that triflinglie handled. Your deare selfe can best witnes the maner, being done in loose sheetes of paper, most of it in your presence, the rest, by sheetes, sent unto you, as fast as they were done. In summe, a young head, not so well stayed as I would it were, (and shall be when God will) having many many fancies begotten in it, if it had not ben in some way delivered, would have growen a monster, & more sorie might I be that they came in, then that they gat out. But his chiefe safetie, shalbe the not walking abroad; & his chiefe protection, the bearing the liverye of your name; which (if much much good will do not deceave me) is worthy to be a sanctuary for a greater offender. This say I, because I knowe the vertue so; and this say I, because it may be ever so; or to say better, because it will be ever so. Read it then at your idle tymes, and the follyes your good judgement wil finde in it, blame not, but laugh at. And so, looking for no better stuffe, then, as in an Haberdashers shoppe, glasses, or feathers, you will continue to love the writer, who doth excedinglie love you; and most most hartelie praies you may long live, to be a principall orna-ment to the familie of the *Sidneis*.

Your loving Brother
Philip Sidnei [8]

8. *Works, I*, 3–4.

The question we must ask ourselves, of course, is "Did he mean it?" Older opinion tended to accept the letter at face value and hence not really to bother reading further. Recent comment has discounted it. Ringler, for example, sees it unmistakably as a polite disclaimer:

> With his usual gentlemanly self-depreciation he called his work 'a trifle, and that triflingly handled'; but the trifle was a volume of some 180,000 words, and the intricacy of its design and finish of its parts show that it was planned and executed with the greatest of care. The manuscripts reveal that even after it was finished he made minor revisions on at least five different occasions before 1584, when he began the complete recasting and rewriting of the narrative that remains as the unfinished *New Arcadia*.[9]

We can agree, as I think we must, without dismissing the letter as altogether useless. In the absence of evidence to the contrary, there seems no reason to doubt that a request from his sister may have set Sidney to writing. Once started, he may well have used the many opportunities a long prose romance offered to deliver himself of the "many many fancies" which clamored for expression. Such a procedure he seems almost to confess in the *Defence of Poesie*, and had clearly followed in *Astrophil and Stella*. The autobiographical element alone might suffice to make him restrict circulation of the manuscript to his sister and her acquaintance. That Sidney did not at first envisage the popularity of his "idle work," though merely an assumption, seems a reasonable one; his other great works were ahead of him, he had only *The Lady of May* done in this vein to judge by, and his friends seem to have kept their enthusiasm for that within bounds. How could he predict its popularity? How could he then help writing for a limited audience?

Sidney may well have commenced what was to be so appreciable a labor with a more modest objective. A fledgling author began with pastoral. He might well have considered a literary exercise done for the family as part of his training as a courtier,

9. Page xxxvi.

as Castiglione recommends: "Let him [the Courtier] be versed in the poets, as well as in the orators and historians, and let him be practiced also in writing verse and prose, especially in our own vernacular; for, besides the personal satisfaction he will take in this, in this way he will never want for pleasant entertainment with the ladies, who are usually fond of such things." [1] Though Sidney's "exercise" is hardly the one Castiglione thought of, it could have begun as such. Thus the letter may not be such an extreme case of *sprezzatura*—a careful craftsmanship and an amateur pose, which Castiglione sees as the crowning glory of the courtier in life as well as art—as at first it appears to be. Discounted, it should not be altogether devalued.

The radical disagreement about the Old *Arcadia* seems to me to be caused by the confusion of two related but essentially different questions: (1) Is the Old *Arcadia* comic or serious? In other words, into what genre did Sidney design it to fit? (2) How seriously did he regard the writing of it? In spite of its length, is it still an offhand job? Or carefully wrought? The simple fact that a comedy, even a frivolity, may be seriously and carefully conceived really does seem to require repetition. Similarly a tragi-comedy may be conceived as a "Look Ma! No Hands!" show-piece. Neither of these separate questions can be left unanswered in a study of the Old *Arcadia* but they must be answered separately. The second question would seem at first blush a biographical rather than critical one, and unanswerable as well. It is neither. The spirit in which Sidney wrote and in which he desired us to read is of the greatest importance, as we shall later see. And it can reasonably be inferred from the text. We need not flee to biography.

From the text alone it is difficult to account for the wide disparity of views about the Old *Arcadia*. Assumptions brought to it must be responsible for some of the confusion. Evaluation of the prefatory letter is only one area of prejudgment. Virtually all scholars (and the original version has had few readers who were

1. *The Book of the Courtier*, trans. Charles S. Singleton (Anchor Books, 1959), p. 70.

not) have come to it from a reading of the composite *Arcadia* and/or the New. Their response is usually preconditioned. They are bound to think of the Old as a rough draft. After the bewildering variety of the New the Old is bound to seem plain or, to the sympathetic, classically simple. Since it is unflattering to Sidney to think he wrote thousands upon thousands of words with neither change nor improvement in style or wisdom, changes and improvements in both have naturally been detected. If the New seems an epic, the Old must be one in miniature. This kind of inevitable back-pressure has been applied to the Old *Arcadia* since its discovery.

A second source of prejudice has operated. Perhaps within his own lifetime, certainly from immediately after his death, Sidney has been regarded as the patron saint of Renaissance chivalry. Naturally enough, those elements in his work which reveal his peculiar chivalric sanctity have been dwelt upon. Those that conflict with it have been ignored. The conclusion seems inescapable that, had we known nothing of Sidney's life, most of the comment on the *Arcadia*, Old and New, would hardly have taken the form it has, if indeed it would have been written at all.

A third barrier between the modern reader and either version of the *Arcadia* is the style. Sidney's prose style stands at the opposite extreme from our own. Older critics called it bad, more recent ones call it dated, of historical interest. Almost all who read the *Arcadia* with pleasure come to apologize for the style sooner or later. As a result, the romance has been thought of as primarily a trellis for the flowers of rhetoric, a monument to the mistake of making "concessions to contemporary taste for tinsel and excessive ornament." [2] The style has been a barrier to the meaning, a circumstance that no work of art can survive unmaimed.

This unlucky concatenation of circumstances has smothered an unbiased examination of the original version of Sidney's romance. The present essay proposes to resist these distorting pressures as much as possible, in order to analyze and describe the romance clearly. For it is analysis and not evaluation which is most needed.

2. J. J. Jusserand, *The English Novel in the Time of Shakespeare*, trans. Elizabeth Lee (4th ed. London, 1901), p. 255.

Only then can the romance be properly placed in its historical context. The Old must be considered apart from the New, apart from the Sidney legend. The style must be allowed to do what it was intended to do, not reproached for failing to do what it cannot and was not created to do.

2. Theme and Structure

A studied complexity of structure and a carefully developed
theme are not usually characteristic of the literary amateur hastily
dashing off a jeu d'esprit. He prefers to write from the heart, to
offer the public his sensitivity, or, failing that, his wit, rather than
his organizational powers. He may aridly imitate conventional
forms, but diffuseness is more apt to be his ruling vice. Sidney, who
took pains to establish his amateur standing, has often been accused of both imitation and diffuseness, haste and a too-ready wit.
The *Arcadia* has been sometimes thought a story of gentle people
and courtly deeds unfolding at random in a mist of noble sentiment, with a fairy-tale ending in the last few pages. The eclogues
appear merely as a matter of literary custom, and instead of reliev-
ing the monotony they intensify it. The Old *Arcadia*, especially,
is said to betray the haste and frivolity of its genesis. Its structure
is simple and unchallenging, its theme obvious.

Until very recently this charge stood largely unrefuted. Now,
however, through the labors of two excellent scholars, we need
not ask whether Sidney's romance has a form but rather what in
detail that form is and why Sidney chose to employ it. Walter R.

Davis, in a recent article,[1] analyzed the structure of the New *Arcadia* in illuminating detail. William Ringler, in the introduction to his edition of the *Poems,* has pointed out the careful five-act structure of the original version and Sidney's reason for adopting it:

> Sidney's artistic ideal was to achieve a maximum of variety and complexity within a clearly articulated structure. He achieved this, and overcame the formless meandering of late Greek, medieval, and renaissance long prose tales, by embodying the diverse materials of romance in dramatic form. The *Old Arcadia* is a tragi-comedy in five acts, with a serious double plot (the two pairs of noble lovers with Basilius, Gynecia, and Euarchus) combined with a comic underplot (Dametas and his wife and daughter). The action is carried on by a small group of characters (there are only eighteen major actors) and is unified in both place and time. . . . The renaissance Terentian five-act structure is followed with its movement of protasis, epitasis, and catastrophe. . . . Sidney produced in prose a pastoral tragicomedy before the earliest examples of the genre, the *Aminta* and *Pastor Fido* of Tasso and Guarini, were available in print.[2]

No one need remain any longer in doubt about the broad outlines of the first version of Sidney's romance. But the besetting sin in criticism of the *Arcadia* has been generalization. What is still greatly needed is a detailed examination of Sidney's use of the classic five-act structure. For here, as elsewhere, what Sidney borrowed is finally less important than the use to which he put the borrowing. This use I chronicle in some detail. The uniqueness of Sidney's romance seems to demand it. For we shall find that if the Old *Arcadia* is a tragicomedy, it is one of a very special sort, lacking several of the elements one usually expects to find in the classic five-act form.

The differences between Sidney's mythical kingdom and a stereotyped literary Arcadia are evident from the first page, even from the first sentence:

---

1. "Thematic Unity in the New *Arcadia,*" *Studies in Philology,* 57 (1960), 123–43.
2. Ringler, pp. xxxvii–xxxviii.

Arcadia amonge all the Provinces of *Grece* was ever had in sin-
guler reputation, partly for the sweetnes of ye Aire and other
naturall benefittes: But, principally, for the moderate & well
tempered myndes of the people, who, (fynding howe true a Con-
tentation ys gotten by following the Course of Nature, And
howe the shyning Title of glory somuche affected by other
Nacions, dothe in deede help litle to the happines of lyfe) were
the onely people, which as by theire Justice and providence, gave
neyther Cause nor hope to theyre Neighboures to annoy them,
so were they not stirred with false prayse, to truble others quyett.
Thincking yt a smalle Rewarde for ye wasting of theire owne
lyves in ravening, that their posterity shoulde longe after saye,
they had done so: Eeven the *Muses* seemed to approove theire
good determinacion, by chosing that Contrie as theire cheefest
reparing place.[3]

The "sweetness of ye Aire and other naturall benefittes," traditionally the principal stock-in-trade of the pastoralist, are here
mentioned only to be put aside in favor of the feature attraction of
Arcadia, a docile, tractable working class. Arcadia is a colony of
the muses not because of its bubbling brooks and its grass of a
uniform height, but because of its stable political situation. Good
government, not shrubbery, makes the arts flourish, and Sidney
makes his concern for social order apparent from the first. Arcadia's Duke, Basilius, only barely passes political muster—"a
Prince of sufficient skill, to governe so quyett a Contrie." After
he and his Duchess, Gynecia, and two daughters—"the elder
Pamela, the younger *Philoclea*"—are introduced, Sidney tells of
Basilius' folly in believing the oracle and of his even greater foolishness in seeking to escape it by flight into—to use Sidney's revealing term—a desert. Basilius' first-rate political blunder is

---

3. *Works, 4,* 1. All subsequent references to the Old *Arcadia* will be by page
number only, in parentheses at the end of the quotation. In all quotations from
the several versions of the *Arcadia*, I have regularized all superscribed letters.
and expanded all contractions. I have throughout this essay quoted the text at
some length. I apologize to those who know it well, and hope they will not mind
skipping over quotations which many readers may need in following the argument.

pointed out to him at length by his trusty counselor Philanax. Basilius' intention to retreat into "a Solitary place" is an unprincely failure of nerve, according to Philanax, who counsels in effect that better the known danger than the unknown. Basilius seeks a security greater than virtue, wisdom, and perseverance can offer; greater, that is, than life permits. Rather, says Philanax, "Let youre Subjectes have yow in theyre eyes, Let them see the benefit of youre Justice daily more and more, and so must they needes rather like of present suretyes, then uncerteyne Chaunges, Lastly, whether youre tyme calle yow to live or dye, doo bothe like a Prince" (5). The issue, then, is clearly put by Philanax in terms of action or retreat. The rustication of the princesses seems to him a further error. The oracle had said, it will be remembered, "Thy Elder care shall from thy carefull face / By Princely meane bee stolne, and yet not lost; / Thy Younger shall with Natures bliss embrace / An uncouth Love" (2). Virtue is its own, and its only, defense, says Philanax. A cloistered virtue wilts in the light of day: "O, no, hee can not bee good, that knowes not whye hee ys good, but standes so farr good, as his fortune may keepe him unassayed, but, coming to yt his rude simplicity ys eyther easily chaunged, or easily deceyved" (5). Basilius endures this unexceptionable advice with no more ill grace than princes customarily exhibit on such occasions, then does just as he wishes. He divests himself temporarily of his sovereignty, leaving it in Philanax' hands. Thus begins the complex sequence of events in Arcadia; at the same time the formal exchange of speeches between sovereign and regent-to-be has introduced a central theme of the romance, the temptations of passivity and the need for resolute action. The opening would surely have been familiar to Sidney's first readers. Basilius' dilemma is the one which had begun *Gorboduc* as it was to begin *Lear*, the spectacle of the foolish ruler abdicating his responsibilities.

Next the two heroes of the piece, Pyrocles and Musidorus, appear on stage. A very short biography explains their presence in Arcadia and hints at the prowess the reader can expect them to display. Pyrocles, with "eyther evell or good fortune," immediately falls in love with Philoclea, a likeness of whom he has glimpsed in a portrait of the royal family dutifully displayed by Pyrocles' host Kerxenus. His resulting fondness for dawdling in the isolated (and forbidden) area of Arcadia where the two princesses are secluded draws upon him the rebukes of his friend Musidorus:

> A mynde well trayned and longe exercysed in vertue, (my sweete and worthy Cossen) dothe not easily chaunge any Course yt once undertakes, but uppon well grounded and well weyed Causes: For, beeying witnes to yt self of his owne Inwarde good, yt fyndes no thinge with oute yt of so highe a pryce, for wch yt shoulde bee altered . . . I have marcked in yow, (I will not say an alteracyon) but a Relenting truely and slaking of ye mayne Carryer yow had so notably begun . . . yow subject youre self to solitarynes, the slye Enimy yt moste dothe seperate a man from well doyng.   [10–11]

In reply, Pyrocles reproaches Musidorus for ignoring the manifold blessings of Arcadia, especially its gorgeous scenery. He then confesses his love for Philoclea and his unalterable intention to disguise himself as an itinerant Amazon warrior in order to gain at least her presence and perhaps even her regard. This is altogether too much for his friend, who explodes in several pages of mingled excoriation and cheap but heartfelt advice, finally agreeing, since he cannot hope to change Pyrocles' mind, to help him to his desires. This debate between the two friends, more elaborate than that between Philanax and Basilius, still turns on the same opposition of forces: the demands of duty and the active life on the one hand, and the pursuit of one's desires and hopes into a life of retirement on the other. Each of the "serious" double plots begins with a formal debate on the same subject. Before penetrating the forbidden area any further, Pyrocles arms himself for his new life by changing his clothes. Sidney uses this turning point in the story to indicate that Pyrocles is not foregoing altogether a life of active self-assertion but rather transferring his endeavors from the field of courtly battle to that of courtly love—for it is a mockery of the typical epic "arming-scene" that he chooses to draw:

And to begyn with his heade, thus was hee dressed; His heyre,
which the younge men of *Greece* ware very longe, (accoumpting
them moste beutyfull, that had yt in fayrest quantity) lay uppon
the uppermoste parte of his foreheade in Lockes, some curled,
and some, as yt were forgotten: with suche a Careles care and
with suche an arte so hyding arte, that hee seemed hee woulde
lay them for a Patern whether nature simply or nature helped by
cunning bee the more excellent, the Rest wherof was drawne
into a Coronet of golde wyers, and covered with fethers of dy-
vers Coloures, that yt was not unlike to a hellmett, suche a glitter-
ing shewe yt bare, and so bravely yt was helde up from the heade.
Uppon his body hee ware a kynde of Dublett of skye coloured
Satyn, so plated over with plates of Massy golde, that hee seemed
armed in yt: His sleeves of the same in steade of plates, was
covered with purled Lace.   [23]

And so it goes on until he is completely clothed. Thus attired and
thus befriended he plunges into the desert.

When he has come to a sufficiently solitary place, Cleophila (for
so Pyrocles now calls himself) sits down and sings amidst her sobs
the frequently remarked song "Transformde in shewe, but more
transformde in mynde," which epitomizes for the reader the
change which has come over the young prince:

> Transformde in shewe, but more transformde in mynde,
>   I cease to stryve, with duble Conquest foylde;
> For, woe ys mee, my powers all (I fynde)
>   With owtewarde force, and inward treason spoylde.
>
> For, from withoute, came to myne eyes the blowe,
>   Whereto, myne Inwarde thoughtes did faintly yeelde:
> Bothe these conspirde pore Reasons overthrowe,
>   False in my self, thus have I lost the feelde.
>
> And thus myne eyes are plaste still in one sighte,
>   And thus my thoughtes can thinck but one thing still:
> Thus, reason to his servantes gives his righte,
>   Thus ys my power transformed to youre will.
> What marvell then I take a Womans hewe?
> Since, what I see, thincke, knowe, ys all but yow?   [25]

The victory of passion over reason and the unnatural reversal which Sidney gently mocked in the "arming scene" quoted above are here made explicit to the reader, and Pyrocles is made explicitly aware of them. The consequences to be expected from such a surrender of the bastions of reason are quick to follow. Dametas appears. After he and his witch of a wife and ungainly daughter have been described, and his rise to power over the two princesses explained as still another failure of Basilius' judgment, Dametas is introduced into the presence of the sorrowing Cleophila. His threats to her (the feminine pronoun will be used for Cleophila henceforth) eliciting only firm resistance, he runs to Basilius for help and the Duke thus meets the Amazonian object of his future warmest desires. Cleophila's cover story works even more smoothly on Basilius than she could desire, for he not only welcomes her into the presence of her beloved and transposed namesake but begins to fall in love with her himself. The two princesses, when they come on stage, are described very much as Cleophila was a few pages before. All their garments are full and plain in the Greek fashion, Pamela has a jewel with an impresa on it just as Cleophila does, Philoclea's titillating exposure of almost bare skin at crucial places is very much like that wanton "smalle of his Legg" which Cleophila's flowing gown is cut to display. The later description is clearly meant to recall the former and to compromise further the manly vigor of the enterprise, weakened as it is by the last song. To an unsympathetic Musidorus the picture can hardly escape scorn, but to the transformed shepherd Dorus whom Cleophila meets upon excusing herself it has the ring of truth. For Musidorus also has been transformed by love:

Come Shepearde weedes become youre Masters mynde,
    Yeelde owteward shewe, what Inwarde chaunge hee tryes:
Nor bee abashed, synce suche a guest yow fynde,
    Whose strongest hope in youre weyke comforte lyes.

Come Shepeard weedes attend my woofull Cryes,
    Disuse youre selves from sweete *Menalcas* voyce:
For others bee those Tunes which sorrowes tyes,
    From those clere notes which freely may rejoyce.

> Then powre oute pleynte, and in one worde say this:
> Helples his pleynte, who spoyles him self of blis.   [36]

The song is similar to Pyrocles' lament of two scenes ago and is meant to recall it. Both lament a drastic change in costume and social position, and a still more upsetting loss of self-control and hence of inner harmony. Cleophila seems puzzled and demands of Dorus "what sodeyn chaunge, had thus sodeynly chaunged him? whether the goddess of those woodes had suche a power, to transforme every body, or whether in Deede, as hee had allwayes in all enterpryzes moste faythfully accompanyed her, so hee woulde continew to matche her in this new *Metamorphosis*" (37–38). As the whole world including Cleophila knows from his conventional behavior and appearance, love has struck Musidorus down in turn. The scene, based on the most familiar of plots—Cupid's revenge— obviously recalls the scene discussed earlier in which Pyrocles diffidently confides his love to a scornful Musidorus. Pyrocles taunts Musidorus: "Remember, that love ys a passion, and that a worthy manns reason must ever have the Masterhod" (38). The two scenes, repetitions of essentially the same behavior in the two friends, are typical of Sidney's use of parallel scenes, and of parallel elements within scenes (like the two changes of name and of apparel, the two songs lamenting the change, the two false life histories, and the initial unpleasantness of Basilius to both) for purposes of comic and ironic comparison.

After Dorus has been introduced to the pastoral court and given a shepherd's job under Dametas, all the main characters are on stage and ready to be stricken by love. Basilius now feels the full force of the Wanton Boy:

> There hard by the Lodge walked hee [Basilius], carrying this unquyet contention aboute him, but, passion ere longe had gotten the absolute Masterhood, bringing with yt the shewe of present pleasure fortifyed with ye autority of a Prince, whose power mighte easily satisfy his will ageanst ye farr fett (thoughe true) reasons of the Spirite, whiche in a man not trayned in the way of vertue, hathe but slender worcking: So that ere longe hee utterly gave him self over to the Longing desyer, to enjoy *Cleophila*.
> [41]

He is recalled suddenly from his reverie by the frantic shepherds
who call him in their flight to preserve his daughters from the lion
and the bear suddenly come amongst them. We are then told that
both Dorus and Cleophila had been similarly occupied by love
when the surprise invasion took place. Cleophila, about to apostro-
phize, holding Philoclea's hand in her own, gets out only, "O
Love, sithe thow arte inchangeable to mens estates, howe arte
thow so Constant in theyre tormentes?" (42) before the mon-
strous lion and the she-bear arrive. Philoclea falls into Cleophila's
arms from fear and is held there until the last possible moment by
the willing Amazon, who then releases her beloved and chases the
lion, which has now begun to chase Philoclea.

> But *Cleophila*, seeyng how greedily the Lyon went after the
> Praye (shee her self so much desyered) yt seemed all her Spirites
> were kindled with an unwonted feare, so that, equalling the
> Lyon, in swiftnes, shee overtooke him, as hee was redy to have
> seized him self of this beutyfull chase: And disdeynfully saying,
> are yow become my Competitour?, thrust the Lyon throughe the
> brest. [43]

The role of Cleophila as hunter is not altogether metaphorical.
The melodramatic chase is a graphic illustration of precisely what
the noble prince does throughout the first three books; Philoclea
is the "Praye" of his pursuit, and both princes' courses often seem
to be uncomfortably like the lion's. To make the comparison still
clearer, Sidney puts Gynecia at the tail of the procession, running
after Cleophila with the anxiety of a brand-new passion for her.
Her feminine intuition has seen through to the man at once, and
Cleophila's prowess in facing the lion has both confirmed her intuition and engendered her passion. Sidney's comment on the
tableau of this chase permits no doubt about the thematic significance of this fairy-tale interruption: "yt was a newe sighte
fortune had prepared to those woodes, to see these three greate
Personages thus rone one after the other: Eche carryed away with
the vyolence of an Inwarde evell" (44). The inner convulsion
each of the lovers has bewailed in his speeches and songs is here
externalized, the action reinforces the speeches, or, more precisely,

the melodrama complements the rhetoric. The theme becomes a pageant. The pageant is also, of course, the first stage of the complication. If the reader cherishes doubts about the theme of the first book—and ultimately of the whole romance—they should be dispelled by Sidney's comment on the frenzied concern of Basilius, Gynecia, and Philoclea (father, mother, and daughter) for Cleophila's trifling wound, received in the battle with the lion: "For yt seemed that Love had purposed, to make in those solitary woodes, a perfect Demonstration of his unresistable force, to shewe that no Dezart place can avoyde his Darte hee must flie from him self that will shonne his evill" (45). Here there should be no question that the sequence of passionate seizures has been carefully arranged to demonstrate this most conventional of themes. As Sidney comments very near the end of the first book: "For in deede, Fortune had framed a very stage play of Love amonge these fewe folkes, making the Olde age of *Basilius* the vertue of *Ginecia,* and the simplicity of *Philoclea,* all affected to one" (50).

The first book—or act—is, then, far from artless. Basilius' initial unwisdom, carefully exposed and discussed in the exchange of speeches between Basilius and Philanax, starts a sequence of events which is to bring both civil chaos to Arcadia and emotional perturbation to all the royal characters who live there. Sidney makes clear that Basilius' mistake is his attempt to know the future— which cannot be known— and to avoid the dictates of fortune— which cannot be avoided. The Duke's initial choice of pastoral passivity, rather than princely fortitude, leads to the "unnatural" transformation of the two princes and to the necessity of their using subterfuge to woo their loves. Basilius' folly likewise demeans his two daughters by subjecting them to a rude rustic clown and hence increases their willingness to follow the two princes out of captivity. The happenings of the remainder of the romance prove to be an elaborate confirmation of the truth of Philanax' advice, and the placement of his speech at the beginning of the romance shows Sidney's clear intention to integrate the formal oratorical occasions, the set pieces of rhetoric, with the thematic development. The description of Arcadia at the beginning of the first book in terms of its political balance rather than its natural advantages makes it clear that Sidney's version of Arcadia demands of its ruler a life of action, that his romance is going to illustrate the dangers rather than the pleasures of pastoral retirement. It then proceeds to do so. The characterization of love almost completely in terms of the reversal of the "natural" relationship of reason and passion in the human personality indicates that Sidney's concern is rather more with the pains of love than with its pleasures. He then illustrates these pains. The triumph of love so carefully traced out in each of the characters takes its first form in precisely balanced and arranged passionate speeches and songs (first to oneself or a friend, next to the beloved), coming in its second stage to the active pursuit of one's desires, graphically illustrated by the chase of the lion and the bear. Thus the private and the public worlds run parallel courses of dissolution throughout the romance, courses begun with careful calculation in the first book. No incident, no song, no speech exists simply for the sake of melodrama or of rhetorical display; each contributes to a steady thematic progression.

Are the eclogues similarly integrated? Sidney seems to regard them as light-hearted interludes calculated, as he says at the end of the first book, "to ease yow fayre Ladyes of the tedyousnes of this longe discourse" (51). The First Eclogues fall into five more or less independent parts. The first element is the contest between Dorus and Lalus in praise of their beloved Kalus. It is of that most traditional kind which opposes a suitor rich but ugly (Lalus) to one who though poor is fair (Dorus). Dorus seizes the occasion to woo Pamela under another name, a procedure which he employs to great effect in later books. The central theme upon which the two competing shepherds ring their tedious changes is the powerlessness of reason in the face of the divine passion of love. So with Dorus:

> Howe ofte when reason sawe Love of her harnished,
>   With Armor of my harte hee cryed, O, vanitye?
> To sett a Perle in steele, so meanely varnished?
> Looke to thy self, reache not beyonde humanity?

> Her mynde, beames, state, farr from thy weyke winges
>   banished
> And Love whiche Lover hurtes ys inhumanity.
>
> Thus reason sayde, but shee came, reason vanished,
>   Her eyes so mastering mee, that suche objection
> Seemde but to spoyle the foode of thought longe famished. [56]

The theme of an inward surrender of the proper dominance of reason over passion, treated in the songs and speeches of Book I, is here introduced again by Dorus: "No thralles like them, that Inwarde bondage have" (58). Lalus repeats these sentiments and all is set above the constant *basso continuo* of not altogether stylized Petrarchan frustration and despair. The first part, then, rehearses two of the themes of Book I in another literary form.

The second element of these eclogues, a damnation of Cupid to discount the praise, is clearly intended to balance the first; the protagonist against love here is Dicus: "*Dicus*, whether for certeyne mischaunces of his owne, (or oute of a better judgment whiche sawe the bottome of thinges) did more detest and hate love, then the moste Envyous man dothe in him self cherysh and love, hate" (60). Characteristically, Sidney emblematizes the sentiments Dicus is shortly to express:

Nowe hee came (as a man should say) Armed, to shewe his Malice, for in the one hand hee bare a whipp, in the other, a naked *Cupide*, suche as wee comonly sett him forthe: But, on his Brest hee ware, a paynted Table, wherein hee had given *Cupide* a quite newe forme, making him sitt upon a payre of gallows like a Hangman, aboute whiche there was a Rope very handsomely provyded; hee him self paynted all ragged and torne so that his Skinne was bare in moste places, where a man mighte perceyve his body full of eyes, his heade horned with the hornes of a Bull, with longe eares, accordingly, his face oulde and wrinckled & his feete Cloven. In his Right hand hee was paynted holdinge a Crowne of Lawrell, in his lefte a purse of money, and oute of his mouthe hange a lase, whiche helde the pictures of a goodly man and an excellent fayre woman: And with suche a Countenaunce he was drawne, as yf hee had perswaded every man by those Intisementes, to come and bee hanged there. [60]

The exaggerated passion of the previous contest could hardly be more graphically opposed. It is characteristic of Sidney, too, to place his elaborate tableau in a dramatically effective position, to oppose verbal extravagance with a visual demonstration of the opposite point of view. With the miseries of love still fresh in his mind from the labors of Lalus and Dorus, the reader can hardly withhold a measure of agreement from Dorus' characterization of the joys of love. When Dicus comes to sing his song, one finally feels that he has hit upon a sane man, one who may restore some measure of perspective to a world sick with love:

> Pore Paynters ofte, with silly *Poettes* joyne,
>> To fill the worlde with straunge but vayne Conceyptes:
>
> One bringes the Stuff, the other stampes the Coyne,
>> Whiche breedes nought else but glosses of Deceiptes:
>>> Thus Paynters *Cupid* paynte, thus *Poettes* doo,
>>> A naked god, blynde, younge, with Arrowes twoo.
>
> Is hee a God, that ever flies the Lighte?
>> Or naked hee disguysd' in all untruthe:
> Yf hee bee blynde how hitteth hee so righte,
>> Or ys hee younge, that tamed oulde *Phebus* youthe. . . .
>
> No, no thinge so; an oulde false knave hee ys.   [61]

Dicus goes on to refute each of the accepted attributes of Cupid, concluding with:

> Millions of yeares this oulde Drivell *Cupid* lives,
>> While still more wretche, more wicked hee dothe prove;
> Till nowe at lengthe, that *Jove* him office gives,
>> At *Junos* sute, who muche did *Argus* love:
>>> In this oure worlde, a hangman for to bee:
>>> Of all those fooles, that will have all they see.   [62]

The two extremes of extravagant praise and unqualified damnation do not, as one might expect, cancel each other out. Dicus' strong condemnation puts the triumph of love of Book I in a slightly different light, at the same time less dignified and more ominous, but it in no way explains how to resist the irresistible force. Sidney leaves the reader convinced that much of the elaborate protestation of affection he has read comes under the heading of "straunge but vayne Conceyptes," but he does not specify how much. The reader is left to decide how much real feeling—if any —is meant to emerge through the several levels of literary stylization in Book I proper and in the preceding laudatory contest to which Dicus' discourse more immediately refers. The reader is gently reminded by Dicus' violent disagreement that the eclogue is compounded of various kinds of contests in which it is not sincerity that is valued but the ability to plead with equal facility on either side of the question. Thus Lalus and Dicus assume roles already selected for them by pastoral tradition, and thus the older Dicus pleads the case of the antilover. Yet, as Sidney indicates in his ambiguous description of Dicus' motives quoted earlier, it is not clear whether he speaks from intellectual conviction or whether the grapes have soured. The conviction in the poem seems to go beyond what the dramatic context demands, to color the previous book.

Dicus damns the Boy, but he fails to provide a defense against him, as Histor points out in the third—and central—element in the First Eclogues, the story of Plangus and Erona, or more accurately of Antiphilus and Erona. Erona does precisely what Dicus has counseled: she makes war on Cupid. In return for her sacrilege in destroying Cupid's graven images, he involves her in a degrading love and an impossible dilemma. Dicus has provided a text, and the tale the example. Its principal event has the same theme as the romance as a whole—the triumph of love—a theme of which the first book offers an organized and integrated series of instances. The tale is even more closely related to Book I because the two disguised princes figure in it.

The fourth action of the first eclogue, the verse dialogue between the old shepherd Geron and the young one Philisides, is fully as traditional as the first two sections and as well integrated into the thematic progression of book and eclogue. It debates the consolations—such as they are— of age as an assuagement of love. Though the arguments on both sides are inevitably among the oldest known to mankind, the verse is lively and the debate spirited:

G. Upp, upp *Philisides*, Let sorowes goo,
    Who yeeldes to woo, dothe but encrease his smarte.
Doo not thy hart, to playntfull Custome bringe,
    But, let us singe, sweete tunes doo passyons ease,
    And olde man heare, who woulde thy fancyes rayse.

P. Who myndes to please the mynde drownde in Annoyes?
    With outeward Joyes, whiche inlie can not sincke,
As well may thinck, with Oyle to coole the fyer,
    Or with desyer, to make suche foe a frende,
    Who dothe his sowle to endles mallice bend.

G. Yet sure, an ende, to eche thing tyme dothe give,
    Thoughe woes now live, at length thy woes must dye,
Then vertue trye, yf shee can worcke in thee,
    That whiche wee see, in many tyme hathe wroughte
    And weykest hartes to Constant temper broughte.

P. Who ever taughte a skilless man to teache,
    Or stopp a breache, that never Canon sawe,
Sweete vertues Lawe, barres not a Causefull moane,
    Tyme shall in one, my lyfe and sorowes ende,
    And mee perchaunce youre Constant temper lende. [68]

After an interchange of two more stanzas, Geron takes the offensive for six stanzas and expresses fully the arguments against love which have been presented thus far: it deprives one of self-control and hence of freedom, usurping the mind and using its energies for its own further harassment. Philisides' rejoinder is to the point: "O Godds how longe this oulde foole hathe anoyde? / My wearyed eares . . ." (70). Old age is moral, according to Philisides, because it is past the time for anything else. Geron chooses to ignore the insult and stress again the serious consequences of love:

Passyon beares hye, when puffing witt dothe blowe,
    But ys in deede a Toye, yf not a Toye,
Trewe Cause of evills, and Cause of Causeles woe,
    Yf once thow mayste that fancyes glosse destroy,
Within thy self thow soone wilt bee asshamed,
    To bee a Player of thyne owne Anoy.   [71]

The fourth section of the eclogues, then, develops the themes of love versus passion, of the need for resolute action, and of love's perversion of the active element in man's nature, in still another traditional pastoral context, the debate of youth and old age.

The metrical experiments with which Dorus and Philoclea bring the eclogues to a close elaborate the reason-passion theme still further. Both comment on their paradoxical abasement which is also an advancement toward their true desires, on the chaotic perturbation of heart and the constant vexation of spirit which is love's last best gift to a troubled mankind. Love, they have found, does not discriminate between the high and the low, strikes all equally. The concealed wooing which hides under their sometimes slightly dark conceits serves to lead the reader's attention back to the main story, and the comments of the royal spectators on the princely skill at eclogues fully restore the dramatic context necessary for a smooth transition to Book II.

The contents and direction of the second book are summarized in the first sentence: "In these Pastorall pastymes a great Nomber of dayes were spent [sic] to followe theyre flying Predecessors, while the Cupp of poyson which was deeply tasted of all this Noble Company had lefte no synew of theyres, withoute mortally searching into yt" (87). The reader has seen love triumph; now he will see it gloat. The book pursues the private sufferings of each of the characters in a series of rhetorical scenes which find their dramatic consummation in the much-discussed peasants' revolt. Hardest hit of the royal Arcadians is Gynecia, and to her sufferings we are first introduced. In the frenzy to which her predicament—a "fountayne of daunger" Sidney calls it—impels her, she cries out:

O Desartes Dezartes how fitt a guest am I for yow, synce my hart ys fuller of wylde Ravenous beastes then ever yow were, O vertue, how well I see, thow werte never but a vayne name, and no essentiall thinge which haste thus lefte thy professed Servaunt when shee had moste neede of thy lovely presence; O Imperfect proportion of Reason, whiche can to muche foresee, and so litle prevent . . . yet yf my desyer how unjust soever yt bee, mighte take effect, thoughe a Thowsande Deathes followed yt, and every deathe were followed with a thousand shames, yet, shoulde not my Sepulchre receyve mee withoute some Contentment. [87–88]

We need not dwell on the reason-passion contention at the base of her complaint, but should observe that she explicitly makes the connection (advanced as an explanation of the lion and bear scene at the end of Book I) between the pursuit of her own desires and the "wylde Ravenous beastes" running through the "Desartes." More important still is the frankness with which she recognizes the absolute predominance of passion in her own behavior. She will do anything for satisfaction. It is to this level that the rest of the characters are to be reduced during the course of Book II. Notice in passing that Sidney has here, as with Philanax' speech in Book I, placed a crucial speech at the beginning of a book, set forth the text as it were, which he goes on to gloss.

Cleophila's song, when Gynecia stumbles upon her in the woods, is a confession that "Reason, in vayne, now yow have lost my harte." There is no Arcadian grass growing under Basilius' feet either, and very soon he confesses his own abject slavery to Cleophila: "See in mee ye power of youre Beauty, whiche can make oulde age, to aske Counseill of yowthe? And a Prince unconquered to become a Slave to a straunger?" (92). Philoclea is next: "in the meane tyme, the sweete *Philoclea* founde straunge unwonted motions in her self: And yet, the pore sowle coulde neyther descerne what yt was, nor whether the vehemency of yt tended. Shee founde a burning affection towardes *Cleophila*, an unquyet desyer to bee with her, and yet shee founde that the very presence kyndled her desyer" (93). Dorus then begins his ruse of making love to Pamela through Mopsa. Obviously superior though his parts and address are, it is his tale of the two princes (and the consequent revelation of his aristocratic birth and prospects) which procures that "Secrett Consent" Pamela soon yields to the impassioned pleas delivered via Mopsa. At this point in the story all the lovers have confessed themselves to the objects of their desires except Cleophila and Philoclea. Philoclea has advanced in awareness of her ailment sufficiently to recant a former pledge to chastity which she had inadvisedly written on marble.

Her prayer to Diana has much in common with her mother's earlier imprecations against the conditions of life and love, but a kinder fate is in store for her. She is sent by her father to plead for him with Cleophila (that is a stratagem Cleophila has imposed on Basilius) and their common passion soon comes out with the tearful sympathy: "beholde here before youre eyes *Pyrocles* Prince of *Macedon*, whome onely yow have broughte to this falle of fortune, and unused *Metamorphoses* whome yow onely have made neglect his Contry, forgett his Father, and lastly forsake hym self" (114). The cup of poison has now been drained to the dregs by the noble company and its dire results are apparent.

In the remainder of the book Sidney points out the consequences such wholesale neglect of duty has for the kingdom. He describes the rebellion. The "complication" of the parallel plot begins. Immediately the second "complication" begins to obtrude upon—and interact with—the first. The rebellion interrupts Gynecia as she is pleading with Cleophila, it imposes itself on Dorus' pastoral lament with Philisides, it drives Basilius out of his lodge and into his rusty armor; together the aristocrats gain a temporary respite but their strength is obviously insufficient to bring such a desperate matter to conclusion. Cleophila saves the day, of course, but only after Sidney interrupts the tumult in midcourse and explains the genesis of the uprising. His explanation is almost too patently clear: the usual birthday celebration for Basilius drew together a crowd that "emboldened with the Dukes absented maner of Living" let its gripes grow into revolt. Thus Philanax' predictions are borne out exactly, and the political philosophy so obvious in the beginning of the first book is reintroduced strongly at the close of the second. And just as at the end of the first book the nobles' pursuit of one another was limned out by the introduction of wild beasts which they had come to resemble, so here the logical result of the abandonment by the royal circle of duty and social position which the second book spells out is illustrated by the metamorphosis of the once peaceful and tractable citizens of Arcadia into a herd of savages. The elaborately rhetorical confessions of the slaves of passion are shown to have a very unpleasant real-life result. Action conflicts with word. As

Sidney later wrote, however, the art of language, like a sword, can save one's country or kill one's father. Pyrocles proceeds to use it to save the country. Since this speech will be discussed at some length later, it is enough to mention here that Sidney so arranges his narrative that the formal rhetorical occasion comes at a critical point in the drama and is a logical outgrowth of the dramatic development of the romance. The book closes with Basilius' premature attempt to unravel the oracle, a further reference back to the events at the beginning of Book I.

The Second Eclogues, like the First, concern themselves with the same themes as the prose section they follow. The first sequence reduces to a harmless symbolic dance the rebellion just concluded:

> The Rude tumulte of the *Phagonians* gave occasyon to the honest Shepeheardes, to bringe theyre Pastoralles this day with a Daunce whiche they called *The Skirmish betuixt Reason and Passyon.* . . .

Reason. Thow Rebell vyle, come, to thy Master yeelde;
      (*And the other that mett with him answered*)
Passion. No Tyrant, no, myne, myne shall bee the feelde.
R.   Can Reason, then a Tyrant coumpted bee?
P.   Yf Reason will that Passyons bee not free.
R.   But Reason will, that Reason governe moste:
P.   And Passyon will that passyon rule the Roste.
R.   Youre will ys will but Reason, Reason ys:
P.   Will hathe his will, when Reasons will dothe mysse.
R.   Whome passyon leades unto his deathe, ys bent:
P.   And lett hym dye, so that hee dye content.
R.   By Nature yow, to Reason faythe hathe sworne:
P.   Not so; but Fellowlike together borne.
R.   Who passyon dothe ensewe lives in anoye;
P.   Who passyon dothe forsake, lives voyde of Joye.
R.   Passyon ys blynde, and treades an unknowne trace:
P.   Reason hathe eyes, to see his owne evell Case.

> *Then (as they approached nearer) Twoo of Reasons syde (as yf they shott att the other) thus sange.*

R.	Dare passyons then abyde in Reasons lighte?
P.	And ys not Reason dymmed with passyons mighte?
R.	O Foolish thinge, whiche glory doest destroy.
P.	O gloryous Tytle of a Foolish Toye.
R.	Weykenes yow are, dare yow with oure strengthe feighte?
P.	Bycause, oure Weykenes weykeneth all youre mighte.
R.	O sacred Reason helpp oure vertuous Toyles?
P.	O passyon pass, on feeble Reasons spoylles.
R.	Wee with oure selves abyde a dayly stryfe:
P.	Wee gladly use the sweetness of oure Lyfe.
R.	But, yet our stryfe sure peace in ende dothe breede?
P.	Wee now have peace, youre peace wee doo not neede.

> *Then did the twoo Square Battells meete, and (in steade of feighting) embrace one another, singing thus.*

R.	Wee are too stronge, but, reason, seekes not blood;
P.	Whoo bee too weyke, do fayne they bee too good.
R.	Thoughe wee can not orecome, oure Cause ys Just:
P.	Lett us orecome, and lett us bee unjust.
R.	Yet, passyon yeelde, at lengthe to Reasons strooke:
P.	What shall wee wynn by taking Reasons yooke.
R.	The Joyes yow have shall bee made permanent:
P.	And so wee shall with greef Learne to repent.
R.	Repent in Deede, but, that shall bee youre Blisse:
P.	Howe knowe wee that, synce present Joyes wee misse.
R.	Yow knowe yt not, of Reason, therefore knowe yt:
P.	No Reason yet, had ever skill to showe yt.

> Then Let us bothe to Heavenly Rules give place:
> Whiche *Reasons* skill, and *Passyons* doo deface. [129–30]

The orthodox injunction at the end of the debate—"Then Let us bothe to Heavenly Rules give place"—has little effect on the princely spectators. The Duke bestows his praise and blame, chooses between the "reason" team and the "passion" team solely on the basis of what he thinks likely to please Cleophila. She, unable to take her eyes off Philoclea, has paid no attention to the contest. Philoclea is equally occupied in gazing at Cleophila, even though she knows it will infuriate her jealous mother. The irony of giving good advice about reason's government of passion to such as these could hardly be plainer, if one is fully observant of context. Only Dorus is sufficiently attentive to engage Dicus in an eclogue on the subject of falling in love. Dorus, in response to Dicus' request, describes the progress of passion in a long, conceited verse paragraph.

Sighte ys his Roote, in thoughte ys his progressyon,
 His Chyldehood wonder, Prentiship, attention,
His youthe Delighte, his Age the sowles oppressyon.
 Doubt ys his sleepe, hee waketh in Inventyon,
Fancy ys his foode, his Cloathing all of Carefullnes,
 Beuty his Booke, his play Lovers Discention,
His eyes are curyous searche, but wylde with warefullnes.
 His wynges Desyer ofte Clipte with Desperatyon,
Largess his handes coulde never skill of sparefullnes,
 But howe hee dothe by mighte, or by perswasyon,
To Conquer and his Conquest howe to ratify,
 Experyence Doubtes, and Schooles holde Disputatyon. [132]

The remainder of the eclogue repeats Dicus' praise of the quiet life and Dorus' mingled praises of passion and complaints of its usurpation of reason.

In the eclogue between Plangus and Boulon which is repeated by Histor, the struggle between passion and reason is projected onto a cosmic scale. Plangus and Boulon are figures in the long prose digression in the center of the First Eclogues. Plangus, whose desperate love for Erona is frustrated at every turn, begins the eclogue. After an initial stanza which demands to know how long his torments are to last, he transfers his sense of outrage to the cosmos:

Ah where was first, that Crewell Cunning founde,
 To frame of earthe a vessell of the mynde
Where yt shoulde bee the self destruction bounde,
  What needed so hye spirites suche Mansions blynde?
  Or wrapt in flessh, what doo they here obtayne?
   But gloryous Name of wretched humane kynde,

Balles to the starres, and Thralles to fortunes raigne,
    Turned from them selves infected with theyre Cage
Where deathe ys fearde, and lyfe ys helde wth payne,
    Lyke Players placed to fill a filthy stage,
        Where Chaunge of thoughtes one foole to other shewes
        And all but Jestes, save onely sorowes rage?
                      [139-40]

Boulon's reply to this exasperation at Erona's, and more generally
man's, predicament is orthodox, but not perhaps so dramatically
effective as Plangus' condemnation:

O Man take heede, how thow the goddes do moove,
    To Causefull Wrathe, whiche thow canst not resist,
Blaspheymous wordes the Speaker vayne dothe prove,
    Alas, whyle wee are wrapt in Foggy Myst,
        Of oure self Love, (so passyons doo deceyve)
        Wee thincke they hurte, where moste they doo
        assist.

To harme us wormes, shoulde they by Justice leave,
    His Nature, nay, hym self for so yt ys,
What glory from oure Losse can wee receyve,
    But still oure daseled eyes theyre way do myss,
        Whyle that wee doo at his sweete scourge repyne,
        The kyndely way to beate us on to bliss.

Yf shee must dye then hathe shee lost the lyne,
    Of loathsome dayes, whose losse how canst thow mone,
That doest so well theyre myseryes defyne,
    But, suche wee are with inward Tempest blowne,
        Of wyndes cleane Contrary, in waves of will,
        Wee moane that Losse, (which had) wee did
        bemone.   [141]

The eclogue is entirely within its own dramatic context, yet it
does, as we have seen before in the eclogues, comment on the
larger themes of the main story. That this was Sidney's intent the
comment following the close of the eclogue clearly illustrates:

So well did *Histors* voyce express the passyon of *Plangus*, that
all the Princely beholders were stricken into a silent Considera-

cyon of yt: In deede every one making that hee hearde of an other, the Ballance of his owne Trubles. [144]

The eclogues, here at least, function much as does the play within the play in later Elizabethan drama. The confusing tale Histor then goes on to tell connects the eclogues to the main story by still another path, in telling the thrilled reader about the dragon and giant slaying adventures of Pyrocles and Musidorus. For the rest, the tale occupies itself with the distress caused by love's striking in the wrong places, just as it does in the main narrative. The remaining metrical experiments by the two princes, whatever poetical merit the reader chooses to assign them, further elaborate the crippling effect of passion on reason, the paradoxical self-torture of the unfulfilled love affair. The eclogues close with all the principals in bed but unable to sleep, perforce content "to meditate uppon theyre private desyers."

Typical of Sidney's continuous concern for smooth articulation of the movements of his romance is the first sentence of Book III. It picks up precisely where the Second Eclogues left off, even repeating some of the same phrases:

> The next day which followed a Night full of passyons, and yet brought in yt self newe matter to encrease them (Tyme uppon Tyme still adding groweth to a well rooted inclination) while the *Duke* in the after noone tyme was buysy aboute *Appollos* Rytes, *Cleophila*, to whome the not enjoying her Frend *Dorus*, had beene one of her burdenous greeffes, took holde of this oportunity; And, called her beloved Cossyn with her went to the same place, where first shee had Reveyled unto hym her inclosed passyon, and was by hym as yow may remember with a Frendly sharpenes reprehended. [159]

The friends' return to the same spot to review their passionate pilgrimage seems to be a conscious attempt by Sidney to point up the distance they have traveled. At bottom the conference has been called to agree on strategy in the serious campaign for consummation which is the central dramatic concern of Book III. Dorus has coaxed a love token, a glove, from Pamela; he is sufficiently encouraged to change his note from tragic to comic in the song with which he decorates this occasion. Cleophila remains despairing, her song neatly inverting the phrases of Dorus'. As on the occasion of their previous meeting on that ground, the praise of friendship takes up a good deal of time, but they finally get down to business: how to carry off the two princesses. Dorus has already made his plan—he and Pamela will make for the nearest seaport, whence to his kingdom—and, more important, has obtained Pamela's consent to this defiant venture. After its successful conclusion, he will then return with an army to succor Pyrocles. Pyrocles, strengthened by joy in his friend's good hope, and perhaps tempted by the hope of a way out of his own troubles, finally brings himself to a parting. His sorrow is mollified by the prospect of action. In desperation he tries to think of what *he* can do until the army arrives. The reader, on the other hand, can hardly help wondering what will happen when the army does arrive. The two princes evidently intend, in plain words, to wage war in order to commit rape, to exploit Basilius' folly by stealing his daughters. The third book is the history of this campaign.

Cleophila's troubles begin with Basilius, who has decided after his religious exercises that it is Cleophila he most adores, not Phoebus Apollo. The confession ending in the song "Phaebus Farewell, a sweeter Sainte, I serve" produces no suggestion of compliance from the sweeter saint, but when Basilius confides to her (167 ff.) that he means to leave the forest and belatedly take Philanax' advice, that he means to upset the whole apple cart so carefully pushed by the two princes, Cleophila is constrained to a more loving reply. She persuades him to stay in the forest by dangling the carrot of future surrender. The rigid causal framework Sidney has built up again makes the reader pause at the implications of her action. There is every reason to believe that if Basilius had returned to his lawful throne all the subsequent tumult in Arcadia would have been avoided, the status quo ante restored. By persuading Basilius to ignore the dictates of traditional wisdom, Cleophila makes herself clearly responsible for what follows. She shows some awareness of what she has done, though no regret.

Synce that the Stormy Rage of passyons darcke,
   (Of passyons darcke made darck by Beutyes Lighte,)
With Rebell force hathe closde in Dongeon darcke,
   My mynde ere nowe led forthe by *Reasons* lighte,
Synce all the things which gives my eyes theyre lighte,
   Do Foster still the fruite of Fancyes Darcke.
     So that the wyndowes of my Inward Lighte,
     Do serve to make my Inwarde powers Darcke.

Synce, (as I say) bothe mynde and Sences darcke,
   Are hearde, not helped, with pearsing of the Lighte,
While that the Lighte may shewe the horrors darcke
   But can not make resolved Darcknes Lighte.
     I like this place where at the Least the Darcke,
     May keepe my thoughtes from thoughte of wonted
      lighte. [169]

Context is once again important; the darkness-light conceit is suggested by the cave to which Cleophila has retreated. She is not alone there. Gynecia lies at the farthest end, prostrate with passion. The eclipse of reason by passion, the subject of Cleophila's rhetoric, is also bodied forth by the tableau of Gynecia's cave of passion. She discovers Cleophila and in a violently passionate, extravagantly rhetorical scene offers herself to him, threatening dire punishment if he does not take her then and there. He cannot think of any alternative for the moment, and Sidney leaves him hanging to the cliff to shift the spotlight to Dorus.

The young shepherd elaborately deceives Dametas, Mopsa, and Miso by playing on the ruling passions of each, and carries off Pamela. It is the comic climax of the romance, the moment all readers look forward to, when the fools are all paid off in their own coin. At the same time the elopement itself is a wholly serious action, one of the disasters predicted by the oracle which triggered the removal to the forests. Sidney focuses his comic and serious plots on the same action. Two climaxes are fused into one. Pamela's second thoughts (and the reader's) as she rides away (185 ff.) are not ill founded, as the scene of Dorus' attempted rape proves. At the moment he decides to rape her the mob arrives and balks his resolution. Sidney then leaves Dorus

abruptly and returns to Pyrocles, who has in the meantime hit
upon a device of his own—the assignation trick. It works, and he
gains the satisfaction which no one else in the romance is able to
contrive. Philoclea's second thoughts (197 ff.) are meant to recall
those of Pamela but happily for Pyrocles no mob appears inad-
vertently to defend her honor. She surrenders, and the joys which
follow are the very center of the romance. To this favor all the
Arcadians wish to come. The process begun when Pyrocles looked
at the picture of Philoclea has now put Basilius and Gynecia in
the cave, Pamela in desperate straits with Musidorus, and Pyrocles
himself realizing his fondest dream.

With consummation so fresh in mind, marriage cannot be far
behind. It is not; it is the subject of the Third Eclogues. Again
Sidney takes pains to articulate the parts of his romance; the first
sentence of the Eclogues stands in ironic contrast to the passionate
spectacle of fine language with which Pyrocles has won Philoclea
in the scene just ended: "*Lalus,* not with many paynted wordes
nor false harted promyses had wonne the Consent of the beloved
Kala, but, with a true and simple making her knowe hee loved
her, not forcing hym self beyonde his reache to buye her affection" (288). Lalus treats her especially well, Sidney points out,
on the way to the church. He has, furthermore, taken her there
with the consent of both sets of parents: "And so with Consent
of bothe Parentes (withoute which neyther *Lalus* woulde aske,
nor *Kala* graunte), Theyre Mariage day was appoynted, whiche
because yt fell oute in this tyme, I thincke yt shall not bee Im-
partinent to remember a litle oure Shepeheardes, while the other
greater persons are eyther sleeping or otherwyse occupied"
(228). Sidney could hardly make his ironic contrast any clearer.
The old friend of *honest* love, Dicus, supplies the marriage hymn,
of which the first stanza at least must be quoted:

> Lett Mother *Earthe,* now deck her self in flowers,
> > To see her Ofspring seeke a good encrease,
> Where justest Love dothe vanquish *Cupids* powers,
> > And Warre of thoughtes ys swallowed up in peace,
> > > Whiche never may decrease:
> > > But like the Turtles fayre

Live One in Twoo, a well united payre,
Whiche, that no Chaunce may stayne,
O *Hymen* longe theyre Cupled joyes mentayne.

[229]

In the ten stanzas that follow, all the evils which plague the protagonists of this strange stage-play of love are cited as being cured by the elixir of marriage; lust, jealousy, carking worry, vanity, all disappear in this orthodox relationship. All the other shepherds, friend and foe, agree that he has "sunge well & thriftely" (232). Nico's song against jealousy in the marriage state and Pas' reminder that there should be no double standard pave the way for Philisides' song, in which the teachings of Sidney's friend Languet about the necessity of hierarchical order are elaborated. (All this praise, remember, is highly ironical; our hero and heroine are not married.)

The autobiographical element introduced reappears more strongly in the Fourth Eclogues. Here it gives way to the eclogue between Geron and Histor in which Geron defends marriage ("Holly Mariage, sweete and surest meane, / Oure Foolish Lustes in Honest Rules to stay" [242]), and Histor points out that the average wife—far unlike Kala—is an irritable scold interested only in keeping up with the Joneses. It is tempting, though without means of proof, to see Sidney speaking to himself in this praise of marriage, to see him seeking a way himself out of the malaise of passion he has so well described: "Marry therefore, for Marryage will Destroy, / Those passyons which to youthfull hedd do Clyme, / Mothers and Nurses of all vayne Annoy" (245). Book IV opens:

> The Everlasting Justice (using oure selves to bee the punisshers of oure faultes, and making oure owne actions the beginninge of oure Chastisement, that oure shame may bee the more manifest, and oure Repentance followe the sooner,) tooke *Dametas* at this present (by whose folly the others wysdome mighte receyve the greater overthrowe) to bee the instrument of reveyling the secrettst Connying: So evill a grounde dothe evell stande upon, and so manifest yt ys, that no thing Remaynes strongly, but that whiche hathe the good foundacyon of goodnes. [247]

We have seen that Sidney pays special attention to the opening sentences of each of the books; this one presents in capsule form the entire book, in which justice arrives to exact its penalty from gratification. After the low comedy of Mopsa, Miso, and Dametas has played itself out, the serious business of the book begins. Dametas surprises the happy sleeping couple *in flagrante delicto*, steals Pyrocles' sword, locks them in, and advertises their guilt to the world. Hard on this news, the Duke's death is made known. The comic sequence of events which brought it about is then related. Once again the two plots are focused on the same incident. Basilius' ironic praise of his delightful night with his wife of twenty years precedes a partial reconciliation almost immediately destroyed by Basilius' drinking of the sleeping potion. That Basilius' consummation should have turned so rapidly to ashes indicates the unpleasant results passion holds out to its victims henceforth in the romance. It is Gynecia, of course, who bears the brunt of the burden, tearing her hair in despair until Basilius awakens in the last few pages. The populace too, in an absolute about-face from its mood at the end of Book II, joins Gynecia in a paroxysm of grief. The people's grief, we may presume, is no less heartfelt than Gynecia's, although it involves an unbecomingly abrupt change of feelings for both. It is only with Philanax that the reader can fully sympathize. His affection for his prince, far outweighing his own ambition for power, blends with bitter regret that his own advice was not taken at the first: "O that the wordes my moste faythfull Duty delivered unto yow, when yow first entred this solitary Course, mighte have wrougthe asmuche perswasion in yow, as they sprange from Truthe in mee?" (267). Again we see Sidney recalling the reader's attention to Philanax' crucial speech at the beginning of Book I. The rigid cause-and-effect sequence, which the carefully constructed plot supports, could hardly be plainer.

Pyrocles, awakened by the commotion arising from Dametas' alarm, discovers that he is now—to use Sidney's phrase—a Prisoner *for* Love rather than *of* Love. In the debate on suicide between Pyrocles and Philoclea which follows his unsuccessful attempt at it, Philoclea takes the Christian position, Pyrocles the Stoic. In the end it is Love that triumphs again, and Pyrocles is taken in his shirt by Philanax.

The reader now rejoins Musidorus, who is fighting with the remnant of the Phagonian Rebels. This marauding band was "guyded by the everlasting Justice to bee Chastizers of *Musidorus* broken vowe," just as Dametas was selected as a Divine rod to punish Pyrocles. Pamela, virginity intact, does not regard the band in this light. She is resolute in her sense of rectitude, in marked contrast with her sister's confidence in the righteousness of consummated true love. "For howe can I want Comfort," Pamela says, "that have the true and Living Comfort of my unblemisshed vertue? And how can I wante honor, as longe as *Musidorus* (in whome in deede honor ys) dothe honor mee?" (291). This is gall indeed to Musidorus, and he dispatches a quick but contrite prayer that when the time comes again he will be found deserving of such virgin praise. After a night of chaste mutual comfort they are captured by a search party sent out by Philanax, their guard is disposed of, and they are sent back to face punishment with the other lovers.

The political consequences of the attempted elopements and of Basilius' folly become apparent (and the political and private worlds join) with the arrival of the demagogue Tymantus, "a Man of Middle age, but of extreme Ambition" (300). His plan for usurpation is to call Philanax a usurper, and it works to the extent of leaving Arcadia in "Tumult uppon Tumult" as Book IV closes.

The tumults are so great as to prompt the shepherds to withdraw still further into the forest for the Fourth Eclogues. After a conventional translation of civil strife into trouble for the sheep, and Klaus' and Strephon's utterly uninspired confession of their hopeless passions, Philisides begins his tale and songs. In them Sidney is clearly autobiographical.[4] The tantalizing lyric outcries

---

4. Goldman, following Friedrich Brie (*Sidneys Arcadia, Eine Studie zur Englischen Renaissance* [Strassburg, 1918]), comments: "Near the beginning of the fourth eclogue there is an autobiographical passage which seems a very original touch until one discovers that it follows rather closely a similar life story told by one of Sannazaro's shepherds at the beginning of the *settima prosa* of the Italian *Arcadia*." (*Sidney and the Arcadia*, p. 175).

in several of the previous eclogues, which the reader is often tempted to read autobiographically, give way here to unmistakable personal reference. The initial prose passage should be quoted in its entirety:

The name of *Samothea* ys so famous that (telling yow I am of that) I shall not neede to extend my self further in telling yow what that Contry ys: But there I was borne of suche Parentage as neyther lefte mee so greate that I was a Marck for envy, nor so base yt I was subject to Contempt, brought up from my Cradell age with suche Care as Parentes are wont to bestow uppon theyre Children whome they meane to make the maynteyners of theyre Name. And assoone as my memory grewe stronge enough to receyve what might bee delyvered unto yt by my senses; they offered Learning unto mee, especially that kynde that teacheth what in truthe, and not in opinyon ys to bee embrased and what to bee eschewed. Neither was I barrd from seeyng the Naturall knowledg of thinges so farr as the narrowe sighte of man hathe pearsed into yt: And bycause the myndes Commaundement ys vayne withoute the body bee enhabled to obay yt, my strengthe was exercysed with Horsmanship, weapons, and suche other qualityes, as besydes the practize carryed in them selves some servisable use, wherein, so I proffited that as I was not excellent, so was I accompagnable. After that by my yeares or perchaunce by sooner priviledg then yeares comonly graunt, I was thought able to bee myne owne Master, I was suffered to spende some tyme in travell, that, by the Comparyson of many thinges I might rypen my Judgment: Synce greatnes, power, Riches, and suche like standing in Relation to an other (who dothe knowe no thing but his owne) dothe not knowe his owne. Then beeyng home returned and thought of good hope (for the worlde rarely bestowes a better Tytle uppon yowthe) I continewed to use the Benefites of a quyet mynde, In truth (I calle hym to witness that knoweth hartes) even in the secrett of my Sowle bent to Honesty: Thus farr yow see, as no pompous spectackle of an untrubled Tenor of a well guyded lyfe. But alas what shoulde I make Patheticall exclamations to a moste true event? So yt hapned that Love, (whiche what yt ys, youre owne feeling can best tell yow) diverted this Course of Tranquility, which though I did with so muche covering hyde, that I was thought voyde of yt, as any man: yet my wounde which smarted in my self brought mee in fyne to this Chaunge, muche in state, but more in mynde.   [312–13]

All the details of Sidney's life, and the almost laconic rhetorical question, "But alas what shoulde I make Patheticall exclamations to a moste true event? So yt hapned that Love . . . ," seem to be presented in just the spirit Sidney would choose for a directly personal plea. Few would contest as attributes of Sidney himself the twin gifts of Venus' fire and Diana's chastity which are bestowed on the dreamer. Especially characteristic is the conviction that love is—in a strictly social sense—degrading; that it endangers one's role. The elegiacs that follow offer, besides their general applicability to Sidney's desperately unhappy and frustrated love affair, one topical reference:

Unto the Caytiff wretche whome long affliction holdeth;
And now fully beleeves help to bee quyte perisshed.
Graunt yet graunt yet a looke to the last monument of his
      anguish.
            O yow (alas so I fynde) Cause of his onely Rewyn.
Dread not a whitt (o goodly crewell) that pitty may enter,
      Into thy hart by the sighte of this Epistle I sende.
And so refuse to beholde of these straunge woundes the Recitall,
      Least yt might thee allure home to thy self to returne,
(Unto thyself I do meane those graces dwell so within thee,
      Gratefullnes, sweetenes, Holylove, Harty regarde,)
Suche thinge can not I seeke, Dispayre hathe given mee my
      answer,
      Despayre, moste tragicall Clause to a Deadly Request.
Suche thinge can not hee hope that knowes thy determinate
      hardnes,
      Hard lyfe, a Riche Marble, hard, (but a fayre) Dyamond.
                                                              [318–19]

The "Rich" sonnets in *Astrophil and Stella* offer parallel instances. The problem this identification presents is that Penelope Devereux was not married to Lord Rich until the summer of 1581, by which time the Old *Arcadia*, if scholars are correct, was finished. It is possible that these verses were inserted in the Fifth Eclogues after they were first written, but the autobiographical nature of the Eclogues as a whole, into which these elegiacs fit so nicely, makes a later addition unlikely. The completion date of the Old *Arcadia* may thus be later than heretofore supposed. Sidney, wishing to record his own despair upon learning that his beloved was going to marry someone else, could hardly have chosen a more appropriate time than this, when his two protagonists have themselves arrived at a similiar seemingly hopeless situation.

The elegy for Basilius which Dicus then pronounces, and Agelastus' farewell to the sun of the kingdom, both serve (as Dicus says) to "leave particuler passyon, and joyne in bewailing this generall Losse of that Contry" (320).

This "generall Losse" is, as we might now expect, the subject of the first sentence of the last book:

> The daungerus Devision of Mens myndes, the Ruynous renting of all estates had now broughte *Arcadia* to feele the pangues of uttermoste perill (suche Convulsions never Coming but that the lyfe of that government drawes nere his necessary peryod) when to ye honest and wyse *Philanax* equally distracted betwixt Desyer of Revenge and Care of the States establishment there came unlooked for a *Macedonian* gentleman: who in shorte but pithy maner delyverd unto hym that the renoumed *Euarchus* Kinge of *Macedon* having made a longe and tedyous journey, to vizitt his oulde Frende & Confederate the *Duke Basilius*, was nowe come within half a myle of the Lodges. [327]

Sidney unites both the confusion and the hope of its cure in his opening sentence. Although the oratory of Tymantus the demagogue keeps matters in doubt for a short while, Philanax' clever speech persuades the citizenry to accept Euarchus as their temporary ruler. The people, "tyred allready with theyre Divisions," show themselves amenable to returning, albeit painfully, to normality. Euarchus, a Mirror of Princes, takes the stage, and through him Sidney provides an amplified restatement of the standards of good government which Philanax had first set down in Book I and which Basilius and the others had so grievously neglected:

[Philanax comes upon Euarchus] taking his Rest under a Tree, with no more affected pompes, then as a Man that knewe (howe so ever hee was exalted) the beginning & ende of his Body was earthe. But first yt were fitt to bee knowne what Cause mooved this puisant Prince in this sorte to come to *Arcadia: Evarchus* did not further exceede his meanest Subject with the greatnes of his fortune, then hee did surmount the greatnes of his fortune, with ye greatnes of his mynde. In somuche that those thinges which often tymes the best sorte thinck rewardes of Vertue, hee helde them not at so hye a pryce, but esteemed them Servauntes to well dooyng: The Reward of vertue beeyng in yt self, on which his Inward love was so fixed, that never was yt dissolved into other desyers, but keeping his thoughtes true to them selves, was neither beguyled with the paynted glasse of pleasure, nor dazeled with ye false lighte of Ambition. This made the Lyne of his actions streighte, and allwayes like yt self, no worldly thing beeynge able to shake the Constancy of yt; whiche among many other tymes yeelded some proof of yt self. When *Basilius* the Mightyest Prince of *Greece* next to *Evarchus* did sodenly with-oute the advyse or allowance of his Subjectes (withoute eyther good showe of reasonable Cause, or good provision for likely accidentes in the sighte of the worlde) putt hym self from ye worlde: As a Man that not onely unarmed hym self but woulde make his nakednes manifest. This measured by the myndes of moste Princes, even those whome great actes have entitled with the holy name of vertue, woulde have beene thought a sufficyent Cause (where suche oportunity did offer so great pray to theyre handes) to have soughte the enlarging of theyre Dominions: wherein they falsely putt the more or less felicity of an estate. But *Evarchus* that had conceyved what ys evill in yt self no respect can make good, (and never forgatt his office) was to meyntayne the *Macedonians* in the exercyse of goodnes and happy enjoying theyre naturall lyves: Never used warr (whiche ys meyntayned with the Cost and blood of the Subject) but when yt was to defend theyre Righte, whereon theyre well beeyng de-pended: For this Reconing hee made, howe farr so ever hee ex-tended hym self, Neighboure hee must have: And therefore as hee kept in peace tyme continuall Discipline of warre, and at no tyme woulde suffer injury, so hee did rather stand uppon a just moderacyon of keeping his owne in good and happy Case, then multiplying desyer uppon desyer (seeking one enemy after an other) putt bothe his honor and peoples safty in the continuall dyce of Fortune. So that having this advauntage of *Basilius* contrey layde open unto hym, in steade of laying an unjust grype uppon yt (which yet mighte have bene beutyfyed with the noble name of Conquest) hee streighte Considered the universal Case of *Greece* deprived by this meanes of a princely piller, he wayed and pityed the pityfull Case of the *Arcadian* people: Who were in worse Case then yf deathe had taken away theyre Prince, for so yet theyre necessity woulde have placed some one to the helme. [331–32]

The folly of Basilius is reinforced by the strong irony of Euarchus' original errand:

These Rightly wyse and temperate Consideracyons mooved *Evarchus*, to take his Laboursome Journey to see whether by his authority hee might drawe *Basilius* from this burying him self alyve, [the pun here is surely intentional], and to returne ageane to employ his oulde yeares in doyng good, the onely happy action of mans lyfe: Neyther was hee withoute a Consideracyon in hym self to provyde the Mariage of *Basilius* twoo Daughters, for his Sonne and Nephewe ageanst theyre returne. [332–33]

Thus are the public and private plots united, and the adventures of the two princes shown to have been self-defeating. From now on, the reader observes the events in Arcadia with the knowledge that not an adverse Fortune but human folly is responsible for them. Yet if it is possible to oppose the dictates of passion, it is by no means easy. Gynecia's cries of anguish on the night before the trial, although described as "blaspheymous repyning ageanst her Creation," are not readily answered: "O Goddes? (woulde shee crye oute) why did yow make mee, to Distructyon? yf yow loved goodnes why did yow not give mee a good mynde? Or yf I can not have yt withoute youre guifte, why doo yow plaigue mee?" (340).

The famous trial scene with which the Old *Arcadia* concludes is perhaps Sidney's most successful attempt to combine rhetorical declamation, abstract debate of theme, and the pleasures of *opsis*. The spectacle ought really to be acted: Euarchus in the seat of judgment; Basilius' coffin draped with black on the catafalque just before him; defendants and accuser in their most splendid costumes facing each other across the bier. The two noble princes, the pathetic queen, accused all three of the greatest crimes; the most just of judges; the most violently self-righteous of prosecutors. Philanax, construing the late happenings into a vast plot against the state; the two princes pleading the irresistible force of love and the most honorable of intentions toward the princesses; Euarchus dispensing justice with utter impartiality—Philoclea to a nunnery, Gynecia to be buried alive, violent ignominious death for our heroes. The slaves of passion, named and described with growing disfavor from the beginning of the fourth book, are here openly condemned. Rape, rebellion, and murder are finally given their right names. Reason has reasserted itself, in the person of Euarchus, over the passion which has grown to dominate even the formerly judicious Philanax. The trial is the thematic as well as the dramatic climax of the romance, and to it Sidney brings the same carefully symmetrical structure we have seen prevailing elsewhere in the romance: the two princes each attempting to rouse the populace to his princess, defending himself with warmth against Philanax' vicious attacks; the two princesses each defending her lover and her own conduct in a passionate letter; Philanax equally violent against them all; between them, spatially as well as thematically, the judicious Euarchus discounting the exaggerations of passion; the passions of all coming in the end to death. The pageant is carefully balanced and symmetrically arranged. The awakening of Basilius, which brings about perhaps the fastest recognition scene and joyful dénouement in English fiction, also provides the kind of sensational event upon which, as we have seen, Sidney likes to close the various sections of the romance. The oracle which inspired the retreat to the forest has now fulfilled itself, and the court moves back to town. All passion spent, the status quo restored, everyone—hopefully—lives happily ever after.

The progression of the major themes through the five books ought now to be clear. First there is the love versus reason theme:

in the first book everyone falls in love; in the second they endure the sufferings it brings, and bring themselves to confess their passions to the loved ones; in the third the stratagems of love are carried out and some kind of climax is reached in each affair; the last two books mete out the punishment for the gratifications of the third book. The fourth relates the failures of the schemes begun in the third, the fifth passes judgment on the conduct of the characters in the first four and re-establishes the rule of reason. The theme of friendship is elaborated in the first book (in the confession of Pyrocles to Dorus and later in that of Dorus to Pyrocles), in the third (when they meet to make a plan of battle), and in the fifth (when they face death together, and debate on the nature of life after death). Between these focal points it recedes into the background. It is worth noting, too, that love and friendship work together more than they conflict, a departure from their traditional opposition. The political philosophy which suffuses the entire romance is pre-eminent at the beginning of Book I when Basilius' initial errors are committed; the consequences of his mistakes first appear at the end of Book II, when Cleophila temporarily diverts them. The happenings in Book III cause a further eruption at the end of Book IV which is finally healed at the same time that private passion is brought under reasonable control by the coming of Euarchus in the final book. Throughout the romance the parallel rupture of traditional relationships on the political and personal levels is emphasized.

These themes we have observed to predominate in the eclogues as well. The careful articulation of eclogues and prose sections has been pointed out. The skillful use of songs to crystallize action or emotion has been remarked. The clever use of the basic division of the eclogue into two opposed positions to dramatize the conflict of reason and passion further unites the eclogues and the prose sections. Symmetry, parallelism, and contrast have emerged from our examination as Sidney's basic structural devices. The Old *Arcadia*'s characteristic fault, if we choose to call it that, is too tight and predictable an organization, not too loose a one. The perfectly obvious painstaking care with which the parts of the romance are put together precludes any verdict of an offhand jeu d'esprit. It seems almost certain that Sidney had the organization of the whole in mind when he began, although to be sure a few separate songs or eclogues or prose passages may have been inserted later. Not only the specific passages which foreshadow later events, like Gynecia's dream of her dead husband in Book II, but the whole careful relation of predictions in the earlier books and events in the later, the symmetrical buildup of passion to the central climax at the end of Book III and its subsequent deflation in the second half of the romance, proclaim a work intricately planned and meticulously executed. The immaturity some critics have detected in the Old *Arcadia* is certainly not apparent in Sidney's very considerable powers of construction. The intricate plot of the Old, cassically simple in its five-act structure,[5] precisely organized in its smaller units, has not received sufficient praise.

5. Sidney's reasons for choosing a five-act plan need further discussion. The New *Arcadia*, with its five acts swamped by precisely that episodic construction Aristotle excoriates, testifies that Sidney did not adopt a five-act structure from sheer love of classical precedent. Nor does his interest in the stage of his time, as shown in the *Defence* for example, seem sufficient of itself to account for a classical form. Furthermore, the form of classic tragedy and comedy must have seemed at first a hopelessly inadequate principle of organization for the endless plot of a romance like *Amadis*. Only by rigorous choice of incident—only by preclassicizing his plot as it were—does Sidney make his dramatic structure work. And even so, the Old *Arcadia* is vastly more complex than *Aminta*, for example. It lacks, too, some of the fundamental elements its structure leads us (and would have led the Elizabethan reader) to expect. It has, for example, no *peripeteia* as that word is traditionally used. After the seduction, fortunes do begin to decline precipitously, but this is not the ironic reversal Aristotle had in mind. This reader is hard pressed to find any real *anagnorisis:* neither the two princes nor Basilius really has the capacity for it. *Katharsis* is absent, too. Pity we feel, though hardly real fear. Finally, one looks in vain for a "great action" unless the princes' campaign of rape be so construed. All this is far from denying that in broad outline Sidney used the tragic form. But he adapted it, he did not copy it.

3. The Speeches

Sidney's romance, neither diffuse nor careless, is still vulnerable to attack for its style. Why did he cover his neoclassic trellis with such flowery ornament? His theme is clearly expressed and clearly developed; what did he hope to add? The traditional answer has been that, having decided on his matter, he proceeded to decorate it with the accepted flowers of rhetoric and, pleased with his skill in arranging them, he lost all sense of restraint, laid on his tropes with a trowel. This verdict seems to me no more accurate than the claim that the Old *Arcadia* is a careless youthful toy. If the style could be demonstrated to be as carefully calculated as the structure, and as carefully integrated with theme and structure as they are with one another, then perhaps we might revise our opinions of the Old *Arcadia*.

The main outlines of the story are now fresh in the reader's mind. The romance is built up of a series of scenes, each of which is the occasion for several more or less formal speeches; between these scenes Sidney's narrative to his sister and her friends runs on in a less elevated, more direct style. These rhetorical occasions are carefully integrated with the sudden outbreaks of melodramatic violence deliberately placed throughout the narrative, and the two elements—the melodramatic adventure and the oratory—develop and advance the theme of the conflict of reason and passion. Clarity of explanation required that a fundamental ingredient of the theme be ignored—the humor. This essential yeast of Sidney's rhetorical style must now be considered. For on a closer look, Sidney's intention, in the formal exchanges of oratory by which his characters advance toward the consummation of their desires, is not altogether serious or straightforward. Arcadians and Arcadianism, we shall find, cannot always be accepted at face value. Both must be examined in context. The scene must be considered as both a dramatic and a stylistic unit, and in detail. Context is crucial.

Critics of Sidney have, of course, pointed out the speeches which interlard the narrative. A few students have dissected them with care into their component parts and pointed out the tropes and schemes that comprise these parts. But the relationship among the speeches, the speakers, the spirit in which they are spoken, and the point in the romance at which they occur all seem to have been forgotten. Only when these things are taken into account does the exact nature of Sidney's use of rhetorical style really become clear. It is not enough to trace out the several parts of the classical oration, to name all the figures of language he employs, and then to rest easy thinking these conclusions a full explanation. They are not. Such a procedure alone is not only incomplete but misleading: it implies that the Old *Arcadia* is simply a rhetorical showpiece. Sidney's work emerges, to be sure, from a tradition of rhetorical showpieces, the late Greek romances, and has sometimes been regarded as just such another. In this view, the story is simply a skeleton for gorgeous language. But we have seen already that Sidney's romance is more complex than this superficial description indicates. Establishing as fact Sidney's very frequent use of formal rhetorical theory is only the first step in understanding his use of it as a literary technique. Does the awareness that a character's speech on a certain occasion follows a recognized organization and employs the appropriate diction and rhetorical devices teach us anything in itself? It is at best a clue to the organization of the work, not its whole explanation. Rhetorical theory is, for the Old *Arcadia* at least, an imperfect tool of literary analysis.

A rigorous examination of the romance from the standpoint of rhetorical theory turns soon into a hopeless muddle in which the speeches are resolutely laid down on a chosen Procrustean bed of precept. If we wish to analyze a speech into its component parts, for example, which "arrangement" shall we use? We can follow the seven-part schematization which Sidney's old friend Thomas Wilson advances in *The Arte of Rhetorique* (Entrance, Narration, Proposition, Division, Confirmation, Confutation, Conclusion)[1] since Sidney seems to have followed it in the *Defence of Poesie*. Or, building on the certainty that Sidney remembered the six parts distinguished by Cicero,[2] we may look for Wilson's seven parts less the Proposition. Or since we are told that Sidney translated the first two books of Aristotle's *Rhetorica* we might look at that famous treatise for a hint as to Sidney's rhetorical theory:

A speech has two parts. You must state your case, and you must prove it. . . . Of these two parts the first part is called the Statement of the case, the second part the Argument. . . . The current division is absurd. For "narration" surely is part of a forensic speech only; how in a political speech or a speech of display can there be "narration" in the technical sense? or a reply to a forensic opponent? or an epilogue in closely-reasoned speeches? Again, introduction, comparison of conflicting arguments, and recapitulation are only found in political speeches when there is a struggle between two policies. They *may* occur then; so may even accusation and defense, often enough; but they form no essential part of a political speech. . . . It follows, then, that the only necessary parts of a speech are the Statement and the Argument. These are the essential features of a speech; and it cannot in any case have more than Introduction, Statement, Argument, and Epilogue.

1. Ed. G. H. Mair (Tudor and Stuart Library, 1909), p. 7.
2. *De Oratore* 2.309-35, and elsewhere.

. . . We ought only to bring in a new name if it indicates a real species with distinct specific qualities; otherwise the practice is pointless and silly.[3]

Or, following the *Ad Herennium* as explained by Wilbur S. Howell, we can admit that there are no hard-and-fast rules:

The *Rhetorica ad Herennium* analyzes the six parts of the oration when it discusses invention; and then, when it comes to arrangement, as the second main part of rhetoric, it says in effect that arrangement in theory consists of placing in each part of the oration what should be placed there, whereas arrangement in actual practice consists in knowing under what circumstances to omit one or more of the standard parts of the oration or when to rearrange their standard order.[4]

Some of the speeches in the Old *Arcadia* seem to fit into each of these categories, some into none. Who is to choose? Since there is no single standard and we hardly know which, if any, individual arrangement Sidney tried to follow, we can only examine the text, forcing Sidney's dialogue into predetermined frames with reluctance and with Aristotle's caveat about pointless and silly divisions ringing in our ears. Neither is it always easy to classify a speech by type: funeral oration, petition, forensic speeches of various kinds are easy to spot but many others do not fall naturally into a recognized category. And once we have named them we must still ask ourselves how they are used.

So our task is twofold: we must see whether Sidney is actually following the precepts of formal rhetoric, and, more important, we must explore his use of them in a work of imaginative literature. An attempt to analyze the Old *Arcadia*'s speeches by citing chapter and verse in the rhetorical manuals of the time proves to be not only of limited use but of endless duration. A general analysis of the speeches, as far as possible in the language of everyday

3. *Rhetorica*, trans. W. Rhys Roberts, 3. 1414 a–b, in *The Works of Aristotle*, ed. W. D. Ross (Oxford, 1924), Vol. 9. It is John Hoskins, in *Figures of Rhetoric*, who first mentions Sidney's lost translation of Aristotle.
4. *Logic and Rhetoric in England, 1500–1700* (New York, 1961), p. 72. *Ad C. Herennium: De Ratione Dicendi (Rhetorica ad Herennium)*, English trans. Harry Caplan (Loeb Classical Library, 1954), 3. 9–10.

literary discussion, seems adequate for the purposes of this essay. I have considered only those oratorical occasions which seemed to me to illuminate Sidney's use of a rhetorical style.

Sidney, with Elizabeth's anger at his own attempt to counsel his Sovereign fresh in his mind, must have drawn the opening scene of the Old *Arcadia* with sardonic pleasure. Basilius asks advice of Philanax only "for fashions sake": his mind, as often the case with his real-life counterparts, was already made up. Philanax' speech (3–5), given "with a true harte and humble Countenance," and important as we have seen it to be in the thematic progression of the romance, is a vain effort from the beginning. Both subject and ruler seem to be acting out a ritual, a stock situation in the imaginative representation of monarchy, which even Philanax must suspect to be quite futile. Certainly the reader, coming to the Old *Arcadia* from the *Mirror for Magistrates* or *Gorboduc*, would have been greatly surprised at a tale which started out with a sensible monarch taking good frank advice to heart. He would have expected exactly what does transpire: a foolish prince ignores good advice and thereby begins a chain reaction of folly and suffering. Philanax' speech, though in an unmistakably high style, suits its dramatic context perfectly. On such a grave occasion no one would expect anything else. It is a passably good example of a formal state speech in Elizabeth's reign, as the following series of brief quotations will show. Philanax begins:

> Moste Redoubted and beloved Prince, yf aswell yt had pleased yow at yor goyng to *Delphos*, as nowe to have used my humble service, bothe I shoulde in better season and to better purpose have spoken, and yow perhaps at this tyme shoulde have bene, as no way more in daunger, so, undoubtedly muche more in quyet-nes. I woulde then have saide . . .

His Entrance made, Philanax goes on to employ the old rhetorical device—Aristotle and Cicero both discuss it—of telling his audience at length what, in other circumstances, he might have said:

> These thirty yeares past have yow so governed this Realme, that, neither youre Subjectes have wanted Justice in yow, nor yow

obeydience in them, and youre Neighboures have founde yow so hurtlesly stronge, that they thought yt better to rest in youre frendship then make nowe tryall of youre enmity.

In a seven-part form the Narration should end here; but instead of a single Proposition Sidney has several sentences, amplifying the same point:

Yf this then have proceeded oute of the good Constitution of youre State, and oute of a wyse providence generally to prevent all those thinges, which mighte encomber youre happynes, why shoulde yow now seeke newe Courses, since youre owne example comfortes yow to continew on.

The caveat with which the speech began—"wisdome and vertue bee the onely destinyes appointed to man to followe"—is repeated.

And that yt ys moste certeyne, no Destiny nor influence, whatsoever can bringe manns witt to a higher poynte then wisdome and goodnes.

A third amplification:

Why shoulde yow deprive youre self of governing youre Dukedome, for feare of loosing youre Dukedome, like one that should kill him self for feare of deathe?

At this point in the speech it seems clear that Sidney is not following a seven-part form. He is far closer to Aristotle's simpler four-part form. His apology at the beginning is an Introduction. Philanax' statement about what he would have said before Basilius left for the oracle had he been given a chance, plus his description of thirty years of tranquility, together constitute a Statement. The series of Propositions is really the first Argument, which is concluded by:

Lastly, whether youre tyme calle yow to live or dye, doo bothe like a Prince.

A second Argument, that the two princesses cannot be protected by sequestration in the forest, is summarized by:

O, no, hee can not bee good, that knowes not whye hee ys good.

The Epilogue would be:

> Thus farr hathe youre Comaundement and my zeale drawne mee
> to speake, whiche I like a man in a valley may discerne hilles, or
> like a pore passinger may espy a Rock, so humbly submitt to
> youre gracyous Consideracion: Beseeching yow to stand wholly
> uppon youre owne vertue, as the surest way, to meynteyne yow
> in that yow are and to avoyde any evell which may bee imagined.
>
> [3–5]

Which system of classification is used seems to me not crucial,
so long as one sees the larger sections of the speech: the two
parallel arguments—one for Basilius and his kingdom, one for the
princesses—that virtue is the only defense against mutability.
Aristotle's division seems clearer, though doubtless the addition of
a few epicycles could make the speech fit a seven-, six-, or five-part
pattern.

The really important quality of the speech is clear, whatever
the categorization: it is a formal address to one's sovereign, frank
but ornate. There would have been no question of this in an
Elizabethan reader's mind. None would have felt it to be exaggerated, "literary," or a concession to an extravagant taste. Fortu-
nately this contention can be, if not proved, at least advanced
strongly. Consider this similar passage from another context:

> Most feared & beloved, most swete & gracious Soveraine To seke
> out excuses of this my boldnes & to arme the acknowledging of a
> faulte with reasons for it might better shewe, I knew I did amisse
> then any whitt diminish the attempt especially in your judgement
> who able lively to discerne into the nature of the thing done, it
> wer folly to hope with laying on better colours to make it more
> acceptable. Therfore carying no other olive branches of inter-
> cession, but the lying myself at your feete, nor no other insinu-
> acion either for attention or pardon but the true vowed sacrifice
> of unfeined love, I will in simple & direct termes (as hoping they
> shall only come to your mercifull eyes) sett down the over flow-
> ing of my minde in this most important matter importing as I
> think, the continewance of your safety, & as I know the joyes of
> my life. And because my wordes I confesse shallow, but comming
> from the cleere well-spring of most loyall affection have already

delivred unto your gracious eares, what is the general somme of my traveyling thoughtes. Herein I will now but onely declare what be the reasons that make me thinke the mariage . . . unprofitable for you. Then will I answere your objections of those feares which might procure so violent a refuge, the good or evill which might come unto you by it, must be considered, either according to your state or your person. To your Estate, what can be added to the being an absolute borne & accordingly respected princesse? But as they say, the Irishmen are wont to tell them that dye, they are ritche, they are feare, what nede they to dye? So truely to you indued with felicities byond all others (though shorte of your desertes) a man may well aske, what maketh you in such a calme to chaunge course, to so helthfull a body to applye such a weary medecine? what hope can recompense so hazardous an adventure? [5]

A candid reader will admit it to be just such another piece of rhetoric as Philanax' speech though in this case it is Sidney speaking in real life to his Queen about her proposed marriage with the Duke D'Alençon.[6] Placed in such a context, the style of Philanax' speech cannot justly be called "applied"; it is as integral a part of Sidney's romance as any style can be. It is not only decorous, it is—as we have just seen—realistic.

A closer look at the first scene between Pyrocles and Musidorus reveals an altogether different but equally decorous rhetorical context. When Pyrocles is on the point of confiding to his friend the stupendous news that he is in love, Musidorus suddenly seizes the initiative and reproaches him for his abstracted behavior and prolonged walks in the forbidden part of the forest. Musidorus' text is his beginning *sententia*:

> A mynde well trayned and longe exercysed in vertue, (my sweete and worthy Cossen) dothe not easily chaunge any Course yt once undertakes, but uppon well grounded and well weyed Causes: For, beeyng witness to yt self of his owne Inwarde good, yt fyndes no thinge with oute yt of so highe a pryce, for which yt

5. *Works*, 3, 51.
6. Goldman comments: "The speech of Philanax clearly recalls the tone of Sidney's remonstrance to Elizabeth on the question of the French Marriage" (*Sidney and the Arcadia*, p. 160).

shoulde bee altered: Even the very Countenaunce and behavyor
of suche a man dothe shewe forthe Images of ye same constancy
by meynteyning a right harmony betwixt yt, and the Inwarde
good, in yeelding yt self sutable to the vertuous resolutions of the
mynde.

He then applies his moralization to Pyrocles:

This speeche, I direct to yow, Noble frende *Pyrocles,* the excellency of whose mynde and well chosen course in vertue, yf I doo
not sufficiently knowe, (havinge seene suche rare Demonstracyons
of yt) yt ys my weykenes, and not youre unworthynes: But as in
deede I knowe yt, and knowyng yt, moste derely love bothe yt,
and him that hathe yt, so must I needes say, that since oure late
comming into his Contrey I have marcked in yow, (I will not
say an alteracyon) but a Relenting truely and slaking of ye mayne
Carryer yow had so notably begun and allmoste performed.
And yt in suche sorte as I can not fynde sufficyent reasons in my
greate love towardes yow howe to allowe yt: For, to leave of
other secrett argumentes which my acquayntance with yow
makes mee easily fynde, this, in effect to any man, may bee manifest, that whereas yow are wonte in all the places yow came, to
give youre self vehemently to knowledg of those thinges which
mighte better youre mynde, to seeke the familiarity of excellent
men in Learning and Souldyery, and lastly to putt all these thinges
in practize, bothe by continuall wyse proceedinges and worthy
enterpryses as occasions fell for them. Yow, now, leave all these
thinges undone, yow let youre mynde falle a sleepe, besydes
youre Countenaunce trubled which surely comes not oute of
vertue, (for vertue like the cleare heaven ys withowte Clowdes)
and lastly which seemeth straunge unto mee, yow haunte greately
this place: wherein besydes the Disgrace yt mighte falle of yt,
(whiche that yt hathe not allredy fallen uppon yow, ys more
rather luck then providence, the *Duke* having sharply forbiden
yt) yow subject your self to solitarynes, the slye Enimy yt
moste dothe seperate a man from well doyng.   [10–11]

Pyrocles is crushed by this condemnation, of course, yet not so
taken aback that he cannot reply in a speech even longer and more
carefully organized than that of his friend. The Entrance is a
brief acknowledgment of Musidorus' praise:

Excellent *Musidorus,* in the prayses yow gave mee in the beginning of youre speeche I easily acknoulledge the force of youre
good will unto mee.

The Narration explains why Musidorus was deceived:

For, neyther coulde yow have thought so well of mee, yf extremity of love had not somethinge daselled youre eyes, Nor yow
coulde have loved mee so entierly, yf yow had not beene apte to
make so greate, (thoughe undeserved) Judgmentes of mee. And
eeven so must I say of those Imperfections, to whiche, thoughe I
have ever throughe weykenes beene subject, yet, yow by the
dayly mending of youre mynde have of late bene able too looke
into them, which before yow coulde not discerne.

The Exposition summarizes his point:

So that the Chaunge yow spake of falles not oute by my ympayr-
ing, but by youre bettering, and yet under the leave of youre
better Judgment I must needes saye thus muche (my Deare
Cossyn) that I fynde not my self wholly to bee Condempned,
bycause I doo not with a Continuall vehemency followe those
knowlledges which yow calle ye betteringes of my mynde.

The Division develops the argument that his solitude has thera-
peutic value:

For, bothe the mynde yt self must, (like other thinges) some
tymes bee unbent, or else yt will bee eyther weykened or broken,
and these knowlledges, as they are of good use, so are they not all
the mynde may stretche yt self unto: who knowes whether I
feede my myndes with higher thoughtes?, truly, as I knowe not
all the particularityes, so yet, see I the boundes of all these knoul-
ledges, but the workinges of the mynde I fynde muche more
infinite then can bee ledd unto by ye eye, or imagined by any that
distract theyre thoughtes withowte them selves, and in such Contemplacyons, or as I thincke more excellent I enjoye my solitarynes, and my solitarynes perchaunce ys the Nurse of these
Contemplacyons. Egles wee see flye alone, and they are but
sheepe which allway heard together: Condempne not therefore
my mynde some tyme, to enjoy yt self, nor blame not, the taking
of suche tymes as serve moste fitt for yt.

Halfway through the Division he interrupts his own argument:

> And here *Pyrocles* sodenly stopped, like a man unsatisfyed in him self, thoughe his witt mighte well have served to have satisfyed an other: And soo looking with a Countenaunce as thoughe hee desyered hee shoulde knowe his mynde, withoute hearing him speake, to breathe oute some parte of his Inwarde evell, sending ageane new blood to his face, hee continewed his speeche in this maner.

A new justification for his conduct has just occurred to him which makes him break in upon his argument and change his defense into a speech of praise:

> And Lorde, deare Cossyn (sayde hee) dothe not the pleasantnes of this place, carry in yt self sufficyent Rewarde, for any tyme lost in yt or for any suche daunger that mighte ensewe? Doo yow not see how every thinge Conspires together to make this place a heavenly Dwelling? Doo yow not see the grasse, howe in Coloure they excell the Emeraudes every one stryving to passe his fellowe, and yet they are all kept in an equall heighte? And see yow not the rest of all these beutyfull flowers, eche of whiche woulde requyr a mans witt to knowe, and his lyfe to express? Doo not these stately trees seeme to meynteyne theyre florisshing olde age with the onely happynes of theyre seate beeyng clothed with a Continuall springe, bycause no beauty here shoulde ever fade? Dothe not the Ayer breath health whiche the Byrdes, (bothe delightfull bothe to the eare and eye) do dayly solempnize with the sweete consent of theyre voyces? Ys not every Eccho here a perfect Musick? and these fressh and delightfull brookes, how slowly they slyde away, as, lothe to leave the Company of so many thinges united in perfection, and with how sweete a Murmer they lament theyre forc[ed] departure: Certeynly, cer-teynly Cossyn yt must needes bee, that some Goddess this Dezert belonges unto, who ys the sowle of this soile, for, neyther ys any lesse then a Goddess worthy to bee shryned in suche a heape of pleasures, nor any less then a Goddess coulde have made yt so perfect a Moddell of the heavenly dwellinges.   [11-13]

This eulogy, probably the most quoted passage in the romance, is usually thought typical of the idyllic tranquility of Arcadia. A glance at the rhetorical context exposes the error. The sudden interruption and midcourse change in type of speech show this elaborate praise to be only a new rhetorical weapon which, occurring to Pyrocles on the spur of the moment, has been pressed into immediate service to gain the victory in a friendly debate. The scenery holds no more interest for Pyrocles than for any of the other characters. Their principal, even their exclusive, interest is in each other. So here with Pyrocles; he aims not at praising the scenery but at deceiving his friend. Sidney assumed in his audience a sufficient knowledge of rhetoric to perceive this. Any doubts the careful modern reader has are resolved by Sidney's description of Musidorus' response to this oratorical gambit:

> But *Musidorus* had all this while helde his looke fixed uppon *Pyrocles* countenaunce and with no less loving attention, marcked, howe his wordes proceeded from him; But, in bothe these hee perceyved suche straunge diversityes, that they rather increased newe Doubtes, then gave him grounde to settle any judgement. For besydes his eyes, sometyme eeven greate with teares the ofte chaunging of his Coloure with a kynde of shaking unstedfastnes over all his body, hee mighte see in his Countenaunce some greate determynacion mixed with feare: And mighte perceyve in him store of thoughtes rather stirred then disgested, his wordes interrupted continually with sighes, which served as a Burthen to eche sentence, and the tenor of his speache (thoughe of his wonted phrase) not knitt together to one constant ende but rather dissolved in yt self, as the vehemency of ye Inward passion prevayled, whiche made *Musidorus* frame his answer nearest to that humor which shoulde soonest putt oute ye secrett. For having in ye beginning of *Pyrocles* speeche (whiche defended his solitarynes) framed in his mynde a Reply ageanst yt, in the prayse of Honorable action in shewyng that suche kynde of Contemplacyon ys but a gloryous tytle to Idlenes: That in action a man did not onely better him self, but, benefitt others. That the Goddes woulde not have delivered a sowle into the body, whiche hathe armes and legges only instrumentes of Dooynge, but that yt were intended, the mynde shoulde employ them, and that the mynde shoulde best knowe his owne good or evell by practize: whiche knowledge was the onely way to en-

crease the one & correct the other, besydes, many other better argumentes, whiche the plentyfulnes of the matter yeelded to the sharpenes of his witt. When hee founde *Pyrocles* leave that, and falle to suche an affected praysing of the place, hee lefte yt like-wyse, and joyned therein with him, because hee founde him in that humor, utter more store of passyon.   [13]

Sidney is perfectly explicit: Musidorus must switch tactics in reply to Pyrocles' new gambit. Further undercutting of this famous elaborate praise of the Arcadian climate (after Musidorus has neatly turned Pyrocles' oratorical flank by praising the company of one who can praise solitude so persuasively and sweetly) emphasizes how far back Sidney the narrator stands from this purple passage. Pyrocles says:

But I merveyle at the excessive prayses yow give to this Dezart, in truthe yt ys not unpleasant, but, yet, yf yow woulde returne unto *Macedon,* yow shoulde see eyther, many heavens, or fynde this, no more then earthely: And, even *Tempe,* in my *Thessalia,* where yow and I to my greate happynes were brought up to-gether ys nothinge inferior unto yt. But, I thincke yow will make mee see that the vigor of youre witt can shewe yt self in any sub-ject, or else yow feede sometymes youre solitarynes, with the Conceyptes of the *Poetts:* whose liberall pennes can as easily traveyll over mounteynes as Mole hilles, and so like well disposed men, sett upp every thinge to the highest Noate, especially, when they putt suche wordes in the mouthe of one of these Fantasticall mynde infected people, yt Children and Musicians calle Lovers.
   [14]

A pointing finger in the margin could hardly have made Sidney's warning more explicit—read the full-blown rhetoric in the roman-tic context, remember who is talking. Now since almost everyone in the romance biologically capable of doing so falls in love, violently, passionately in love, and since they are poets to a man, the reader ought to be braced for speeches "set up to the highest Note." Here at the beginning of the romance Sidney takes pains to indicate the spirit in which we are to read. He alerts us to the constant rhetorical maneuver in which his characters are engaged, and if we ignore the warning we shall constantly misread the

Arcadia,[7] taking as Sidney's heartfelt philosophy what is intended as primarily rhetorical attack and defense by one of his characters.

We shall, for example, be surprised at the next round in the two friends' debate. The mention of the word "love" throws Pyrocles into a fit, and this seizure forces from him—to his intense relief—the confession that he is in love. "Nowe the Eternall goddes forbidd . . . cryed out *Musidorus*" (14). The vehemence is, of course, part of the oratorical game. No one, audience, Musidorus, or anyone else, could have had the slightest doubt about Pyrocles' condition. Love's signs were as egregious as those of the plague, and as well known. Pyrocles, "having broken the yce," narrates his troubles at length to his friend. When he has done he places himself at the feet of the stern judge, his friend Musidorus, who has had time to collect his tropes and schemes and replies with a free-wheeling exhortation. He first praises his friend indirectly:

> And ys yt possible, that this ys *Pyrocles* the onely young Prince in the Worlde formed by Nature, and framed by education, to the true exercyse of vertue,? or ys yt in deede some *Amazon Cleophila*, that hathe counterfeited the face of my frend in this sorte to vexe mee? For likelyer sure I woulde have thoughte, that my owtewarde face mighte have beene disguysed, then that the face of so excellent a mynde coulde have beene thus blemisshed? O, sweete *Pyrocles* seperate youre self a litle, yf yt bee possible from youre self, and let youre owne mynde looke uppon youre owne proceedinges, so shall my woordes bee needeles & yow best instructed.

He reminds Pyrocles of his father's hopes:

> See with youre self, how fitt yt will bee for yow in this youre tender youthe, (borne so great a Prince, and of so rare not onely

---

7. As does Boas, for example, when he refers to this scene in the Old as "A too prolonged sentimental debate" (*Sir Philip Sidney*, p. 63). Goldman, too, seems to miss the point: "Even the right to love is argued bitterly between the two heroes —Musidorus reproaching his friend for desertion of the life of heroic effort, and seeking to win him to it again by this lively exposition of the strenuous philosophy which they had once held in common: 'A mind wel trayned . . .' Pyrocles defended his new devotion to love as best he could, but made little immediate impression upon Musidorus, who was prepared to answer him stoutly, '. . . having in the beginning of *Pyrocles* speech . . .' Further on, the argument is renewed with even greater zeal" (*Sidney and the Arcadia*, pp. 164–65).

expectation, but proof) desyered of youre oulde Father & wanted of youre native Contry, (nowe so nere home) to direct youre thoughtes from the way of goodnes, to loose, nay, to abuse youre tyme?

And of his wider fame:

Lastly, to overthrowe all the excellent thinges yow have done, which have filled ye worlde with youre fame, as yf yow shoulde drowne youre ship in the longe desyered haven, or like an yll player, shoulde marr ye last acte of his tragedy: Remember, (for I knowe, yow knowe yt) that yf wee will bee men, the reasonable parte of youre sowle, ys to have absolute Comaundement, ageanst which yf any sensuall weykenes aryse, wee are to yeelde all oure sounde forces to the overthrowyng of so unnaturall a Rebellyon. Wherein, how can wee want corage, synce wee are to dealle ageanst so weyke an Adversary, that in yt self, ys no thing but weykenes: Nay, wee are to resolve, that yf reason direct yt, wee must doo yt, and yf wee must doo yt, wee will doo yt.

Sententia gives way to an attempt at shaming Pyrocles:

For, to say I can not, ys Chyldish, and I will not, womanish: And, see, how extremely every way, yow endaunger youre mynde, for to take this womanly habite, (withoute yow frame youre behavyour accordingly) ys wholy vayne, youre behavyour can never come kyndely from yow, but as the mynde ys proportyoned unto yt: So that yow must resolve, yf that yow will play youre parte to any purpose, (what sover peevish Imperfections are in that sexe) so soften youre harte for to receyve them, the very first downestepp to all wickednes. For, doo not deceyve youre self, my deare Cossen, there ys no man sodenly eyther excellently good, or extremely evill, but growes eyther as hee holdes him self up in vertue, or lettes him self slyde to vicyousnes.

Finally Musidorus gets to the point:

And let us see, what power ys the Author of all these trubles, forsoothe, Love, Love, a passyon, and the barest and fruitlessest of all passyons, feare breedeth witt, Anger ys the Cradle of Corage, Joy openeth and enhableth the harte, Sorow as yt closeth yt, so yet, draweth yt inwarde to looke to the correcting of yt self, and so, all of them generally, have power, towarde some good by the direction of reason. But this basterd Love, (for in deede the name of Love ys unworthely applyed to so hatefull an humor) as yt ys ingendred betuixt lust and Idlenes, as ye matter yt worckes uppon ys no thing but a certeyn base weykenes whiche, some gentle fooles calle a gentle harte: As his adjoyned Companyons bee, unquietnes, longinges, fonde Comfortes, faynt discomfortes, hopes, Jealosyes, ungrounded rages, Causeles yeeldinges, so ys the highest ende yt aspyers unto, a litle pleasure with muche payne before, and greate repentance after: But that ende, (how endles yt ronnes to infinite evills) were fitt ynoughe for the matter wee speake of, but, not for youre eares, in whome in deede, there ys so muche true disposicion to vertue. Yet thus muche of his worthy effectes in youre self ys to bee founde, that yt utterly subvertes the Course of Nature, in making reason give place to sence, and man, to woman.

His last stage of argument is a shaky attempt at historical defini-tion:

And truely, hereuppon (I thinck) yt first gott the name of Love, for in deede the true Love hathe that excellent nature in yt, that yt dothe transforme the very essence of the Lover, into the thinge loved, uniting, and as yt were incorporating yt, with a secrett, and Inward worcking, and herein doo these kyndes of Love imi-tate ye excellent. For, as the Love of heaven makes one heavenly, the love of vertue vertuous, so dothe the love of the Worlde make one become worldly, and this effeminate love of a Woman, dothe so womanish a man, that, yf yow yeelde to yt, yt will not onely make yow a famous Amazon but a Launder, a Distaff spinner, or whatsoever other vyle occupacyon theyre idle heades can im-agyn, and theyre weyke handes performe: Therefore, to truble yow no longer with my tedyous, but, loving wordes, yf eyther yow remember, what yow are, what yow have beene, or what yow must bee, yf yow Consider, what yt ys, that mooves yow, or with what kynde of Creature yow are mooved, yow shall fynd ye cause so smalle, the effectes so daungerus, youre self so unworthy to ronne into the one, or to bee driven by the other, that, I doubte not, I shall quickly have occasyon, rather to prayse yow, for having Conquered yt, then to give yow further Counsell howe to doo yt.   [15-17]

He is having a wonderful time, it is plain to see, needling his friend; though the arguments are indisputably sound, the only phrase with the ring of sincerity is the one about tedious but loving words.[8] The content for this kind of speech had attained a certain regularity by Sidney's time, and Musidorus follows the pattern with care. Wilson, for example, lists the following common ingredients in such a speech:

Praise or condemnation
Expectation of all men
Hope of victorie
Hope of renowne
Feare of shame
Greatnesse of reward
Rehearsall of examples in all ages, and especially of things lately done.[9]

This kind of list formed the basis for the good advice Musidorus so enjoys delivering. One hopes his own enjoyment satisfied him,

8. This passage is discussed in a recent article by P. Albert Duhamel ("Sidney's *Arcadia* and Elizabethan Rhetoric," *Studies in Philology*, 45 [1948], 134–50). He points out that Musidorus' speech is calculated to convince: "Sidney presents Musidorus in a series of closely reasoned arguments showing that Pyrocles' behaviour is unfitting. These arguments are clearly drawn from several difficult topics which are thus employed in their classical manner as sources of probative material and not as affording hints for the expanding of the material" (p. 147). Pyrocles' reply, he points out, is meant to be seen as lame in comparison with Musidorus' attack. But he reads the passage as wholly serious and so fails to observe that Musidorus' strong arguments are ironically compromised by his subsequent behavior, that though Musidorus knows a lot about rhetoric he has yet to learn much about love. Thus we cannot confidently conclude that Sidney was making a strong case for arguments he believed sovereign for the disease of love. Zandvoort comments on this passage: "We may be sure that these words were assigned to Musidorus not by way of a rhetorical declamation, but as an expression of Sidney's inmost conviction. More even than the sensuous bias, the desire for action was characteristic of Sidney's mind" (*Sidney's Arcadia*, p. 150). But if Sidney firmly held these beliefs to be an answer to Pyrocles' predicament, why do they not help Musidorus when he too is struck down by Cupid? Sidney doubtless believed in a life of resolute heroism, but such resolution is repeatedly shown as ineffectual against the blind god. That the passage is intended as primarily comic it is impossible to doubt. Even Wolff, who was not averse to a serious reading, calls it "the high-water mark of Sidney's humor" (*Greek Romances*, pp. 330 ff.).

9. *Arte of Rhetorique*, p. 63.

because Pyrocles was not listening: "*Pyrocles* mynde was all this while so fixed uppon an other Devotion, that, hee no more attentively marcked his frendes discourse, then the Chylde, that hathe leave to play, marckes the last parte of his Lesson" (17–18).

The speeches, however, must go on, so we find that Pyrocles has heard enough to reply: "yet the very sounde having lefte the generall poyntes of his speeche in his mynde, the respect hee bare to his frende, broughte forthe this Answer" (18). His central device defending love is the hoariest chestnut in the history of rhetoric—he praises mother. This short speech of praise, offering all the traditional arguments in defense of woman, is concluded with:

> But, to tell yow true, I doo bothe disdayne to use any more wordes of suche a Subject, whiche ys so praysed in yt self, as yt needes no prayses, and withall, feare leste my Conceipte (not able to reache unto them) bringe forthe wordes, which for theire unworthynes may bee a Disgrace unto them, I so inwardly honor. Let, this suffise, that they are Capable of vertue, and vertue (yow youre self say) ys to bee loved, and I too, truely: But this I willingly confess, that yt likes mee muche better, when I fynde vertue in a fayre Lodging, then when I am bounde to seeke yt in an yll favored Creature, like a Pearle in a Doungehill.   [18–19]

After he has caught his second wind, his arguments are cleverer but less convincing:

> And, pore Love (sayde hee) Dere Cossyn, ys litle beholding unto yow, since yow are not contented to spoyle yt of ye honor, of the highest power of the mynde, which notable men have attributed unto yt, but yow deject yt, belowe all other passions (in truthe) some thinge straungely; Synce, yf Love receyve any disgrace, yt ys by ye Company of those passyons yow preferr unto yt. For those kynde of bitter objections, as, that Lusty Idlenes, and a weyke harte shoulde bee as yt were the matter and forme of love, rather tuche mee, (*Musidorus*) then Love: But, I am good witnes of my owne Imperfections, and therefore will not defend my self, but, herein I must say, yow deale contrary to youre self, for, yf I bee so weyke, then can yow not with reason stirr mee up, as

yow did by the remembrance of myne owne vertue, or yf in deede I bee vertuous, then must yow Confess, that love hathe his worcking in a vertuous harte, and so no doubt hathe yt what soever I bee. For, yf wee love vertue, in whome shall wee love yt, but in vertuous Creatures, withoute youre meaning bee, I shoulde love this worde of *Vertue*, when I see yt written in a Booke.

He attempts to turn the tables on his friend:

> Those trublesome effectes yow say yt breedes bee not the faultes of Love, but of him, that loves, as an unable vessell to beare suche a power, lyke evell eyes not able to looke on the sunne, or like a weyke brayne soonest overthrowne with the best wyne. Eeven that heavenly love yow speake of ys accompanyed in some hartes with hopes, greeffes, Longinges and Dispayres, and in yt heavenly love synce there are twoo partes, the one the Love of yt self, the other, the excellency of the thing loved, I (not able at the first leape, to frame bothe in my self) doo now like a diligent worckman, make redy the cheef Instrument, and first parte of that great worcke which ys love yt self: whiche, when I have a while practized in this sorte, then, yow shall see mee turne yt to greater matters. And thus gently, yow may, yf yt please yow, thincke of mee neyther doubte yow, because I werre a womans apparrell, I will bee the more womannish, since I assure yow (for all my apparell) there ys no thing I desyer more, then fully to proove my self a man, in this enterpryse: Muche mighte bee sayde in my defence, muche more for love, and moste of all for that Devyne Creature, which hathe joyned mee and love together. But these Disputacions are fitter for quyett Schooles then my trubled braynes, which are bent rather in deedes to performe then in wordes to defend the noble desyer yt possesseth mee.   [19–20]

The dubious Neoplatonism upon which he builds his house of cards is weak even in his own eyes, as the last sentence of the speech shows. Pyrocles begins to tire of the game, to plead a domination by real feeling, but Musidorus will not let him alone. His dismissal of the sophistry of Pyrocles' speech, "O Lorde, (saide *Musidorus*) howe sharpp witted yow are to hurt youre self" (20), is immediately parried by a Pyrocles who, despite his plea of exhaustion, still has a good deal of disputation in him: "No aunswered hee, but yt ys the hurte yow spake of, which makes mee so sharpp witted." The long series of exchanges that follows, essentially the same kind of stylized "can-you-top-this?" flyting so prevalent in the eclogues, finally brings Pyrocles to his knees: "The lengthe of these speeches before had not so muche cloyed *Pyrocles, thoughe hee were very Impacyent of longe delibera-cions,* as this last farewell of him, hee loved as his owne lyfe, did wounde his sowle" (21) (italics after "*Pyrocles*" mine). Musi-dorus' victory over his friend, basically a rhetorical one as we have seen, causes them both to collapse in a tearful embrace. Pyrocles' frantic confession of defeat convinces Musidorus of the hopeless-ness of his friend's case. Musidorus then decides, since satisfaction of his passion is the only possible antidote, to help Pyrocles to it. He reverses his oratorical posture and charges Pyrocles to be ever faithful to his mistress. Indicating once again that this florid senti-ment is not always to be taken *au grand serieux*, Sidney describes Pyrocles' relief in a restrained humorous aside: "*Pyrocles* harte was not so oppressed with the twoo mighty passions of Love & unkyndenes, but, that yt yeelded to some myrthe at this Com-aundement of *Musidorus*, that hee shoulde love *Philoclea*" (22).

The more closely one reads a scene like this, the more one admires Sidney's skill in manipulating the various devices of rhetoric for comic effect. Attention to context and speaker pre-vents attribution to Sidney of the linguistic excesses of his char-acters, and in this way exposes the humor more clearly. For the comedy in the Old *Arcadia* depends primarily on the manipula-tion of style for its effect. The scene we have just examined gently mocks several stock situations: the old war-horse contest between love and friendship on the one hand, and love and reason on the other; the first agonies of romantic love; above all, those "cheap tricks" of rhetoric which Sidney has so often been accused of abusing. Sidney's original Wilton audiences must have seen this clearly and been thoroughly amused. Perhaps even the modern reader can smile when, a short time after this scene ends, the roles are reversed and Musidorus has fallen violently in love with Pamela, to the consternation of Pyrocles:

Why, howe now Dere Cossen saide shee yow that were even now so highe in the pullpett, ageanst Love, are yow now become so meane an Auditor? Remember, that love ys a passion, and that a worthy manns reason must ever have the Masterhod. I recant, I recant, cryed *Musidorus*. [38]

The inevitable has come about, Cupid has triumphed; the vehement rhetorical reproaches of conventional wisdom evaporate in the face of real feeling and understanding sympathy.

The critic is tempted at first to call the whole scene straightforward parody, but the remainder of the romance proves such a classification much too one-sided. In the first place, the themes beneath the profuse language are the serious themes of the romance. Sidney would hardly have taken the trouble to develop them so rigorously if he had not intended them seriously. Secondly, the speeches are good enough to generate some real emotion in their own right. We are convinced by the end of Book I that both princes are seriously in love. Yet there is no denying the comic effect of much of their behavior, and no denying—as the foregoing analysis shows—that Sidney intended it. If we consider the speeches out of context and ignore the comic intent, our conclusions will be consistently wide of the mark. Brother Simon Scribner, for example, discussing Sidney's use of rhetorical question, has this to say about the famous "blades-of-grass" passage quoted a short while ago:

It is evident here that much more than mere description is achieved. Through the use of rhetorical question, Sidney is able to give a renewed impression of the poetical nature of Arcadia, of its effect on the heroes of the story, and while moving the narration to a climax, to prepare (by the evident emotion of the passage, witnessed to by the iteration), for the surrender of the heroes to its charms, and to those of its inhabitants.[1]

Knowing that the speech was a rhetorical maneuver allows us to see that the heroes do not have the slightest real concern with the poetical nature of Arcadia, or with the charms it undeniably pos-

---

1. Brother Simon Scribner, *Figures of Word-Repetition in the First Book of Sir Philip Sidney's Arcadia* (Washington, D.C., 1948), p. 23.

sesses, except insofar as these "natural benefits" can help them to their desires. Not Sidney but Pyrocles is using the rhetorical question and his real purpose is not to celebrate the "poetical nature" of Arcadia but to pull the wool over the eyes of his friend. The "evident emotion" of the passage is an ambiguous quality at best.

The fact is that the attentive modern reader, thus far along in the Old *Arcadia*, should be frankly puzzled about how seriously to take it. If he accepts every speech as wholly sincere he may become bored by the actors of the romance and even irritated at its creator. If he continues in his first reaction, "He can't be serious," he is going to be amused but not edified, and without any doubt Sidney wanted to edify his reader. Some middle ground has to be found if we are to read the remainder of the Old *Arcadia* with anything like pleasure. At this point we must be content with recognizing that the style is more skillful than has heretofore been supposed, that its exaggerated artfulness is put to dramatic use.

The straightforward comedy which Dametas brings with him offers a less ambiguous illustration of Sidney's spoofing of stock rhetorical situations. When the Principal Herdsman surprises the newly made Cleophila, he blusters "like him, that playes *Hercules* in a play and god knowes never had *Hercules* fancy in his heade: . . . Am not I *Dametas?* why, am not I *Dametas?* . . . Thow woman, or boy, or bothe, or whatsoever thow bee, I tell thee there ys no place for thee, get thee gone, I tell thee yt ys the *Dukes* pleasure, I tell thee yt ys Mr *Dametas* pleasure" (28). Cleophila remembers how to play out a comic scene when she is plunged in the middle of one:

> *Cleophila* coulde not chuse but smyle at him, and, yet taking her self with the maner, spake these wordes to her self: O *Spirite*, (saide shee) of myne, how canst thow receyve my myrthe in the mydest of thyne agonyes, and thow myrthe how darest thow enter into a mynde so growne of late thy professed enimy? [28]

Dametas goes on in the very top of Seneca his style: "Thy spirite, (sayde *Dametas*) dooest thow thincke mee a Spirite? I tell thee, I am the *Dukes* officer, and have the charge of him & his Daughters" (28–29). Cleophila's reply—"O Perle (saide sobbinge

Cleophila) that so vyle an Oyster shoulde keepe thee?"—elicits:
"By the Combecase of *Diana*, sware *Dametas*, this woman ys
madd. Oysters and Pearles? Doest thow thincke I will buy Oysters? I tell ye gett thee packing, or else I must needes bee offended"
(29). If Sidney could thus parody the Senecan rants he heard at
the Inns of Court, it seems reasonable to surmise that he could see
how ridiculous his own supposed "Arcadianism" would sound if
presented without qualifications and that he was neither ignorant
of nor averse to the comic possibilities it offered.

This supposition becomes a certainty in the second book. Gynecia begins with a not unmoving apostrophe to the sun and whatever other powers are responsible for her predicament:

> O *Sunne* saide shee whose unspotted lighte directes the stepps of
> mortall Mankynde, arte thow not ashamed to imparte the Cleare-
> nes of thy presence to suche an overthrowne worme as I am? O
> yee heavens, which continually keepe the Course allotted unto
> yow, can none of youre Influences preveyle somuche uppon the
> miserable *Ginecia*, as to make her preserve a Course so long em-
> brased by her? O Desartes Dezartes how fitt a guest am I for
> yow, synce my hart ys fuller of wylde Ravenous beastes then
> ever yow were, O vertue, how well I see, thow werte never but a
> vayne name, and no essentiall thinge which haste thus lefte thy
> professed Servaunt when shee had moste neede of thy lovely
> presence; O Imperfect proportion of Reason, whiche can to
> muche foresee, and so litle prevent, Alas, alas saide shee, yf there
> were but one hope for all my paynes, or but one excuse for all
> my faultynes: But wretche that I am, my torment ys beyonde all
> succor, and my evill deserving dothe exceede my evell fortune.
> For no thinge else did my husband take this strange Resolution to
> live so solitarily, For no thing else did the wyndes delyver this
> straunge guest to my Contry, For no thing else have the Des-
> tinyes reserved my lyfe to this tyme: But that I onely, moste
> wretched I shoulde become a plague to my self and a shame to
> woman kynde; yet yf my desyer how unjust soever yt bee,
> mighte take effect, thoughe a Thowsande Deathes followed yt,
> and every deathe were followed with a thousand shames, yet,
> shoulde not my Sepulchre receyve mee withoute some Content-
> ment: But alas, sure I am not that *Cleophila* ys suche, as can

answer my Love, And yf shee bee, how can I thinck shee will synce this mysguysing must come needes for some foretaken Conceipte, And eyther way, wretched *Ginecia*, where canst thow fynde, any small ground plott for hope to dwell uppon? No, no yt ys *Philoclea* his hart ys sett uppon, yf hee bee a hee, yt ys my Daughter whiche I have borne to supplant mee; But, yf yt bee so, the lyfe I have given the ungratefull *Philoclea*, I will sooner with these handes bereve thee of then my Byrthe shall glory shee hathe bereved me of my desyers? In shame there ys no Comforte, but, to bee beyonde all bondes of shame? [87–88]

The reader may think the language exaggerated but the feeling is sincere. Her willingness to die a "thowsande Deathes" to effect her desires, especially, is the very leitmotiv of all the Arcadians struck down by Love. Like them, she is painfully aware of the "Imperfect proportion of Reason." Yet the reflecting reader can hardly prevent his sympathy for her from being at least slightly weakened by her ludicrous predicament, overcome as she is by love for a false Amazon who is making love to her daughter. When she meets Cleophila, she hardly allows time for an exchange of civilities before she is down on her knees before her:

> *Cleophila* help mee, O *Cleophila*, have pitty on mee? *Cleophila* ran to her, merveiling what sodeyne sicknes had thus possessed her. And beginning to aske her the Cause of her sorowe and offering her service . . . O *Cleophila, Cleophila* sayde shee doest thow offer me phisick, whiche arte my onely poyson? or wilte thow doo mee service, whiche haste allredy broughte mee into eternall slavery? [90]

Is this intended as moving pathos? It is usually read as such, for Gynecia is the one character in the Old *Arcadia* most critics would agree is fully "third-dimensional." [2] Yet duchesses, even tragic ones

2. Zandvoort, for instance, comments: "Unlike the characters of Pamela and Philoclea, hers is almost fully developed in the original version; and the alterations which Sidney thought it necessary to make in her case are slight. . . . Such as they are, they seem to betray a certain sympathy of the author with the tragic figure of this passionate queen, a desire to uphold her dignity, which is absent in his treatment of her husband Basilius" (*Sidney's Arcadia*, p. 89). He then quotes J. J. Jusserand's description of her as "the worthy contemporary of the strongly passionate heroes of Marlowe's plays."

and even in pastoral romances, did not usually throw themselves at the feet of visiting Amazons, or indeed of visitors of any kind. The usual procedure if a violent scene were needed was for the visitor to throw himself at the feet of the duchess. Sidney's inversion leads us to suspect a comic intent.

But Sidney's comic qualification of her pathos does not stop here. Her outpouring of passionate regard is interrupted by her husband who, not surprisingly for one in his state of mind, immediately sends her home:

> But assoone as *Basilius* was ridd of his wyves presence, falling downe on his knees, O Lady sayde hee, whiche have onely had the power to stirr up ageane those flames which had so long layen deade in mee: See in mee ye power of youre Beauty, whiche can make oulde age, to aske Counseill of yowthe? And a Prince unconquered to become a Slave to a straunger? And when yow see that power of youres Love, that at leste in mee since yt ys youres (allthoughe in mee yow see no thing to bee loved). Worthy Prince answered *Cleophila*, (taking him up from his kneeling) bothe youre maner, and youre speeche are so straunge unto mee, as I knowe not how to answer yt better then with sylence: yf sylence please yow (saide the *Duke*) yt shall never displease mee, since my harte ys wholy pledged to obay yow, otherwyse yf yow woulde vouchesafe myne eares suche happynes, as to heare yow, they shall but Convey youre wordes to suche a mynde, whiche ys with the humblest degree of reverence to receyve them.   [92]

It is impossible to overlook the implicit comparison of this confession of affection to the one which Gynecia has just made on *her* knees. Now, however seriously we may choose to regard Gynecia, there should be unanimous consent from readers that Basilius shows himself to be a silly ass as soon and as often as possible. Yet there is nothing in his speech itself to indicate that he suffers any less than Gynecia, that our sympathy should be less intense. In fact, both speakers and both speeches are slightly ridiculous, as their juxtaposition shows.

Cleophila's predicament is more ludicrous still. For she is both wooer and wooed, and what she indignantly refuses to grant Basilius she must passionately plead for from Philoclea. As Basilius'

pursuit becomes even warmer, Cleophila's rejection of his importunities becomes increasingly ironical. For when she has to act
the opposite part, the pleading lover, she does it with a deadly
earnestness made still more amusing by the elaborate rhetorical
devices employed.

Look for example at her behavior at the end of the second book,
when Philoclea comes to her forced to intercede for her father in
a matter about which she would like to speak for herself. The two
lovers meet by the river bank, where Cleophila has been writing
a plaintive verse in the sand with a willow wand. This in itself is
so patently a stock situation that we must be suspicious of a joke.
Cleophila, like Gynecia and Basilius earlier in the book, hardly allows her visitor to open her mouth before she pours out her
troubles:

> At lengthe, *Philoclea* having a while mused, how to wade betwixt
> her owne hopeles affection, and her Fathers unbrydled hope, with
> blusshing Cheekes, and eyes cast downe to the grounde shee began
> to say: My Father, to whome I owe my self, and therefore must
> performe all Deutyes unto. When *Cleophila* streight embracing
> her, (and warranted by a womanly habite ofte kissing her)
> Desyered her to stay her sweete speeche, (For well shee knewe
> her Fathers arraunt, and should receyve a sufficyent answer):
> But, now shee demaunded leave, not to loose this longe soughte
> for Comodity of tyme, to ease her hart thus farr, that yf in her
> Agonyes her Desteny was, to bee condempned by *Philocleas*
> mouthe, at least *Philoclea* might knowe, whome shee had
> condempned.   [113–14]

The ironic similarities with Basilius' and Gynecia's cries for aid
are apparent enough, though in her passionate excitement Cleophila seems unaware of them. She apologizes to Philoclea in the
most fulsome manner for the informality of her situation: "Moste
beloved Lady, the incomparable Worthynes of youre self joyned
to the greatenes of youre estate, and the Importance of the thinge
whereon my lyfe consisteth dothe requyre, bothe lengthe of tyme
in the beginning and many Ceremonyes in ye uttering my enforced speeche" (114). This introduction is comical in itself,

when one thinks of the unceremonious haste of the embrace a moment before, and it gains more comic force when it is followed by the pompously egotistic, rhetorically inflated confession of who she is. The Entrance is elaborate:

> But the smalle oportunity of envyous occasyon with the malicyous eye hatefull Love dothe cast uppon mee, and the extreme bent of my affection, whiche will eyther breake oute in wordes or breake my hart, compell mee not onely to embrace ye smallest tyme, I may obteyne, but, to lay asyde all respectes due to youre self in respect of my owne lyfe, whiche ys nowe or never to bee preserved: I do therefore vowe to yow hereafter, never more to omitt all dutyfull formes, Doo yow now onely vouchsafe, to heare the matters of a moste perplexed mynde, yf ever the sounde of Love have come to youre eares, or yf ever yow have understood what force yt hathe had, to Conquer the strongest hartes, and chaunge the moste setled estates.

Now comes a series of characterizations of himself:

> Receyve here not onely an Example of those straunge Tragedyes, but one, that in hym self hathe conteyned all the particularityes of theyre mysfortune: And from henceforthe beleeve yt may bee, synce yow shall see yt ys, yow shall see I say, a Living Image and a present Story of the best Patern, Love hathe ever shewed of his worckmanship. But, alas, whether goest thow my toungue, or how dothe my harte consent to adventure the reveyling my nerest tuching Secrettes, but, spare not my speeche, here ys the Author of my harmes, the witnes of thy wordes, and the Judge of thy lyfe.

He finally reveals his identity in a climactic outburst:

> Therefore ageane I say, I say, O onely Princes attend here a myserable mirackle of affection, beholde here before youre eyes *Pyrocles* Prince of *Macedon*, whome onely yow have broughte to this falle of fortune, and unused *Metamorphoses* whome yow onely have made neglect his Contry, forgett his Father, and lastly forsake hym self. My sute ys to serve yow, and my ende ys to doo yow Honor, youre fayre face hathe many marckes in yt of amasement at my wordes: Thinke then what his amasement ys, from

whence they come, synce no wordes can carry with them the lyfe of the Inward feeling. Yf the highest love in no base person may beare place in youre judgement then may I hope, youre beuty will not bee withoute pity: yf other wyse yow bee (alas but let yt never bee so) resolved, yet shall not my deathe bee withoute Comfort, receyving yt by youre sentence.   [114–15]

Here Pyrocles sounds to the reader more like Dametas than like a prince. Philoclea, relieved that Cleophila is of noble birth, is more gratified still to find him a man. Her fluttered spirits obscure for her what is only too apparent to the reader: that Pyrocles is not so in love, not so transported by the occasion, as to neglect the order of his discourse. It is a carefully amplified self-dramatization which in the dramatic context makes him seem a foolish prig.

Dorus, too, has a difficult time supporting his heroic role. In order to obtain Pamela's notice he is forced to adopt the humiliating subterfuge of pretending love to Mopsa. Mopsa, an antidote not only to desire but to its usual veneer of noble sentiment as well, gives Dorus no ready occasion to betray his true self. But he perseveres, and soon Pamela notices "eyther great ignorance or a second meaning" in what he says:

And ys yt onely the fortune, (moste beutyfull *Mopsa*) sayde hee of wretched *Dorus*, that, fortune must bee the measure of his mynde? Am I onely hee, yt bycause I am in mysery, more mysery must bee layde uppon mee? Must that, whiche shoulde bee Cause of Compassyon, become an Argument of Cruelty ageanst mee?: Alas excellent *Mopsa* consider, that a vertuous Prince requyres the Lyfe of his meanest Subject & the Heavenly sonne disdaynes not to give lighte to the smallest worme? O *Mopsa*, yf my harte coulde bee as manifest to yow as yt ys uncomfortable to mee, I Doubt not the heighte of my thoughtes shoulde well counterveyle the Lowlynes of my quality. Who hathe not hearde of the greatnes of youre estate? who sees not that youre estate ys muche excelled with that sweete uniting of all Beutyes which remayneth & dwelleth with yow: who knowes, not, that all these are but Ornamentes, of that devyne sparck within yow, whiche beeyng descended from heaven, coulde not else where pick owte so sweete a Mansyon? But, yf yow will knowe what ys ye Bonde that oughte to knitt all these excellencyes together, yt ys a kynde of mercyfullnes, to suche a one, as ys in sowle devoted to those perfections. [95]

Pamela finds nothing inappropriate in the language of Dorus' discourse if it is really addressed to her, but for the reader the luster on the self-pity is dimmed by all those "Mopsa's." Even Mopsa dimly perceives that this paragon of gentility is trifling with her feelings:

> *Mopsa,* who allredy had had a certeyne smackering towardes *Dorus,* stoode all this while with her hande some tyme before her face, but Comonly (with a certeyne speciall grace, of her owne) wagging her Lippes and grenning, in stede of smyling: But all the wordes hee coulde gett of her was . . . in faythe yow Jeste with mee, yow are a mery man, in deede? But *Pamela* did not somuche attend *Mopsas* interteynement as shee markd bothe the matter *Dorus* spake, and the maner hee used in uttering yt, and shee sawe in them bothe a very unlikely proportion to Mistris *Mopsa.*
> [95–96]

Pamela, through the pattern of double-talk they have established, asks Dorus to produce his social credentials, and he replies with his tale of metamorphosis (98ff.). It recalls of course Pyrocles' confession of identity and confirms our impression that neither of our heroes is unduly modest. Dorus tells his tale at some length, and ends it with an apology for its brevity:

> Pardon therefore, (moste excellent Princess) yf I cutt of the Course of my Dolorous tale, synce yf I bee understood I have sayde ynoughe for the defence of my basenes. . . . Hee ended thus his speeche, but withall began to renewe his accustomed playntes & humble Intercessyons to *Mopsa,* who having no greate Battell in her Spirit, was allmoste broughte asleepe with the sweete delivery of his Lamentacyons. [101]

The reader, as I think Sidney intended, cannot help wondering whether Mopsa's peasant horse sense has not triumphed over Dorus' aristocratic self-congratulation. Pamela, once she sees Dorus as a social equal, is a pushover for his sweet talk. Not so stout Mopsa. Even when Dorus pleads his case with verse and music, her head is not turned:

> *Mopsa* . . . yet beeyng farr spent towardes *Dorus,* shee an-
> swered *Pamela,* that for all his quaynt speches shee woulde keepe
> her honesty close ynoughe: And that as for ye hye way of
> Matrimony, shee woulde go never a furlong furder, till my Mas-
> ter her Father did speake the whole worde hym self.   [102]

Even coming from Mopsa this is still good advice, advice Pamela
would have done well to heed. Wisdom is not all with the upper
classes, even in Arcadia. In a scene like this we can still object, of
course, to Dorus' inflated rhetoric. But we should not mistake
Sidney's intention in employing it. He is not simply drawing a
touching love scene with comic relief. He has distanced himself
from Dorus' speech, used it to characterize Dorus in a not altogether flattering way, and commented on it indirectly through
the obvious butt of his joke, the fetching Mopsa. Nor does
Pamela's gracious condescension emerge unscathed: Mopsa can see
through Dorus even if Pamela cannot. Thus the high rhetorical
style is manipulated for dramatic effect, is made an instrument to
comment on theme and characterization, is thoroughly and skill-
fully integrated into the narrative structure. In this larger view,
the "ornament" is not excrescent.

Formal oratory can be placed in an appropriate dramatic context far more simply than the speeches we have examined thus far.
Cleophila's placatory speech to the rebel mob at the end of Book
II is an obvious example. The narrative calls for a speech to save
the day; Cleophila bravely makes one, and a shrewd and direct
one, too:

> And unadvysed thinge yt ys, and I thincke, not heretofore seene,
> O *Arcadians,* that a woman shoulde give Counsell to men, a
> Straunger to the Contrey people, and that lastly in suche a pres-
> ence a private person as I am shoulde possess the Regall throne?
> But the strangenes of youre action makes that used for vertue,
> whiche youre vyolent necessity imposeth, for certeynly a woman
> may well speake to suche men, who have forgotten all manly
> governement: A Straunger may with reason instruct suche sub-
> jectes as neglect due poyntes of subjection. And ys yt merveyle
> this place ys entred into by an other, synce youre owne *Duke,*
> after xxx yeares government, dare not shewe his face to his fayth-

full people? Heare therefore O *Arcadians*, and bee asshamed, ageanst whome hathe this zealous rage bene styrred? whether have yow bent those manfull weapons of youres in this quyet harmeles Lodge? There are harboured no *Troianes* youre auncyent Enimyes, nor *Persians*, whome yow have in present feare? Here lodge none but suche, as eyther yow have greate Cause to love, or no Cause to hate? But, none other moste sure can yt bee, ys yt I? O *Arcadians* ageanst whome youre anger ys armed? Am I the marck of youre vehement quarrell? yf yt bee so, that Innocency shall not bee a stopp for furye? yf yt bee so, the Lawe of hospitallity may not Defend a Straunger fled to your Armes for succour: Yf lastly yt bee so, that so many valyant mens Corages can bee enflamed to the myscheef of one hurtles woman, I refuse not to make my lyfe a sacrifice to youre wrathe. Exercyse in mee youre indignation, so yt goo no furder, I am content to pay the great favoures I have receyved among yow, with the usury of my well deserving lyfe: I present yt to yow here, O *Arcadians* yf that may suffyse yow, rather then yow (called over the worlde the wyse and quyett *Arcadians*) shoulde bee so vayne as to attempt that alone, (which all youre Contry will abhorr) then yow shoulde shewe youre selves so ungratefull, as to forgett the fruite of so many yeares peaceable government, or so unmercyfull as not to have any fury over mastered with the holy name of youre Naturall *Duke*. For, suche a hellish madnes (I knowe) will never enter into youre hartes, as to attempt any thing ageanst his person, which no Successor (thoughe never so hatefull to hym) will for his owne sake leave unpunished: Neyther can youre wonted valure bee turned to suche a basenes, as instede of a *Duke* delyvered unto yow by so many Royall Auncestors, to take the Tyrannous yoke of youre fellow subject, in whome the [innate] meanes will bringe forthe Ravenous Covetusnes, and the newnes of his estate suspectfull Cruelty. Imagyn what coulde youre enimyes more wishe unto yow, then to see yow with youre owne handes overthrowe youre estate: O what woulde the first *Arcadians* youre worthy predecessors saye, yf they lived at this tyme, and sawe theyre ofspring defacyng suche an excellent Monarchy? whiche they with muche laboure and bloode wysely establisshed? No no, youre honest hartes will never so gratify youre hatefull Neighboures, nor so degenerate from youre famous Auncesters. I see in youre Countenaunces now vertuously settled no thing but Love and Duty to hym, (who onely, for youre sakes dothe embrace the government) the uncerteynty of his estate made yow take Armes: Now yow see hym well with the same Love lay them down. Yf now yow ende, (as I knowe yow will) hee will take no other accoumpte of yow, but, as of a vehement, I must confess over vehement affection, the onely Countenaunce shoulde proove a wickednes, But yt ys not so, I see very well, yow began with zeale, and will ende with reverence.   [123–24]

This speech has been much remarked, as showing the typical attitude of the Elizabethan governing class toward the fickle mob over whom they attempted to rule, and as illustrating the great importance which a training in oratory could have in carrying out the practical business of governing. Cleophila, it is said, righteously indignant at the canaille, reads them the riot act of Tudor political philosophy in plain language and at the same time cleverly offers them a peaceful way to save face.

But Cleophila is, we should remember, at least partly to blame for the rebellion in the first place. The confused determination upon which the mob acts includes the danger that "a Straunge Woman had now possest theyre Prince and government" (121). Sidney, of course, has no use at all for His Despised Poor, and their opinions can be automatically classed as contemptible; yet, as Basilius never tires of saying, singing, and versifying, Cleophila *has* gained absolute masterhood over him. All he has *is* at her command. The mob could hardly have made a more accurate determination, unless they had fixed on the Duke himself. And indeed they have. But they are easily fooled out of their fell purpose by Cleophila, who feels no obligation to be wholly honest in persuading them. She says, for example: "Here lodge none but suche, as eyther yow have greate Cause to love, or no Cause to hate? But, none other moste sure can yt bee, ys yt I? O *Arcadians* ageanst whome youre anger ys armed? Am I the marck of youre vehement quarrell? yf yt bee so, that Innocency shall not bee a stopp for furye? yf yt bee so, the Lawe of hospitallity may not Defend a Straunger fled to your Armes for succour." The Arcadians, of course, do have cause to hate her; she has bewitched their Duke, their Duchess, and their Princess. The irony is amusing, as well as serious, but it is unquestionably intended: with the help of his cousin, this self-righteous orator is shortly to make plans for introducing into Arcadia the foreign army which he scornfully mentions and dismisses in his speech. His disguised identity is the very opposite of "Innocency," and what he thinks of the laws of hospitality can safely be left to the reader's perspicacity. Impeccable as the reproaches to the mob may be in themselves, Cleophila is hardly the person to make them. Here, too, the formal oratorical style is dramatically decorous: not only does the situation call for a speech, but the speech itself is made to comment ironically on both speaker and situation. The style becomes an integral part of the romance.

It would be heretical to look upon the famous celebration of the joys of love and friendship and the sorrows of their conflict, which opens the third book, as anything but noble sentiment, pure and unalloyed. The late C. S. Lewis has voiced the opinion of modern admirers of the romance when he says that we read the *Arcadia* not for the instruction and not for the style, but for the nobility of its sentiment.[3] Yet we have seen by now that the two princes are not such paragons of virtue, such soap-opera heroes, as they are usually made out to be. We should not be surprised to find them human here too, underneath their gorgeous discourse. The setting of the scene is idyllic in the best Arcadian manner:

> There [in the same glade where they had formerly talked of love] sitting downe amongst the sweete flowers whereof that Contry was very plentyfull, under the pleasant shade of a Brode-leaved *Sicamor*, they recoumpted one to an other theyre straunge Pilgrimage of passyons, omitting no thinge which the open harted Frendship ys wonte to lay forthe, where there ys Cause to comunicate bothe Joyes & sorowes: For, in Deede there ys no sweeter Taste of Frendship then the Cuppling of theyre Sowles in this Mutuality eyther of Condoling or Comforting. Where the oppressed mynde, fyndes yt self not alltogether miserable,

3. *English Literature in the Sixteenth Century*, pp. 338 ff.

since yt ys sure of one, which ys feelingly sory for his misery: And the joyfull spendes not his Joy eyther alone or there where yt may bee envyed, but may freely send yt to suche a well grounded object, from whence hee shall bee sure to receyve a sweete reflection of the same Joyes. [159]

The scene set and the appropriate moral reflections amplified, the two princes are free to resume their favorite pastime: "Then woulde there aryse betuixt them Loving Debates of theyre Ladyes Beautyes, of theyre owne Constancyes, and some tymes gloryously stryve whether had bene the moste wretched" (159). Sidney likes to deflate his two heroes in subordinate clauses, and he seldom does so more adroitly than here. The glories of friendship so painstakingly amplified, balanced, opposed, and alliterated in the preceding lines lose in nobility and sentiment but gain in humor as we learn to what glorious strife they have led. All the inflated sentiment in the world about love and friendship does not conceal their single-minded and practical pursuit of their desires.[4]

The "Loving Debates" which follow show this single-mindedness clearly (the quibble seems to be intentional; the princes love one another, debate about love, and love to debate). The two friends begin with good-natured banter about Fortune's unequal treatment of them:

Alas, sayde *Cleophila,* (when shee had a while pawsed after her frendes Musick) Can yow not joye sufficyently in youre joyes, but yow must use youre joyes, as yf yow woulde vauntingly marche over youre frendes myseryes? Bee happy still my *Dorus,* but wishe the same happe to hym, whome good will dothe make to place muche of his hope in yow. Not the same happ (sayde *Dorus* smyling) *Philocleas* happ I freely graunte yow, but I pray yow lett not youre *Amazon* eyes bee busyed upon the Lady *Pamela,* For youre Lookes have an attractive power in them, and

4. Even Goldman seems to have sensed this, though he ascribes it to Sidney's love for noble, manly action: "But once they both accept love as part of their active life, every step of their double courtship is directed with energy and strategy toward the achievement of their ends. It is interesting to note that the women, in love and out, display the same irrepressible energy in seeking to achieve their ends" (*Sidney and the Arcadia,* p. 165).

youre harte ys not made of the hardest Metell: And are yow affrayed of that (sayde *Cleophila*) from henceforthe bee not, for hardly are Starres seene in daylight, but I woulde fayne knowe, what assurance yow have of ye Chaunging favor of Fortune. I have hearde of them that dreamed muche of holding greate Treasures, and when they awaked founde no thinge in theyre handes but a Bedstaff: Glad woulde I bee to bee assured of youre well beeyng, for mee thinckes, the goddes bee too unequall to Mankynde, yf they suffer not good to come from one Kynesman to an other, by a secrett confusion as wee fynde daily evell dothe by manifest infection. Therefore, synce youre Joy was suche as yow woulde fynde in youre harte to singe yt, doo now for my sake vouchesafe to say yt: My Joyes are suche, saide *Dorus* as neyther suffer in them selves uncerteynty, nor are in daunger by inconstancy, Lett mee therefore, Doo no wronge to my Motherly Destenyes (whiche have woven mee so blessed a webb) by ungratefull forgetting theyre favoures. And since I have often tyered ye *Muses* with the hidyous Tune of my Dolefull affectes, I will nowe sawce those Sorowes with some more pleasaunt exercyses.

Dorus then sings his "Comycall" tune ("The Merchaunt Man"), which Cleophila requites with a "Tragicall" inversion of the same phrases. Cleophila then takes Dorus in her arms and implores him to tell of his adventures. He complies:

Alas (saide *Dorus* with a chaunged Countenaunce) the Cruell Schoole master makes the silly Chylde thincke a litle play greate sporte, and howe muche the more wee neede greate help, smalle help, seemes the greater unto us: For longe beaten in mysery yt makes us measure oure myndes by oure powers and not by oure wisshes, and the harte stuffed with wofullnes, ys glad greedily to sucke the thinnest ayer of Comfort: Farr am I (God knowes) from the place, where I hope to stoppe, But yet well advaunced I am from thence where I tooke my start. Then did hee declare unto her the Discourse of all that, with whiche heretofore, fayre Ladyes, I have trubled yow . . . [the narrator then recounts Dorus' adventures]. And therefore now saide *Dorus* my Dere Coszen to whome Nature began my Frendship, Education con-

firmed yt and verture hathe made yt eternall, here have I discovered the very foundacyon whereuppon my Lyfe ys buylt:
Bee yow ye Judge betwixt mee and my fortune. The vyolence
of Love ys not unknowne unto yow, and I knowe my Case shall
never want pitty in youre Consideracyon. Howe all the Joyes
of my harte do leave mee in thinckinge, I must for a tyme bee
absent from yow. The eternall Truthe ys witness unto mee, I
knowe I shoulde not so sensibly feele the Panges of my last Departure: But this enchauntment of my Restles Desyer hathe suche
aucthority in my self above my self, that I am become a Slave
unto yt. I have no more freedome in myne owne Determina-
cyons, my thoughtes are all bent to carry away my burdenous
blisse. Yet moste beloved Coszen, rather then yow shoulde
thincke I doo herein vyolate that holy bande of true Frendship
wherein I unworthy am knitt unto yow, Comaunde my staye:
Perchaunce, the force of youre Comaundement may worck suche
impressyon, which no Reason of my owne can imprint unto yt,
for the Goddes forbid, the fowle worde of abandoning *Pyrocles*
mighte ever bee objected to the faythfull *Musidorus*. But yf yow
can spare my absence, whose presence no way serves yow, and
by the Devision of these twoo Lodges ys not ofte with yow,
Nay yf yow can thincke my absence may (as yt shall) stand yow
in stede by bringing suche an Army hether, as shall make *Basilius*
willing or unwilling to knowe his owne happ in graunting yow
Philoclea: Then I will cherefully goo aboute this my moste
desyered enterpryse, I shall thincke the better half of yt allredy
atcheeved beeyng begun in the fortunate hower of my Frendes
Contentment.

The narrator supplies for us the appropriate gestures and expressions:

These wordes as they were not knitt together with suche a
Constant Course of flowynge eloquence as *Dorus* was wonte to
use, so was his voyce interrupted, with sighes, and his Countenaunce with enterchaunging Coloure dismayde: So muche his
owne harte did fynde hym faulty, to unbynde any way the
continuall use of theyre dere frendshipp. But, Oh feminine Love,
what power thow haste in mens hartes? Many tymes hee had bene
desyerous to signify his happy success and finall determinacyon
with *Pamela:* But his harte woulde never serve to come to this

poynte, till one worde emboldened an other kyndely to discover
to his Frende his owne unkyndenes.

Dorus has, it appears, taken the words out of Cleophila's mouth:

Cleophila, who had beefore purposed to make the like declara-
cyon uppon what slippery grounde her hope stoode, and yet
how farr her hopes in *Philoclea* were advaunced, how farre by
Ginecia they were hindered; when this last Determinatyon of
Dorus strake her attentive eares, shee stayed a great while oppressed with a Deade amasement. There came streighte before her
mynde, made tender with wooes, the Images of her owne Fortune, her tedyous longinges, her Causes to dispayer, the Comber-
some folly of *Basilius,* the enraged Jelosy of *Ginecia* her self a
Prince withoute Retinewe a Man anoyed with the trubles of
womankynde, Loathsomely Loved, and daungerusly Loving, and
now for the perfecting of all her Frende to bee taken away by
hym self to make the losse ye greater by the unkyndenes. But,
within a while shee resolutely passed over all inward objections,
and therefore preferring her Frendes proffitt to her owne desyer,
with a quyet but harty Looke shee thus answered hym. Yf I bare
thee this Love (vertuous *Musidorus*) for myne owne Sake, and
that oure Freendship grewe bycause I for my parte mighte
rejoyse, to enjoy suche a Freend, I shoulde nowe so throughly
feele myne owne Losse, that I shoulde Calle the heavens and
earthe to witnes, howe cruelly yow robbe mee of my greatest
Comfort, measuring the breache of Frendshipp, by myne owne
passyon.

She now proceeds to deny feeling the perturbation she has, in fact,
just felt:

But bycause, in deede I Love thee for thy self, and in my judgment, Judge of thy worthynes to bee beloved, I am content to
leave all that which mighte please my self. I am content to buylde
my pleasure upon thy Comforte, and then will I deeme my happ
in Frendship greate when I shall see thee whome I Love, happy;
Lett mee bee sure, thow Lovest mee still, the onely pryce of true
affection: Goo therefore on worthy *Musidorus* with the guyde
of vertue, and service of fortune, Lett thy Loves bee Loved, thy
Desyers prosperus, thy escape safe, and thy Journey easy, Let

every thinge yeelde his help to thy Desert. For my Parte, absence shall not take the frome myne eyes, nor afflictions shall barre mee from gladding in thy good, nor a possessed harte shall keepe thee from the place yt hathe for ever allotted unto yow.

The narrator explores Dorus' perplexity at Cleophila's apparently superior fellow-feeling:

But *Cleophila* (who had now looked to the uttermoste of yt and establisshed her mynde uppon assured Determynacyon) my onely Frende sayde shee, since to so good towardnes youre Curtuous Destenyes have conducted yow, Lett not a Ceremonyall Consideracyon of oure mutuall Love bee a Barr unto yt? I joy in youre presence, but I joye more in youre good, that Frendship bringes forthe the fruites of enmity which preferrs his owne tendernes before his Frendes Domage, For my parte, my greatest greef herein shall bee, I can bee no further servisable unto yow.

This is too much for Dorus:

O *Cleophila* (sayde *Dorus* with his eyes eeven covered with water) I did not thincke so soone to have displayed my Determynacyon unto yow, but to have made my way first into youre Loving judgment, But, alas as youre sweete Disposicyon drewe mee so farr, so dothe yt more strengthen mee in yt: To yow therefore bee the due Comendacyon given who can conquer mee in Love ànd Love in Wysdome. As for mee, then shall goodnes turne to evell, and ingratefullnes bee the token of a true harte when *Pyrocles* shall not possess a Principall seate in my sowle, when the name of *Pyrocles* shall not bee helde of mee in devoute Reverence.

The narrator's dry reflection sets the stage for the end of the scene:

I thincke, they woulde never have come to the Cruell instant of parting, nor the yll Faring worde of Farewell, had not *Cleophila* seene a farr of the oulde *Basilius* who had beene every where to seeke her synce hee had ended his Sacrifyce: And nowe beeyng come within Compass of discerning her, hee began to frame the Lovelyest countenaunce hee coulde, stroking upp his Legges,

setting his Bearde in due order & standing bolt upprighte. Alas
(sayde *Cleophila*) beholde an evill for tooken of oure sorowfull
Departure, yonder, see I one of my furyes which dothe dayly
vexe mee, Fare well, Farewell my *Musidorus*, the goddes make
fortune to wayte on thy vertues, and make mee wade throughe
this Lake of wretchednes: *Dorus* burste owte into a fludde of
teares wringing her fast by the hande. No no, saide hee I goo
blyndfolde whether the Course of my yll happ carryes mee, for
nowe too late my harte gives mee, this oure separating can never
bee prosperus: But, yf I Live, attend me here shortly with an
Army.   [160–66]

That Sidney's final intention in a scene like this was partly, if
not primarily, comic seems to me undeniable. Underneath the
ceremonial celebration of friendship and of the still greater power
of "female love," the two princes meet and plan their campaign
of seduction, trying all the while to outdo each other in affection,
misery, and nobility of language. Their real feelings and desires
are repeatedly contrasted with the noble emotions they profess.
Sidney has made no secret of this contrast; it is all implied in his
description of the "Loving Debates," a description which ends
("But yf I Live, attend mee here shortly with an Army") on a
note of practical civil disobedience. If we construe Sidney's intention here as an earnest attempt to create nobility of sentiment by
an unremitting application of gorgeous flowers of rhetoric we
shall miss all the fun. We shall feel he has lost his sense of stylistic
proportion, when the whole purport of his romance is to show
how ridiculous his characters are when they lose theirs.

A sense of proportion—in love, in language, in life—is what the
Arcadian court most needs. They are all ridiculously without restraint. Basilius, seeking out Cleophila when she has parted from
Dorus, greets her with a rant out of *Hercules furens* no less silly
than that of Dametas which we have already discussed:

Yow mighte have seene *Basilius* humbly swell, and with a Lowly
looke stand uppon his tipptoes; suche diversity her wordes delivered unto hym. O *Hercules* (answered hee) *Basilius* afrayde?
or his blood Colde that boylles in suche a Furnace? Care I who ys
with mee, while I enjoy youre presence? Or ys any place good

or badd to mee, but as yt pleaseth yow to bless or Curse yt?
O lett mee bee but armed in youre good grace, and I Defye what
ever there ys or can bee ageanst mee: No, no, youre Love ys
forcible, and my Age ys not withoute vigor.   [168]

Cleophila is bored with Basilius but not with emotional or rhetorical scenes: "*Cleophila*, assoone as hee was departed went towardes
Pamelas Lodge in hope ageane to have seene her frend *Dorus*, to
have pleased her self with a newe paynefull farewell" (169). Her
pain comes from another quarter, however; she runs into Gynecia,
who is just at the beginning of a frantic apostrophe to Darkness
(Gynecia is in a cave):

O Darcknes (saide shee) whiche dothe lightsomely mee thinckes
make mee see the picture of myne inward Darcknes, synce I have
chosen thee to bee the secret witnes of my Sorowes, Lett them
receyve a safe receypte in thee, and esteeme them not tedyous:
But, yf yt bee possible, lett the uttering them bee some discharge
to my overladen brest. Alas, Sorowe, now thow haste the full
Sacke of my Conquered Spirites, rest thy self a while, and sett
not still newe fyers to thyne owne Spoylles: O accursed Reason
how manye eyes haste thow to see thy evills and howe dumbe,
nay blynde arte thowe in preventing them? Forlorne Creature
that I am, I woulde I mighte bee freely wicked, since wickednes
dothe prevayle. But the Foote steppes of my over troden vertue
ly still as bitter accusacyons unto mee; I am devyded in my self,
how can I stande? I am over throwne in my self who shall rayse
mee, vyce ys but A Nurse of Newe Agonyes, and the vertue I
am devorced from, makes the hatefull Comparyson the more
manifest. No, no vertue either I never had but a shadowe of thee,
or thow thy self are but a shadowe. For how ys my sowle abandoned? How are all my powers layde waste? My desyere ys
payned bycause yt can not hope, and yf hope came, his best
shoulde bee but myscheef, O straunge mixture of humane myndes,
onely somuche good lefte, as to make us Languish in oure owne
evills: Yee infernall Furyes (for yt ys to late for mee to
awake my Deade vertue or to please my Comfort in the Angry
godes) yee infernall Furyes (I say) ayde one that dedicates her
self unto yow. Lett my Rage bee satisfyed since the affect of yt
ys fitt for youre service: Neyther bee afrayed to make mee too

276

happy, synce no thing can come to appease the smarte of my
guylty Conscyence, I desyer but to asswage the sweltering of my
hellish Longing dejected *Gynecia?*   [172]

Again one hesitates over how to read it. No one can fail to feel
sorry for her; yet Cleophila does:

> *Cleophila* no sooner hearde the Name of *Gynecia* but, that with
> a Colde sweate all on her, as yf shee had bene redy to treade
> uppon a deadly stinging adder, shee woulde have withdrawne her
> self, but her owne passyon made her yeelde more unquyett
> motyons then shee had done in Commyng. So, that shee was
> perceyved . . .   [172–73]

This time Gynecia is both distraught and angry:

> O saide *Gynecia*, howe good Leysure yow have to frame these
> scornefull answers? ys *Gynecia* thus to bee dispysed? Am I so vyle
> a worme in youre sighte? No, No, trust to yt harde harted
> Tygre, I will not bee the onely Actor of this Tragedy, synce I
> must falle, I will press downe some others with my Ruyns? synce
> I must burne, my spytefull Neighboures shall feele of my fyer?
> Doest thow not perceyve that my diligent eyes have persed
> thorowe ye Cloudy Maske of thy Disguysement? Have I not
> tolde thee O foole (yf I were not muche more foole) that I
> knowe thow wouldest abuse us with thy owtewarde shewe? Wilt
> thow still attend the Rage of Love in a womans hart? The Girle
> thy well chosen Mistris perchaunce shall defend thee, when
> *Basilius* shall knowe howe thow haste sotted his mynde with
> falsehood, and falsely soughte the Dishonor of his howse: Beleeve
> yt beleeve yt unkynde Creature I will ende my myseryes with
> a Notable example of Revenge, and that accursed Cradell of
> myne shall feele the smarte of my wounde, thou of thy Tyranny,
> and lastly (I Confess) my self of myne owne worke.   [173–74]

As well as possibly supplying a source for a much-discussed
Shakespearian line,[5] she calls a spade a spade. Cleophila *is* abusing
them with her outward show, she *has* besotted Basilius' mind with
falsehood (the last example of this in the scene immediately pre-

5. York says to Margaret, the she-wolf of France, in *3 Henry VI:* "O tiger's
heart wrapt in a woman's hide!" (I.iv.137).

ceding), she *has* falsely sought the dishonor of his house. But the matrix of these bald truths is a theatrical tantrum which compromises what Gynecia says. A promise of satisfaction of her one desire tricks her into spending a night of passion in the same cave— but with her husband. Basilius' enthusiasm for his assignation with the woman he supposes to be Cleophila is, like everything else in Arcadia, extravagant.

Blessed bee thow O Nighte sayde hee that haste with thy sweete winges shrowded mee in the vale of blisse? Yt ys thow that arte the first begotten Chylde of tyme, the day hathe beene but an usurper upon thy delightfull inheritance? Thow invitest all Living thinges to Comfortable Rest, thow arte the stopp of stryfe, and the necessay Truce of approching Battells . . . O *Basilius* saide hee the rest of thy lyfe tyme hathe bene but a Dreame unto thee, yt ys now onely thow begynnes to live, nowe onely thow haste entered into the way of blisfullnes? Shoulde fancy of Mariage keepe mee from this Paradyse, or opinion of I knowe not what promyse bynde mee from paying the righte Dutyes of nature and affection? O who woulde have thoughte there coulde have bene suche difference betwixt women? Bee not Jelous no more, good *Gynecia*? but yeelde to the preheminence of more excellent giftes? support thy self uppon suche marble pillers as shee dothe? Deck thy brest with those Alablaster bowells that *Cleophila* dothe: Then accompanyed with suche a litle perhapps thow mayste recover the possession of my otherwyse included Love. But alas *Gynecia*, thow canst not shewe suche evidence, therefore thy Plea ys vayne.   [256–57]

The Duke's ludicrous demonstration that beauty lies in the mind of the beholder causes a great deal of suffering. The suffering (which swiftly follows) is real enough, but so is the humor, and the reader is left to puzzle out the relationship between the two.

In the clearly comic scenes, a rant by Dametas, for example, the spirit in which we are to read is fairly obvious. Sidney tells us himself that it is laughter not pity which he wishes to evoke. Yet the similarities of these comic speeches to those of the serious characters make at least one reader suspicious that the ludicrous can often be found as easily in the one place as in the other. It is a mistake, I think, to consider one wholly serious and the other simply a comic complement.

The most important love scene in the Old *Arcadia* is Pyrocles' seduction of Philoclea. It is the only true consummation scene in the Old *Arcadia*'s wide spectrum of love-making and merits comment for this if for no other reason. Pyrocles, having beguiled the Duke and Duchess into their tryst (and hence indirectly caused the Duke's "death" and the succeeding political turmoil), makes his way to Philoclea's chamber. He has bolted all the doors to the lodge, or at least all those he knows about. Sidney makes pointedly clear his state of mind:

> [Pyrocles] with panting breathe and sometymes sighes not suche as sorowe (restrayning the inward parts) dothe make them glad to delyver: But, suche as the Impacyence of desyer with the unsurety of never so sure hope ys wonte to breathe owte.
>
> [217–18]

Through the open door to her chamber he gets his first glimpse of "her beutyes eclipsed with no thinge but with a fayre smock," as she lies on her bed. Conveniently enough, she is complaining about Pyrocles' neglect. He is struck dumb:

> And with suche a pace as reverent feare dothe teache, hee came to her bedd syde: where kneeling downe, and having prepared a longe Oration for her, his eyes were so filled with her sighte, that as yf they woulde have robbed all theyre fellowes of theyre services, bothe his harte faynted, and his Toungue fayled in suche sorte, that hee coulde not bringe forthe one worde, but referred her understanding to his eyes Language.   [219]

Conventionally surprised to see him, she is not unduly harsh:

> But, shee in extremity amased to see hym there at so undue a season, and asshamed that her beutyfull body made so naked a prospect drawing in her dilicate Lymmes into the weyke guarde of the Bedd, & presenting in her face to hym, suche a kynde of pityfull Anger, as mighte shewe this was onely a faulte.   [219]

We expect a speech of reproach, but hardly the one she gives. For she upbraids him not for surprising her in her bed at a compromising hour but, as she supposes, for coming to torment her trusting love further:

> O *Cleophila,* or *Pyrocles,* (for whether Name I use, yt muche skilles not, synce by the one I was first deceyved and by the other now betrayed). what straunge motyon ys the guyde of thy Crewell mynde hether? Doest thow not thincke the day tormentes thow haste given mee sufficyent, but, that thow doest envy mee the Nightes quyett? wilt thowe give my Sorowes no truce, but, by making mee see before myne eyes, howe muche I have lost, offer mee due Cause of Confirming my Complaynt? Or ys thy harte so full of Rancoure, that thow doest desyer to feede thyne eyes, with the wretched spectackle of thyne overthrowne enemy? and so to satisfy the full measure of thy undeserved Rage with the receyving into thy sighte the unrelevable Ruyns of my desolate lyfe? O *Pyrocles, Pyrocles,* for thyne owne vertues sake Lett myseryes bee no Musick unto thee, and bee content to take to thy self some Coloure of excuse, that thow diddest not knowe, to what extremity thy Inconstancy or rather fallshoode hathe broughte mee.   [219-20]

To leave her in torment is the furthest thing from Pyrocles' mind, as he hastens to tell her in a speech even more indirect than her own. She is, beneath the poetic prose, asking to be asked; he now lets her know that the time is right:

> *Pyrocles,* (to whome every sillable shee pronounced was a Thunderbolt to his harte) egally distracted betuixt amasement and sorowe, abasshed to heare suche a stopp of his desyres, (greeved with her payne but tormented to fynde hym self the Author of yt) with quaking lippes and pale cheare, Alas, Dyvine Lady sayde hee: youre Displeasure ys so Contrary to my desert, and youre wordes so farr from all expectation, that I have leste abillity nowe I have moste neede, to speake in ye Cause, upon which my self dependeth. For my truthe ys so undoubtedly Constant unto yow, my hart ys so assured witness to yt self of his unspotted faythe, That, (having no one thing in mee wherowte any suche Sacriledge mighte aryse) I have nothing like wyse in so direct thinge to say for my self, but sincere and vehement protestatyons: For in truthe there may moste wordes bee spent, where there ys some probabillity to breede on bothe sydes Conjecturall allegacyons.

280

But so perfect a thinge ys my Love in yow as yt suffers no questyon, so yt seemes to receyve Injury by any addicyon of wordes
unto yt, yf my Soule coulde have beene polluted with Treachery,
yt woulde like wyse have provyded for yt self due furniture of
Colourable answers: But as yt stoode upon the naked Confidence
of his untouched Duty, so I must Confess yt ys alltogether unarmed ageanst so unjust a vyolence as yow lay uppon mee. Alas,
lett not the paynes I have taken to serve yow, bee now ac-
coumpted Injuryous unto yow? Let not ye Daungerus Conning
I have used to please yow, bee deemed a Treason ageanst yow;
Synce I have deceyved them, whom yow feare, for youre sake,
Do not yow Destroy mee for theyre sake. What can my wordes
furder express? I have ridd them bothe oute of the howse, There
ys none here to bee eyther hynderers or knowers of the perfecting the mutuall Love which once my Love wrought in yow
towardes mee, but onely the Allmighty powers, whome I Invoke
to bee the tryers of my Innocency; And yf ever my thoughtes
did receyve somuche as a faynting in theyre true affection, yf
they have not continually with more ardoure from tyme to tyme
pursewed the possession of youre sweetest favoure, yf ever in
that profession they receyved eyther spott or falshoode, then lett
theyre most horrible plaigues falle uppon mee. Lett myne eyes
bee deprived of theyre Lighte which did abase ye heavenly
Beames that strake them, Lett my falsifyed toungue serve to none
use, but to bemone myne owne wickednes? Lett my harte em-
poysoned with detestable Treason bee the seate of infernall
Sorowe? Let my Soule with the endless anguish of his Conscience
become his owne Tormentor?   [220–21]

Pyrocles seems not struck wholly dumb: his real message—the
family and servants are out of the way, the doors are locked, and
the coast is clear—is plain enough. In a situation so clearly defined
the reader expects at least a token expression of shocked surprise
from the lady, and so Philoclea's next speech seems to be:

O false Mankynd, (cryed oute the sweete *Philoclea*) howe can an
Impostumed harte, but yeelde forthe evill matter, by his mowthe?
Are oathes there to bee beleeved where vowes are broken? No,
no, who dothe not feare due recompencing plaigues, dothe litle
feare, the Invoking of plaigues will make them come ever a whitt

the sooner. But alas, what ayleth this newe Conversion? Have yow yet an other sleighte to play? Or do yow thincke to deceyve mee in *Pyrocles* forme, as yow have done in *Cleophilas?* Or rather now yow have betrayed mee in bothe those, ys there some thirde Sexe lefte yow? Into whiche yow can transforme youre self, to enveigle my Simplicity? Enjoy, enjoy the conquestes yow have allredy wonne, and assure youre self yow are come to the furthest poynte of youre Cunning: For my parte unkynde *Pyrocles*, my onely Defence shall bee Beleef of nothinge, My Comfort my faythfull Innocency, and the punishment I desyer of yow shall bee youre owne Conscyence.

But by the end we see that she is still accusing Pyrocles of trifling with her feelings. This finishes off the prince: "*Philocleas* hard percevering in this unjust Comdempnacyon of hym did so over-throw all the mighte of *Pyrocles* mynde, (who sawe that tyme woulde not serve to make proof by Deedes, and the better wordes hee used the more they were suspected of deceiptfull Cunninge)" (221). Neither deeds nor speeches will serve, so Pyrocles faints dead away like the heroine in a "penny dreadful." *This* will show her the depth of his feelings! And it does. She rushes to the other extreme—rapturous penitence:

O unfortunate suspicyons (sayde shee) the very meane to lose that, wee moste suspect to lose? O unkyndenes kyndenes of myne which turnes an Imagined wronge with an effectuall Injury? O folly, to make quarrells my Supplications, or to use hate as the Mediator of Love? Chyldish *Philoclea?* haste thow throwne away the Jewell wherein all thy pryde Consisted? haste thow with too muche haste overronne thy self? Then woulde shee Renewe her kisses and yet not fynding the Lyfe returne Reduble her playntes in this maner: O Devyne Sowle sayde shee, whose vertue can possess no less then the highest place in heaven, yf for my Eternall plaigue thow haste utterly lefte this moste sweete man-syon before I followe thee with *Thisbyes* punishment of my Rash unwarynes, Heare this protestacyon of myne, that ys, the wronge to thee, proceeded of a moste syncere but unresistable affection; So ledd with this pityfull example yt shall ende in the mortall hate of my self, and yf yt may bee I will make mee a Tombe of thy memory.   [222]

Needless to say, even at a time of extreme anxiety she is aware of the sources and analogues of her predicament in the long tradition of romantic literature. Now, she sees, is the time for a tragic but infinitely romantic end. Purely by chance, however, Pyrocles opens his eyes at precisely the crucial moment and she, forgetting modesty in relief, throws herself into his arms. The blazon which Sidney inserts—as having passed briefly through our hero's mind just before he lies down beside her—increases the suspense until finally we leave them in their happy plight.

One cannot belittle the style of this scene. It is subtle, amusing, and touching. But its purpose is not to reveal the elevated sentiments and delicate palpitations of the lovers. It is exactly the reverse of such a rhetorical chromo. Its exaggerated rhetoric serves as a decorous covering for the real interest of both parties—satisfaction of physical desire. The extreme indirection of the language would to a reader of the time in no way hide the basic situation of proposition and reply around which the scene is built. The expressions of limitless regard each offers to the other are intended to be counters in the question-and-answer game as much as outpourings of real feeling.

The first real trial of Pyrocles' affection comes when he awakens and finds that Dametas has locked the door, making him and Philoclea prisoners *in flagrante delicto*. To prove that he does indeed value her more than his own life, he resolves on suicide as the only salvation of her honor. Again the reader half expects a romantic tragedy: he kills himself, she awakens and, finding him dead, kills herself—a Pyramus and Thisbe ending after all. But as luck would have it, Dametas has stolen Pyrocles' sword and he cannot find another lethal weapon with which to carry out his resolve. Casting about in desperation, he finally wrenches a bar from the window and—after this soliloquy—plunges the bar into his side:

O barre blessed in that thow haste done service to the Chamber of the Peragon of lyfe, since thow couldest not serve mee to make a perfect escape, yet, serve my turne I pray thee that I may escape from my self? Therewithall yet, once looking to fetche the last repast of his eyes, and newe ageane transported with the pityfull

Case hee lefte her in, kneeling downe, hee thus prayed unto *Jupiter*. O greate maker and greate Ruler of the worlde, (sayde hee) to thee doo I sacrifice this bloode of myne, and suffer (O *Jove*) the errors of my youthe to passe away therein, and lett not ye sowle by thee made, and ever bending unto thee bee ever rejected of thee: Neither bee offended, that I do abandon this body, to the government of whiche thow haddest placed mee withowte thy Leave. Synce howe can I knowe, but that thy unsearcheable mynde ys I shoulde so doo, synce thow haste taken from mee all meane longer to abyde in yt: And synce the Difference standes, but in a shorte tyme of dyinge (thow that haste framed myne harte enclyned to doo good) How can I in this small space of myne benefit somuche all the Humane kynde, as in preserving thy perfectest worckmanship, thy Cheefest honor? O Justice yt self, howe soever thow determeynest of mee, Lett this excellent Innocency not bee oppressed? Lett my Lyfe pay her losse? O *Jove* give mee some signe, that I may dye with this Comfort. And pawsing a litle (as yf hee had hoped for some token) And when soever, to the eternall Darknes of the earthe shee dothe followe mee, Lett oure Spirites possess one place, and lett them bee more happy in that uniting: with that stryking the Barr uppon his harte syde, with all the force hee had, (and falling withall uppon, to give yt the more throwgher passage) . . .   [272–73]

So should a hero die. But not this hero: "the Barre in truthe was too blunt, to doo the facte, allthoughe yt persed his skynn, and bruysed his Ribbes very sore, so that, his breathe was allmoste past hym" (273). Sidney completely deflates the carefully built rhetorical crescendo.

Philoclea, awakened by the noise Pyrocles cannot avoid making as he falls senseless to the floor, revives him and lectures him on the sin of suicide, and on her determination to take her own life if he takes his. Their disputation on suicide is full-dress (273 ff.), Philoclea taking the negative Christian position and Pyrocles the positive pagan position. At the end, "*Pyrocles* was not so muche perswaded as delighted by her well conceyved and sweetely pronounced speeches." Now, this is an odd sentiment to assign to Pyrocles if Sidney meant the scene to be at all serious. Much as the Tudors admired rhetorical skill, one can hardly imagine such admiration as among Pyrocles' thoughts on this occasion, if he is really in deadly earnest. It is as if Juliet on the balcony were to reflect, "My! he speaks well!" A modern reader has trouble deciding whether the two lovers are in a comic pickle or a serious jam. It is certainly a trifle hard to accept it without even smiling, as does John F. Danby when he writes, "Suicide in the *Arcadia* is an extreme falling-away from the frame of patience—a final sin." [6] It can hardly be so somber.

By the time of the great trial scene of Book V events have become wholly serious. The use of a rhetorical style here presents less of a problem than anywhere else in the Old *Arcadia*. The context of the law court clearly calls for all the weapons in the armory of oratory. The law court was one place where a formal speech and only a formal speech would be decorous. Sidney's intention, too, is much less likely to be mistaken. Before going on to the trial proper, though, we should at least note in passing three occasions for oratory which lead up to it. Philanax' petition to Euarchus (333–36) is an oration in which the conventional subdivisions can be marked off.[7] Its unction is just what the occasion demands. Euarchus' speech of acceptance of the protectorate is one of the few clear-cut attempts at direct characterization in the Old *Arcadia*. The direct honesty of the speech is that of the man:

> I understand (saithe hee) Faythfull *Arcadians* by my Lord *Philanax*, that yow have with one Consent chosen mee to bee the Judge of the late evills happened, Orderer of the present Dis-

6. *Poets on Fortune's Hill: Studies in Sidney, Shakespeare, Beaumont and Fletcher* (London, 1952), p. 66.

7. Using tears for an Entrance, and the device of a living tragedy for the Narration, he uses a brief Proposition ("*Arcadia* fynding her self in these desolate Termes dothe speake, and I speake for her to thee, not vaynely, puisant Prince?"), explains himself more fully in his Division (down to "to take uppon yow"), skips the Confirmation and Confutation as he explains ("The perticularityes bothe of theyre Statutes and Demaundes yow shall presently after understand"), and "can for Conclusion say no more but this . . ." Should this all seem a trifle forced to the reader, he should be reminded that speeches just like this were used every day in Sidney's England. For Sidney's courtly audience, this would have had almost a colloquial ring, since it was the most common of courtly speeches—the petition.

orders and finally Protector of this Contry, till therein yt bee seene what the Customes of *Arcadia* requyre: Hee coulde say no further beeyng stopped with a generall Crye, that, so yt was, giving him all the Honorable tytles and happy wisshes they coulde imagyn. Hee beckened unto them for sylence, and thus ageane proceeded, Well (sayde hee) how good choyse yow have made, the attending must bee in yow, the proofe in mee: But, by-cause yt many tymes falles oute wee are muche deceyved in others, wee beeyng the first to deceyve oure selves I am to re-quyre yow, not to have any overshooting expectation of mee, the moste crewell adversary of all honorable Doynges, nor promyse youre selves wonders oute of a sodeyne liking.

Euarchus reminds the populace, just as every mirror of princes reminds the ruler, that he is but mortal:

But Remember that I am a Man, that ys to say a Creature, whose reason ys often darkened with error; secondly that yow will lay youre hartes voyde of foretaken opinyons, else what soever I doo or say will bee measured by a wronge Rule, like them that have the yealow Jaunders every thing seeming yealow unto them. Thirdly whatsoever Debates have risen among yow may bee utterly extinguisshed, Knowing that even among the best men are diversityes of opinyons which are no more in true Reason to breede hatred, then one that loves Black, shoulde bee angry with hym yt ys Clothed in white.

Then follows a curious sentence:

For, thoughtes and Conceyptes are the very apparell of the mynde.

Does he mean that the style is the man? If so, Sidney may be commenting on his character through the character's own mouth:

Lastly, that yow doo not easely judge of youre Judge, but since yow will have mee to Comaunde, thincke yt ys youre parte to obay: And in Rewarde of this I will promyse and protest unto yow that to the uttermoste of my skill, bothe in the generall Lawes of nature, speciall of *Greece*, and particuler of *Arcadia* (wherein I must Confess I am not unacquaynted) I will not onely see ye passed evills duely punished, and youre weale hereafter

286

establisshed, but, for youre Desyer in yt yf neede shall requyer I will employ the forces and treasures of myne owne Contry. In the meane tyme, this shall bee the first order I will take, that no man under payne of greevous punishment name mee by any other Name, but Protector of *Arcadia:* For I will not leave any possible Coloure to any of my Naturall Successors to make Clayme to this which by free election yow have bestowed uppon mee, and so I vowe unto yow to depose my self or yt, assoone as the Judgement ys passed, the *Duke* buryed, and his Lawfull Successor appoynted. For the first wherof (I meane the trying, whiche bee guilty of the *Dukes* deathe, and these other haynous trespasses) bycause youre Customes require suche haste, I will no longer delay yt, then till to morowe, assoone as ye Sunne shall give us fitt oportunity: Yow may therefore retyer youre selves to youre Rest, that yow may bee the Redyer to bee present at these so great important matters.   [338–39]

It is, we might observe, one of the most effective speeches in the romance, a clear proof that Sidney knew how to use the art of persuasion directly when he chose to. It serves as a touchstone of sincere feeling amidst all the full-blown oratory into which the reader is immediately plunged.

Pyrocles and Musidorus, on the night before the trial, seek to "enhable theyre myndes agenst all extremitys." It is a moving scene, yet the alert reader cannot help reflecting, while they comfort one another and praise their friendship, on the inappropriateness of the sentiments they express. Pyrocles, for example, blames their ill fortune on an unpropitious heaven, and Musidorus reproaches him:

O blame not the heavens sweete *Pyrocles*, saide *Musidorus*, as theyre Course never alters, so ys there no thing done by the uncharitable Ruler of them but hathe an everlasting reason for yt: And to say the truthe of these thinges wee shoulde dealle ungratefully with *Nature* yf wee shoulde bee forgetfull Receyvers of her good giftes, & so diligent Auditors of ye Chaunces wee like not. Wee have lived and have lived to bee good to oureselves, and others, oure sowles which are putt into the sturring earthe of oure bodyes have atcheved the causes of theyre hether comming, they have knowne and honoured with knowledg the cause of theyre

287

Creation: And for many men (for in this tyme place and fortune yt ys lawfull for us to speake gloriusly) yt hathe beene behovefull that wee shoulde live.   [344–45]

The sentiment, a combination of Stoic fortitude and an ill-judged Christian moral complacency, is inoffensive enough in itself. But does it really fit our two heroes? They have had other honorable adventures, true, but they certainly ought not to be quite so self-satisfied about their career in Arcadia. They leave—so far as they know—a dead duke, a ruined queen, two princesses dishonored, and a tumultuous kingdom ruled by a foreign king, as mementoes of their sojourn there. As we have seen, neither prince is wont to hide his light, but a reader may perhaps be forgiven for thinking them more pleased with themselves than the occasion warrants. They are not, they make clear, repentant in the slightest. Pyrocles says:

Add this to youre Noble speeche my dere Cosen (saide *Pyrocles*) that yf wee complayne of this oure fortune, or seeme to oure selves faulty in having one hurt the other, wee shewe a repentance of the Love wee beare to these Matcheles Creatures, or at least a Doubt yt shoulde bee over dearly boughte. Whiche for my parte (and so dare I answer for yow) I calle all the goddes to witness, I am so farr from that, no shame, no torment nor deathe coulde make mee forgoo the least parte of the inwarde honor, essentiall pleasure and living lyfe I have enjoyed in ye presence of the faultles *Philoclea*.   [345]

They fall next to speculating on the immortality of the soul, and it is worth observing that Sidney changes the style to conform to the nature of the occasion:

Certeynly (answered *Pyrocles*) I easely yeelde, that wee shall not knowe one an other, and muche less these passed thinges with a sensible or passionate knowledg, for the Cawse beeyng taken away the effect followes. Neyther doo I thincke wee shall have suche a memory as now wee have, whiche ys but a relique of the sences, or rather a printe the senses have lefte of thinges passed in oure thoughtes. But yt shall bee a vitall power of that very intelligence, whiche as while yt was here, yt helde the cheef seate of oure lyfe, and was as yt were the last resorte, to which of all oure knouledges the highest appealle came, and so by that meanes was never ignorant of oure actions (thoughe many tymes rebelliusly resisted, allwayes with this prison darckened): Somuche more beeyng free of that prison, and returning to the lyfe of all thinges where all Infinite knowledg ys, yt can not but bee a righte intelligence which ys bothe his name and beeyng of thinges bothe present & passed, Thoughe voyde of imagening to yt self any thing, but even growne like to his Creator hathe all thinges with a Spirituall knowledge before yt. The Difference of which ys as harde for us to conceyve, as yt hathe beene for us when wee were in oure Mothers wombes to comprehend (yf any body coulde have toulde us) what kynde of lighte wee now in this worlde see; what kynde of knowledge wee now have: Yet, nowe wee doo not onely feele oure present beeyng, but wee Conceyve what wee were before wee were borne, thoughe Remembraunce make us not doo yt but knowledg. [346]

For the Old *Arcadia*, this is straightforward, ratiocinative prose. It contrasts markedly with the princes' usual inflated discourse. Out go the parenthetical expansions, the parallelism and antithesis, the alliteration, the various plays on single words; in their place is a dignified, reasonably lean prose.

Although the princes are resolute for death, they have not given up hope for their princesses. Musidorus, while being led to the judgment seat, tries to rally the crowd to Pamela and hence upset the trial:

And ys yt possible O *Arcadians* (sayde hee) that yow can forgett youre naturall Duety yow owe to youre Princess *Pamela?* Hathe this soyle beene so litle beholding to her noble Auncestors? Hathe so longe a tyme rooted no Love in youre hartes that live? Where ys that faythe to youre Princes blood, whiche hathe not onely preserved yow from all daungers heretofore, but hathe spredd youre fame to all Natyons in the worlde? where ys that Justice the *Arcadians* were wonte to florish in, whose Nature ys to render to every one his owne?

Pyrocles had *calmed* the mob with same argument, loss of reputation, in Book II. Musidorus goes on to demonstrate an unwonted solicitude for Basilius' affairs:

Will yow now keepe the Right from the Prince, who ys the onely giver of Judgment, the key of Justice and Lyfe of youre Lawes? Doo yow hope in a fewe yeares, to sett up an other Race, which no thinge, but lengthe of tyme can establish? Will yow rewarde *Basilius* Children with ungratefullnes, the very poyson of Manhood? Will yow betray youre longe settled reputation with the fowle name of Traytors? ys this youre Mourning for youre *Duke* to encrease his Losse with his Daughters misery? Imagyn youre Prince to looke oute of the heavens unto yow, what doo yow thincke hee coulde wish for more at youre handes, then that yow doo well by his Children? And what more honor I pray yow can yow doo to his obsequyes, then to satisfy his sowle with a Loving memory, as yow do his body with an unfelt solempnity? what have yow done with the Princes *Pamela? Pamela* the just inheritrix of this Contry, *Pam:* whome this earthe may bee happy, that yt shoulde bee hereafter sayde shee was Borne in *Arcadia: Pamela* in her self youre ornament, in her education youre Foster Chylde and every way youre onely Princess? What accoumpt can yow render to youre selves of her. Truely I doo not thincke that yow all knowe what ys become of her, so soone may a Dyamonde bee lost, so soone may the fayrest light in the worlde be putt oute.

His concluding advice is ironical in view of his behavior toward Pamela:

But looke, Looke unto yt O *Arcadians,* bee not willfully robbed of youre greatest treasure, make not youre selves Ministers to private ambitions, who doo but use youre selves to putt on youre owne yokes; What soever yow determyn of us, yet lett not *Basilius* Daughters bee straungers unto yow; Lastly howsoever yow barr her from her publique Soveraignty, which yf yow doo (litle may wee hope for equity when Rebellion raignes) yet deny not that Chyldes Right unto her, that shee may come and do ye last Duetyes to her fathers body. Deny not that happynes (yf in suche a Case there bee any happynes) to youre late *Duke,* that his body may have his last tuche of his dearest Chylde.   [351–52]

Finally, Musidorus pleads, if the crowd is to be so hardhearted as still to judge Pamela, at least let her view her father's dead body. That spectacle will turn their heads even if his exhortations cannot. Like Antony holding up Caesar's slashed and bloody toga, Musidorus is not unaware of the power of pathetic *opsis*. But the crowd will not be drawn and, learning that they intend no violence to Pamela, her lover subsides.

Knowing the rivalry of the princes (and Sidney's fondness for parallelism) we expect a few words from Pyrocles. He chooses to address them to Euarchus, having seen his friend fail with the mob. The pose he chooses is that of the suppliant but dreadfully honest penitent:

> In this sorte with a lowely behaviour and onely then like a Sup-plyant, hee spake to the Protector. Pardon mee moste Honoured Judge (saide hee) that uncommaunded I begin my speeche unto yow, since bothe to yow and mee these wordes of myne shall bee moste necessary: To yow, having the sacred exercyse of Justice in youre hande, nothinge apertaynes more properly then Truthe nakedly and freely sett downe. To mee (beeyng invironed aboute with daungerous Calamityes) what can bee more Convenyent & comfortablle then at least, to bee at peace within my self, in having discharged my Conscyence in a moste behoovefull verity: Understand therefore & truly understand that the Lady *Philoclea* (to whose unstayned vertue yt hathe beene my unspeakeable misery that my Name shoulde become a Blott) yf shee bee accused, ys moste unjustly accused of any Dishonorable facte, whiche by my meanes shee mighte bee thoughte to have yeelded unto, what soever hathe beene done, hathe bene my vyolence.

At the brink of admitting that he has raped her, he draws back. By a clever qualification, he invokes God without technically blaspheming:

> Which notwithstanding coulde not prevayle ageanst her Chas-tity, but whatsoever hathe beene informed, was my force, and I attest the heavens, (to blaspheyme which I am not now in fitt tyme) that somuche as my Coming into her Chamber was wholly unwitting unto her. This youre wisdome may with all Consider (, yf I woulde lye, I woulde lye for myne owne behoof) I am not so oulde as to bee weary of my self: But the very stinge of my Inward knowledg, joyned with the Consideracyon I must needes have, (what an infinite Losse yt shoulde bee to all these, who

Love goodnes in good folckes, yf so pure a Chylde of vertue
shoulde wrongefully bee destroyed) compelles mee to use my
Toungue ageanst my self and receyve the Burden of what evell
was uppon myne owne Dooyng. Looke therefore with pityfull
eyes uppon so fayre Beames, and that mysfortune which by mee
hathe fallen unto her, help to repayre yt with youre publique
Judgment.

Modesty does not prevent his lecturing Euarchus upon a judge's
duty:

Since who so ever dealles crewelly with suche a Creature shewes
hym self a hater of Mankynde & an Envyer of the worldes blisse.
And this petition I make even in the name of Justice that before
yow proceede ageanst us, I may knowe howe yow conceyve of
her Noble thoughe unfortunate action, and what judgment yow
will make of yt.   [352–53]

The end of saving Philoclea justifies for him the means—a clever
and calculated perjury. The "Truthe nakedly and freely sett
downe" is the last thing he wants Euarchus to know.

Philanax as prosecutor changes from the just and loving counselor seen heretofore into a vindictive monster. This change has
bothered some critics, but seems to me to have been adequately
explained by the vicious personal abuse which was a common
practice in the law courts of Sidney's time. Sidney once again
suits his style to the occasion. Philanax, as prosecutor, is acting a
part, just as we have seen the two princes doing to a lesser degree.
It is as well to remember though that Sidney takes care to provide
a realistic motivation for Philanax: when he steps out to face
Gynecia, he thinks he is facing the murderer of his beloved duke:

Philanax incontinently stepped forthe, and shewyng in his
greeved eyes, that hee did thirst for her blood, began a well
thoughte on discourse of her (in his judgment) execrable wickednes.   [354]

Gynecia, who now interrupts him, tries to forestall the predictable tirade of abuse by confessing to Basilius' murder and
pleading for death (354). The reader, although he knows she
has given a false confession, cannot help sympathizing with her.

She has not had the courage to confess her real crime—lust for Cleophila—but she has admitted to herself that this crime was an indirect cause of Basilius' accidental death, and that she is thus partly responsible for it.

The popular clamor of pity her speech evokes is rigorously set aside by her judge, Euarchus:

At lengthe, the Reverent Awe they stoode in of *Euarchus*, broughte them to a silent wayting his determination, who having well Considered the abhominacyon of the facte, attending more the manifest proof of so horrible a trespas confessed by her self and prooved by others, then any thing Relenting to those tragicall phrases of her (apter to sturr a vulgar pitty, then his mynde, whiche hated evill, in what Coloure soever hee founde yt): Having conferred a while with the Principall men of the Contry and demaunded theyre allowance hee indefinitely gave his Sentence. That whereas bothe in private & publique respectes this woman had moste haynously offended (in private) bycause Mariage beeyng the moste holy Conjunction that falles to Mankynde oute of whiche all famelyes & Consequently all societyes do proceede, which not onely by Community of goodes but Community of Children, as to knitt the myndes in a moste perfect union whiche who so breakes dissolves all humanity, No man living from the Daunger of so neare a Neighboure: Shee had not onely broken yt, but broken yt with deathe, and ye moste pretended Deathe that mighte bee. In publique Respect, yt, the *Princes* person (beeyng in all *Monarchiall* governementes the very knott of the peoples wellfare and lighte of all theyre Doynges, to whiche they are not onely in Conscyence but in necessity bounde to bee Loyall) shee had traytorusly impoysoned hym, (neyther regarding the Contryes proffett, her owne Duty, nor the Rigor of the Lawes): That therefore aswell for the due satisfaction to Eternall Justice and accomplishment of ye *Arcadian* Statutes, as for the everlasting Examples of all Wyves and Subjectes, shee shoulde bee presently conveyed to close prison, and there bee kept with suche foode as might serve to sustayne her alyve, untill the day of her husbandes buryall. At which tyme shee shoulde bee buryed quick in the same Tombe with hym, that so his murder mighte bee a Murder to her self, and shee forced to keepe Company with the body from which shee had made so

> detestable a severance: And lastly deathe mighte redress theyre
> disjoyned Conjunction of Mariage. [355–56]

Once again Sidney gives us a pathetic speech—Gynecia's plea—
and contrasts its sentimental verdict with the harsh reality of the
moral decision it has glossed over. Euarchus, the only character
in the Old *Arcadia* who consistently refuses to be persuaded by
elaborate speeches, here again pleads directly to the case.

The proceedings against the two princes are again delayed
when they question the jurisdiction of the court over them as
strangers and more especially as absolute princes.[8] The court
quickly rules that the willing visitor voluntarily puts himself
under the laws of the host country. "As for theyre beeyng Princes,
whether they were so or no, the belief stoode but in theyre owne
wordes whiche they had so dyversly falsifyed, as they did not
deserve beleef" (358). Their brave devices have brought them to
this, that their word is worthless in open court. Philanax then
opens the prosecution against Pyrocles with the most elaborate
speech thus far in the romance (358–64). His spontaneous gestures
are carefully rehearsed.

> But *Philanax* that was even shorte breathed at the first with the
> extreme vehemency hee had to speake agenst them stroking once
> or twyce his foreheade, and wyping his eyes which eyther wept,
> or hee woulde at that tyme have them seeme to weepe, looking
> first uppon *Pyrocles* as yf hee had proclaymed all hatefullnes
> ageanst hym humbly turning to *Euarchus* (who with quyet
> gravity shewed greate attention) hee thus began his Oration.

One might note here that the speech is specifically called an
"Oration" at the end (Pyrocles bears with impatience "the lengthe
of his Oration") as well as here at the beginning. He next launches
into his Entrance:

> That which all men (who take uppon them to accuse an other) are
> wonte to desyer moste worthy Protector, to have many prooffes
> of many faultes in them they seeke to have condempned, that ys
> to mee in this present action my greatest Comber, and anoyaunce:
> For the Nomber ys so greate and the quality so monsterus of the

8. Both delaying tactics are, of course, standard forensic practice.

Enormityes this wretched young man hathe committed, that
neyther I my self can tell where to begin (my thoughtes beeyng
confused with the horrible multitude of them) neyther do I
thincke youre vertuous eares will bee able to endure the reporte
of them. But will rather imagyn, yow heare some Tragedy invented of the extremity of wickednes, then a just recitall of a
wickednes in deede committed: For suche ys the disposicion of
ye moste synceare Judgmentes, that as they can beleeve meane
faultes, and suche as Mans nature may easely slyde into, so when
they passe to a certeyne degree, nay, when they pass all degrees of
unspeakeable naughtynes then fynde they in them selves a hard-
nes to give Creditt, that humane Creatures can so from all humanity bee transformed. But in myself the strengthe of my Love
to my deade Master will help the weyknes of my memory, in yow
youre excellent Love of Justice will force yow to vouchsafe attention: And as for the matter yt ys so manifest, so pityfull evidences lye before youre eyes of yt, that I shall neede to bee but a
breef recoumpter and no Retoricall Enlarger of this moste harme-
full myscheef. I will therefore (in as fewe wordes as so huge a
Trespas can bee conteyned) deliver unto yow the Some of this
miserable facte.

With this specious promise of brevity, he begins his Narration:

Leaving oute a great nomber particuler tokens of his naughtynes,
and onely tuching the essentiall poyntes of this dolefull Case.
This Man whome (to begin withall I knowe not howe to name)
synce beeyng come into this Contry unaccompanyed like a lost
Pilgrim, from a Man grewe a woman from a woman a Ravissher
of woemen, thence Prisoner & nowe a Prince: But this *Tymophirus*, this *Cleophila*, this what yow will (for any shape or Tytle
hee can take uppon hym that hathe no restraynt of shame)
having understood the Solitary lyfe my late Master lived, and
considering how open hee had layde hym self to any Trayterus
attempt, for the first Maske of his falshoode disguysed hym self
like a woman. Whiche beeyng the more simple and hurtles sex
mighte easyer hyde his subtill harmefullnes and presenting hym
self to my Master the moste Courteous Prince yt lyved, was
receyved of hym with so great gratyousnes, that mighte have
bounde not onely a gratefull mynde, but might have mollifyed
any Enimyes rancor: But this venymous Serpent admitted into

his bosome, as Contagion will fynde a fitt body for yt, so had hee
quickly falne into so nere acquayntance with this naughty woman
(whome even now yow moste justly condempned) that this was
her Right hand, shee sawe with no eyes but his, nor seemed to
have any lyfe but in hym. So glad shee was to fynde one more
conning then her self in covering wickednes with a modest vaile.
What ys to bee thoughte passed betwixt twoo suche vertuous
Creatures (wherof the one hathe confessed murder and the other
Rape) I leave to youre wyse Consideration.

Again and again Philanax pleads strong emotion as excuse for a
haste and brevity which never materialize:

For my harte hastens to the miserable poynte of *Basilius* murder.
For the executing wherof with more facility, this young
Nymphe of *Dianas* bringing up, fayned certeyne Rytes shee had
to performe: So furyous an Impiety had carryed hym from all
Remembrance of goodnes, that hee did not onely not feare the
goddes as the beholders and punisshers of so ungodly a villany,
but did blaspheymusly use theyre sacred holy name as a Minister
unto yt. And forsoothe, a Cave hereby was chosen for the
Temple of his Devotions a Cave of suche Darcknes as did prog-
nosticate hee went to please the Infernall powers: For there this
accursed Caytif uppon the Aulter of falshood sacrifyed the lyfe
of the vertuous *Basilius,* by what meanes hee trayned hym thether,
alas I knowe not, for yf I mighte have knowne yt eyther my lyfe
had accompanyed my Master or this fellowes deathe had preserved hym. But this may suffise that in the mowthe of the Cave,
where this fellow had his Lodging and Chappell (when allredy
Master Shepeherd his Companyon had conveyed away the un-
doubted Inheritrix of this Contry) was *Gynecia* founde by the
deade Corps of her husband (newly impoysoned,) apparelled in
the garmentes of the younge Lady: And redy (no questyon) to
have fledd to some place according to theyre Comforte, but that
shee was by certeyne honest Sheepeheardes arrested. While in
the meane tyme (bycause there shoulde bee lefte no Revenger
of this bloody myscheef) this Noble *Amazon* was vyolently
gotten into the Chamber of the Lady *Philoclea:* where by the
mingling of her shame with his mysdeede hee might enforce her
to bee accessary to her Fathers death, and under the Countenaunce of her and her sister (ageanst whome they knewe wee

woulde not Rebell) seaze as yt were withoute grype into theyre Trecherus handes the Regiment of this mighty Province. But the Allmighty eye prevented hym of the ende of his myscheef by using a villayne *Dametas* hande to inclose hym in there, where with asmuche fortefication as in a howse coulde bee made hee thought hym self in moste security.

The Proposition follows:

Thus see yow (moste Just Judge) a short and simple story of ye infamus misery, falne to this Contry, in deede infamus, synce by an effeminate Man wee shoulde suffer a greater overthrowe then oure mightiest enimyes have ever bene able to lay uppon us.

His Division, Philanax confides, will be in two parts:

And that all this which I have sayde ys moste manifest aswell of the murdering of *Basilius* as the Ravishing of *Philoclea* (for those twoo partes I establish of my accusation) who ys of so incredulus a mynde or rather who will so stopp his eyes from seeying a thinge clearer then the lighte, as not to holde for assured so pallpable a matter, for to begin with his moste crewell mysdeede, yt ys to bee imagined that *Gynecia* (a woman thowghe wicked yet witty) woulde have attempted and atchieved an enterpryse no less hazardus then horrible without having some Counsellours in the beginning and some Comforter in the performing: Had shee who shewed her thoughtes were so over Ruled with some straunge desyer, as in despite of good nature and Womanhood to execute that in deedes whiche in wordes wee can not heare withoute trembling, Had shee I say, no practize to leade her unto yt? Or had shee a practize withoute Conspiracy? Or coulde shee Conspire withoute some body to Conspire with? And yf one were, who so likely as this, to whome shee comunicated (I am sure) her mynde (the worlde thinkes) her body.

Gynecia's word, he maintains, is now worthless:

Neither lett her wordes (taking the whole faulte uppon her self) bee herein any thinge avaylable, for to those persons, who have vomited oute of theyre sowles all remnauntes of goodnes there restes a certeyne pryde in evill; And having else no shadow of glory lefte them, they glory to bee Constant in Iniquity: And that

(God knowes) bee helde oute to ye last gaspe withoute reveyling theyre accomplishes as thinckinge greate Corage ys declared in beeyng neyther affrayed of ye goddes nor asshamed of the worlde.

With good judgment, he soon shifts from the more to the less sympathetic target:

But let *Gynecias* action dye with her self what can all the Earthe answer for his coming hether? whye alone, yf hee bee a Prince? Howe so Richely Jewelled yf hee bee not a Prince? why, then a woman, yf now a Man, why nowe *Tymophirus* yf then *Cleophila?* Was all this play for no thinge? or yf yt had an ende, what ende? but the ende of my dere Master? Shall wee doubt so many secrett Conferences with *Gynecia?* suche fayned favoure to the oversoone beguyled *Basilius?* A Cave made a Lodging, and the same made a Temple of his Religion? Lastly suche chaunges and traverses, as a quiett Poett coulde scarce fill a poem with all were directed to any less scope then to this monsterus Murder? O snaky ambition which can wynde thy self into so many figures to slyde thether thow desyerest to come? O Corrupted Reason of Mankynde, that can yeelde to deforme thy self with so filthy desyers? And full graceles bee those Myndes whome so unnaturall desyers doo not with theyre owne uglynes sufficyently terrify? But yet even of favoure let us graunt hym thus muche more, as to fancy that in these foretoulde thinges Fortune mighte bee a greate Actor perchaunce to an evell ende? yet, to a lesse evell ende all these intangled devises were intended? But I beseeche youre Ladyship my Lady *Tymophirus* tell mee what excuse yow can fynde for the Chaunging youre garmentes with the *Duchess* that very instant shee was to finish her execrable practize? Howe can yow Cloake the lending of youre Cloake unto her? was all that but by chaunce too? Had the starres sent suche an influence unto yow as yow shoulde bee just weary of youre Lodging and garmentes when oure *Prince* was destyned to this slaughter? What say yow to this O shamefull and shameles Creature? Fitt in deede to bee the Dishonor of bothe sexes. But alas, alas, I spende too many wordes in so manifest and so miserable a Matter? They must bee fowre wylde horses which (according to oure Lawes are the executioners of Men which murder oure prince) which must decyde this questyon with yow.

Philanax admits that his anger has impelled him to a premature conclusion halfway through his Division:

> Yett see, so farre had my zeale to my beloved Prince transported mee, that I had allmoste forgotten my second parte and the seconde abhominacyon, I meane his vyolence offered, I hope, but offered to the Lady *Philoclea:* wherewith (as yt had well become his Womanhoode) hee came raving to the Judgment seate. In deede oure Lawes appoynt not so crewell a deathe (alltho Deathe too) for this facte as for the other: But whosoever well wayes yt shall fynde yt sprounge oute of the same fountayne of myschevous naughtynes. The killing of the Father, Dishonouring the Mother & Ravishing the Chylde: Alas coulde not so many benefites receyved of my Prince, the Justice of *Nature,* the Righte of hospitallity bee a brydle for thy Lust, yf not to thy Crewelty? Or yf thow hadst as surely thow haste, a harte recompensing goodnes with hatred coulde not his deathe (which ys the last of Revenges) satisfy thy mallys? But thow must heape uppon yt the shame of his Daughter? were thy eyes so stony, thy Brestes so Tygrish as the sweete and beutyfull shewes of *Philocleas* vertue did not astonish thee? O wofull *Arcadia,* To whome the name of this Mankynde Courtizen shall ever bee remembred, as a Procurer of thy greatest Losse.

The brief Confirmation repeats the basic promise of the Entrance:

> But, too farr I fynde my passion, yet honest passion hathe guyded mee. The Case ys every way too muche unmesurable.

The Confutation I construe as beginning here:

> It resteth in yow O excellent Protector to pronounce Judgment, whiche yf there bee hope that suche a younge man may proove proffitable to the worlde who in the first exercyse of his owne determeynacyons farr passed the Arrauntest Strumpett in luxuriusnes, the Coningst Forger in falshood, A Player in disguysing, a Tygre in Crewelty a Dragon in ungratefullnes, let hym bee preserved like a Jewell to doo greater myscheef? yf his yowthe bee not more defyled with trechery then the Eldest mans age, lett I say his yowth bee some Cause of Compassyon: yf hee have not every way sought the overthrowe of Humane society, yf hee

have done any thinge like a Prince, let his naming hym self a Prince breede a Reverence to his base wickednes. Yf hee have not broken all Lawes of hospitality and broken them in the moste detestable degree yt can bee, let his beeyng a Guest bee a sacred protection of his more then savage doynges: Or yf his whorish beuty have not beene as the highe way of his wickednes let the picture drawn uppon so poysonus a wood bee reserved to shewe howe greatly coloures can please us.

In his Confutation, Philanax introduces and attempts to demolish all the excuses advanced, or obvious and likely to be advanced, by the accused: his youth—corrupted; his noble birth—belied by his conduct; his status as a stranger—forfeit by treachery to his host; his beauty—whorish. His Conclusion begins:

> But yf yt ys (as yt ys) what shoulde I say more? a very spirit of Hellish naughtynes, yf his acte bee to bee punished and his de-fyled person not to bee pittyed, then restore unto us oure Prince by duly punisshing his murderers. For then shall wee thincke hym and his name to live when wee shall see his killers to dye, Restore to ye excellent *Philoclea* the honor by taking oute of the worlde her dishonour: And thincke that at this day in this matter are the eyes of ye worlde uppon yow, whether any thinge can sway youre mynde from a true administration of Justice. Alas, thoughe I have muche more to say, I can say no more, for my Teares & Sighes interrupt my speeche, and force mee to give my self over to private sadnes.

The narrator's comment on these crocodile tears further confirms Philanax' adherence to formal divisions in his speech:

> Thus when *Philanax* had uttered the uttermoste of his mallice, hee made sorowe the Cause of his Conclusion.

As the reader has no doubt observed, Philanax neglects none of the devices of rhetoric. His well dramatized sadness we have already noted. His modest description of his speech as the truth nakedly and freely set down is a basic device to relieve the sus-picion of insincerity which an obviously prepared speech always generates. The name-calling and the careful choice of adjectives for the unfavorable stock response they will call up, the abuse based on the change of sex, all spring to the eye. The elaborate use of tropes and schemes is scarcely less apparent. How much of Philanax' righteous indignation is oratorical posturing is difficult to decide. He has sufficient motive, in his love of Basilius, to hate Pyrocles, and the anger which prompts him to come to a premature conclusion halfway through the Division seems unfeigned. But it too may be a rhetorical stratagem. His speech is, as prosecution speeches are by nature, completely and violently one-sided.

Yet if we were in Philanax' position would our version of the story be essentially different? His reconstruction of events, suffused though it is with vilification, is the one the world would logically adopt. When he says that the two princes resist the charge "thinckinge greate Corage ys declared in beeying neyther affrayed of ye goddes nor asshamed of the worlde," is he not voicing the same sentiments the princes agreed on as a Stoic defense the night before the trial? Philanax accuses Pyrocles of "killing of the Father, Dishonouring the Mother & Ravishing the Chylde": he clearly did the third (consent was immaterial, the central factor being the princess' marriageability) and the second and first followed at least partly from his campaign to accomplish the third. Pyrocles is obviously not the insane rapist and murderer Philanax makes him out to be, yet we ought not dismiss all the Prosecutor's arguments when we discount his passion.

Pyrocles' rebuttal is splendid. As resolute as Philanax, Pyrocles contains his anger in a speech that is (except for the denial of Philoclea's consent) honest and true:

> My accusers tale may well beare witnes with mee moste Rightfull Judge in how harde a Case and invironed with how many trubles I may esteeme myself. For yf hee who shewes his toungue ys not unacquaynted with rayling was in an Agony in the beginning of his speeche with the multitude of his matters hee had to lay unto mee, wherein not withstanding the moste evill coulde falle unto hym, was that hee shoulde not do so muche evill as hee woulde: How combred do yow thincke I may acknoledge my self, who in thinges no less importing then my lyfe must bee myne owne advocate withoute leysure to answer or foreknowledg what shoulde bee objected. In thinges I say promoted with so

cunning a Confusion, as having mingled truthes with falshoodes, surmyses with certeyntyes Causes of no moment with matters capitall scolding with complayning I can absolutely neyther graunt nor deny. Neither can I tell whether I come hether to bee judged, or before judgment to bee punisshed, beeyng compelled to beare suche unworthy wordes farr more greevous then any deathe to mee: But since ye forme of this governement allowes suche Toungue liberty unto hym, I will picke aswell as I can oute of his Invective those fewe poyntes which may seeme of some purpose in ye touching of mee. Hoping that as by youre easy hearing of mee yow will shewe that allthoughe yow hate evill yet yow wish men may proove them selves not evill, so in that hee hathe sayde, yow will not waye somuche, what hee hathe sayde, as what hee hathe prooved.

Pyrocles' quiet passion is a perfect dramatic foil to Philanax' torrential abuse.

Remembring that Truthe ys simple and naked, and that yf hee had guyded hym self under that Banner, hee needed not oute of the way have soughte so vyle and false disgracinges of mee, ynoughe to have made the untruest accusation beleeved. I will therefore using truthe as my best eloquence repeate unto yow asmuche as I knowe in this matter, and then by the onely clearenes of this Discourse, youre wisdome (I knowe) will fynde the Difference betuixt Caveling supposicion and direct declaration: This Prince *Palladius* and I beeyng inflamed with love (a passion farr more easily reprehended then refrayned) to the Twoo pereles Daughters of *Basilius*, and understanding howe hee had secluded himself from ye worlde that (Lyke princes) there was no access unto hym, wee disguysed oure selves in suche formes as might soonest bringe us to ye revealing of oure affections. The Prince *Palladius* had suche event of his dooynges, that, with *Pamelas* consent, hee was to convey her oute of the thraldome shee lived in to receyve the subjection of a greater people then her owne, untill her Fathers Consent might bee obtayned. My fortune was more hard, for I bare no more [love] to the Chaste *Philoclea*, then *Basilius* deceyved in my sexe shewed unto mee: Insomuche that by his importunacy I coulde have no tyme to assayle the Constant Rock of the pure *Philocleas* mynde till this pollicy I founde. Taking (under coloure of some Devotions) my

Lodging to drawe *Basilius* thether with hope to enjoy mee which lykewyse I revealed to the *Duchess* that shee might keepe my place, and so make her husband see his error: while I in the meane tyme (beeyng delivered of them bothe) and having so lockt the dores as I hoped the Imaculate *Philoclea* shoulde bee succourles, my attempt was suche, as even now I confessed, and I made prisoner there, I knowe not by what meanes, when beeyng repelled by her devyne vertue I woulde faynest have escaped. Here have yow the Thridde to guyde yow in Labyrinth this man with his toungue had made so monsterus.

The labyrinth metaphor emphasizes the marked contrast between Pyrocles' narrative, unencumbered by the more obvious arts of language, and the elaborate rhetoric of Philanax:

Here see yow the true discourse which hee (mountbanck facyon) dothe make so wyde a mouthe over: Here may yow conceyve the Reason why the *Duchess* had my garment, bycause by her goyinge to the Cave in the Mooneshyne Nighte shee mighte bee taken for mee. Whiche hee useth as ye knott of all his wyse assertions, so, that as this Duble mynded fellowes accusation was duble, Duble lykewyse myne Answer must needes bee to the murder of *Basilius* and vyolence to the Inviolate *Philoclea:* For the first, O heavenly goddes, who woulde have thought any mowthe coulde have beene founde so immodest, as to have opened so sleighte prooffes of so horrible matters. This first argument ys a question, who woulde imagyn, that *Gynecia* woulde accomplish suche an acte withoute some accessaryes, and yf any? who but I? Truly I am so farr from imagining any thinge, that till I sawe these mourning tokens, and hearde *Gynecias* confession I never imagined the *Duke* was deade: And for my parte so vehemently and more like the maner of passionate then guylty folckes, I see the *Duchess* persecute her self, That I thincke Condempnacyon may goo too hastily over her, considering the unlikelyood (yf not impossibility) her wisdome and vertue so longe nourisshed, shoulde in one moment throwe downe yt self to the uttermoste ende of wickednes. But, whatsoever shee hathe done (which as I say I never beleeved) yet howe unjustly shoulde that aggrevate my faulte? shee founde abrode, I within dores: For (as for the wearing of my garment I have toulde the Cause) shee

seeking (as yow say) to escape, I locking my self in a howse,
withoute perchaunce the Conspiracy of one pore Straunger
mighte enable her attempt? or the fortification of the Lodge (as
the trim man alledged) might make mee hope to resist all
Arcadia?

Pyrocles replies directly to Philanax' discrediting of Gynecia's
testimony:

And see how injuryously hee seekes to drawe from mee my
cheefest Clearing by preventing the Credit of her wordes where-
with shee hathe wholly taken the faulte uppon her self: An honest
and unparciall Examiner, her wordes may condempne her, but
may not absolve mee? Thus voyde of all probable allegacyon the
Craven crowes uppon my affliction, not leaving oute any evell
that ever hee hathe felte in his owne sowle to charge my youthe
withall: But who can looke for a sweeter breathe oute of suche
a stomack or for hony from so filthy a spyder? What shoulde
I say more? yf in so inhumane a matter which hee hymself
confesseth syncerest Judgmentes are lothest to beleeve, and in
the severest Lawes, proofes clearer then the sunne are requyred,
his Reasons are onely the skome of a base mallice, my answers
moste manifest shyning in theyre owne Truthe. Yf there re-
mayne any doubt of yt (bycause yt standes betuixt his affirming
and my Denyall) I offer, nay I desyer, and humbly desyer, I may
bee graunted the Tryall by Combatt: By Combatt, wherein let
hym bee armed, and mee bee in my shyrt, I doubt not Justice will
bee my shielde, and his harte will shewe yt self as fainte as yt ys
false.

In replying to the second of Philanax' charges, Pyrocles comes
to the crucial point in his defense, the force of love:

Nowe come I to the second parte of my offence towardes ye
younge Lady, whiche I confess, and for her sake hartely lament:
But in fyne I offered force to her (Love offered more force to
mee) lett her Beuty bee compared to my yeares, and suche
effectes will bee made no myrackles. But synce yt ys thus as yt ys,
(and that Justice teacheth us not to love punishment, but to flee
yt for necessity) the salve of her Honor, I meane, as the worlde

will take yt (for else in truthe yt ys moste untouched) must bee my Mariage, and not my deathe: Synce the one stoppes all mouthes the other becomes a doubtfull fable. This matter Requyers no more wordes, and youre experience (I hope) in these Cases shall neede no more; For my self, mee thinckes I have shewed allredy too muche love of my lyfe, to bestowe so many.

He closes by preaching a love of truth he does not always practise:

But certeynly yt hathe beene love of truthe which coulde not beare so unworthy falshood, and love of Justice that will brooke no wronge to my self nor other: And makes mee now even in that respect to desyer yow to bee mooved rather with pitty at a Just Cause of teares, then with the bloody teares this Crocodile spendes, who weepes to procure deathe & not to lament Deathe. Yt will bee no honor to *Basilius* Tombe to have guiltless bloode sprinckled uppon yt? And muche more may a Judge overweigh hym self in Cruelty, then in Clemency. Yt ys hard, but yt ys excellent, where yt ys founde, a Right knowledge when Correction ys necessary, when grace dothe more avayle: For myne owne Respect, yf I thought in wysdome, I had deserved deathe I woulde not desyer lyfe, for, I knowe nature will condempne mee to dye, thowgh yow doo nott. And longer I woulde not wish to drawe this Breathe, then I can kepe myself unspotted of any horrible Cryme: Onely I can not nor ever will deny the Love of *Philoclea,* whose vyolence wrought vyolent effectes in mee.
[364–67]

Within limitations of time, place, and convention his reply is just what he says it is, "Truthe . . . simple and naked." But it is also truth without consequences. Nothing he says excuses him from responsibility for the consequences of his unbridled passion. His defense is the force of love, a constraint so great that its subject ceases to exist as a moral being. When he says, "But in fyne I offered force to her (Love offered more force to mee) lett her Beuty bee compared to my yeares, and suche effectes will bee made no myrackles," it is for him both explanation and excuse. His argument does not extend beyond the personal effect on him and his cousin and their loves.

When the enraged Philanax returns to the attack, he stresses exactly what Pyrocles (in accordance with the good rhetorical dictum that if you cannot answer an objection do not mention it at all) has ignored: the effects on Arcadia of this incursion:

> Beholde moste noble Protector, to what estate *Arcadia* ys come, since suche Men may Challenge in Combatt ye faythfullest of Nobility, and having merited the shamefullest of all deathes dare name in Mariage the *Princesses* of this Contry. Certeynly my Masters I must say yow were muche oute of Taste, yf yow had not rather enjoy suche Ladyes, then bee hanged; But, the one yow have asmuche deserved, as yow have dishonored ye other. But now my speeche must bee directed to yow good Master *Dorus*, who with *Pallas* help pardy are lately growne *Palladius*. Too muche, too muche this sacred seate of Justice grauntes unto suche a Fugitive bondslave, who in stede of these examinacyons shoulde bee made confess with a whipp that which a halter should punish: Are not yow hee Sir, whose sheepehooke was pre-pared to bee oure Scepter, in whome lay the knott of all this Tragedy? Or else perchaunce they that shoulde gayne litle by yt were dealers in the Murder: yow, onely that had provyded the fruites for youre self knewe no thing of yt, knewe no thinge? hathe thy Companyons here infected thee with suche impudency, as even in the face of all the worlde to deny that which all the worlde perceyveth? The other pleades ignorance and yow I doubt not will alledg absence: But, hee was ignorant when hee was harde by, and yow had framed youre absence just ageanst the tyme the acte shoulde bee committed. So fitt a Lievetenaunt hee knewe hee had lefte of his wickednes, that for hym self his safest meane was to convey away the Lady of us all: Who (once oute of the Contrye) hee knewe, wee woulde come with Ollive braunches of intercession unto her, and falle at his feete to be-seeche hym, to leave keeping of sheepe and vouchsafe the tyrannising over us.   [371–72]

This is exaggerated, to be sure, yet what would have happened had Musidorus escaped and returned with his army? Philanax has just cause for anger, an anger so great that speaking against Musi-dorus he becomes "so overgon with rage, that hee forgatt in his oration his precyse Methode of Oratory." He does too; he launches directly into his Division, omitting, as he says, "my cheef Matter of the *Dukes* Deathe." His anger here is real enough.

Musidorus, in his reply, attacks both Philanax' arguments and his oratorical pose. The speech is disappointing after Pyrocles' defense, a blend of vituperation and false coloring no better than the abuse it seeks to answer:

> O Goddes (saide hee) and have yow spared my lyfe to beare these injuryes of suche a Drivell? Is this the Justice of this place, to have suche men as wee are submitted not onely to apparant falshood, but moste shamefull Revyling? But marcke I pray yow the ungratefullnes of the Wretche, howe utterly hee hathe forgotten the Benefites bothe hee and all his Contry hathe receyved of us: For, yf men ever may Remember theyre owne noble Deedes, yt ys then when theyre just defence, and others unjust unkyndenes dothe requyte yt.

Dorus adduces benefits conferred:

> Were not wee the men yt killed the wylde Beastes, whiche otherwyse had killed the *Princesses*, yf wee had not succoured them? Consider I pray yow yf yt please yow, where had beene *Tymophirus* rape or my treason, yf the sweete beutyes of the earthe had then beene devowred? eyther thincke them now deade, or remember they live by us. And yet this Telltale full often can acknowledg the loss they shoulde have by theyre taking away, while maliciusly hee overpasseth who were theyre preservers. Neither let this bee spoken by mee, as yf I meant to Ballance this evill with that good, for I must Confess, that the saving suche Creatures was rewarded in the acte yt self: But onely to manifest the parciall jangling of this vyle Pickthanck. But yf wee bee the Traytors where was youre fidelity, O onely toungue valyant gentleman, when not onely the younge *Princesses*, but the *Duke* hym self was defended from uttermoste perill, partly by mee, but principally by this excellent younge Mans bothe wisdome and valeure.

His argument is shot through with holes. The chase they gave to the princesses promises a worse conclusion than that of the lion and the bear. They saved the kingdom from an uprising of which they themselves were a partial cause:

Were wee (that made oure selves ageanst hundreds of armed men openly the shieldes of his lyfe) like, secretly, to bee his poysoners? Did wee then shewe his lyfe to bee dearer to us then oure owne, bycause wee mighte after robb hym of his lyfe to dye shamefully?

They defended Basilius, true, but hardly for his sake alone:

Truly, truly, Master Orator, whosoever hathe hyered yow to bee so buysy in theyre matters, (who keepe honester Servauntes then youre self) hee shoulde have bid yow in so many Raylinges bringe some excuse for hym self, why in the greatest neede of youre Prince (to whome yow pretend miraculus good will) yow were not then as Forwarde to doo like a Man youre self, or at least to accuse them that were slack in that service? But comonly they use theyre feete for theyre Defence whose toungue ys theyre weapon; Certeynly a very simple subtilty yt had beene for us, to repose oure lyves in ye Daughters when wee had killed the father? But as this Gentleman thinkes to wynn the reputation of a gallant speaker (by leaving nothing unsayde which a filthy mowthe can imagyn) so thincke I (or ellse all wordes are vayne) that to wyse mens judgment oure Clearenes in ye *Dukes* deathe ys sufficyently notoryous. But at length, when the Merchaunt hathe sett oute his gylded bagage, lastly hee comes to some stuff of importance, and saythe I conveyde away the *Princess* of this Contry? And ys shee in deede youre *Princess?* I pray yow then, whome shoulde I wayte of else, but her that was my Mistris by my professed vowe? and Princess over mee while I lived in this soyle? Aske her, whye shee went aske not mee why I served her, synce (accoumpting mee as a *Prince*) yow have not to doo with mee, taking mee her Servaunt, then take withall that I must obay her. But yow will say I perswaded her to flee away, certeynly I will for no deathe deny yt, knowyng to what Honoure I shoulde bring her, from the thraldome by suche fellowes Counsell as yow shee lived in: Shall perswasion to a *Prince*, growe treason ageanst a *Prince?* yt mighte bee error in mee, but falshood yt coulde not bee, since I made my self partaker of what soever I wisshed her unto: who will ever Counsell his kinge yf his Counseyll bee judged by the event? and yf yt bee not founde wyse shall yt bee thoughte to bee wicked? But yf I bee a Traytor I hope yow will graunte mee a Correlative to whome I shall bee a Traytor: For the *Princess* (ageanst whome the treasons are considered) I am sure will avowe my faythfullnes, withoute that yow will say, I am a Traytor to her bycause I lefte the Contry, and a Traytor to the Contry, bycause I went with her?

Musidorus has saved his strongest argument for last:

Here do I leave oute my just excuses of Loves force, whiche as the narrow hart hathe never had Noble rowme ynoughe in yt to receyve so yet, to those Manlike Corages, that by experience knowe how subject the vertuous myndes are to love a moste vertuus Creature (witnessed to bee suche by the moste excellent giftes of Nature) will deeme yt a veniall trespass to seeke the satisfaction of honorable desyers: Honorable, even in the curyousest poyntes of honor, whereoute there can no disgrace nor disparagement come unto her. Therefore (O Judge) which I hope doste know what yt ys to bee a Judge, that youre ende ys to preserve & not to destroy mankynde, that Lawes are not made like Lymetwigges or nettes to catche every thinge that tucheth them: But rather lyke sea Marckes to avoyde the Shippwrackes of ignorant passingers synce that oure doynge (in the extreymest interpretation) ys but a humane error. And that of yt yow may make a profitable event (wee beeyng of suche estate as theyre Parentes woulde not have misliked theyre affinity) yow will not I trust at the perswasion of this Brabler, burne youre howse to make yt cleane: But, like a wyse Father, turne even the faulte of youre Children to any good, that may come of yt, synce that ys the fruite & ende of all Judgmentes. [373–75]

The real ground of his defense develops logically from Pyrocles' remarks about the force of love. Musidorus says plainly what Pyrocles only implies—"my just excuses of Loves force." He proclaims that passion—of the noble sort he feels, at least—not only will triumph over every other consideration both of person and of state, but that it should so triumph. Those who feel differently are simply unequipped to understand the mysteries of noble virtuous love. This adolescent doctrine can hardly be regarded as Sidney's own. It tells us rather that Musidorus as a hero has definite limitations, that he cannot repent because he cannot really understand what he has done wrong. Musidorus develops, more explicitly than Pyrocles, the theme that whatever is irresistible cannot be immoral, but in no particular does he answer Philanax' indictment.

We have throughout the romance looked in vain for the moral center, for the author's mature, considered view of the happenings in Arcadia. With Euarchus' verdict, it seems that we finally have it:

> This weighty matter wherof presently wee are to determeyn, dothe at the first Consideracyon yeelde twoo important Doubtes. The firste
>> Whether these men bee to bee judged. The seconde
>> Howe they are to bee judged.

He first disposes of the question of the heroes' privileged princely position:

> The first Doubt aryseth bycause they give them selves oute for *Princes* absolute, a Sacred name, and to which any vyolence seemes an Impiety: For how can any Lawes which are ye bondes of all humane society bee observed, yf the Lawe givers & Lawe Rulers bee not helde in an untouched admiration? But hereto all thoughe all redy, they have bene sufficyently answered yet, thus muche ageane I will repeate unto yow. That whatsoever they bee or bee not, here they bee no *Princes* synce betuixt *Prince* and *Subject*, there ys as necessary a Relation, as betweene father and sonne. And as there ys no Man a Father but to his Chylde, so ys not a Prince a Prince, but to his owne Subjectes, therefore ys not this place to acknowledge in them any principallity, withoute yt shoulde at ye same tyme by a secrett Consent, confess subjection: yet hereto may bee objected, that the universall Civility, the Lawe of Nations (all mankynde beeyng as yt were Coinhabiters or worlde Citizens together) hathe ever requyred publique persons shoulde bee (of all partyes) especially regarded: Since not onely in peace but in warres, not onely *Princes*, but Herauldes and Trompettes are with greate reasons exempted from injuryes.

Next he points out that Pyrocles and Musidorus have abrogated the laws whose protection they seek:

> This poynt ys true, but, yet so true, as they that will receyve the benefites of a Custome must not bee the first to breake yt, for then can they not Complayne, yf they bee not helpt by that, which they themselves hurt: Yf a *Prince* do actes of hostility withoute denouncing warre, yf hee breake his oathe of Amity, or innumerable suche other thinges contrary to the Lawe of Armes, hee must take heede howe hee falleth into theyre handes whom hee so wrongeth, for then ys Curtesy the best custome hee can clayme: Muche more these men, who have not onely lefte to doo like *Princes*, but, to bee like *Princes*, not onely entered into *Arcadia*, and so into the *Arcadian* Orders, but into Domesticall services, and so by making them selves private, deprived them selffes of respect due to theyre publique Calling. For no proportion yt were in Justice, that a Man might make hym selfe no *Prince* when hee will do evell, and mighte a newe create hym self *Prince* when hee will not suffer evell: Thus therefore by all Lawes of Nature and Nations, and specially by theyre owne putting them selves oute of the Sanctuary of them, these younge Men can not in justice avoyde the judgment but like private men must have theyre Doynges eyther cleared excused or condempned.

Euarchus makes clear the basis of judgment: the laws of Arcadia, not speculative reasoning. The first is universally accepted, the second open to individual interpretation:

> There resteth then the second poynte, Howe to Judge well: And that must undoubtedly bee done, not by a free Discourse of Reason and skill of philosophy, but must bee tyed to the Lawes of *Greece* and municipall statutes of this Kingdome. For allthough oute of them these came and to them must in deede referr theyre Ofspringe, yet bycause Philosophicall discourses stande in the generall Consideration of thinges, they leave to every man a scope of his owne interpretacyon. Where the Lawes (applying them selves to the necessary use) foulde us within the Boundes assured, which once broken, mans nature infinitely raungeth: Judged therefore they must bee, and by youre Lawes Judged.

This contention strikes at the heart of the princes' defense, for they admit to breaking the law but adduce a higher power (and in Musidorus' case a higher law)—chivalrous love. Euarchus continues:

> Nowe the action offereth yt self to due Ballance betwixt the accusers twoo foulde accusation, and theyre answer accordingly applyed: The questyons beeynge, the one of a fact simply, the other of the quality of a facte. To the first they use direct Deny-all, to the second, qualification and excuse: They deny the Murder of the *Duke,* and ageanst mighty presumptions bringe forthe some probable answers, whiche they do principally fortify with the *Duchess* acknouledging her self onely culpable. Certeynly as in equallity of Conjectures wee are not to take holde of the worste, but rather to bee glad wee may fynde any hope, that Mankynde ys not growne Monsterus (beeyng less evell undoubtedly, a guilty man shoulde escape, then a guiltless parrish) so yf in the rest they bee spottless, then ys yt no furder to bee remembred: But yf they have aggrevated these suspicions with newe evills, then are those suspicions so farr to shewe them selves, as to cause the other poyntes to bee thorowly examyned and with less favoure weighed, since this no man can denye, they have beene accedentall yf not Principall Causes of the *Dukes* death.
>
> Nowe then wee are to determeyn of the other matters which are layde to them, wherein they doo not deny the facte, but deny or at least dimenish the faulte.

Euarchus penetrates Musidorus' juvenile reasoning without pausing:

> But first I may Remember (thoughe yt were not first alledged by them) the services they had before done, truly honorable and worthy of great Reward, but, not worthy to counterveyle with a followyng wickednes: Rewarde ys proper to well doynge, ponishment to evell doynge, which must not bee confounded, no more than good & evill are to bee mingled. Therefore yt hathe beene determeyned in all wysdomes, that no man bycause hee hathe done well before, shoulde have his present evilles spared, but rather, so muche the more punished: As having shewed hee knewe howe to doo good, woulde ageanst his knouledge bee naughte.

The Speeches

Allowances made, he summarizes the offenses to which the two have confessed:

> The facte then ys nakedly withoute passion, or parciality, to bee viewed, wherein hee that termes hym self to bee *Tymophirus,* denyes not hee offered vyolence to the Lady *Philoclea:* An acte punished by all the *Grecian* Lawes, with beeyng throwne downe from a hye Tower to the earthe, a Deathe which dothe noo way exceede the proportion of the Trespas. For, nothing can bee ymagined more unnaturall, then by force to take that, which beeynge holyly used, ys the Roote of humanity, the beginning & meynteyning of Living Creatures, wherof the Confusion must needes bee a generall Rwyn: And synce the wickednes of Lust ys by oure Decrees punished by deathe, (thoughe bothe so consent) muche more ys hee whose wickednes so overflowes, as hee will compell an other to bee wicked. The other younge Man hee confesseth, hee perswaded the Princess *Pamela* to flee her Contrey, and accompanyed her in yt, withoute all questyon, a Ravishment no less, then the other: For, allthoughe hee ravisshed her not from her self yet hee ravisshed her from hym yt owed her which was her Father. This kynde ys chastized by the loss of the heade, as a moste execrable thefte, for yf they must dye, who steale from us oure goodes howe muche more they who steale from us that, for whiche wee gather oure goodes.

Euarchus reminds the two young men of the responsibilities of rank, theirs and their princesses':

> And yf oure Lawes have yt so in ye private persons muche more forcible are they to bee in *Princes* Children? Wheare one steales as yt were the whole state, and well beeyng of that People, tyed by the secrett of a longe use to bee governed by none but the next of the blood. Neyther lett any man merveile oure Auncesters have bene so severe in these Cases, since the example of the *Phenecian Europa,* but especially the *Gretian Helen* hathe taughte them, what destroyng fyers have growne of suche sparckles: And allthoughe *Helene* was a wyfe, and this but a Chylde, that booteth not, since the Principall Cause of marying wyves ys that wee may have Children of oure owne. But lett us see howe these younge menn (truely for theyre persons worthy of pity yf they have pityed them selves) doo goo aboute to miti-

313

gate ye vehemency of theyre Errors: Some of theyre excuses are comon to bothe, some peculier, onely to hym that was the Shepeheard bothe Remember the force of Love, and as yt were the mending up the matter by theyre Mariage.

Now Euarchus replies to Musidorus' central argument, the force of love:

> Yf that unbrydeled Desyer which ys intituled Love mighte purge suche a sicknes as this, surely wee shoulde have many Loving excuses of hatefull myscheefes: Nay, rather no myscheef shoulde bee committed that shoulde not bee vailed under the name of Love. For aswell hee that steales mighte alledg the Love of money hee that murders the Love of Revenge, hee that rebells the Love of greatnes as the Adulterer ye Love of a woman: since in all speeche they do affirme they Love that which an yll governed passyon makes them to follow. But love may have no suche priviledge.

He proceeds to expound a definition of love, and its proper effects, far more likely to resemble Sidney's own:

> That sweete and heavenly uniting of the myndes, which properly ys called Love, hathe no other knott but vertue: And therefore, yf yt bee a Right Love, yt can never slyde into any action yt ys not vertuous.

To the proposed solution of marriage, Euarchus replies:

> The other and in deede more effectuall reason ys, that they may bee marryed unto them, and so honorably redress the Dishonor of them, whome this matter seemeth more to tuche: Surely, yf the questyon were, what were convenyent for ye parties, and not what ys just in the never chaunging Justice, there might bee muche sayde in yt. But herein wee must consider that ye Lawes looke howe to prevent by due examples, that suche thinges bee not done: For, yf the Governoures of Justice, shall take suche a scope, as to measure the force of the Lawe by a shewe of Convenyency, and measure that Convenyency not by the publique Society (but by yt which ys fittest for them to offend) younge men, stronge men & riche men shall ever fynde private Convenyences, how to cover suche committed disorders, as to the publique shall not only bee inconvenyent but pestilent.

Once again, the two heroes have ignored the larger implications of their acts:

> This Mariage perchaunce might bee fitt for them, but very unfitt for the state yt were to allowe a Paterne of suche procurations of Mariage, and thus muche doo they bothe alledge: Furder goes hee that went with the Princes *Pamela*, and requireth ye benefitt of a Counsellor, who hathe place of free perswasion & ye reasonable excuse of a Servaunt that did but wayte of his Mistris. Withoute all question as Counseilors have greate Cause to take heede how they advise any thinge directly opposite to the forme of that present governement, especially when they doo yt simply, withoute publique allowance; So yet ys this Case muche more apparant, since neyther shee was an effectuall *Princess* (her Father beeyng then alyve, and thoughe hee had bene deade) shee not come to the yeares of authority, nor hee her servant in such maner to obay her, but by his owne preferment, first belonging to *Dametas* and then to the *Duke*. And therefore yf not by *Arcadian* Lawes yet by howsholde orders bounde to have done nothing withoute his agreement.

All objections dealt with, Euarchus passes sentence:

> Thus therefore, since the Deedes accomplisshed by these Twoo are bothe abhominable, and inexcusable, I doo in the behalf of Justice, and by ye force of *Arcadian* Lawes pronounce: That *Tymophirus* shall bee throwne of, from a hye Tower, to receyve his deathe by his Falle, *Palladius* shall bee beheaded, the tyme before the Sunne sett, the place in *Mantinea*, the executioner *Dametas* which office hee shalle execute all the dayes of his lyfe, for his beastly forgetting the carefull Duty owed to his Charge: This sayde hee turned hym self to *Philanax* and twoo other of the Noble men comaunding them to see the Judgment presently performed. [375–80]

The direct, legalistic prose of the entire speech needs no comment, except perhaps that the character who is the undeniable ethical touchstone of the romance speaks a language almost without ornament. The division of the argument is explicitly explained stage by stage. Facts (as Euarchus understands them) and not abuse are its sole subject, justice its only purpose. Euarchus is not—so far as he knows at this point—a party to the dispute, nor is he in love. He speaks as a rational man, and as a responsible public person. And, like no one else, he states both sides of the question.[9] As a result of the these circumstances, his speech is an abstract, impersonal, explicit analysis of the themes which until now we have had to extract from ambiguous dramatic contexts. It is Euarchus who spells out the reader's second thoughts about the adventures in Arcadia.

The last great speech of the Old *Arcadia* sets forth the moral judgment implicit in the entire romance. After the princes' identities are revealed, Euarchus from his grief adds a personal condemnation as well: "Nay I can not in this Case acknowledg yow for myne, for never had I Shepeheard to my Nephewe, nor never had woeman to my sonne, youre vyces have degraded yow from beeyng *Princes* & have disanulde youre Birtheright" (383). Upon this Musidorus loses his temper and curses his uncle—an outburst in character with his previous speech. Pyrocles, also in character, rebukes his cousin for his impatience and his misplacement of blame, then falls on his knees and begs pardon from his father and begs also the life of his cousin. Euarchus is firm and rises from the judgment seat, and things are at an absolute impasse— when, of course, Basilius wakes up.

Fairy tale endings are traditionally not to be scrutinized in the

9. The relationship between Philanax' and Euarchus' styles is an almost perfect illustration of the contrast drawn by Aristotle between the orator who attempts to gain his case by working on the emotions of his hearers, and the orator who depends on the merits of the case. Philanax emphasizes the emotional overtones of the case rather than dwelling on the proven facts (c. *Rhetorica* 2.1401 b). Euarchus, on the other hand, sticks to enthymemes. Aristotle had written: "The only question with which these writers here deal is how to put the judge into a given frame of mind. About the orator's proper modes of persuasion they have nothing to tell us; nothing, that is, about how to gain skill in enthymemes" (*Rhetorica* 1. 1354 b). Earlier, he had cautioned: "It is not right to pervert the judge by moving him to anger or envy or pity—one might as well warp a carpenter's rule before using it" (*Rhetorica* 1. 1354 a). Euarchus' proofs, it might be noticed, are all "non-artistic," that is they are what we would call evidence rather than argument (for a full discussion of this distinction see Howell, *Logic and Rhetoric*, p. 69); Philanax, on the other hand, develops "artistic" proofs, that is, those depending on his skill in invention, and rather neglects the strong "non-artistic" ones to which Euarchus restricts himself.

light of reason, yet after this one has married the princely couples and forgiven the Duchess and Duke, the reader cannot help recalling Euarchus' speech. The Duke's murder, he had said, was not the central issue. Justice was demanded for ravishing the princesses. Not private accommodation but justice. Does Basilius' belated consent set all right? What are we to make of the "tragicomic" dénouement?

From the common perception that the Old *Arcadia* includes several formal speeches on traditional subjects, we have moved to describe some of them: a love-versus-friendship debate, declaration of love (several examples), lament (several examples), a debate on suicide, one on facing death and on immortality, a placatory speech to a wild mob, an inflaming speech to a docile mob, and all the panoply of a state trial. We have seen that these usually follow the general precepts for organizing a speech, though we have not adopted a single framework and forced them all into it, nor have we analyzed a speech into its parts unless something of importance seemed to follow from such a proof of its careful organization. Rather, an attempt has been made to show how painstakingly these rhetorical occasions are integrated into the narrative and thematic progression of the romance. Sidney's careful observance of decorum or careful transgression of it has been pointed out. We have tried to show how the various speeches were humorously compared and contrasted, and to suggest how Sidney the narrator distanced himself from the verbal pyrotechnics of his characters. He laughs at them with us. The ambiguity which this humor infuses into the themes of the romance has, hopefully, been made apparent to the reader. He should by now wonder how seriously he is to read the *Arcadia*. For the nobility of sentiment for which this work is famous seems often, upon closer analysis, to include a large measure of farce on the one hand and humbug on the other. Their presence raises new questions about Sidney's attitude toward both passionate love and the elaborate language that usually accompanied it in his own time.

4. Sidney the Narrator

An age that cherishes the memory of Henry James can hardly be expected to allow Sidney the narrator to escape unscathed. The spectacle of an author frankly telling a tale *in propria persona*, commenting on it as it flows from his pen in asides to his "Dear Ladies," obviously regulating the unfolding of the narrative, makes the modern reader as uncomfortable as James felt in the loquacious I've-got-no-secrets company of Trollope. Sidney seems in many places to give the show away, to tell us twice over how we should feel. Myrick comments: "In the original version, where Sidney so often disregards the principles of the *Defence*, he frequently drops his role of 'maker' and comments upon the story." [1] But, as we have seen, the "message" of the Old *Arcadia* may not be quite so obvious, the reader's response not so clearly predictable, as has formerly been thought. It is logical, then, to seek in Sidney as narrator a figure more complex than the chatty, brotherly, facile moralizer he at first seems to be.

The narrator of the Old *Arcadia* is ostensibly Philip Sidney—no *persona* is involved. He tells the tale to his sister and her friends. If he were writing today he would probably eliminate

1. *Sidney as Literary Craftsman*, p. 243.

all his parenthetical assertions and simply report, or seem to report, what happened. There would be no asides to his "Dear Ladies." The mask of "maker" would never slip from his face. Not having our advantages, he lets it slip so often it is difficult to tell when it is up and when down. He seems not to have taken a great deal of care to keep the two roles separate, not to have acknowledged, in fact, any fundamental separation at all. "Maker" and "Commentator" is a misleading dichotomy for the Old *Arcadia*. Instead, we might distinguish first a narrator who is essentially a reporter, who describes the scenes to his "Dear Ladies" as if he were watching a play. His principal function at times seems to be that of a man changing a play into a prose romance. Scenery, pose, gesture, expression, all are given through his "comment." In this way, his interruptions could be said to heighten the dramatic vividness, not to detract from it. This kind of comment Myrick would presumably construe as legitimately belonging to the "maker." But the narrator also annotates, both implicitly and explicitly, what he describes. He is omniscient, he has seen the play before. He has also written, produced, and directed it. He even plays a part in it. In none of these roles is he less of a "maker" than in any other, and the "product" results from the complex interaction of these roles upon one another, not from any single one.

To be more explicit: we have first the basic story of the princes' adventures in Arcadia, in which Love pursues its inevitable triumph. The narrator simply describes this. He is powerless to change it, though he clearly would like to at certain points. He sympathizes with the characters much as he would had they been created by somebody else. But he knows what is going to happen, and try as he does to put a good face on some of the dastardly deeds, he cannot change the fundamental facts. Even when he becomes bored with their speeches he cannot shorten them: at one point when Basilius is reopening his heart to Cleophila he remarks on Basilius' discourse, "with many other suche hony wordes, which my penn growes allmoste weary to sett downe" (168). This is simply to say that Sidney, once he has made his initial assumption, that his characters are violently in love, does not interfere with the events which he—as "maker" and "com-

319

mentator" and "actor"—sees as inevitably following from this assumption. The consequences of passion are in no way softened. There is only one exception to this, the happy ending. (It is a vital exception, of course.) But by not otherwise softening the effects of passion, Sidney avoids the very thing to which James so objected in Trollope: the author's confession that he could make things turn out differently if he wanted to. The narrator's comments and regrets have precisely the opposite effect here; they emphasize the inevitability of the "Pilgrimmage of Passion" passing before us. Sidney at one point even says he is simply re-telling what is contained in official records: "And doubt yow not, fayre Ladyes, there wanted no questioning how thinges had passed, but bycause I will have the thanckes my self, yt shall bee I yow shall heare yt of, And thus the Auncyent Recordes of *Arcadia* say, yt fell owte" (47). Too much ought not to be made of this mythical authority, for it is not seriously or repeatedly introduced, but it does indicate that Sidney intended to place himself in the role of an omniscient narrator reporting a story whose main events are unalterable. Occasionally he rearranges speeches uttered in haste or emotion. He gives in full the text of songs which only run rapidly through the mind of his characters: "But doo not thincke (Fayre Ladyes) his thoughtes had suche Leysure as to ronne over so longe a Ditty: The onely generall fancy of yt came into his mynde fixed uppon the sence of the sweet Subject [Philoclea]" (226). But he does not change any of the essentials of the story or radically alter the character of his personages.

The narrator also comments on the action being played out before him. Sometimes Sidney is a modest narrator: "In what Case pore *Gynecia* was, when shee knewe the voyce and felt the body of her husband? Fayre Ladyes, yt ys better to knowe by imaginacyon, then experyence?" (214). Occasionally he seems personal, almost autobiographical, as when Pyrocles and Philoclea are tucked in bed at the end of Book III: "Hee gives mee occasyon to leave hym in so happy a plighte, least my Penn mighte seeme to grudge, at the due Blisse of these pore Lovers, whose Loyalty had but smalle respite of theyre fyery Agonyes" (227). At other times, he seems to be the impersonal mouthpiece of conventional wisdom. The first sentence of Book IV, "The Everlasting Justice" etc., is one of innumerable examples. The Old *Arcadia* is larded with sententiae, many of them voiced by this speaker of conventional wisdom. They are part of the romance in a way that such speculations as the one quoted, about Gynecia's disappointment at finding her lover become her husband, are not. They supply a moral framework within which the action can be judged. Critics have, of course, objected to this. Aristotle's dictum that "the poet should speak as little as possible in his own person for it is not this that makes him an imitator," [2] developed into the modern preference for "showing" over "telling," has caused the Old *Arcadia* to be ranked beneath the New because in the Old the second method allegedly predominates over the first. Muir writes, for example: "In some ways the old *Arcadia* is more directly didactic than the new. Sidney cut out the narrator's moralizing, often transferring it to one or other of the characters in the story." [3] Yet the moral orientation which the narrator provides is essential to the reader's evaluation of the action. The narrator performs, in fact, the function Aristotle looked for from the chorus.[4]

Not all of the narrator's moralizings are the expected opinions. The beginning sentence of Book IV, though conventional, is still in its context surprising and strong; as we have shown in Chapter 2, it colors the whole of our reading of the book which follows. It is misleading to view these as pointless asides of a garrulous narrator. This difference between the narrative poses does not lend itself to absolute demonstration but will, I am confident, become obvious with a close reading. The important point to be made is that sometimes Sidney stands distanced from the narrator or, to put it another way, his comments upon the action are often so general or traditional as to be rather part of the narrative than personal asides. It is a mistake to make out a complete distinction between the "real" Sidney and "Sidney the narrator," for the distance between them frequently changes. But there are differ-

---

2. *Aristotle's Theory of Poetry and Fine Art*, trans. S. H. Butcher (4th ed. London, 1920), p. 93.

3. "Sidney," p. 21.

4. If the narrator is in some way a chorus, Sidney has an Aristotelian shield: "The Chorus too should be regarded as one of the actors; it should be an integral part of the whole, and share in the action" (Butcher, p. 69).

ences between the two nevertheless. Sidney's tongue is more fully in his cheek at some times than at others.

The first Pyrocles-Musidorus scene, for example, shows a narrator who describes its humor without betraying an understanding of it. He is careful to make the comedy clear for us but he does not acknowledge it openly or seem even to be aware of it. He goes on, much in the manner of one of Swift's narrators, being precise about details and oblivious to larger issues. When Pyrocles, in the midst of his passionate confession to his friend of his noble love for Philoclea, reveals his real motive in a moment of heat, the narrator reports it without emphasis along with the praises of heavenly love which have preceded it: "And thus gently, yow may, yf yt please yow, thincke of mee, neyther doubte yow, because I werre a womans apparrell, I will bee the more womannish, since I assure yow (for all my apparell) there ys no thing I desyer more, then fully to proove my self a man, in this enterpryse" (19–20). There can be little doubt that Sidney placed this here as a parenthetical ironic comment on the extravagant language Pyrocles uses to describe his love, but the narrator is specifically made blind to it. At other times, his perception of the comedy is partial, and deliberately understated. He is closer to the author but not coincident with him, as when Musidorus reverses his stand against Pyrocles' falling in love: "*Pyrocles* harte was not so oppressed with the twoo mighty passions of Love & unkyndenes, but, that yt yeelded to some myrthe at this Comaundement of *Musidorus*, that hee shoulde love *Philoclea*" (22). Another example leaves us in doubt as to how widely the narrator is willing to be caught smiling. In the midst of the suicide debate which follows the seduction, Pyrocles pretends to agree to Philoclea's demand that he stay alive in order to humor her: "*Pyrocles* who had that for a Lawe unto hym not to leave *Philoclea* in any thinge unsatisfyed, allthoughe hee still remayned in his former purpose, and knewe the tyme woulde growe shorte for yt" (275). When Dorus, questioned in Book I about his desires for employment, replies (so that he can remain close to Pamela) that his mind is "wholly sett up on pastorall affaires" (49) the ironic dismissal of the pastoral element is passed on by a tongue-in-cheek narrator without comment. Such a dismissal of what at least purports to be the central concern of the story—pastoral affairs—is likely to escape a modern reader but presupposes, one must think, a considerable meeting of minds between Sidney and his anticipated audience. Otherwise such persistent ironic shorthand simply would not succeed.

Sometimes Sidney comments wryly on his characters in asides which take the reader fully into his confidence. He describes Pyrocles' awakening after his night with Philoclea: "But, so yt was yt *Pyrocles* awaked, grudging in hym self, that sleepe (though very shorte) had robbed hym, of any parte of those his highest Contentmentes" (269). He is even more obvious in his reflections on his clowns, as when Dametas is hastening on to his buried treasure:

> Many tymes hee cursed his horses want of Consideratyon that in so ymportunate a Matter woulde make no greater speede, many tymes hee wisshed hym self the back of an Asse to help to carry away his newe soughte Riches: An unfortunate wissher, for yf hee had aswell wisshed the hedd, yt had beene graunted hym, at lengthe, beeyng come to the Tree whiche hee hoped shoulde beare so golden Ackornes. [177]

Sometimes the mockery is made more indirect by being put into the mouth of the character: Mopsa, for example, after she has been told about the wishing tree by Dorus, "Conjured hym by all her precyous Loves, that shee mighte have the first possession of the wisshing Tree, assuring hym, that for the enjoyng of her hee shoulde never neede to Clyme farr" (184).

The moral is sometimes explicitly drawn, sometimes left entirely up to the reader. In the fifth book, for example, Philanax goes to meet Euarchus, who has paused just inside the boundary to make clear his peaceful intent. Philanax finds the great King "taking his Rest under a Tree, with no more affected pompes, then as a Man that knewe (howe so ever hee was exalted) the beginning & ende of his Body was earthe" (331). The moral is unmistakable: privilege does not extend beyond the grave, better not abuse it on this side. Then on the next page we read:

> These Rightly wyse and temperate Consideracyons mooved *Euarchus*, to take his Laboursome Journey to see whether by his authority hee might drawe *Basilius* from this burying him self

alyve, and to returne ageane to employ his oulde yeares in doyng good, the onely happy action of mans lyfe: Neyther was hee withoute a Consideracyon in hym self to provyde the Mariage of *Basilius* twoo Daughters, for his Sonne and Nephewe ageanst theyre returne. The tedyus expectation of which joyned with the feare of theyre miscarrying (having beene long withoute hearing any newes from them) made hym the willinger to ease that parte of Melancholy with chaunging ye objectes of his wearyed sences.   [332–33]

The full context is given to demonstrate how unobtrusively this tremendously ironic and important fact—that the two princes and princesses would have been married anyway—is offered to the reader. The really important moral is not drawn at all, is almost hidden in fact.

Even these few examples show that the narrator does not remain at a fixed distance either from his characters or from his audience. This easily confuses the modern reader, who soon learns that such a narrator cannot be trusted. We cannot follow his lead always, and cannot feel sure that we are understanding the moral orientation of the romance.

This untrustworthy narrator is one of the real difficulties of the romance. The narrator accepts Euarchus as the all-wise king and moralizes, as we have just seen, on his countless evidences of wisdom and probity. Yet the same narrator also seems to be in full sympathy with the heroic seductions carried out by the princes. His praise of them is too frequent throughout the romance to need documentation. The reader is bound to think his attitude inconsistent; in the first half of the romance he is all for love, in the second all for justice.[5] It is tempting to postulate a narrator quite separate from Sidney, a *persona* who accepts the

5. This problem has been discussed apropos of the *Arcadia* by Kenneth T. Rowe, and a verdict of fundamental inconsistency brought in ("Romantic Love and Parental Authority in Sidney's Arcadia," University of Michigan, *Contributions in Modern Philology*, No. 4 [April 1947], p. 16). There, of course, the problem is easier to solve. The inconsistency results from the grafting together of two fragments of fundamentally different intent. In the Old, the remedy comes harder. Here the reader does seem to be clubbed from behind by a surprise ending à la Herman Wouk.

tale uncritically as a pastoral romance of serious, intentional, noble sentiment, and to place Sidney the author outside him altogether. We could then introduce Sidney into the romance with Euarchus and the inconsistency would be solved. But this postulation ignores the many instances of Sidney in propria persona. It fails to notice, also, the instances in which the narrator seems to see further than Euarchus does. The narrator comments, for example, on the irony of Euarchus' sitting in judgment on his son and nephew: "In suche shadowe or rather pit of Darckenes the wormish mankynde lives that neyther they knowe howe to foresee nor what to feare; and are but lyke Tennys balles tossed by the Rackett of the higher powers" (358). The opposite position—that Sidney is frank and frankly himself at all times—is as easy to refute.

The reader can never lay his hand on a constant rule, applicable to all situations. He must read carefully, of course, but even then the author's attitude toward his creation remains often puzzling, sometimes frankly ambiguous. Sidney is always getting up from his seat in the audience, climbing on stage to act a scene, turning to comment on it in an aside, arranging his characters in specific poses and facial expressions, and then going back to his seat for the next scene. Much as we would like him to stay put, he will not. This movement makes the romance much harder to interpret, but it also offers the possibility of an ultimate meaning a little more bracing than the predigested Tudor political philosophy and over-cooked Petrarchan passions which are usually given as its raison d'être. For these various roles affect one another in interesting combinations. The basic action laid down by Sidney the "maker" proceeds from a single action—Basilius' withdrawal—without outside help. The narrator makes the traditional observations, often so obvious that they cause a good deal of irritation, but neglects to comment on facts he relates which are of great interest to the careful reader of the primary, unchangeable story. Immediately the two kinds of "morals," the obvious ones drawn by the narrator and those implicit in the logic of the plot, begin to be compared in the reader's mind. Sidney the "maker" begins to question the adequacy of traditional wisdom about his chosen subject of love.

The unreliable narrator introduces several difficulties of interpretation. First of all, the comedy is weakened, for we are not always sure when to laugh or how hard. L. C. Potts has written that "the first requisite of a comic narrative is that it should be precise; the finest shades of character should stand revealed, and the situation must be clear."[6] Sidney is sometimes imprecise. Potts also sensibly points out that all comic narrators moralize, that comic illumination is part of the role. Sidney's fault is perhaps not intrusion but maladroit intrusion. More generally, the ambiguous narrator is at the root of the confusion as to how seriously the romance is to be taken. Doubtless it is true, as Wayne C. Booth has recently said, that "It is only by distinguishing between the author and his implied image that we can avoid pointless and unverifiable talk about such qualities as 'sincerity' or 'seriousness' in the author."[7] But what do we do if we cannot distinguish between them? The thesis of Booth's brilliant book, that an author ought not to allow this confusion to occur, may be correct but hardly helps in deciding when author and "implied image" coincide and when they do not. The presence of an undependable narrator means that the romance lacks a completely reliable control, for no other character is adequate to this function. This lack is not acute when the narrator's traditional moralization is sufficient for interpretation of the events he describes, but when his comments move us in one direction and the logic of events the opposite way, the reader is bewildered. This bewilderment may, of course, be intended[8] but if we suspect it to arise from inadvertent shifts of narratorial distance and posture we shall be seriously disoriented in the world of Arcadia.

Such disorientation has not been felt by many of Sidney's commentators. The license of romance has operated to excuse Sidney the narrator from anything like a consistent moral scrutiny of his own tale. This moralistic point of view, it will be immediately objected, simply does not apply to a romance. A modern reader must do as the Elizabethans did and accept the superficial moral with gusto. He must read for the rhetoric. He should not make

6. *Comedy* (London, n.d.), p. 67.
7. *The Rhetoric of Fiction* (Chicago, 1961), p. 75.
8. See below, Chapter 6, for a discussion of this.

rhetorical mouthpieces into moral beings; he should not seek out subtleties where they do not exist. But if they do exist? They obtrude themselves on any reader who is willing to credit Sidney with a moral judgment beyond the kindergarten level.

The didacticism of the Old *Arcadia* has been commonly misunderstood because the dialectic nature of the romance has been overlooked. The teller's ambivalent character has been ignored. Speeches have been quoted to prove that Sidney believed this or that, and a following speech which presents the opposite case has been ignored, or dismissed—if it disagreed with the commentator's theory—as token opposition erected only to be demolished. Sidney was, obviously, often more convinced by one side than by the other, but the contest, both in his own mind and in the romance, is not so one-sided as conventional moralists on the prowl for examples of virtue often proclaim. There are no easy answers to Gynecia's outcries, for example, no ready solutions for Cupid's blindness. The affirmative statement never wholly cancels out the negative one preceding it. The first stays in mind to color and add depth to the second. The proposed resolution of the two opposing forces of the romance, reason and passion, is Christian marriage. But circumstances combined to make Sidney see it as a not wholly harmonious synthesis, a sometimes inadequate compromise with passion. He clearly indicates this in the irresistible force of passion which leads up to the near-catastrophe a happy ending so narrowly averts. The proper moral is drawn, but in the teeth of contradictory evidence. We are meant to "take" the moral solution, but with the remembrance of the forces with which it must contend fresh in mind.

Sidney's fondness for dialectic in his literary practice has been obscured, as I see it, by ignoring the great sophistication of his attitude toward rhetoric. That the Old *Arcadia* uses rhetoric is common knowledge. That it is also *about* the use of rhetoric seems to me equally important. We might go so far as to say that, obliquely at least, the Old *Arcadia* addresses itself to the main point of defense in the *Defence* that rhetoric (or poetry—the two are almost synonymous in this case) is a neutral weapon, lending itself alike to good uses and bad. Cleophila/Pyrocles, for example, calms the rebel mob with the same arts she/he uses in trying to excite the mob to desert Euarchus and rally to the two princesses. Gynecia uses the same language to express her anguish as her husband does to voice his ludicrous infatuation. The many instances of ironic qualification of the speeches, which together create the tension between speech and action, show Sidney aware of the opportunity for deception that rhetorical training offered. The constant conflict in *Astrophil and Stella* between the direct language of real passion and the feast of cold compliment with which literature in his time set it out recurs repeatedly in the Old *Arcadia*. Most often it is not Sidney but one of his characters who employs the arts of rhetoric, and the reader watches it in the devil's work as often as not. The reader is not fooled. He is specifically intended to remain undeceived.

The *Defence* reveals how closely poetry and rhetoric were linked in Sidney's mind. Sidney's literary method in the Old *Arcadia* (and in *Astrophil and Stella* too) is, however, diametrically opposed to the rhetorical. It is dialectical through and through. The reader watches rhetoric persuade others while Sidney aims to persuade him through dialectic. A little reflection shows the informing traits of the romance to be clearly dialectical. Zandvoort has remarked Sidney's fondness for analyzing a proposition into two opposite points of view.[9] Many of the rhetorical "occasions" are in fact disputations or debates. The soliloquies present, for the most part, a character arguing with himself or with the universe. The fundamental organizing principle of the eclogues is a division into two opposing camps, on both trivia and large issues. In its largest sense, the romance may be fairly described as a dialectic between reason and passion, in which each side, through an often-changing personification, uses all the devices of rhetoric to prevail over the other. Thus rhetoric, as widely as Sidney uses it, is always kept at a safe distance. Its flowers are—as it were— always smelled by somebody else. It is in this sense that the Old *Arcadia* is about rhetoric, about its abuses and, to be fair, its beauties as well.

Sidney must have felt he could rely on his original small, so-

9. *Sidney's Arcadia*, p. 172.

phisticated audience properly to separate narrator and rhetorical excess. He could depend on their personal knowledge of himself to supply the needed control. He did not have to write it in. It may well be that the shifting in the New of some narrative comment to characters in the romance, which has been called an evidence of Sidney's growth as a storyteller, is actually an attempt to provide direction for the needs of a larger and anonymous audience.

A sense of the original audience excuses us from thinking that the asides to his "Fayre Ladyes" crash the barriers of fictional form. For the Old *Arcadia* is not a pastoral romance pure and simple, but rather a pastoral romance told by a brother to his sister. The recurrent references to his audience and to himself remind the reader of the larger context of the romance—that it is from an aristocratic brother to an aristocratic sister, that it is to be read with the lightness of touch not to be looked for in an adolescent's whole-hearted absorption in Sir Walter Scott. The reader often feels himself in the place of the fair ladies, at a third remove from what is happening in Arcadia. The asides are still another attempt by Sidney to indicate the spirit in which we are to read.

The sense of a particular audience is part of the romance. The introductory letter should be accepted to this extent at least—a general, heterogeneous audience was not envisaged. Rather we should picture a Wilton fireside. The comedy is immeasurably improved when the work is read aloud. It might be as well to think of it as something like closet drama. Set speeches or a rapid exchange of repartee were probably given dramatic heightening, perhaps divided into parts, during the reading. The songs would almost certainly have been sung. Although delivery is often the subdivision of rhetoric most briefly dealt with by writers on the subject, it is always stressed, often with poetry as an example of the advantages it offers. Aristotle, for example, comments in *Rhetorica:*

This [the proper method of delivery] is a thing that affects the success of a speech greatly; but hitherto the subject has been neglected. Indeed, it was long before it found a way into the arts

329

of tragic drama and epic recitation: at first poets acted their tragedies themselves. It is plain that delivery has just as much to do with oratory as with poetry.[1]

Unquestionably, a reader or group of readers would have heightened the comedy, just as they would have reinforced the psychology of each scene by the gestures Sidney describes.

Youthful Sidney has been taken to task by Zandvoort as a clumsy, immature storyteller,[2] and even those who praise the narrative technique of the Old do so because it is so simple and straightforward. Actually it is neither clumsy nor straightforward. The plot, as we have shown, is artful to a fault. The manner of telling may in the last analysis be equally so. If we call Sidney clumsy because he overworks the phrase "as yow shall shortly heare," [3] while ignoring, for example, the great skill with which he interweaves narration and speech, we shall distort both his skill at the time of writing the Old and his rationale in the revision. His narrative style has obvious faults—witness the cliff-hanger stratagem. But denied the grace of these warhorses, who would be saved? There are easier ways to tell a love story if that is all one wants to do. That was *not* all Sidney wanted to do. He was concerned to make clear his complex—perhaps contradictory—feelings about that love story, or more precisely that kind of love story. I suggest that this concern prompted him to develop a complex use of the narratorial pose which English prose fiction had not up to that time possessed.

The Sidney one imagines as author of the Old *Arcadia* emerges as less a plaster saint than is usually thought. He becomes, though, a shrewder author. For the dialectical approach is far superior to the rhetorical for an imaginative work. An intelligent reader is never insulted by an author's moralization if he is informed of the desperate paradox it attempts to solve. The author becomes the preacher only when he sets up his tray of simple solutions for the problems endemic to mankind. The genuinely persuasive part of his work states the paradox, not its solution. Sidney clearly saw

1. 3. 1403 b.
2. *Sidney's Arcadia*, pp. 67 and passim.
3. Ibid., p. 84.

this as an artist, if he did not always admit to it as a man. His romance is not simply a rhetorical statement of the good old truths, though there are enough of them in it. Rather it shows how perilous a life those truths have in a world "by love possessed." The Old *Arcadia* is a dramatic statement of the fundamentally paradoxical relation between passion on the one hand and a livable public and private order on the other. For Sidney knew that though the rhetorician can never admit to doubt, the poet—if he is wise—will never pretend to certainty.

5. Rhetorical Style

Defenders of Sidney's *Arcadias* have been somewhat embarrassed by the Arcadian style. Except for the plea of time and place, and the claim for enrichment of the language, they have had little of value to say in recent years about this crucial issue. The strongest statement an admirer of Sidney seems willing to hazard is Lewis' claim that no one in other respects equipped to understand the romance was ever defeated by the style.[1] The adverse critics of the romance agree for the most part that both versions "bewray a want of inward touch." It will be convenient to have these standard condemnations of the Arcadian style before us, since they have fixed the traditional image of the *Arcadia* in the public mind.

J. W. H. Atkins writes:

> He avoids . . . the devices of Euphuism, the more obvious absurdities of bombastic, pedantic phrase, as well as those "tricks of alliteration" and other "far-fetched helps" which "do bewray a want of inward touch." His excesses, on the other hand, are those of a poet who forgets that he is now committed to prose. He enters upon a pedestrian task, unprepared to forego poetical flight; and, freed from the restraints which verse imposes, he strains even the limits of a more willing prose. With coherence

1. *English Literature in the Sixteenth Century*, p. 341.

of structure he is not greatly concerned. His sentences, long and rambling, are yet incapable of expressing his wealth of thought, and are, therefore, expanded by frequent parentheses. When he aims at emphasis, he occasionally employs Lyly's trick of antithesis . . . his favourite artifice is that of a jingle of words, which lacks effect as it lacks dignity.[2]

Greg is equally strong: "Arcadianism was little if at all better than Euphuism. It is just as formal, just as much a trick, just as stilted and unpliable, just as painful an illustration of the fact that a figure of rhetoric may be an occasional ornament, but cannot by any degree of ingenuity be made to serve as a basis of composition." [3] J. J. Jusserand points to the central objection in both these adverse verdicts: "by the side of these graceful flowers [the unquestioned felicities of style in a few purple passages], how many others are faded! What concessions to contemporary taste for tinsel and excessive ornament!" [4] Sidney could and did write good prose elsewhere, but in the *Arcadia* he let himself be carried away by the gaudy fad Lyly had started. So Krapp writes:

One is surprised that Sidney, having written so well here [in the *Defence of Poesie*] should write so badly in the *Arcadia*. But the prose style that seemed adequate for a critical essay, perhaps seemed inadequate to Sidney for a work of a higher and imaginative kind. Though he regarded the essence of poetry as inherent in the subject, with other Elizabethan stylists he shared the opinion that an elevated theme, like that of the *Arcadia*, called for a rhetorical and artful style. Time has not altogether justified Sidney in this opinion, and his significance in the development of English prose would have been vastly increased if he had written his most important work with the sound feeling for prose style which he exhibited in the *Apologie*.[5]

The *Arcadia* is considered by these critics to be Sidney's Great Mistake. He has paid an extreme price for his extreme fashionability.

2. *Cambridge History of English Literature*, 3, 402–03.
3. W. W. Greg, *Pastoral Poetry and Pastoral Drama*, pp. 151–52.
4. *The English Novel in the Time of Shakespeare*, p. 255.
5. George Philip Krapp, *The Rise of English Literary Prose* (New York, 1915), pp. 365–66.

Some students of the *Arcadia* have chosen to interpret Sidney's elaborate style as a deliberate attempt to prove that English had come of age by using in English all the devices of language so admired by the humanists in the classical tongues. M. Genouy, for example, takes this view,[6] as does R. F. Jones, in a specifically linguistic study.[7] Sidney himself seems to contradict this view in the letter to his brother already quoted where, just before the mention of his "toyful booke," he writes, "So yow can speake and write Latine not barbarously I never require great study in Ciceronianisme the cheife abuse of Oxford, *Qui dum verba sectantur, res ipsas negligunt.*" [8]

The tacit assumption by most critics concerning the style of the *Arcadia*, Old and New, has been that Sidney's first aim was to tell a story, and that for this purpose a straightforward style would have been far superior to the heavy rhetorical ormolu he finally chose. The style, in this view, is so much dead weight. But this assumption prejudices the case before we have got through the first page. Nor need we assume at the start that the Old *Arcadia* is a rhetorical diploma-piece, a simple imitation of the highly rhetorical genre of the Greek romance. If we strip the style from its context and cut up isolated passages into the most discrete units that Renaissance rhetoric discriminated, we should not be surprised that our verdict is "applied and excessive ornament." If we agree to ignore Sidney's larger intention, we shall then be able to agree that the context is irrelevant. As Eugene M. Waith has perceptively written: "Without a doubt, this is formal, tricky, stilted, and unpliable writing, just as Greg says it is, but the situation it expresses is also formal, tricky, stilted, and unpliable. It is useless to single out the style for disapproval, since it is an inseparable part of the literary form." [9]

If we are to understand the original *Arcadia*, we must consider style in its widest sense—all the ways in which language can be

6. *L' "Arcadia" de Sidney*, p. 159.

7. "The Eloquent Language," ch. 6 of *The Triumph of the English Language* (Stanford, 1953).

8. *Works*, 3, 132.

9. *The Pattern of Tragicomedy in Beaumont and Fletcher*, Yale Studies in English, 120 (New Haven, 1952), 76.

used for expressive effect. The simple rhetorical Noah, naming the tropes as they march by, is hopelessly lost. We have seen in earlier chapters that we must keep in mind elements not immediately connected with style in its narrower sense: context, previous and subsequent scenes and their language, the general rules of decorum, the distance of the narrator from his charcters, and so on. It is self-defeating to remove figures of speech, lush descriptive passages, carefully arranged speeches, from their contexts and then to complain that Sidney is laying his ornament on with a trowel. The dramatic context, the spirit in which something is said, is as important in the original *Arcadia* as in Shakespearean comedy.

A few scholars have at least attempted to relate style and context. Krapp, for example, writes:

> The style of the *Arcadia* was carefully chosen to fit the subject.
> Sidney's purpose being to write a sustained and elevated narra-
> tive, one also in which the events moved with the freedom and
> often the apparent confusion of the complications of life, he
> appropriately took as a basis of his style a long and complicated
> sentence structure.[1]

But this one-to-one relationship between style and subject is far too simple, supported neither by the style as a whole nor by the subject of either *Arcadia*. Still more impressionistic is Stanley Harkness, in an article cataloguing Sidney's crimes against the canons of prose style:

> Some of them [Sidney's stylistic errors] are doubtless inad-
> vertent; most of them are unquestionably deliberate. The aban-
> don, even wantonness, which results is surely one of the qualities
> which Sidney sought for his extravagant romance.[2]

I no more than Harkness "wish to appear to palliate Sidney's offenses against the integrity of sentence-architecture,"[3] but surely it is too simple to equate a supposed freedom of the fancy with a wanton abandon in matters of syntax.

1. *English Literary Prose*, p. 374.
2. *The Prose Style of Sir Philip Sidney*, University of Wisconsin Studies in Language and Literature, 2 (Madison, 1918), 57-76, 76.
3. Ibid., p. 70.

The Old Arcadia

A real advance in describing the style of the *Arcadia* was made by S. L. Wolff, who pointed out that Sidney's style so varies from page to page that one cannot speak of a single Arcadian style:

> Sometimes it is touched with Euphuism, sometimes with Petrarchanism, sometimes with the Catalogue, Summary, and Splitting Constructions of late Latin rhetoric. . . . But its prevailing characteristics are 'epideictic'; a fondness for the oratory, the theatrical terminology, the antithesis, and the oxymoron, which give such a specific flavor to Greek Romance.[4]

The final result, for Wolff, was "an effect of rhetorical strain throughout." [5] But his awareness of the presence of several styles in the *Arcadia* prevented him from making the perhaps too-ready generalizations common before his time. Unfortunately, Wolff was not willing to see in its extensive use of rhetoric anything more than a straightforward imitation of the rhetorical display pieces of late Greek romance. Anyone who has read his discussion of the two *Arcadias* is compelled to acknowledge enormous stylistic borrowings. The fundamental figures of speech—the stylistic constants—are for the most part the same in Sidney and in the Greek romances of Heliodorus and others: parallelism of various kinds (isocolon, parison, paromoion), ploce, alliteration, antithesis as both trope and scheme, the several types of personification. Rhetorical scenes, extravagant displays of stylized emotion, all are to be found in the genre before Sidney. But the comedy of the Old *Arcadia* is largely Sidney's addition and the irony entirely so. The elaborate rhetorical maneuver described above in Chapters 3 and 4 is Sidney's characteristic innovation against the traditional background of the genre. The background must constantly be kept in mind, but primarily because only against it can we clearly distinguish Sidney's aim within the genre.

The first—really the only—scholar to concern himself with the style of the Old *Arcadia*, R. W. Zandvoort, allowed Sidney more originality than Wolff was willing to concede. His chapter on "The Style of the Two Arcadias" [6] begins with the comment, "Sidney's style, like his story, seems to have baffled critics by its

4. *The Greek Romances*, p. 354.
5. Ibid., p. 365.
6. *Sidney's Arcadia*, pp. 165 ff.

remarkable diversity, and any attempts thus far made to define it have been one-sided and inadequate." He distinguishes between narrative sections and "flights of poetical prose" (by the density of tropes and schemes) and warns, apropos of one of the latter:

> Though a passage like this is not by any means unique, a wrong impression is often produced by critics detaching similar poetical fragments from their surroundings and presenting them as typical samples of what is called "Arcadianism." The latter term had better be avoided altogether, as it suggests a definite and consistent type of style, which is the very opposite of what we do find in the *Arcadia*.[7]

We must accept the general framework and artistic philosophy or read no further. So much should be said for both Sidney and his sources. Can we say more? Can we say that the "easy" ornaments, the persistent devices of balance, contrast, and antithesis which are the heart of the stylistic problem of the *Arcadia*, Old and New, should be justified the same way? Could most of them be eliminated? Would not all the speeches be more persuasive without them? No single answer will suffice. The separate devices must be taken up one by one, in light of Sidney's larger purposes as we have come to understand them. Whether ornaments are superficial or not depends, obviously, on what we see beneath the surface.

A reasonable assessment of Sidney's Arcadian style in this narrower sense of "rhetorical ornament" seems to me to depend heavily on what knowledge and conception of rhetorical theory one attributes to Sidney. Deciding what he really thought about the theory and practice of rhetoric—as opposed to analyzing his cleverness in manipulating the individual devices of rhetoric—is no easy matter. Even to define the term "rhetoric" itself, a necessary preliminary, is far from simple. Like style—one of its elements in the manuals of the time—rhetoric can be a narrow study or a wide one. It can, like Cicero's *De Oratore*, place the art of persuasion in its widest context, fabricating an ideal orator who, stuffed with the accumulated knowledge of every field of endeavor, combines the shrewd Roman politician and the Platonic philosopher. Or,

7. Ibid., p. 168.

like Peacham's *The Garden of Eloquence*, it may concern itself with stylistic ornament only, distributing to logic and to political philosophy the more difficult of its former tasks. There are treatises for almost every shade of opinion between these two extremes, and hardly any two use exactly the same terminology, or if they do it is often for different elements. The influences of these treatises one on another are so interwoven that the amateur is soon bewildered. As a result, the term "rhetorical" can mean almost anything. From a purist's point of view all styles are "rhetorical," all are calculated to persuade. The relationship between rhetorical theory and practice and imaginative literature is more confusing still. The importance of this relationship is obvious, but it has been found so shifting and inconstant that generalization beyond individual cases seemed risky and inaccurate.

Sidney's position is especially perplexing. He obviously sustained an unusual interest in rhetoric—the Old *Arcadia* leaves no doubt on this point—yet his attitude toward its use, judging from the romance, is ambivalent at best, often ironical in the extreme. His fictional characters use several different styles, some elaborate, others not, and one hesitates to identify the author with any single one. This makes it extremely difficult to place him in the development of rhetorical theory. His treatise on poetry should shed light on his conception of rhetoric and its relation to literature, but this *Defence of Poesie* is itself a thoroughly rhetorical combination of fundamentally contradictory arguments which perplex us still further. It is true we can assume Sidney's knowledge of the basic texts on rhetoric. We know he planned to translate the first two books of Aristotle's *Rhetorica*, and Cicero was in the Shrewsbury curriculum when he was at school there.[8] He would have read the *Ad Herennium,* the authentic *De Inventione, Orator,* and *De Ora-*

---

8. According to George William Fisher, *Annals of Shrewsbury School* (London, 1899), p. 43, the curriculum in 1578 was as follows:
 For Latin Prose:—Tully, the *Commentaries* of Caesar, Sallust, Livy, and two little books of Dialogues drawn out of Tully's *Offices* and *Lodovicus Vives* by Mr. Thomas Ashton.
 For Latin Verse:—Virgil, Ovid, Horace, and Terence.
 For Greek:—Greek Grammar of Cleonarde, Greek Testament, Isocrates, and Xenophon's *Cyropaedia.*

tore. He knew Thomas Wilson and must have known his *Arte of Rhetorique*. With the other treatises of his time he probably had at least a layman's acquaintance. But we do not know from external sources to what extent he followed any one rhetoric, and the *Arcadia* itself can be made to exemplify almost any of the contemporary treatises. An additional complication is the degree to which Sidney imitated not formal treatises on rhetoric but works like the late Greek romances which offer illustrations of rhetorical precepts. Most of the comment on Sidney's style has ignored these complications, simplifying either the rhetorical precepts available to Sidney, or his use of them, or often both.

Sidney is usually made out to be a Ramist, that is, one who, following Ramus, would assign to logic the categories of arrangement and invention which had traditionally been two of the five arts of rhetoric. Aristotle had held that "rhetoric is a combination of the science of logic and of the ethical branch of politics; and it is partly like dialectic, partly like sophistical reasoning." [9] Ramus felt this brought about an unnecessary duplication of logic's function and restored to it all but style and delivery. As Howell has concisely expressed it:

> To Aristotle and Cicero, dialectic was the theory of learned communication, rhetoric of popular communication, and thus both arts needed the two former processes [invention and arrangement] while rhetoric needed the two latter [style and delivery] in particular. To Ramus, dialectic was the theory of subject matter and form in communication, rhetoric the theory of stylistic and oral presentation.[1]

This divorce of meaning and style rendered rhetoric merely the art of ornamenting plain language; relieved of its organizational and ratiocinative responsibilities, it ran wild—in Arcadia. "Sidney's Arcadian figures," Wimsatt and Brooks write, "became standard Ramist rhetorical illustrations in England." They point out the paradox that the simplified theoretical rhetoric which Ramus and Talon introduced, "the 'Arcadian' rhetoric, should

9. *Rhetorica*, trans. W. Rhys Roberts, 1. 359 b.
1. *Logic and Rhetoric*, p. 165.

soon come to be taken as the very embodiment of rhetorical floridity." "The explanation of this latter fact," they add, "lies in the principle that a pure rhetoric (that is, a rhetoric of elocution detached from invention and disposition—of style detached from sense), no matter how simplified or restricted, is inevitably an excessive and artificial rhetoric. Far more 'difficult' writers than either Lyly or Sidney—Shakespeare, for instance, or Donne—employ the whole range of both figures and tropes without being 'flowery.' " [2]

Such an explanation of Sidney's rhetorical views agrees nicely with a reading of Sidney's style in the *Arcadia* as superficial, applied, excessive, a carpet of flowers which seduces our senses but leaves our minds untouched. As Crane has written:

> The *Arcadia* is profusely ornamented with tropes and with those figures, common to the romances, which attempt to arouse the feelings, whereas there are very few figures of the type upon which John Lyly mainly depended, those derived from the processes of dialectical investigation and directed to the reason. [3]

For the Ramist, rhetoric came more and more to be the opposite of plain speaking. Wilson, for example (who, though not technically a Ramist, represents the same stylistic emphasis), writes: "by plaine teaching, the *Logician* shewes himselfe, by large amplification, and beautifying of his cause, the *Rhetorician* is alwaies knowne." [4] Rhetoric became not only the cosmetic of language but its inflator as well; it taught Sidney copious verbal embroidery.

Yet on closer examination this tidy explanation of Sidney's historical position has little to recommend it. In the first place, the cupboard where the "logical" arts of invention and arrangement are kept is largely irrelevant to imaginative literature. That they are not included in "rhetoric" does not mean they are ignored altogether. Sidney, for example, quite clearly used both these arts to the full in the Old *Arcadia*. Many speeches are carefully organ-

---

2. William K. Wimsatt, Jr., and Cleanth Brooks, *Literary Criticism, A Short History* (New York, 1957), pp. 224–25.

3. W. G. Crane, *Wit and Rhetoric in the Renaissance* (New York, 1937), p. 107.

4. *Arte of Rhetorique*, p. 23.

ized in the standard Ciceronian manner, avail themselves of the topics of invention, whether logical or rhetorical. How do we know what art Sidney thought he was drawing upon? The Ramist connection is not needed to explain Sidney's use of rhetoric, obscures in fact his real attitude toward an ornate style. The use of a high style, it should be remembered, had always run the danger of excess, and the study of rhetoric had traditionally tended to concentrate excessively on style. Sidney did not need Ramist precedent to tempt him, if tempted he was. Longinus, for instance, thinks the dangers of excess almost too obvious to mention: "That the use of figurative language, as of all other beauties of style, has a constant tendency towards excess, is an obvious truth which I need not dwell upon." [5] Gorgeous language was the primary vice of the Greek romances, upon which Sidney relied so heavily, and had been the endemic rhetorical delinquency since Isocrates. Style has always been the obvious place to display a fashionable acquaintance with the arts of language. To what extent Sidney followed Ramist precedent we shall never know. We must judge by what he wrote and what he wrote compels no "Ramist" verdict in the sense in which one has been given.

No one can deny that Sidney was abnormally sensitive to the importance of style; he must have known he was writing an excessively ornamented one.[6] How else can we explain his plainer

5. "On the Sublime," in Lane Cooper, *Theories of Style* (New York, 1907), pp. 97-159, 141.

6. Largely ignored in discussions of Sidney as Ramist are the many cautions he must have known against stylistic excess. Castiglione, for example, in the very sentence in which he first uses the famous word *sprezzatura*, cautions against an obviously elaborate style: "[the Count] I have found quite a universal rule which in this matter seems to me valid above all others, and in all human affairs whether in word or deed: and that is to avoid affectation in every way possible as though it were some very rough and dangerous reef; and (to pronounce a new word perhaps) to practice in all things a certain *sprezzatura*, so as to conceal all art and make whatever is done or said appear to be without effort and almost without any thought about it" (*The Book of the Courtier*, trans. Singleton, p. 43). A new word, but an old idea, implicit one might guess in the nature of language. So Aristotle: "We can now see that a writer must disguise his art and give the impression of speaking naturally and not artificially. Naturalness is persuasive, artificiality is the contrary; for our hearers are prejudiced and think we have some design against them, as if we were mixing their

prose? Euarchus, who speaks for Sidney if anyone does, speaks bare prose, letting the "flowers of Rethorique" pass, "onely marcking whether theyre reasons tended" (375). Is it unreasonable to think Sidney expected the same discrimination in his readers? If we must look beyond rhetoric to where reasons tend, then we should not regard Sidney's romance as a formulary rhetoric of Ramist tropes and schemes. We shall only be misled. It is far better to think of Sidney as holding a traditional Aristotelian view of the nature and function of rhetoric, as knowing when enough was enough, and going beyond it only for a purpose.

Was this purpose simply the imitation of a highly rhetorical genre as closely as possible? Was he really, as he confesses in the *Defence*, "sicke among the rest," infatuated with a style he later repudiated? The degree to which Sidney's famous critical essay is a carefully calculated piece of special pleading has not always been recognized. Myrick did students of the period a signal service in elucidating its rhetorical character,[7] but his analysis implied a warning which has gone unheeded; since the *Defence* is a classical oration designed as a reply to Gosson's *School of Abuse*, its arguments were likely to have been selected to vanquish Gosson quite as much as to express with precision Sidney's own views. This concern with gaining a rhetorical victory may explain some of the minor contradictions of the *Defence* [8] and perhaps its occasionally

---

wines for them" (*Rhetorica* 3.1404 b). The truth of this, we may surmise, prompted Sidney to speak with blunt directness in moments of intensest stress. (One thinks of "Give me some food!" or the "For I speak it in earnest" of the letter to Molyneux.) To picture him, in the Old *Arcadia*, assiduously watering the flowers of rhetoric which he had the good sense elsewhere to avoid is a deceptive simplification.

7. See "The *Defence of Poesie* as a Classical Oration," in *Sidney as Literary Craftsman*, pp. 46 ff.

8. For example, late in the essay Sidney is strong against those who contravene the unities: "But if it bee so in *Gorboducke*, howe much more in all the rest, where you shall have *Asia* of the one side, and *Affricke* of the other, and so manie other under Kingdomes, that the Player when he comes in, must ever begin with telling where he is, or else the tale will not be conceived" (*Defence of Poesie, Works, 3,* 38). But earlier, in showing that poetry is not literally true, he scornfully comments: "What childe is there, that coming to a play, and seeing *Thebes* written in great letters upon an old doore, doth beleeve that it is *Thebes?*" (*Works, 3, 29*).

crude contentiousness as well.[9] We should certainly be on guard when we come to the comments Sidney makes which are immediately applicable to the Old *Arcadia,* for they may not represent his considered judgment either.

In a passage in the digression at the close of the *Defence,* Sidney castigates such an affected style as he uses in the Old *Arcadia,* confessing himself at the end to have been "sicke among the rest."[1] The "hony-flowing Matrone Eloquence" he finds "apparrelled, or rather disguised, in a Courtisanlike painted affectation." Inkhorn terms, the cold compliments of stylized Petrarchan affectation, excessive alliteration, overuse of figures of speech, misplaced vehemence, maladroit similitudes, all stand for censure. Who but the academics can be responsible?

> I have found in divers smal learned Courtiers, a more sound stile, then in some professors of learning, of which I can gesse no other cause, but that the Courtier following that which by practise he findeth fittest to nature, therein (though he know it not) doth according to art, thogh not by art: where the other using art to shew art and not hide art (as in these cases he shuld do) flieth from nature, & indeed abuseth art.

An artful argument to be sure, it shows Sidney aware of a need for restraint. Awareness becomes contrition in the next paragraph:

> But what? methinks, I deserve to be pounded for straying from *Poetrie,* to *Oratory:* but both have such an affinitie in the wordish consideration that I think this digression will make my meaning receive the fuller understanding: which is not to take upon me to teach *Poets* how they should do, but only finding my selfe sicke among the rest, to shew some one or two spots of the common infection growne among the most part of writers; that acknowledging our selves somewhat awry, wee may bende to the right use both of matter and manner.

These passages describe a Sidney first wholly intoxicated with language, then sobered after his overindulgence. If they are true,

9. As, for example, in the childish depiction of history and philosophy, or in the cheap sarcasm at the expense of Plato.

1. *Works,* 3, 42–43, from which the unnoted quotations following are taken.

disenchantment with his own prose style may have caused Sidney to leave the New *Arcadia* incomplete. Such an explanation would mean a rather abrupt change of feelings on his part, since he is if anything more ornate, more methodically ornate, in the New than in the Old. But he could hardly have finished the story in plain language after several hundred thousand words of rhetorical elaboration; nor would he have wanted it to be published, even were he protected by a thick layer of false modesty. The rhetoric, in this view, would presumably have been altogether seriously intended in both versions.

Yet such a conclusion is hardly inevitable. If the *Defence of Poesie* was written before the New *Arcadia* was undertaken, as Ringler maintains,[2] then the self-dispraise can hardly be sincere. Sidney may, rather, have considered the *Defence* the wrong context for a frank and extended discussion of his playful infatuation with rhetoric. Easier far, and more oratorically effective, to confess a sickness among the rest, and from this pose of candor plead for a reformation.[3] This explanation agrees with the evidence we have found in the Old *Arcadia* that Sidney often uses an elaborate style for comic purposes. According to this view, Sidney was from the first aware of the dangers of excess. Like anyone sensitive to language in that time, he enjoyed playing with it, perhaps even too much, at too great length, so that an apology was necessary. But he was never swept entirely off his feet by a tidal wave of fashion. He preserved his sense of proportion, even when his characters did not. Ramism, a theoretical readjustment among the schoolmen, may have augmented fashionable excess but did not alter Sidney's attitude toward it. The precepts of classical rhetoric which he adduces against stylistic excess were in his mind from his days at school.

Sidney was not, then, convinced that the best style is the gaudiest. His romance is a veiled comment on the abuse of easy orna-

2. Pp. xlix, 365.

3. Aristotle writes: "The best way to counteract any exaggeration is the well-worn device by which the speaker puts in some criticism of himself; for then people feel it must be all right for him to talk thus, since he certainly knows what he is doing" (*Rhetorica* 3. 1408 b).

ments by others. But Sidney, like a much greater contemporary, undeniably enjoys the figures while he mocks them. He is not averse to putting them to work. Frequently. If he did preserve his stylistic sanity, as has been maintained, why did he use throughout those "easy" ornaments which have so troubled later readers?

Why, for example, does he organize his sentences in balanced and antithetical elements? He aims, I think, to create on an elementary stylistic level the same division into opposites which on a higher level we have called a dialectical method. Sentence structure echoes the symmetry of the whole work and of its larger constituent parts. When Pyrocles is described in the phrase, "hee rather coulde not help, then did not knowe his faulte" (11), the antithesis embodies a fundamental paradox of the romance. And repetition intensifies the paradox. In the comic dialogue later in the same scene, there is the following interchange:

Alas, lett youre owne brayne disenchaunt yow, saide *Musidorus*.
My harte ys to farr possessed, sayde *Pyrocles*, but the head gives yow direction and the harte gives mee lyfe answered *Pyrocles*.

[20]

The examples of this type of paradox are endless and many of them, I grant, are insignificant. But they fit perfectly into a romance whose structure and plot are built on a basis of balance and contrast.

The constant use of personification, as several critics have remarked, was not unusual in an age where inanimate nature was still in a real sense alive. A recent commentator on *Astrophil and Stella* notes that Sidney most often personifies abstraction "rather than natural objects or mythological figures." "No other element of Sidney's style," he remarks, "is so surely responsible for the energy of *Astrophel and Stella*." [4] This is true of the Old *Arcadia* as well. Sidney constantly injects metaphors which imply action; emotions and ideas, sins and virtues are embodied, made to move. Although characters often stand and declaim, their speech conveys vivid motion. Sometimes a phrase one would call simple pleonasm

4. Robert L. Montgomery, *Symmetry and Sense: The Poetry of Sir Philip Sidney* (Austin, Texas, 1961), pp. 91–94.

turns out to state a paradox and to animate the struggle between its two opposites. Musidorus, for example, in the first speech quoted, does not say that "solitude leads to evil" but that "yow subject youre self to solitarynes, the slye Enimy yt moste dothe seperate a man from well doyng." Pleonastic it may be, but it does vivify the moral struggle Musidorus wishes to convey.

The jingles of sound are harder to explain. Alliteration, it seems agreed, is not offensive in the Old *Arcadia*.[5] The various devices of word repetition often seem a vice. Their contribution to the humor is not large, nor does Sidney seem to take much advantage of the punning opportunities afforded him, by using the same root in two different senses. It has been suggested that the devices of word repetition in the *Arcadia* were valuable in "emphasizing ideas and the movement of thought, as, for instance, by accentuating parallel or antithetical structure," [6] but such an explanation can be partial at best. Sheer infatuation with language probably explains the remainder.

The quoted passages unfortunately do not fully reveal the extent to which Sidney depends on descriptive adjectives for characterization. Whether or not these descriptive adjectives can be properly called epithets is debatable. They are not always the same. Basilius, for example, is the "Pore *Basilius*," or "the good oulde *Basilius*." Pamela is usually but not always "the vertuous *Pamela*," Philoclea often but not always "unmatched," still more often "sweet." But the technique is the same, even when the affliction of "the afflicted *Cleophila*" is ludicrous, or when it is Mopsa whose epithet is "the pretty Pigg." Sidney sometimes uses these epithets ironically (Pyrocles, for example, in his defense speech, describes how he unsuccessfully attempted "to assayle the Constant Rock of the pure *Philoclea's* mynde") but not with any methodical intention that I can detect. The adjectives used for

5. Zandvoort writes: "Alliteration is by no means absent from the *Old Arcadia*, but in most of the passages where it occurs it is no more obtrusive than in many a piece of modern prose" (*Sidney's Arcadia*, p. 170).

6. Sister Miriam Joseph, C.S.C., *Shakespeare's Use of the Arts of Language*, Columbia University Studies in English and Comparative Literature, 165 (New York, 1947), 307.

general description must be obvious to the reader. By them Sidney
constantly supplies the accepted opinion about events and attributes, as well as character. When he wants to, he can charge such
adjectives with irony easily enough. The adjectives are used, as a
matter of fact, much as are the sententiae, to supply a constant
framework of orthodox morality.

Sidney has been much criticized for his facile sententiae. Hazlitt,
for example, with his customary freshness of phrase, charged
Sidney with always "reading a pragmatical, self-sufficient lecture
over the dead body of nature." [7] Such a reading ignores the ways
in which this easy guidance by the narrator is ironically undermined or obviously contradicted by events. But even taking this
into account, Sidney can fairly be called excessive in some places.
How much one wishes to consider Sidney as a jejune moralist,
applying old saws to situations whose complexity he was too
young and naïve to understand, depends finally on how one reads
the romance in its entirety. If one is willing to grant Sidney a
real understanding of the enduring nature of his central theme—
human passion—and a consequent awareness that his book of
commonplace maxims is not really the whole answer to mankind's
problems, then the sententiae will be seen as often ironic or obviously inadequate to the occasion. If, on the other hand, one con-
ceives Sidney as accepting wholeheartedly the proverbial wisdom
of his age and stuffing his romance with it, then he must share
Hazlitt's impatience.

The reader's patience has been tried by Sidney's syntax as
well. It is magnificently accumulative; clauses are piled up moun-
tain high. We can call it "primitive" as Zandvoort does, if we
like; judged by prose standards since Dryden, it doubtless is. But
our final attitude is really a matter of taste. Occasionally Sidney
is hard to follow, but finally it is our aesthetic sense, not our
grammatical sense, which is outraged. This offense is partly a
matter of punctuation. Sidney seems to have used very little.[8] He
probably depended on natural breath pauses in reading. Loose

7. "Lectures on the Age of Elizabeth," in *The Collected Works of William
Hazlitt*, ed. A. R. Waller and Arnold Glover (12 vols. London, 1902), 5, p. 322.
8. Ringler, p. lxv.

sentences almost always speak better than they read, especially if the author himself speaks them, so that his speaking and writing rhythms coincide. Listening audiences are usually less alert to syntactical precision within the sentence anyway. Balance and antithesis would then be more noticeable than length or complexity. The narrative sections, plainer in every respect and shorn of a consistent antithetical structure, seem as a consequence to suffer most from clause heaps. Look, for example, at this slice of narrative:

> But the twoo *Princes* having understood the beginning of the matter by *Thermuthis*, taking hym with them, they entred into *Memphis*, as the pore Prince was some fewe myles all redy carryed towardes his Shipp of deathe. Whiche they understanding, and (fearing they shoulde not have leasuer to tell the Kinge, and save hym) they first pursewed after hym, and by force of Armes joyned with the help of some of the Contry who were willing to help theyre Prince, they rescued hym of theyre handes.
> [150]

It is representative of Sidney's narrative style at its most un-adorned.[9] We object to the relation between clauses, the way each clause seems to lean on the previous one like a row of knocked-over dominos, and to the parenthetical elements (which, by the way, seem to bear little relation to the use of the punctuation marks for parenthesis). Here tastes clash. This is the way Sidney and his contemporaries told a plain story. If a modern reader is appalled he can only put down the book. Sidney could be, melancholy comfort, much worse.[1]

Sidney's imagery has not drawn much comment, and indeed it is not remarkable for its inventiveness. Almost all his images have been used in a hundred sonnets between Petrarch and Sidney. What is unusual is the unmistakable pattern established by the constant repetition of images of certain kinds clustered around the

9. Peter MacNaughton Miller ("The Rhetoric of Sidney's Arcadia," unpublished dissertation, Princeton University, 1939) points out, pp. 111 ff., that in the New *Arcadia* the narrative passages are generally much less metaphorical than the speeches. This is clearly true of the Old *Arcadia* as well.

1. See, for example, the "Defense of the Earl of Leicester," *Works*, 3, 61–71.

theme of passionate love. The hastiest reader will admit that love in the original *Arcadia* is passionate love; affection has a very minor role, sentiment (in spite of common belief) almost none. And passion is described in consistently unpleasant terms by all who feel it: the Arcadian language of love is a language of attack, victory and slavery; of burning torment; wounds, poison, disease and death; of violence and compulsion, desire and appetite; above all of the folly of lust. Each of these terms by itself seems simply a Petrarchan cliché; their use is often comically hyperbolic; but the cumulative force and direction are unmistakably serious.

Whether or not it later acquires greater dignity and elevation, love begins in Arcadia as a physical attraction, often expressed as beams from the eyes of the loved one. Musidorus' first acquaintance with Pamela is described in these terms: "beames of ye Princess *Pamelas* beauty, had no sooner stricken into his eyes, but, that hee was wounded with more sodeyn vyolence of Love than ever *Pyrocles* was" (36–37).

The eyes are the channels for an attack pressed in military metaphors. Let me cite a few of the many examples:

Hee [Musidorus] thoughte her fayre Foreheade was a feelde, where her fancyes foughte . . . the lyinge as in Ambush under her Lippes those armed Ranckes, all armed in moste pure white, and keeping the moste precyse order of Military Disciplyn . . . hee was bent to take the vauntage of the weykenes of the watche, and see whether at that season hee coulde wynn the Bullwarck before tymely help mighte come.　　　　　　　　　[189–90]

Pamela founde in her Conscyence suche an accusing of a secrett Consent thereto, that shee thought yt safest way to direct the speeche, leste in Parley, the Castell mighte bee given upp. [102]

[Philoclea to Cleophila] . . . yf my Castle had not seemed weyke, yow woulde never have broughte these disguysed forces? . . . Thow haste then the victory.　　　　　　　　　[115–16]

And yet, O Prince *Pyrocles* . . . what Tryumphe canst thow make of this Conquest? what spoylles wilt thow carry away of this my undeserved overthrowe? Coulde thy force fynde oute no fitter fielde, then the feeoble mynde of a pore Mayde . . .

What neede hadst thow to arme thy face with the inchaunting
Maske of thy paynted passyons? what neede hadst thow to
fortefy thy exellencyes with so exquisite a Cunning in making
oure owne artes betray us? . . . was all this to wynn the unde-
fended Castle of a frende, which beeyng wonne thow wouldest
after Rase? [198]

The cumulative effect of this kind of language is to make love
seem (what perhaps it is) a perpetual, boring rehearsal of male
assault and female surrender. Sidney and his age seemed to tire
of this Petrarchan ritual enactment no more than they tired of
the equally ritualistic single combat between males in armor.

Moreover, even placed as it often is in a comic context, this
ordeal of alternate assault and capitulation is not only unpleasant
but violent, as the following examples show. In the animal chase
in Book I, "Eche [of the lovers is] carryed away with the vyolence
of an Inwarde evell" (44). Gynecia is brought "by the vyolence
of that yll answered passyon . . . purposely to overthrowe her
self" (357). Pyrocles, defending by implication (in his speech in
Book V) all those who are stricken by love in Arcadia, says: "I
beeyng inflamed with love (a passion farr more easily reprehended
then refrayned) . . . But in fyne I offered force to her (Love
offered more force to mee) . . . Onely I can not nor ever will
deny the Love of *Philoclea*, whose vyolence wrought vyolent
effectes in mee" (365–67).

Each of these lovers seems, and talks of himself as, a slave to
passion. Pyrocles early in the first book is referred to as "having
first payde up his late accustomed tribute of Syghes" (18). Basilius
walks about "carrying this unquyet contention aboute him, but,
passion ere longe, had gotten the absolute Masterhood" (41).
Philoclea frequents a grove—"there had shee enjoyed her self
often, while shee was Mistris of her self" (104). Gynecia, about
to offer what our grandparents called "the last favors" to Cleophila, is described as "not unlike the Condempned Prisoner . . .
[who] heares that his pardon ys promysed but not yet signed"
(194–95). The horde of outlaws call Musidorus back from "the
tyrannicall fyer of Lust," when he is nearly "overmastered with

the fury of delighte" (190). He has the opportunity to be so over-powered because Pamela has been "transported with desyer and . . . had never free scope of Judgment" (185).

In a hundred such instances—even in the most exaggerated speeches—Sidney drives home the point that love deprives the lover of his essential individuality. Pyrocles, for example, when he confesses his identity and his love to Philoclea, says:

> Beholde here before youre eyes *Pyrocles* Prince of *Macedon*, whome onely yow have broughte to this falle of fortune, and unused *Metamorphoses* whome yow onely have made neglect his Contry, forgett his Father, and lastly forsake hym self. [114]

The idea that the lovers are unwilling victims of powers they cannot control is implicit in their constant description as being wounded, or diseased, or poisoned; the basic unifying idea in this imagery is the helplessness of the rational will in the face of love. Here are a few of the very large number of instances:

> Alas (saide hee) Prince *Musidorus*, howe crewelly you deale with mee, yf yow seeke the victory, take yt, and yf yow list Tryumphe: Have yow all the reason of the Worlde, and with mee remayne all the Imperfections? Yet suche as I can no more lay from mee, then ye Crowe can bee perswaded by the Swann, to cast of his blacknes. But, truly yow deale with mee like a Phisicion, that, seeyng his patient in a pestilent feyver, shoulde chyde him, in steade of ministring help, and bid him bee sick no more: Or rather, like suche a frend, that vizitting his frende condempned to perpetuall prison, and loaded with greevous fetters, shoulde will him to shake of his Fetters or hee woulde leave him. I am sicke, and sick to the deathe, I am a Prisoner, neyther ys there any Redress, but, by her, to whome I am a slave: Now, yf yow list, Leave him, that loves yow in ye highest degree, but, remember ever, to carry this with yow, that yow abandon youre Frende in his greatest neede. And herewith the deepe wounde of his Love beeyng rubbed a fressh, with this newe unkyndenes, began as yt were to bleede ageane, in suche sorte that hee was unable to beare yt any longer: But, gusshing oute abundance of teares, and Crossing his armes over his wofull harte hee sancke downe to the grounde. [21]

351

[Philoclea] O mee unfortunate wretche (saide shee) what poysonous heates bee these that thus possess mee, how hathe the sighte of this Straunge guest invaded my sowle? Alas what entrance founde this desyer, or what strength had yt, thus to conquer mee? [105–06]

In these Pastorall pastymes a great Number of dayes were spent to followe theyre flying Predecessors, while the Cupp of poyson which was deepely tasted of all this Noble Company had lefte no synew of theyres, withoute mortally searching into yt: yet never manifesting his venemous worck, till once that . . . [87]

[Musidorus counsels Pyrocles] to purge youre heade, of this vyle infection. [21]

But, yow worthy Ladyes, that have at any tyme feelingly knowne what yt meanes, will easily beleeve the possibility of yt, let the ignorant sorte of people give credit unto them that have passed the Dolefull passage, and duely fynde, that quickly ys the infection gotten, whiche in longe tyme ys hardly cured. [45]

The torments of the disease of love burn, consume by passion:

But as yf the opening of her Mouthe . . . wherof her harte coulde not beare the vyolent Issue . . . *Cleophila* rann to her, merveiling what sodeyne sicknes had thus possessed her. . . . *Ginecia* opening her eyes wyldely upon her, pricked with the flames of love and the Tormentes of her owne Conscyence: O *Cleophila, Cleophila* sayde shee doest thow offer me phisick, whiche arte my onely poyson? or wilte thow doo mee service, whiche haste allredy broughte mee into eternall slavery? [90]

[Philoclea] fynding a Mounteyne of burning desyer to have over whellmed her harte, and that the fruites therof having wonne the place, began to manifest them selves with horrible terrors of Danger, Dishonor and dispayre. [103]

But, *Basilius*, who began to feele the sparckles of those flames, which shortly after burned all other thoughtes oute of his harte . . . [32]

[of Gynecia] And this doubtfull Jelousy served as a Bellowse to kyndle the vyolent Coles of her passion. [45]

> [Pyrocles wonders] how am I ye nearer to quenche the fyer
> that Consumes mee? [93]

> [Philoclea] founde a burning affection towardes *Cleophila.*
> [93]

Love is a food, though less often than a burning fire:

> [Pyrocles] suffering all his sences to devoure up theyre cheefest
> foode . . . [280]

The imagery presents the consummation of love unequivocally and repeatedly as the satisfaction of physical desire. Both the passage describing the attempted rape of Pamela and that in which Philoclea is persuaded to give what Pyrocles can never return are wholly in terms of physical gratification. The flights of Platonic fancy are few and ironic. Cleophila's attitude in the following passage is more characteristic:

> Alas, answered *Cleophila,* yf my beauty bee anythinge, then, will
> yt help mee to some parte of my Desyers, otherwyse, I am no
> more to sett by yt then ye Orator by his eloquence, that per-
> swades no body. [24]

Gynecia, in a theatrical but effective passage of naked confession, summarizes the attitude which the imagery consistently enforces:

> yet yf my desyer how unjust soever yt bee, mighte take effect,
> thoughe a Thowsande Deathes followed yt, and every deathe
> were followed with a thousand shames, yet, shoulde not my
> Sepulchre receyve mee withoute some Contentment. [88]

Sidney's love imagery carries an intense message in its orthodox language—that "expense of spirit in a waste of shame" which is the subject of his comedy. It works on the reader even in a comic context; the sheer weight of the repeated comic hyperbole, as well as the speeches not ironically undermined, combine to make the reader feel, as the overpowering final impression of the romance, the disruptive force of passion. To call this "touches of Petrarchanism" is gross understatement. To contend that Sidney was simply parroting the rhetoric of love he knew is equally gross simplification. He did not choose his imagery in a fit of absence of mind, nor was he unaware of its effect, nor reluctant to exploit its connotations.

Sidney has often been criticized for his lack of characterization, a criticism which the similarity of imagery in all the characters' speeches might seem to support. But his final emphasis is on the power of love, not on the individual characters who illustrate it, and this power the language does recreate by constant repetition, through every character's mouth, of carefully selected groupings of traditional images of disorder. So in still another way Sidney, through the style he employs, comments indirectly on the behavior of his characters. An imagery that expresses the havoc caused by passion complements a plot that does the same thing. Pyrocles' plea at the trial that the lover has no control over his actions, is in a sense not responsible for them, is the climactic overt expression of what the imagery has told the reader from the first page.

The syncretism of the imagery should be remarked. The disruption of civil order, the breaking of established relations between man and man, and the turmoil within the human breast are constantly defined one in terms of the other. Of course this had been done before, but seldom with so clear an intention to focus on love as the source of disorder on all three levels of human life. The imagery again parallels the plot exactly.

Sidney's originality is thus of a particular kind, a new combination of traditional images rather than an invention of fresh ones. The conception of love which emerges from the imagery can hardly be called sentimental, nor, for the modern reader, is it likely to seem excessively idealistic. Passion, physical desire, is itself a sickness, and the act of love the universal antidote. To an extent, certainly, Sidney inherited this metaphor from the morally bankrupt Greek romance, but he would hardly have patterned his imagery as he did had it not struck a responsive chord within himself.

Wimsatt and Brooks have recently described Sidney's style in the *Arcadia* in this way:

Rhetorical Style

Sidney's Arcadian rhetoric is likely to seem florid enough to a 20th-century reader. A recent close analysis of this rhetoric has, however, suggested its rather heavy dependence on certain devices of word order (*figures* or *schemes*—such as isocolon, parenthesis, anaphora, antithesis) rather than on the metaphoric and ironic range of the *tropes*. In short, Sidney's rhetoric was what would have been called by a medieval writer in the *Ad Herennium* tradition a rhetoric of "easy ornaments." [2]

A detailed assessment of Sidney's style in these terms would require far more space than we have here, but we should by now be in a position to suggest some ways in which such a statement is and is not true. In the first place, we can say, with the author of the "close analysis" (P. Albert Duhamel), that Sidney is at all events less "easy" than Lyly. [3] Sidney, Duhamel points out (Sidney's characters, one should say), uses the topics of invention for developing proofs rather than for ornament only, as is usual with Lyly. This is, however, rather negative support for the Old *Arcadia*. That Sidney leans heavily on the schemes mentioned we have just seen. But we have also noticed that the rhetorical floridity is itself not calculated to convince the reader directly; it is held at a distance and commented on by the author. It is in the author's indirect comment on the tropes and schemes, and not in the tropes themselves, that the irony most often enters. The depth of vision which ordinarily comes with brilliant metaphor Sidney more often creates with ironic juxtaposition. The "easy" ornaments are technically that, but their effect read in the context of the Old *Arcadia* is less easy, and less easy to interpret, than is generally thought.

The irritation many readers feel at the wealth of easy ornament might, I suspect, subside if they were aware of the distance from it at which Sidney stands. The understanding that the ornament is calculated, not by the author to fool the reader, but by one character to fool another, is bound to affect our estimation of it as excessive.

This explanation does not, however, exonerate Sidney com-

2. *A Short History*, p. 224.
3. "Sidney's *Arcadia* and Elizabethan Rhetoric," p. 147.

pletely from the charge of writing an over-ornate style. As we have pointed out, certain tropes and schemes do overlay almost the entire romance and contribute to its principal fault. We should like to see in the Old *Arcadia*, I think, not a plain style, but a greater distinction among "styles," and a more reliable stylistic norm than Euarchus' relatively plain speech against which to measure them. The degree to which Sidney failed to provide this stylistic control is really the degree to which he was "sicke among the rest."

Even as it is, however, the style is not nearly so annoying as has been thought, once we are clear about what Sidney sought to communicate through it. It has been, finally, a misunderstanding of what the Old *Arcadia* sought to say which has confused our estimation of the style. (The process has, of course, also worked in reverse.) So one of Sidney's biographers writes:

> The real biographical significance of the *Arcadia* consists in its style, which is of the man himself. In its combination of Arcadian and heroic elements, its vagueness as to time and place, in its very confusion of episode, the unreality of its portraiture and the dreaminess of its atmosphere is reflected Sidney's tendency to turn in spirit from the world of things as they were to the world of things as they might be.[4]

He writes of the composite version, but the mistake is as great in Old as in New. The style is of the man, perhaps, in the feeling for symmetry and balance, in the tendency to cast the paradoxes of life into a dialectical form, but beyond this into the misty mid-region of chivalric sentiment we should not go. It is an artificial style, whose elements we match with traits of the author's personality only at great risk. The unity it achieves is that of rhetorical and literary convention, not of a personal attitude toward love and life.

Critics commonly wish Sidney had chosen to write his romance in a much plainer style. Myrick, for example, writes: "Sidney had

4. Malcolm W. Wallace, *The Life of Sir Philip Sidney* (Cambridge, England, 1915), p. 236.

not learned that 'virtue is like a rich stone, best plain set.' " [5] Yet if we took away the style what would be left? The style *is* the story. Sidney both teaches and delights through his manipulation of his elaborate rhetorical style. Without it we should have an uninspired tale of sordid pastoral seduction; losing the Old *Arcadia*'s comedy, we should also lose its essential truthfulness.

5. *Sidney as Literary Craftsman*, p. 183.

6. Comedy – Tragic and Romantic

A "pastoral romance" was the temporary name given to the Old *Arcadia* in Chapter 1 above. We have now come far enough in our investigation to label it more precisely. Sidney wrote, without any doubt, a prose-fictional tragi-comical-heroic-politico-pastoral drama. It is an awkward title, to be sure, but one which does full justice to the complexity of the work. The reader appreciates immediately that Sidney (to use Amos Alonzo Stagg's memorable phrase) "gave of the fullness of his best." Scholarly description can go no further.

Starting from the rear and working our way forward we can fit it into each genre in turn. Perhaps when we reach the front of the line we shall know whether to laugh or cry, whether to confirm our souls in self-control or turn the whole romance over to Momus. First, consider the Old *Arcadia* as a drama, a genre in the forefront of Sidney's mind when he wrote his toyful book. Its five divisions are "books or acts." Characters and narrator frequently refer to the story in theatrical terms. The final personification of the first book is explicit: "For in deede, Fortune had framed a very stage play of Love amonge these fewe folkes, making the Olde age of *Basilius* the vertue of *Ginecia*, and the simplicity of

Philoclea, all affected to one" (50). Again, later in the romance: "The Sunne beginning now to sende some promyse of his Cominge Lighte, making haste (as I thinke) to bee *Spectator* of the following tragedyes . . ." (255). Dametas "thoughte certeynly all the Spirittes in hell were come to play a Tragedy, in those woodes" (262). Gynecia too is apt to dramatize her troubles, as when she taunts the scornful Cleophila: "There ys a fayrer Scene prepared for thee, to see the Tragicall ende of thy hated Lover?" (261).

In Sidney's life there is no dearth of evidence of a strong interest in the stage. Shrewsbury, where Sidney was at school, emphasized drama:

> Allusion has already been made to Ashton's [the headmaster] partiality for dramatic performances, and his skill in arranging them. With such predilections it is not surprising that he should have made them a prominent feature of school life at Shrewsbury. He left it a standing regulation of the school that, on every Thursday, the highest form should, before going to play, "declaim and play one Act of a Comedy"; and the celebrity of the Whitsuntide Plays at Shrewsbury in Ashton's time is strong evidence of the pains he must have taken in training the boys for their performance.[1]

That Sidney's aroused interest persisted the digression on drama at the end of the *Defence* attests.

Several critics have noted Sidney's interest in drama. F. S. Boas describes a stage simile as "an incidental illustration of Sidney's critical interest in the stage of his day." [2] Tucker Brooke, too, noticed that: "The main story, handled in the 'acts,' has much the quality and structure of one of the tragicomedies which Sidney's namesake, Philip Massinger, later wrote for the seventeenth-century stage." [3] Other subsequent influence has been at least mentioned. H. W. Hill, in an imperceptive study of the relation between the *Arcadia* and Elizabethan drama, vaguely points to the great debt later writers of romantic comedy owe to Sidney: "Further investigation on the part of the reader will, I

1. George William Fisher, *Annals of Shrewsbury School*, p. 17.
2. *Sir Philip Sidney*, p. 90.
3. *A Literary History of England*, p. 474.

think, convince him that the more general influence of the *Arcadia* on the Elizabethan drama was to encourage love of nature, lofty conceptions of duty, and refined courtesy." [4] Further investigation, unfortunately, shows none of these influences. As a matter of fact, there has not been much further investigation of Sidney's relationship with the drama of his time. It must have been close. The Old *Arcadia* alone draws on current drama heavily. Not simply Dametas' mock-Senecan rants or the tragic-heroine characterization of Gynecia, but the romance's whole structure shows his knowledge of contemporary and classical drama. The rigorous five-act structure, the choric role which the narrator often plays, the symmetrical division into oracular involvement and dénouement, all betray it. The contemporary drama must have contributed the double plot, but the stock character of the foolish husband [5] and the travesty of the good blunt man which Dametas plays out seem to owe more to the Commedia dell'Arte. The element of masque is strong, too; witness the elaborate staging of the trial scene. Clearly much of this concern with setting may have come from the Greek romances, but it is a mistake to overlook the more obvious pageants that offered a vivid "source" closer to home. The interpolated songs, too, owe much to contemporary stage practice. Finally and obviously, many passages of the Old *Arcadia* strike the reader as designed for quick, easy, and successful transfer to the stage. The basic stylistic unit seems to be not chapter or book but scene; it is individual scenes which impress themselves graphically on the memory.

The extent to which the Old *Arcadia* is a pastoral has been much debated. Sidney's intention has generally been viewed as the antithesis of the pastoral impulse to withdrawal and retreat; and action—heroic or not—is undeniably stressed in the romance. The pastoral elements often strike one as stage setting. In spite of Hill's contention that Sidney's romance encouraged a love of nature, and in spite of the ink spilled over the famous descriptive passages (the "leaves of grass of an equal height" is probably the

4. Herbert Wynford Hill, "Sidney's *Arcadia* and the Elizabethan Drama," University of Nevada Studies, 1–3 (1908–1911), 1–59, 59.
5. See C. S. Lewis, *English Literature in the Sixteenth Century*, p. 337.

best known), the modern reader is not likely to put the author down as a nature lover. Sidney is far more interested in Arcadians than in Arcadia. The details of a dress, the wanton disarray which exposes a patch of white skin, these details catch his attention. His eye for nature seems much more conventionally limited. Outside the eclogues (this is, of course, a large exception) the elements of pastoral are kept to a minimum. Only the setting, the forest, is clearly pastoral, and even here Sidney is different. For Arcadia is not only the forest, the place of retreat; in Sidney's romance, it is the whole country. And a real country, too, not a fairyland. Critics who overlook this important distinction are likely to miss the unity of the Old *Arcadia*, thinking Sidney's political didacticism foisted on his romance. F. S. Boas, for example, writes: "For a time the *Arcadia* turns from a romance into a political treatise on that perennial Elizabethan bogy, the difficulties and dangers of a disputed succession to the throne." [6] In the sense in which he uses the word, the Old *Arcadia* had never been a "romance." Arcadia had never been a pastoral paradise exempt from the political constraints of everyday life in real kingdoms. The political lesson Sidney embodies in Basilius' folly depends upon a fundamental political normality. And it is a lesson offered directly to the reader; there is no allegorical transfer of political realities to the shepherd and his flock. The only purely pastoral transformation—that of Prince Musidorus into Dorus the shepherd—has a quite practical motive, the seduction of Pamela. No one even suggests that Dorus is attempting to escape from the cares of the great world. As for Basilius' escape, it is called folly and cowardice by everyone concerned with the kingdom; the most knowledgeable, Philanax and Euarchus, are the strongest against it. It is not exaggerating to maintain that Sidney's fundamental political concern caused him to write an antipastoral. If the Old *Arcadia* was actually written during a rustication at Wilton, we can only infer from the so-called pastoral temper of the work that the idleness was enforced and uncomfortable. He was bored with the idyllic peace of the Elizabethan countryhouse, not bathing in its golden glow.

6. *Sir Philip Sidney*, p. 72.

Interesting as they are, the political and pastoral facets of the Old *Arcadia* do not pose the crucial question for the modern reader: With what degree of seriousness are we to regard Sidney's romance? It is easy, of course, to call it a comedy. It has a happy ending. Forget that, and one can as easily make it out a tragedy. Its superficial similarities to classical tragedy are apparent. The oracle prompts Basilius to seek out a security which the gods do not permit and he is punished for his folly. The classical structure has been remarked above. The romance has obvious affinities with a political tragedy like *Gorboduc* (a play that Sidney singles out for special praise in the *Defence of Poesie* [7]), which shows the consequences of folly at the apex of the state. Without Euarchus and the happy ending the same kind of civil war which plagues *Gorboduc* (and later *Lear*) could have arrived with Musidorus and his army. This type of sophisticated political morality play stems, of course, from the earlier medieval notion of tragedy as the "fall of illustrious men," and Sidney seems aware of this tradition as well. Basilius, had he died as a result of his folly, might have qualified for inclusion in the *Mirror for Magistrates.* The two princes, leaving their high careers for a commoner's life and a degrading death, would have fitted without trouble. None of these parallels is exact, certainly. But several elements of the older conception of tragedy are demonstrably included in the final effect of the romance. Tragedy in its fullest Shakespearean sense is more difficult to isolate. Pyrocles and Musidorus are prepared, it is true, to give up all for love, and many readers have found them modeling heroic virtue in one guise or another. They unabashedly cast themselves in a tragic role (especially in their dialogue on immortality). Yet even if we regard them with high seriousness, it is questionable whether their heroism, brought into the Arcadian world from the outside as it is, would give them sufficient dignity for a tragic ending had Sidney desired it. Nothing indicates that he did. Euarchus is potentially the most tragic character in the romance once he learns the identity of the prisoners he has just condemned, but this tragic potentiality is neglected entirely.

7. *Works, 3,* 38.

Even without the quick-release ending, the comic intent in much of the Old *Arcadia* is unmistakable. Sidney does not merely introduce comic relief into a tragic drama; his serious figures are ironically undermined as well. If this be admitted, then our conception of Sidney's two heroes will have to be radically modified. For it is undeniable, as one critic writes, "that a comic character must not finally seem to us heroic, and that it must as a whole invite critical judgment rather than arouse strongly sympathetic feeling." [8] Critical judgment has been aroused by the Old *Arcadia* less frequently than sympathetic feeling, to be sure, but the romance demands both, and neither exclusively. If the two are mutually exclusive, then the Old *Arcadia* is fundamentally weakened by demanding both at once.

One way out of this dilemma is to call the romance a tragicomedy. Sidney, of course, expresses opinions on the subject of tragicomedy in the *Defence*. He writes, first:

> Now in his parts, kindes, or *species*, as you list to tearme them, it is to be noted, that some *Poesies* have coupled togither two or three kindes, as the *Tragicall* and *Comicall*, whereupon is risen the *Tragicomicall*, some in the maner have mingled prose and verse, as *Sanazara* and *Boetius;* some have mingled matters *Heroicall* and *Pastorall*, but that commeth all to one in this question, for if severed they be good, the conjunction cannot be hurtfull.[9]

Later, he maintains:

> But besides these grosse absurdities, howe all their Playes bee neither right Tragedies, nor right Comedies, mingling Kinges and Clownes, not because the matter so carrieth it, but thrust in the Clowne by head and shoulders to play a part in majesticall matters, with neither decencie nor discretion: so as neither the admiration and Commiseration, nor the right sportfulnesse is by their mongrell Tragicomedie obtained.[1]

Here, as elsewhere, the precepts of the *Defence* are of limited use in evaluating Sidney's imaginative work. Such a work as the

8. Potts, *Comedy*, p. 116.
9. *Works*, 3, 22.
1. Ibid., p. 39.

Old *Arcadia* could conceivably include both the tragic and comic consequences of being stricken by love. The primary sin in the Old *Arcadia*, if sin is the right word, is a loss of self-control in the throes of love. Such a loss can lend itself easily to either serious or comic treatment for, though potentially the greatest of social dangers, its first and most immediate consequences are almost always ludicrous.

The comic version of *hubris*—frequent in romantic comedy— also works in Sidney's romance.[2] The Old *Arcadia* contains many instances of the punishment Cupid exacts from those who resist him. The First Eclogues are the most obvious extended example, but Dorus, Gynecia, and Philoclea all pay for their various degrees of resistance. The perception behind the myth, that a man seeking to deny the passionate half of his nature courts disaster, is at the heart of Sidney's quarrel with the pastoral attempt at escape. There, too, one attempts to avoid the unavoidable and brings it down upon oneself all the more quickly. The symbol which most fully expresses this foolish attempt to escape the inevitable limitations of man's nature—the oracle—is thus fitting for tragic or comic development, or for both at the same time. There seems to be no intrinsic reason why Sidney should not have attempted such a parallel development. If this purpose were to present the "triumph of love" from Mopsa to Basilius, he could hardly have avoided presenting both the tragic and the ludicrous. If he attempted to show as well the consequences to the body politic of such a triumph, then his plot would have to include the basic elements of the didactic political or historical work, of tragedy, and of comedy. Reduced to barest essentials, the plots of the three types show a basic—perhaps unavoidable—similarity. In each case the status quo (taken for granted as the preferable arrangement) is broken by an eruption of passion which works itself out at human expense leaving, finally, personal happiness or disaster and a society hopefully resolving itself again into a normal civil order. The plot

2. It is predominant in the Greek romances. Habrocomes, for example, the protagonist of *An Ephesian Tale*, remarks at one stage of his sufferings, "Now is the god [Cupid] exacting vengeance of me for my overweening pride" (Xenophon, "An Ephesian Tale," in *Three Greek Romances*, ed. and trans. Moses Hadas, Anchor Books, 1953, p. 118).

of the Old *Arcadia* follows this pattern exactly; it does seem to try to include (if the anachronism will be pardoned) the essential elements of Shakespearean tragedy, comedy, and history.

Yes, the reader will say, but they do not all fit. They *cannot* all fit. They are mutually exclusive. L. C. Potts states the case precisely:

> There are only two literary modes of thought: tragedy and comedy. The nearest other species of literature to these two is the epic. . . . There is an eclectic form of fiction, borrowing certain of the superficial or accidental features of tragedy and comedy, but containing none of the essence of either, and lacking both their pedigree and their philosophical justification: tragicomedy . . . has a popular appeal, and has commended itself to dramatists who like to please their public. There is no great harm in a play or novel that pains and frightens us superficially and not in full earnest, adding yet another thrill—of artificial felicity—by an inappropriate stroke of good fortune in the last act or chapter. But it is not the happy ending that makes a comedy; nor merely the pity and fear that make a tragedy.[3]

I hope that by this stage of our investigation we can dismiss the epic possibility without further consideration. The New may be an epic of sorts, but the Old *Arcadia* certainly is not. But even if we admit the justice of Potts' charge in reference to the Old *Arcadia*—as to an extent we must—we can still make out a rationale for the Old *Arcadia* as a tragicomedy, inferior though it may be. The type from which the Old *Arcadia* most directly derives, the Greek romance, does not demand the whole-hearted emotional commitment which tragic suffering calls forth. Its pathos is highly stylized and highly rhetorical. We are meant to enjoy the language as a tour de force, to be titillated but not profoundly moved. To an extent this is true of the Old *Arcadia*. In such an atmosphere, one feels as less offensive the ironic juxtaposition of fool and suffering woman (Basilius and Gynecia), each speaking the same pathetical rhetoric. We are not meant to feel either amusement or pity deeply because we are not meant to think of the characters as fully three-dimensional. They are types—at best, actors—and

3. *Comedy*, pp. 10–11.

we are not to be wholly caught up in their feelings. They certainly are not; they constantly play for effect and we are meant to see it. This artificiality persists, and indeed is greatly developed, in Jacobean tragicomic drama. Eugene M. Waith, in his study of Beaumont and Fletcher, comments on *The Maid's Tragedy*: "For however inferior *The Maid's Tragedy* may be when compared to *Hamlet*, it is an amazing piece of dramatic contrivance. Admiration for the sheer virtuosity of the play is an important part of the spectator's response." [4] So in the Old *Arcadia*. We are not meant to pierce the artifice to the real world behind it. There is no real world behind it. We do not feel that a contrived surprise ending does real violence to life as we know it, because life as we know it is not what the genre purports to represent. Rather, the world of romance is primarily one of conventions—conventional action, character, and ethics. We accept the fantastic ending as we do in a fairy story. Euarchus' lecture is chastening, and after giving the reader a sufficient scare and pressing the moral, the princes are to be given their fondest desires.

Sidney's fundamental didacticism seems well served by such a reading of the romance. Tragicomedy, though willing to punish the utter villain (Tymantus) and the complete fool (Dametas and company), insists for its protagonists only that they learn their lesson in an egregiously melodramatic scene, thus leaving the reader with a moral taste in his mouth. So Pyrocles and Musidorus, who hold our sympathy throughout, must be chastened but not destroyed. The reader needs to be frightened but not finally disappointed. Such a work, we may suppose, would be calculated to please the delicate sensitivities of Sidney's fair ladies.

An interpretation such as this is very inviting and, provided one is willing to play down the heroic element, seems borne out to some extent by the romance. Certainly it accurately describes what goes on in the Greek romances, which Wolff and others have held to be the immediate ancestors of the Old *Arcadia*. Sidney's version of the genre it fits less well. For if we are not, finally, to accept the work as seriously meant, we are more puzzled

4. *Pattern of Tragicomedy*, p. 25.

than ever by the obvious labor which went into it. Its political philosophy is unavoidably cheapened by such an inconsequential context. The moralizing of narrator and characters loses both depth and application, becomes merely a collection of old saws to be quoted at random. The triumph of love becomes tear-jerking melodramatic pathos. In the end Potts is right—the price of manip- ulated plot and character is unavoidable triviality. We cannot mix mirth and sadness without creating nostalgic sentimentality. The final prohibitive reason why Sidney could not show the same force of love leading to a tragic conclusion in some cases and a ludicrous one in others is the cosmic injustice, the moral (and artistic) chaos such an unraveling would bring about. His con- clusion had to be either a general tragedy or an arranged comic release. His choice of the latter gratifies our tender-heartedness but at the risk of our thinking Sidney the moralist had lost his nerve.

There is another solution to the dilemma. The most profitable attitude toward Sidney's romance, I would suggest, refuses to make allowances for it, reads it as much as possible as we would a comic novel. For it was toward this form that Sidney was groping. That he was occasionally maladroit should not surprise us, since the comic novel as we know it did not yet exist. His successes are considerable, but to see them we must clear our minds of the misapprehensions which have obscured Sidney's prose for so many years. Although elements of realism, topical allegory (conjectural, to be sure), even autobiographical allusions have been pointed out, almost no one has been willing to acknowl- edge that the Old *Arcadia* deals with life in any manner directly. To a reader of Elizabethan romance, Tillyard's voice is quite alone: "The notion, so widespread to-day, that Elizabethan drama dealt with life while Elizabethan romance escaped from it, is as alien to Elizabethan opinion as it should prove itself false to any modern who troubles to read *Arcadia* with sympathetic atten- tion." [5]

Let us take first a brief but broad look at the romance as we

5. E. M. W. Tillyard, *Shakespeare's Last Plays* (London, 1954), p. 12.

have described it thus far. On one level it is a serious explanation of the consequences, public and private, of unbridled passion. On another, it is a sympathetic spoof of the extravagant behavior and inflated language of the traditional literary lover. From Sannazaro, Sidney takes a form which allows him ample opportunity for prose and verse experiment, from the Greek romances the incidents with which to illustrate the effects of love. His heroes look to the medieval romances for their unrelieved heroism. Such syncretism runs the danger of becoming a potpourri, a great jumble; but we have seen how Sidney's cleverly integrated plot avoids this danger.

Still remaining is the problem of conflicting elements, comic spoof and serious passion. We are led to be sympathetic—if smilingly so—toward the princes and princesses, and then we are clubbed by Euarchus' condemnation of them in the last book. As one student of the work has put it: "The result is that the reason is divided while the sympathies remain intact, and the *Arcadia* ends on an effect of ethical confusion." [6] But if we look at the characters of the two princes as in some sense intended to be consistent and credible, this difficulty disappears. If the reader is intended to penetrate their most idealistic declarations of feelings and motives to a base of self-seeking lust beneath, then he is prepared for the condemnation when it comes. It has been building up in his subconscious for some time. Sidney's characters are not, of course, the fully three-dimensional people of modern fiction. But they are not pasteboard rhetorical mouthpieces either. The reader is clearly meant to see them as people with recognizable motives. He is meant to hold them responsible for what they do. They are playing roles, to be sure, and their motivation is often simple: satisfaction of physical passion. But they are sufficiently rounded to serve for a use beyond caricature. So the levity which seems to characterize the early books of the romance does not become serious all of a sudden. To the perceptive reader there is a gradual modulation.

6. Rowe, "Parental Authority," p. 16.

What of the serious true love in the romance? As the comic elements become more serious, the serious passion takes on a steadily increasing ludicrous coloration. The two grow closer together in a unified but steadily and frankly ambiguous definition of the nature of love which would not surprise us in modern fiction but which seems unlikely coming from Sidney. What we expect Sidney to offer us is love as the medieval romances present it. The Old *Arcadia* does not wholly oblige. Once we grant the conventions of falling in love at first sight, the use of an oracle, and the change of identity, then Sidney does not depend on miraculous happenings to show us the triumph of love. Sidney's pairs of lovers are quite as realistically motivated as a character in one of O'Hara's novels. There are, except for Philanax, no radical discontinuities of character, and even in Philanax' case Sidney takes care to supply a realistic motivation. What misleads us is the language the characters use to accomplish their purpose. Once we recognize its complex use we can see Sidney the novelist more clearly.

He stands back from the scene he creates, thereby making it difficult for us to determine precisely what he thought of it. But he clearly was not uncritical. He was not writing simply a love fantasy as that sort of thing was understood in his day. He was trying to make a more profound comment on the enduring paradoxes of passion, and this we hold the legitimate province of the novelist and not of the romancer. Beneath the various kinds of stylization, beneath the burlesque of the language and situations of courtly love in his own time, his purpose was serious. Golden poetic nowithstanding, he was not making men but using "men according as men were." Admittedly he is sometimes carried away with the excess he is gently mocking, as Shakespeare later was. John Palmer has remarked: "Shakespeare will so easily lose the satirical purpose with which he started, and so often provoke us to wonder whether he is ridiculing excess in his characters or sharing their intoxication." [7] It is easy to spot instances where Sidney does the same thing, but they hardly invalidate his pervasive detachment from the full-blown rhetoric. Nor does his love of

7. *Comic Characters of Shakespeare* (London, 1946), p. 4.

language compromise his didacticism. Sidney had written in the *Defence*, one remembers:

> For the representing of so straunge a power in Love, procures delight, and the scornefulnesse of the action, stirreth laughter. But I speake to this purpose, that all the ende of the Comicall part, bee not uppon suche scornefull matters as stirre laughter onelie, but mixe with it, that delightfull teaching whiche is the ende of *Poesie*.[8]

At the heart of modern discontent with the *Arcadia* in either of its forms lies, I would maintain, a suspicion that it has really nothing to offer except traditional morals pointed in obvious ways, and characters who are merely vehicles sagging under the weight of an ideal virtue and ornate rhetoric they are forced to carry through life. The romantic chivalric derring-do of the New, the extravagant passions of the Old, are just what we would expect from the cynosure of chivalry. The average reader, who has read "parts of" the *Arcadia*, Old or New, would probably come away with this impression. If he read as far as the trial scene he would be puzzled by the contradictions implied in Euarchus' verdict but would finally ascribe it to the cheap thrills of tragicomedy.

A further acquaintance with the Old *Arcadia* shows the reader that something more than an obvious Greek or chivalric romance is offered. A few especially credulous students may continue to seek for heroics amidst the many qualifications, but most will be willing to grant Sidney a greater subtlety. Myrick's description of the Old *Arcadia* as "largely a story of love and lovers' devices, thrown against a background of politics in a Greek province"[9] would probably gain general agreement, though here the agreement ends. Some have seen a clearly expressed philosophy in the romance. John F. Danby, for example, remarks:

> Sidney's romance is important because it has such inner coherence—a large, mature, and conscious philosophy. We are protected, with him, from projecting on to him meanings of our own, or finding in him answers to needs of ours he himself did

8. *Works*, 3, 40–41.
9. *Sidney as Literary Craftsman*, p. 128.

not share and did not intend to answer. In his storm we can confidently follow his own moralizations.[1]

But can we? The narrator is, as we have shown, far from reliable, sometimes frankly self-contradictory. If Sidney's philosophy is so plain as Danby would have us believe, why have most readers been unable to agree on what this philosophy is? Sidney's conscious philosophy may be large and mature, but that part which is incorporated into the Old *Arcadia* is far from clear. Is he in favor of heroic self-assertion or against it? Is he defending romantic love or repudiating it? Was he a great admirer of chivalry or its severest critic?

"The whole chivalrous culture of the last centuries of the Middle Ages," Huizinga tells us, "is marked by an unstable equilibrium between sentimentality and mockery. Honour, fidelity and love are treated with unimpeachable seriousness; only from time to time the solemn rigidity relaxes into a smile, but downright parody never prevails." [2] By the late sixteenth century, the progressive decay of chivalry had advanced still further, mockery and seriousness had drawn further apart. Love in this later stage is described by Burckhardt:

> When we come to look more closely at the ethics of love at the time of the Renaissance, we are struck by a remarkable contrast. The novelists and comic poets give us to understand that love consists only in sensual enjoyment, and that to win this, all means, tragic or comic, are not only permitted, but are interesting in proportion to their audacity and unscrupulousness. But if we turn to the best of the lyric poets and writers of dialogues, we find in them a deep and spiritual passion of the noblest kind, whose last and highest expression is a revival of the ancient belief in an original unity of souls in the Divine Being. And both modes of feeling were then genuine, and could co-exist in the same individual.[3]

1. *Poets on Fortune's Hill*, p. 85.
2. J. Huizinga, *The Waning of the Middle Ages* (London, 1924), p. 69.
3. Jacob Burckhardt, *The Civilization of the Renaissance in Italy*, trans. S. G. C. Middlemore (4th ed. rev. New York, 1951), p. 269.

The two modes clearly did coexist in Sidney. In the Old *Arcadia* he forces them to live side by side in the same plot. The rhetorical style and Petrarchan sentiment which characterize the heroes from beginning to end, the standard situations in which the lovers find themselves, bring the whole panoply of traditional courtly love before the reader's eye. But it is introduced only to be gradually undermined and finally wholly repudiated. The language is so gorgeous that it often makes the speaker seem ludicrous or insincere or both. Behind it we see a love which "consists only in sensual enjoyment" and a pair of heroes whose heroism seems to consist primarily of just the audacious unscrupulousness which Burckhardt describes.[4] When Goldman writes that the *Arcadia* shows Sidney's "complete consecration to the ideal of fortitude and honor," and that "The real heroes of the *Arcadia*, Pyrocles and Musidorus, unquestionably represent Sidney's ideal of young manhood," [5] he is contradicting the whole meaning of the Old *Arcadia* and (as we shall see) a good deal of that of the New. He is taking their word for their own worth and their word, as Euarchus makes clear, is wholly unreliable. All the Petrarchan elements upon which this mistaken judgment is based are ironically weakened. The Neo-Platonism each hero affects is constantly belied by his single-minded concentration on bedding his chosen woman. Pyrocles, for example, jumps out of Philoclea's bed, "Having first with earnest kissing the Pereles *Philoclea*, (who then soundly sleeping) was the naturall Image of exact Beuty receyved into his sence" (269). So much for Platonic love. Pyrocles' change of sex, which has bothered Boas and others, was really a stroke of genius which enabled Sidney to focus the silly contradictions of the Petrarchan code on a single character. Boas complains:

4. It is Sidney's *repudiation* of the goal and means of the Petrarchan lover which most critics of the romance have missed. Montgomery, for example, writes: "But it is more noteworthy that Petrarchan psychology thoroughly permeates the prose narrative of the *Arcadia*, even in revision and even in a context where the only laudable goal of love is marriage. Proper and improper lovers alike worship their mistresses as ideal and unattainable. Only the matching of the pairs of lovers at the end violates the usually adulterous code of the Petrarchan situation" (*Symmetry and Sense*, p. 49).

5. *Sidney and the Arcadia*, p. 215, 175.

Thus the tangle of loves [in the Old] arising out of the confusions of sex is completed. This had an irresistible fascination for the Elizabethans which we find it difficult to appreciate today. On the stage it had its origin and partial justification in the acting of women's parts by boys. But in the long-drawn-out narrative of a romance, even Sidney's skill and delicacy of touch find it difficult to make the equivocal 'he she' situation fully palatable.[6]

Actually, the change of sex becomes the center of an increasingly strong ironic comment on the constant pleas for aid and succor which are so strong an element in the psychology of courtly love. The noble impulse to action so often praised as the very mark of Sir Philip is here directed to the agreeable but hardly noble business of seduction. Both heroes, in the end, get caught with their heroic pants down. They constantly deceive themselves as well as their inamoratas. In one of a hundred instances, Pyrocles, after seducing Philoclea, justifies his action with "And as for shame, howe can I bee ashamed of that, for which my well meaning Conscyence will answer for mee to god, and youre unresistable beuty to the worlde" (276). Yet when that "worlde" knocks at the door, he readily confesses, "I was fettered in the moste guilty shame that ever Man was, seeyng what a Paradyse of unspotted goodnes my filthy thoughtes soughte to defyle" (281). When is he lying?

It is the juxtaposition of a rhetorical language moving in one direction and a plot constantly moving in another which gives us our main clue to Sidney's final intention. The language is extremely ornate, always idealistic, crammed with emotional fervor, constantly calling attention to itself. The plot is plain, unobtrusive, moving slowly from sin to retribution. If we strip the idealistic language used by the participants from their behavior, the picture is sordid enough. It seems almost willful misinterpretation to think Sidney unaware of this.

The self-reliance so often seen in the two princes may have once been laudable, but in Arcadia it is clearly not. It has strayed so far,

6. *Sir Philip Sidney*, p. 65.

as a matter of fact, that the behavior it prompts lends itself readily to the most dire interpretations. The princes really are brave, there is no doubt of that; and bravery, whatever historians have said since, had always been the working definition of chivalric honor. Cleophila does brave the mob, Dorus defends Pamela against the band of outlaws. But why do they do so? Sidney had rather a higher conception of honor than simply physical courage, one by which his heroes are tried and found wanting. And, obviously enough, the code of courtly love is sentenced guilty with them.

In the sudden reversal of the reader's judgment embodied in Euarchus' verdict is contained the central "moralization" of the Old *Arcadia*—the substitution of marriage for the adulterous intercourse of the Petrarchan code. Dramatically, the substitution was a gamble. Would the reader's sensitivities be led into a trap he would resent so strongly that he would reject the moral offered? Or would he, his suspicions properly aroused, have foreseen the final justice of such a decision? The crucial factor for an author in a decision like this is perceptively pointed out by Wayne Booth:

> Finally, some of the most powerful literature is based on a successful reversal of what many readers would "naturally" think of as a proper response. Such reversals can only be achieved if the author is able to call to our attention relationships and meanings that the surface of the object obscures.[7]

My opinion is that Sidney's gamble paid off, that he did succeed in calling attention to relationships and meanings beneath the surface of his narrative. Certainly the last two books provide a compelling demonstration of the effects of uncontrolled passion. At one point in the Second Eclogues Cleophila sings:

> The Lyfe wee Leade ys all Love,
> The Love wee holde ys all deathe.   [156]

This is the text which the two concluding books of the romance gloss. They do it well enough so that the final verdict is far from a complete surprise.

7. *Rhetoric of Fiction*, p. 115.

The alternative Sidney provides for passion—the stability of Christian marriage—presumably would not be necessary for heroic paragons. Such perfect princes, their self-control taken for granted, could be heroes utterly uninhibited. It is characteristic of the real "idealization" of the two heroes that such a Platonic course is never even suggested. For men as they are, marriage seemed to Sidney the only plausible alternative to the destruction promised by passion. Faced with the implications of such a solution to the problems of passion, Sidney could hardly avoid a happy ending. It is the only way the solution could be put into practice.

Such at least I conceive to be the "message" Sidney sought to convey. It seems plausible that Sidney, lacerated as he was by his passion for Penelope Devereux, should seek the solace of a rehearsal of his problem and an explanation for it, in writing the Old *Arcadia*. (I hardly see how we can avoid concluding that Sidney was fully in love with her when he wrote the Old *Arcadia*, whatever final dating may be decided upon.) Marriage was for him, I have no doubt, the just and proper solution for such an infatuation.

As a moral man, yes, but as an artist? One wonders. Marriage as a solution certainly fails to satisfy the modern reader, especially as an artistic conclusion to the Old *Arcadia*. For, in fact, it solves nothing. Sidney must have been aware of this too. Who more so? Penelope Devereux was, after all, engaged to marry somebody else—perhaps actually married to him. What then? What if she were unmarried but unwilling too? She seems to have been so. Sidney must have been thrown back on his dilemma as we are today. The melancholy conclusion that eternal frustration is the price of order, fit him though it did, must have offered meager comfort. And besides this, how was he to end the romance? He must marry them off—if marriage was to be the conventional moral drawn—but he could at least show that it was a contrived solution, applied to a problem that in life has no end and no painless solution. This would explain the obvious haste and aplomb with which he wraps things up in a very few pages. Here, as in the lesser sententiae, the moral is drawn a little too obviously to carry complete conviction, though in each case the convention is fundamentally irrefutable.

But conventional wisdom does not always fit life. Though reason wins the rhetorical victories, passion actually determines what happens in Arcadia. It is Sidney's reluctance to provide the conventional, easy answer which many students of the romance have overlooked. Danby, for example, thinks Christian patience emerges as the final lesson from the trial.[8] It brings about, he feels, a kind of spiritual illumination for the princes.[9] One looks vainly for evidence of such illumination in the Old *Arcadia*. Is the marriage more than a pious hope? What are they going to do after the marriage? Would all the patience in the world channel desire into the path of moderation? Sidney was idealistic, perhaps, but not naïve. To preach patience to the lover is, as the Old *Arcadia* demonstrates repeatedly, to charge hell with the proverbial bucket of ice water. The lover has lost control of himself, has ceased—as Sidney makes crystal-clear—to be a moral human being at all. What, after all, brings the happy ending about? Patience? Persistence? No, construed realistically, it is chance, pure chance. Is it oversubtle to think Sidney capable of relishing this final irony?

That passion is at war with society is an ancient profundity, but a profundity nonetheless of the sort upon which real works of art are built. Sidney's Old *Arcadia* does face honestly one of life's insoluble paradoxes. It may even be said to face two, for to Sidney the reality of passion conflicted not only with society but with the conventional means of expressing passion. One of the concerns of the Old *Arcadia* is the language of love.

It was Sidney's saving grace as an artist that he was willing to admit to a strong streak of plain physical desire in his makeup. His work would have been so much cant had he idealized this strong sex drive. For the most part he refused to do so, and his refusal has embarrassed his admirers. Dobell manfully faced the problem when he said, "It can hardly be denied that there was in Sidney's mind a somewhat undue predominance of the sexual element."[1] On a wooden hero of chivalry such evidence of our common

8. *Poets on Fortune's Hill*, p. 70.
9. "The lovers discover more than Love or even Virtue" (p. 70).
1. "New Light," p. 100.

humanity doubtless sits uncomfortably, but it is the very making of Sidney as an artist and perhaps even as a man. For the undeniable fact of his physical passion constantly conflicted with his ideals, sharpening their edge and making him hold them with a more than conventional depth of feeling. When in Sonnet 72 of *Astrophil and Stella* he cries out:

> DESIRE, though thou my old companion art,
> And oft so clings to my pure love, that I
> One from the other scarcely can descrie . . .[2]

he is admitting frankly that the Petrarchan pose does not fit love as he knows it. The idealization of the poet fundamentally opposes the desires of the man.

It is easily seen how this opposition has been built into the Old *Arcadia*. The woods are full of Petrarchan lovers, all spouting devotions set up to the highest note. As men and women, though, they act according to the drives Sidney saw to be common to all creatures. The tension between speech and action, a primary one in the romance, thus proceeds from a basic cleavage in Sidney's own personality. The easy outpourings of exaggerated passion were bound to offend a man who really felt the power of a passion which most only professed. It is in the light of this recognition that we must read the passages where he declares his dissatisfaction with the fashionable language of love. In the *Defence*, for instance, he writes:

> But truly many of such writings, as come under the banner of unresistable love, if I were a mistresse, would never perswade mee they were in love: so coldly they applie firie speeches, as men that had rather redde lovers writings, and so caught up certaine swelling Phrases, which hang togither like a man that once tolde me the winde was at Northwest, and by South, because he would be sure to name winds inough, then that in truth they feele those passions, which easily as I thinke, may be bewraied by that same forciblenesse or *Energia*, (as the Greeks call it of the writer).[3]

2. Ringler, p. 202.
3. *Works*, 3, 41.

Significantly, he does not rule out the possibility of expressing real passion. But it must be done energetically, directly. "Give me some food!" may be an extreme example, but it is that kind of language which seems sincere to Sidney, not the elaborate pattern of double talk which Pyrocles and Philoclea act out before they can climb into bed.

What one really sees in the Old *Arcadia* is an early indication in Elizabethan literature that the rhetorical language of love cannot always be taken seriously, that it is subject to persistent ironical qualification on a large scale. The attitude of Sidney in the Old *Arcadia* is different from the momentary trivializing of a major concern—the "Much ado there was, God wot, / He would love and she would not" of a Nicholas Breton. It is an elaborately patterned questioning of the possible sincerity of an elaborate speech. For the questioning does not stop at the language of love. Ornate language of all sorts is held up to question.

The reader who suspects this to be an oversubtle reading into the romance of a meaning not intended by Sidney must explain the trial speech of Euarchus. We have called attention to the realism of much of the formal oratory of the Old *Arcadia*, but anyone who has read an Elizabethan legal or even quasi-legal document will know that Euarchus' speech is really far too clear to be decretal. Sidney has intentionally put the truth as he saw it in plain and unadorned words. Plain truth does not need rhetoric. Sidney is Aristotelian: "All such [rhetorical] arts are fanciful and meant to charm the hearer. Nobody uses fine language when teaching geometry." [4] It is not an accidental irony that Euarchus comes to the kingdom of Arcadia with a direct proposal of marriage for his son and nephew. *His* wooing would have been as plain as his speech.

Though Sidney admitted to a strong physical desire, his attraction to the idealism of traditional courtly passion was undiminished. He could smile at its obvious artifices while at the same time feeling their power. For he needed the rhetoric of passionate love to express his real feelings quite as much as the poseur needed it to

4. *Rhetorica*, 3. 1404 a.

enliven his. Denis de Rougemont has described this predicament very well:

> The more a man is given to sentiment, the more likely is he to be wordy and to speak well. Likewise, the more passionate a man is, the more likely is he to reinvent the tropes of the rhetoric, to rediscover their *necessity*, and to shape himself spontaneously according to the notions of the 'sublime' which these tropes have indelibly impressed upon us.[5]

The aristocratic impulse in Sidney's nature may have contributed, probably subconsciously, additional force to his need for the traditional rhetoric of love. For lust is a great leveler, and it depends upon the grace and polish of the language with which it is offered to us for its final evaluation. How else, after all, are we to distinguish the fine feelings of the aristocrat from those of the peasant? Whether or not Sidney really thought physical desire the lowest rung on the ladder of love we shall never know. The modern reader is sorely tempted to dismiss the whole ladder as "rationalization," but even if he resists this error there are few unequivocal clues in the Old *Arcadia*. We are meant clearly to sympathize with the characters, stricken as they are by a power beyond their control; the reader is supposed to see that there is genuine feeling behind the flowery protestations of the two princely pairs. Otherwise the tension between speech and action loses its point. But what this real feeling is, we are not told.

One thing is certain. It is not the affectionate companionship which seems to us the stuff of a lasting marriage. Of this there is not a trace in the Old *Arcadia*. Love, for Sidney, was still the grand passion of the chivalric past, and this passion was not built on affection. The lovers are trained for contest not cooperation. Sidney's attitude toward love is far more erotic than domestic, and the in-

5. *Love in the Western World* (rev. ed. Anchor Books, 1957), p. 176. Earlier in his study, he had written: "No European poetry has been more profoundly *rhetorical*, not only in its verbal and musical forms, but also—paradoxical as it may seem—in its actual inspiration, which it obtained from a fixed system of rules. . . . But it is likewise true that no rhetoric has been more productive of high-flown fervour" (pp. 67–68).

fusion of irony in no way lessens its erotic force.[6] Knowing the inglorious end of one's passion seems only to intensify it. Seized as Gynecia is, they would all die a hundred deaths to gain satisfaction. Many of Sidney's later commentators attribute to him a domestic sentimentality more characteristic of Dickens.

Sidney, it appears, was caught in a social and philosophical contradiction not of his own making. Marriage, to a man of his time, provided no alternative to passionate love. It was a matter of dynasty, of money, too important even in the lower strata of society to permit any real deference to the parties concerned. Sidney's own dickering for a wife certainly shows none. Marriage was, in any case, impossible for Sidney with the woman he desired. But—and here we see the man in all his basic honesty—the alternatives of passion were even worse. He did not idealize or romanticize them. Theoretically love of one's lady spurred one on to deeds of prowess, toward glorious adventure, toward fame. But this depended on a passion wholly stylized, on a desire strictly "Platonic." For a really passionate lover, the much more probable rewards were enervated frustration if he failed to win the lady, and slothful ease were he successful.

Thus the struggle between reason and passion, between duty and love in the Old *Arcadia* is built on a fundamental contradiction within the theory of chivalry, an impossible choice between bed and sword.[7] The two heroes make their choice, or rather love makes their choice for them, at the very beginning of our acquaintance with them. They thus renounce the call of duty before we are able to see how ardently they formerly followed it. Half of their chivalry is lopped off before we know them, and makes them to our eyes more the insipid heroes of Greek romance than Sidney intended. In the original romance at least, the values of chivalric honor are not seriously questioned. It is on the love half of the chivalric code that he concentrates in the Old *Arcadia*, love and the havoc it often makes of the more important questions of life.

6. See Huizinga, *Waning of the Middle Ages*, pp. 282 ff.

7. Surely the theft of Pyrocles' sword after his night of bliss with Philoclea allegorizes this choice.

It has not to my knowledge been remarked that love in the Old *Arcadia* is strangely sterile. Within the romance at least, it prompts no deeds, not even a single generous impulse which reaches beyond lover and beloved to the welfare of mankind. Cleophila saves the state for love, and is willing to make war for the same reason. Dorus fights the outlaw band for love and makes peace with them for the same reason. For their loves, the princes will give their all, a noble sentiment without doubt, but in the context of the Old *Arcadia* a vain, misdirected sacrifice. For finally, to Sidney the public world must predominate over the private; personal glory must be harnessed for service to the state. Passionate love in the last analysis can only detract from such a larger goal.[8]

Sidney was not the first to be aware of this internal inconsistency of the chivalric code. Chaucer's *Troilus* would probably be the earliest incontestable example, and there too the focus is on love rather than honor. One would like to think that Sidney saw, in Chaucer's infinitely subtle exegesis of the courtly love drama as it was played in real life, the tragic difference between fine words and fine deeds. So I choose to construe his remark in the *Defence:* "*Chawcer* undoubtedly did excellently in his *Troilus* and *Creseid:* of whome trulie I knowe not whether to mervaile more, either that hee in that mistie time could see so clearly, or that wee in this cleare age, goe so stumblingly after him." [9] In the last quarter of the sixteenth century the problems of adapting the code to a world which it fitted even less well than it had the Europe of the late Middle Ages drew the attention of some of the greatest minds England has ever known. A series of Shakespearean figures, from Falstaff to Thersites, probe chivalric honor. Falstaff's positive, hopeful counterpart is the Red Cross Knight, learning a code of honor that

8. Sidney seems not to have considered the paradox created in the chivalric search for honor by the growth of the Tudor despotism. For the quest for honor and renown, frustrated by an exclusive hierarchy, could easily turn against the public order it ostensibly was created to uphold. It is conceivable that continued denial of office, had Sidney lived longer (or even a larger dose of "honor" as it was seen in the Low Countries warfare), might have made him aware of the limitations of this side of his philosophy as well, and engendered a work similar in intention to Shakespeare's *Troilus and Cressida.*

9. *Works, 3, 37.*

would have astounded his robber-baron ancestors. That Spenser's alternative to passionate love was the same as Sidney's, however different their methods, needs no elaboration here. I do not mean to imply that the Old *Arcadia* is among peers in this company: it is not. But it addresses itself to the same set of problems which troubled greater minds and greater talents. Its fundamental concern is a major concern of its age. It is not simply a latter-day *Amadis*, or a domesticated Greek romance. Nor is it a compendium of fine sentiments for all occasions; if we read it for the sentiment we should hang ourselves.

At all events we cannot call Sidney a romancer. The title novelist fits him far more nearly. But serious novelist though he is, he has written what finally we must read as a comic novel. As things turned out, it was the drama and not prose fiction which was to bring romantic comedy to full flower, but the bud clearly emerges in the Old *Arcadia*. It is not, fundamentally, a tragicomedy, which is wholly serious until the ending, when the author intrudes and solves all problems. Its ironic undercutting, sometimes humorous, sometimes not, is present from the beginning. The comic ending, here as in all high comedy, poses more questions than it answers.

For the first time in the sixteenth century, the contrast between the literary psychology of the lover and his true feelings is made the subject of comedy. When Cleophila tells Basilius: "These bee but those swelling speeches which give the uttermoste Name to every Tryfle . . . Truly Love were very unlovely yf yt were half so deadly as yow Lovers still Living terme yt" (207), she is the direct antecedent of Rosalind, saying: "No, faith, die by attorney. The poor world is almost six thousand years old, and in all this time there was not any man died in his own person, videlicet, in a love-cause . . . men have died from time to time and worms have eaten them, but not for love." [1] If romantic comedy can be said to stem from the decay of the Petrarchan tradition, or more largely to be the end product of the roughly thousand years of courtly love between the late Greek romances and Sidney's lifetime, then the Old *Arcadia* is the first appearance of the last stage. Gynecia and Ba-

1. *As You Like It*, IV. i.

silius in the cave are acting out the first comic death of grand passion.

So the dramatic elements of the Old *Arcadia* with which this discussion began were in the long run to prove the most fruitful for later times. Rhetorical fiction as such reached a dead end with *Menaphon*, modulating into either the jagged but vivid mockery of *The Unfortunate Traveller* or expiring into insipidity. Its tragic potentialities have perhaps a distant descendant in the many heroes who give all for love. Its epic potentiality lived on in the New *Arcadia*.

The reader may be reluctant to concede to the Old *Arcadia* the seriousness of the Shakespearean comedy to which it contributed. Faced with Sidney's didacticism, he is tempted to dismiss it as an overlay of frivolity. Sidney has done something more. He has tried, I feel, to penetrate his own easy advice to an awareness of the paradox of passion with which his moral solution only insufficiently deals. He has made his heroes not only mistaken but necessarily so. The lovers in the *Arcadia* are not their own masters, and they are condemned for their slavery. Necessary as such a condemnation is, it is made with full knowledge of its ultimate futility. Sidney is a realistic moralist. We should think him naïve neither in the results he expects nor in his awareness that exhortation must still be tried.

7. Two Further Questions

An exploratory essay often raises as many questions as it answers. Two in particular seem to be called into the foreground by our discussion: Sidney's use of sources, and the relationship between the Old *Arcadia* and the fragmentary New. Neither can be answered fully. Knowledge of how closely the Old *Arcadia* resembles many other works is invaluable. But the time has come to indicate how the Old *Arcadia* is unlike its sources. Sidney's changes are significant, too. Comparison of Old *Arcadia* and New has received less attention than the sources, though it is scarcely less important. I seek not to compare the two in detail, but rather to alter the conventional basis for their comparison.

Behind each individual source is a long tradition,[1] and it is often difficult to be sure whether a specific work is a source or whether an entire genre has served as more generalized inspiration. This last is often the case in the Old *Arcadia,* which mocks, however gently, a traditional language and range of romantic incident. The specific source for a single incident is often less significant than the use of a whole tradition as a backdrop against which the author gains his comic effects. Thus we are glad to know that Book IX of

1. For a discussion of sources see Davis above, Chapters 1 and 2.

Amadis was a specific quarry, but its incidents are hardly unique; if not there, Sidney would have easily found them, or a sufficient substitute, elsewhere. Boas remarks of a debate in the Old: "In the debate that follows which falls, as it were, into dialogue form, is it fanciful to hear echoes of the disputations in Sidney's Oxford days?" [2] Such echoes are not fanciful at all, are obvious even, but it would be profitless to track down which debates he used, were they preserved. A knowledge of the general tradition is sufficient.

The overlapping of source areas further hinders the establishment of any one-to-one relations between specific source and Sidney's work. Mona Wilson, for example, in an appendix to her study of Sidney, writes of the oratorical sources of Sidney's style: "What then were the channels of infection? These were three: (1) School training in rhetoric; (2) late medieval romance, already influenced by (1); and (3) direct study of the ancients." [3] She feels that the school training was the main influence (or "infection") but her choice is arbitrary. I would place the Greek romances at the top of the list, but this too is an opinion. We just do not know which channel was uppermost in Sidney's mind, nor is our ignorance crucial. To know that the influence reached him somehow is enough. In studying the Old *Arcadia*, genres rather than particular works, and source areas rather than sources, are most important.

Sidney's originality would be illumined more by considering how he differs from these source areas than by searching out which ones supplied particular incidents or techniques. Look for a moment at the Greek romances, which Sidney drew from so heavily. The Greek romance was an essentially trivial genre, evoking a shallow emotional response by a combination of melodrama and rhetorical display. Clever though it may have been, it was "entertainment" in the worst sense of the word. It was not pagan, it was amoral. Wolff writes:

> Now in the Greek Romances, the speeches, and the author's comments upon them, and analyses of the feelings that accompany them, are largely of this sort: they reveal no *ethos*.

2. *Sir Philip Sidney*, p. 74.
3. Wilson, *Sir Philip Sidney* (New York, 1932), p. 308.

... The interest of the rhetoricians who wrote the Greek Romances is not in the ethical choices and avoidances of life ... so much as in sentiment or emotion, with the rhetorical expression of it in set speeches, and the sophistical accounting for it in comment and analysis.[4]

It would be doing Sidney an injustice to fit this noose to the neck of the Old *Arcadia*. For, taking over the basic techniques of rhetorical fiction, Sidney infused them with a strict, pervasive moral consciousness. *Ethos* is everywhere in the Old *Arcadia*. On the smallest scale and on the largest, from sententiae to the trial scene, Sidney has moralized Heliodorus.

Heliodorus' tale, and even more that of Longus, takes place in a political vacuum. Princes and princesses rise and fall as their towns are sacked and their states are overturned, but all for no reason except that fate wills it. Private desires are pursued wholly within the sphere of private life, political ethos is wholly lacking. The structure of romance, as Sidney writes it, is built on political causality. The oracle, a common enough device, is made into an ironical symbol for the facts of political life as Sidney conceived them. We have examined (in Chapter 2) Sidney's careful integration of theme and structure; his predecessors in romance betray slight concern either for theme or structure or for their integration. Their plots are episodic, but without the balance and contrast we have observed in the Old *Arcadia*. The repeated movement from private to public world, from desire to fulfillment to consequence, so masterfully handled in Sidney's romance, appears nowhere in the Greek romances. Sidney makes Arcadia a microcosm of a complete, fully credible state. The setting for the romances Wolff discusses, though it may perhaps faithfully reflect the distintegration of the Mediterranean world at the time,[5] offers no organizing principles, no standard of behavior implicit in the organization of society and against which we are to judge the behavior of the protagonists.

4. *The Greek Romances*, pp. 143–44.
5. See Moses Hadas' introduction to his translation, *Three Greek Romances*, pp. 7 ff., for a discussion of the "implausibilities" of the genre and how they may be explained.

Sensuality pervades the Greek romances, from beginning to end. Longus is frankly erotic. The long delay before Daphnis and Chloe finally consummate their passion aims no higher than titillation. Heliodorus depends more on derring-do and less on bedroom scenes, but there too we look in vain for anything beyond lust. "One and all," Wolff wrote, "they subject the spirit to the sense; one and all they minister to the lust and pride of the eye; one and all they rest in a world of sound and show." [6] Does Sidney do no more? His conception of love begins with lust and pride of the eye, and is comfortably at home in a world of sound and show. His heroes are content to remain in this world and pursue their pyrrhic victory of sense over spirit. Sidney is not. The continual warring of passion and reason in the Old *Arcadia* prepares us for an ethical judgment of Pyrocles and Musidorus which is plainly alien to the spirit of Heliodorus. Sidney's characters do use the Neoplatonic language of Petrarchan convention, true. They seem to reach beyond lust. But this language is ironic, posits a spirituality they fail to live up to. In a real if inadequate sense, the Arcadian characters are moral beings; the characters of Greek romance never rise to this level. Whether or not love was synonymous with passion for Sidney, passion at least has consequences which he recognized and spelled out.

We may be radically mistaken, it is only fair to say, in assuming that because the Greek romances are morally bankrupt for us, they were for Sidney and his contemporaries. Sidney's attitude toward Heliodorus' pair of lovers can be made out as favorable. He praises them in the *Defence*,[7] though how much weight anything in that puzzling essay should carry is, as we have found, not always easy to say. Theagines and Chariclea are loyal to one another, come what may, and this must have struck a responsive chord to one so familiar as Sidney with the dictates of courtly love. If he thought the two Greek lovers in other ways ideal then we must attribute to him a conception of love advanced in no essential from that of the Greeks. Such an attribution leaves unexplained both Euarchus and the trial. Neither the entire Old nor the New *Arcadia* (nor the

6. *The Greek Romances*, p. 191.
7. *Works*, 3, 8, 10.

obvious internal stresses in *Astrophil and Stella*) can be adequately interpreted if Sidney felt the conduct of his own Arcadians to be fundamentally just.

As another opinion of Heliodorus we might in passing quote Underdowne. In the note "To the Reader" prefixed to his translation of the *Ethiopian History*, he finds Heliodorus edifying in the extreme:

> If I shall compare it with other of like argument, I thinke none commeth neere it. *Mort D arthure, Arthur* of little *Britaine*, yea and *Amadis of Gaule*. & account violent murder, or murder for no cause, manhood: and fornication and all unlawful luste, friendly love. This booke punisheth the faultes of evill doers, and rewardeth the well livers. What a king is *Hydaspes?* What a patterne of a good prince? . . . What a lewde woman was *Arsace?* What a patern of evill behavior?[8]

To what extent Underdowne is denigrating the opposition, putting in a moral for sales purposes, is difficult to estimate, but at least possibly he found edification where we are apt to find only amusement.

The differences in plot between Heliodorus and Sidney are more clear-cut. There is no trace in the older romancer of the painstakingly balanced and organized plot Sidney created. The turns and reversals necessary for surprise take Heliodorus' plot first in one direction then another, with no other obvious reason for the alteration of direction. Comparison with Heliodorus illustrates excellently Sidney's not inconsiderable architectonic sense.

Heliodorus' speeches are presented frankly as gorgeous display. We do not see behind them to the fundamental reality of our own world because no fundamental reality is there. Sidney's use of rhetoric, as well as his plot, is remarkable for its differences from its immediate predecessors as much as for its similarities. The rhetorical scenes so common in the earlier romances show none of the careful relation to theme that Sidney gave them. They are display pieces pure and simple. In the Old the dramatic context is signifi-

---

8. Thomas Underdowne, trans., *Heliodorus' An Æthiopian History* (London, 1606).

cant, not simply an obstacle that delays the dénouement and offers occasion for the rhetoric. The context offers the reader implied comment on the rhetoric, interacts with it to intensify the moralization. Sidney's high comedy depends precisely on this undercutting of the rhetoric, and Heliodorus typically displays nothing remotely like it. Even Wolff admits, "The sources of Sidney's humor are . . . quite foreign to Greek Romance." [9] Irony, too, in the degree to which Sidney makes use of it, is lacking in the earlier romances; there is no implied morality to create and animate it. The sentimentality which Wolff points out as characteristic of the Greek romances is bracingly undercut by Sidney's pervasive irony, and the insipidity of the heroes is counterbalanced. Sidney's princes are more active types to begin with, but our laughter at their voluntary exacerbation of the pangs of love relieves us of the tedium we feel when Daphnis, for example, is being tossed, like a jellyfish by the waves, from crisis to pathetic crisis.[1]

The dissimilarities between the Old *Arcadia* and medieval romance are striking. The most obvious general difference is the degree of realism. A comparison with Chrétien de Troyes, Gottfried of Strassburg, or even with Malory, shows that Arcadia is not a fairyland, that its strongest ties are with the England of Sidney's day. Erich Auerbach has written of the milieu of the medieval romance: "Courtly culture gives rise to the idea, which long remained a factor of considerable importance in Europe, that nobility, greatness, and intrinsic values have nothing in common with everyday reality." [2] The whole force and direction of Sidney's life and work bears witness against any such verdict in his case. The Old *Arcadia* shows that nobility—rightly construed—has a great deal to do with everyday reality, that the nobility which neglects the real world is a radically tarnished one. Auerbach per-

9. *The Greek Romances*, p. 333.
1. The Petrarchan lover and, before him, the medieval courtly lover, had always been long-suffering. This element of his character may have descended from Daphnis and his like. Certainly the passivity of the suffering hero is embarrassing, perhaps intentionally ludicrous, in Sannazaro. See, for example, Iacobo Sannazaro, *Opere Volgari*, ed. Alfredo Mauro (Bari, 1961), p. 49.
2. *Mimesis* (Princeton, 1953), p. 139.

ceptively comments that the chivalric feats of arms "accomplished at random, in one place as well as another . . . do not fit into any politically purposive pattern." [3] Such a pattern Sidney supplies in the Old *Arcadia*, and although chivalric bravery is far less apparent than in the New, even in the Old it is measured against a more meaningful social standard than the medieval romance usually offers. The New obviously lends itself to a more profitable and elaborate comparison with medieval romance, since Sidney explicitly considers there the chivalric canon of valor against a stricter moral yardstick, but the difference between the Old and *Amadis*, for example, is too important to go unremarked.

Chivalric seduction, as we see it in the Old *Arcadia*, is followed by serious consequences which the unattached knight-errant would have found an unwonted handicap. The typical castle rescuer commits one deed of valor at a time; each involves a simple choice between good and evil, and usually offers an immediate reward. Percival succors the castle of Belrepeire and Blancheflour rewards him that very night. Sidney's moral world, as well as his political one, is obviously more complex. Euarchus represents a more mature ideal and a higher level of political sophistication than we are accustomed to meet in a courtly romance. His standards of judgment recognize discriminations unknown there. The plot line of the Old *Arcadia* is circular, not a single linear sequence of repetitive adventures but a pattern of related events each affecting the other with the complexity of real life. Such an advance in moral intelligence is not surprising but, in view of the ink wasted on describing Arcadia as the haunt of an ideal chivalry evicted from the harsh reality of Elizabethan politics, it bears mention.

In the Old *Arcadia* Sidney is more interested in the significance of the events he chronicles than in the events themselves; he appears as much concerned with motivation as with deed. The Old *Arcadia* falls far short of being a hair-raising romantic adventure, and even the New is less taken up with narrative per se than most readers suspect. Sidney emphasizes the oratorical displays that

3. Ibid., p. 140.

offer a chance to explore the feelings and beliefs of his characters. Self-analysis as Gynecia illustrates it is often shallow and rhetorical, but it does betray an interest in behavior more advanced than the breathless Boy-Scout enthusiasm for valorous deeds often ascribed to the *Arcadia*. Though the Old *Arcadia* displays (in its main prose story) no wealth of incident even compared with its revised fragment, it does occupy itself—through soliloquy, through change of narratorial distance, through contrast of incident with incident and style with style—with forming the reader's attitude toward the action before him. We do Sidney an injustice if we think of him practising in the Old *Arcadia* a simple form of romantic narration. Enthralling narrative is more often written at the expense of fully rounded characters and credible plot; Sidney is reluctant to sacrifice either element wholly in the Old *Arcadia*, though he often takes liberties with each.

The characters are types to an extent—their names alone show it. The incidents are taken from romance. Yet both elements are constantly pulled earthward; the characters become more real than Sidney first conceived them, and the incidents are so loaded with serious consequences that we forget their initial implausibility. Were Sidney's style less obtrusive it would be easier to think of the Old *Arcadia* as a novel in something like the modern sense, rather than as an idealistically imaginative romance. In expanding its range of incident beyond chivalric encounter in list and bed, Sidney obviously aimed at a closer relationship to day-to-day life than the highly formalized symbolism of the chivalric contest could offer.

Though it may have seemed so, I have not sought to prove the Old *Arcadia* superior to either Greek or medieval romance. But the wealth of detailed similarities between them and Sidney's work has often blinded students to the larger and more significant differences. These differences I have attempted, without invidious intent, to make clear. The changes which an imitative author makes in his sources are, after all, at least as likely to be indicative of purpose as the kind of work imitated.[4] Such is the case here; from sen-

4. See C. T. Prouty, "Some Observations on Shakespeare's Sources," *Shakespeare Jahrbuch*, 96 (1960), 64–77, for a persuasive defense of this contention.

timental erotic romance Sidney fashions moralistic prose fiction.

Sidney's indebtedness to previous prose fiction has been insufficiently marked. Consider, for example, a work which seems to have little enough in common with the Old *Arcadia*, Gascoigne's *The Adventures of Master F.J.* Gascoigne's story in its original form [5] is a plain tale of country-house seduction in which the Petrarchan verses and entreaties introduced into the text are frankly acknowledged as counters in the game of love. Gascoigne's tale has no "moral," nor has the author been accused of an oppressive idealism. Any raison d'être beyond entertainment that the tale has comes from its probable element of autobiography. Sidney's story has its autobiographical elements too, but they are not the most striking resemblance to Gascoigne's novella. Imagine for a moment the Old *Arcadia* as some of Sidney's critics wish he had written it—as a plain tale. Out go the long speeches, the equivocal narrator, the tropes and schemes. Two princes arrive in Arcadia, become enamored of the two princesses of the land, pursue them into retirement, seduce or attempt to seduce them, are caught, tried, sentenced, and then saved by the romantic bell. Outrageously stripped to its barest essentials, the romantic action is not in and of itself edifying, but it is believable, and its credibility is not radically affected by the idealistic rhetoric with which it is loaded. The basic seduction plot persists to contrast with the idealism of the royal lovers' acknowledged motivation. Gascoigne in 1574 had portrayed the Petrarchan conventions fighting under a dubious banner, and Sidney about 1580 does very much the same thing with brighter rhetorical colors. Sidney's idealism intensified the force of the protestations of courtly love, and his rhetorical genius augmented their beauty; but neither prevented his seeing through them to the actualities of human passion as clearly as did Gascoigne. Sidney simply draws the contrast more strongly; he offers a much less cynical attitude toward the Petrarchan pose and language on one hand, and a much stronger, more authentic passion on the other. But he makes essentially the same comparison Gas-

5. The original form is included in George Gascoigne, *An Hundreth Sundrie Flowres*, ed. C. T. Prouty (New York, 1942).

coigne had made; the actuality of passion is juxtaposed with the polite forms for expressing and consummating it.

Sidney's romance is much more often compared to *Euphues* than to *F.J.*, and the superficial resemblances are doubtless clearer: the neo-Greek literary machinery, the two friends' parallel adventures and the inevitable conflict of love and friendship, most of all the style. The differences, less obvious, are perhaps more interesting. Sidney's style is more variable than Lyly's. Lyly's is constant, rides over context like a steam roller; Sidney's is carefully integrated with the context. Lyly does not distance himself from his rhetoric, use its exaggerations for characterization, for dramatic effect. Although beneath the balanced antitheses we may observe his characters about the familiar business of seduction, Lyly fails to point to the inconsistency between word and deed. The "morals" his figures draw remain wholly on the surface; there is no indication of a greater moral intelligence behind them.

The fiction following the Old *Arcadia* gives us little more ethical guidance. Greene's *Menaphon*, if not frankly a parody of Sidney's romance, is a tedious imitation without either Sidney's sense of plot or his concern with the implications of his protagonists' exploits.[6] Lodge's *Rosalynde* is a straightforward Euphuistic pastoral romance, which Shakespeare ironically qualified in a manner unmistakably like Sidney's. Nashe parodies Sidney's use of poetic epithet unmercifully in *The Unfortunate Traveller*, and Jack Wilton's description of Surrey's tournament is a raucous laugh at Sidney, but the work as a whole painfully lacks an ethical center, is a mockery which provides no alternative to the behavior mocked. To my knowledge, Sidney alone offers a carefully constructed plot from which the moral of the work emerges logically and inevitably.[7] Notwithstanding the Old *Arcadia*'s reputation for frivolity, its intellectual and ethical fabric is tougher than that of

6. Kenneth Muir writes of Greene's debt to Sidney: "Later on he was influenced by the Greek romances and by Sidney's *Arcadia* and his style became pastoral and limpid" (introduction to *Elizabethan and Jacobean Prose: 1550–1620*, Pelican Books, 1956, pp. xxi-xxii).

7. His closest follower in this respect, though most students of Sidney would shudder to admit it, is Deloney's *Jack of Newbury*.

its followers, and more comprehensive than those of its Italian predecessors.

If Sidney's syncretistic imitation can be said to move in a single characteristic direction, it is toward an increasing concern with ethical purpose and didactic power. Borrowings become with Sidney increasingly serious; Italian frivolity becomes English morality, low comedy tends to become high. This is precisely what we should expect. We can list Sidney unhesitatingly with the English moralizing translators and imitators, so long as we keep in mind the unprecedented subtlety of his method. He was clearly no Fenton. Neither was he a reborn Heliodorus.

The revised fragment, the New *Arcadia,* is a study in itself. It poses two questions which this essay must acknowledge without fully answering. Why did Sidney revise? Why did he break off his revision? The answers given by critics up to now have proceeded on the assumption that the Old *Arcadia* is an idle frivolity or an immature first draft of the New. Irving Ribner expresses this view in a recent article:

> When Sir Philip Sidney transformed into a model of the Elizabethan prose epic the careless romance he had written to while away the hours of exile at Wilton in 1580, he did so, as Edwin Greenlaw has shown, with the consciousness that he must embody in his work the profoundest of his moral and political ideas.[8]

If this explanation of the relationship between the two is accepted, the reasons for revision seem obvious. Sidney tried his hand at romantic epic in the Old and, finding it skillful, began to write an epic in full earnest, an epic New *Arcadia* which only sudden death prevented his completing. Not he, but death, broke off the epic in midpassage. Why else, with a brilliant prose epic flowing so copiously, would he stop? Conveniently as these explanations fit one another, neither wholly fits the facts. Using what has been

---

8. "Machiavelli and Sidney: The *Arcadia* of 1590," *Studies in Philology,* 47 (1950), 152–72, 152.

learned about the Old *Arcadia* in this essay, I shall try to suggest new answers to both questions.

Why did Sidney revise? Zandvoort, assuming that though Old is less serious than New, both aim to be the same kind of work, stresses the growth of Sidney's powers from the first version to the second.[9] He finds progress in characterization (it is deeper, more realistic), in verisimilitude, in narrative technique (there are fewer clumsy transitions like "As you shall shortly heare"), in plot construction, and (in the "Erona" story, at least) in probability. An aside in the Old, such as "I have not a feeling Insighte enoughe into the matter, to bee able lyvely to express yt," is read as a confession by Sidney that his powers were not yet fully developed.[1] But even if we assume that the interval between the two versions was sufficiently long for any real maturation, either as what Zandvoort calls "thinker" or as "storyteller," to take place, we can still interpret the alterations differently. Change of intention and genre is as plausible an explanation as maturation. An understanding of the Old argues strongly against the charge of immaturity: although the plot of the New may be more elaborate than that of the Old, it is no more skillful, no more mature; while much of the narrative has been handed over to protagonists in the New, this change is not automatically an improvement. The two princesses are assigned some distinguishing characteristics in the New, but none not demanded by the added captivity episode. Most readers have thought the Old more probable than the New *Arcadia*, not less so. Perhaps we should expect a work revised to be not a better version of the same thing, but something basically different and more ambitious.

Those critics who believe that in the New Sidney aimed at the epic have seen the change from Old to New as one of intention not ability. Unfortunately, some have gone on to reason speciously that since the New is an epic and the Old *Arcadia* is not, the Old is inferior and unimportant. Thus Myrick writes:

9. *Sidney's Arcadia*, pp. 71 and passim.
1. Ibid., p. 82.

As to which version is more nearly an heroic poem we have thus
far found a few vague hints. In the use of prose as its chief me-
dium, in introducing considerable bodies of verse, in mingling
matters heroical with matters pastoral, the two versions offer no
contrast. In the avoidance of the supernatural, however, the
Old Arcadia is somewhat less consistent than the *New*, and yet
is not measurably nearer to Minturno's requirements for the
epic. Again, the *Old Arcadia* has nothing that suggests the classic
invocation. Finally, the expository paragraphs with which it
opens do not, like the opening passage of the *New Arcadia*, suggest a poetic example of the kind Sidney discusses in the *Defense*.
In general, therefore, the art of the original version seems less
consistent with itself and with the author's theories than does
that of the *New Arcadia*. . . . The art of the *Old Arcadia* is
therefore comparatively immature.

The inconsistency of the Old in the use of the supernatural is insignificant, amounting to only one instance in an eclogue. The
"classic invocation" which Myrick reads into the New can be
found just as easily in the Old. In fact, the whole chain of reasoning is highly vulnerable. The Old *Arcadia* is inconsistent not with
itself, nor with Sidney's poetic, but only with what Myrick's
thesis demands it should be. So Myrick writes: "In the *Old Arcadia*
there is no parallel to this stately and crowded pageant, embracing the whole range of human life." But perhaps Sidney did not intend a parallel. The Old *Arcadia* is not an inferior epic because it
is not an epic at all. Considering it as such brings the comparison
of the Old and the New full circle to Zandvoort's position again,
that both aim at the same goal.

Myrick continues: "The *Old Arcadia*, on the other hand, by its
more trivial subject, simpler technique, shorter action, narrower
range of characters, and comparative want of episodes, possesses
the epic magnificence to a small degree, or not at all." The technique in the Old is different, but not simpler; there is no "want of
episodes" in the Old—its technique just does not use episodes as
does the New; as for the action of either version, no one, it is perhaps safe to say, has wished it longer than it is. The "more trivial
subject" is love. Myrick writes that, "Warfare and great events are

absent from the *Old Arcadia* . . . these are the very subjects which add dignity to the story." Warfare is absent, certainly, but there is no lack of "great events" if didactic political upheaval can serve rather than chivalric adventure. Such invidious comparison is futile and misleading. To call the art of the New "more conscious than that of the Old, and more consistent with the author's theories," [2] is wholly misguided. The Old is not inferior to the New, it is different. Each version must be considered on its own terms. Broadly speaking, Sidney added in the New the second half of the chivalric ideal—the pursuit of honor. The heroic deeds of the two princes, which we hear about but so seldom see in the Old, are brought directly on stage in the New, and supply the "great events."

The style of the New, too, is closer to the Old *Arcadia* than is usually thought. Muir calls the style of the Old "rough and unpolished" compared to that of the New;[3] Zandvoort, although he admits that "there is little in the style of the revised version that is not actually or potentially present in the first draft," maintains that "most of the stylistic effects are heightened." [4] Zandvoort is closer to the truth, but the heightening is not obtrusive. I do not have space here for the extensive comparisons which documentation of this claim would require, but the reader has only to glance at the extensive side-by-side comparisons that Zandvoort prints [5] to see that the differences between the two are not great. If Sidney thought himself writing an heroic epic in his revision, he did not feel compelled to alter his style radically to suit his new subject. Myrick maintains that Sidney, finding himself "sick among the rest," "revises his original *Arcadia* in the light of critical principles." [6] But the sickness Sidney refers to is his stylistic affectations, and it hardly seems logical to make such a sickness the cause of a revision that is more "sick" still. Dissatisfaction with his style could not have been a major factor in Sidney's decision to revise.

2. *Sidney as Literary Craftsman*, quotations in order occurring on pp. 125–26, 174, 192, 129, 150.

3. "Sidney," p. 15.

4. *Sidney's Arcadia*, p. 175.

5. Ibid., pp. 53 ff.

6. *Sidney as Literary Craftsman*, p. 190.

It is generally agreed that the New *Arcadia* is an epic of some kind, whether heroic, pastoral, or romantic. Each of these kinds would contrast markedly with the Old *Arcadia* as we have come to know it, for none usually permits that ironical detachment from characters and dialogue which we have seen in the Old. If the New *Arcadia* is a serious epic, we must assume Arcadian loves and battles to be as completely idealistic as Goldman and others have thought them. Reading the Old *Arcadia* as in essence a romantic comedy, I find it difficult to believe that Sidney's attitude toward his fictional characters could have undergone so pronounced a metamorphosis. It is not impossible, of course, that Sidney would write a completely serious epic of love, but seeing the pervasive irony which surrounds love in *Astrophil and Stella* and the Old *Arcadia,* one cannot help looking for it in the New. The logical literary kind to which the New *Arcadia* belongs, I should like to suggest—and in this essay it can be no more than a suggestion—is the comic epic. No real outrage is committed against Sidney's revision by this suggestion. It does not preclude a serious meaning any more in the New than in the Old; far from denigrating Sidney's idealism, it may prove him all the more idealistic for holding ideals he saw the world would not tolerate.

There is an interesting passage in the *Defence of Poesie* which may possibly be an autobiographical allusion to the New *Arcadia* (perhaps to the Old as well):

> They [presumably Gosson and the other Puritan critics] say the *Comedies* rather teach then reprehend amorous conceits. They say the *Lirick* is larded with passionat *Sonets,* the *Elegiack* weeps the want of his mistresse, and that even to the *Heroical, Cupid* hath ambitiously climed. Alas Love, I would thou couldest as wel defend thy selfe, as thou canst offend others: I would those on whom thou doest attend, could either put thee away, or yeeld good reason why they keepe thee.[7]

The catalogue of reproaches, at any rate, fits Sidney's work well enough. Yet in the very passage where he seems to admit that he has made Cupid climb to the heroical, the laconic regret with

7. *Works,* 3, 30.

which he refers to the power of love should warn us that he was well aware of Cupid's limitations as hero. It seems logical to think that Sidney's rueful knowledge of the power of love would play a role in the New *Arcadia* just as it did in the Old. Many of the heroes' speeches, too, are transferred bodily to the New from the Old, and it seems inconceivable that the spirit in which we are to read them would differ drastically from one context to the other. Almost all of the Old, as Zandvoort points out, appears in the New in one form or another.[8] Coming from the Old to the New (as Sidney did, after all) it is hard, sometimes, to keep from smiling.

Heroism, as well as love, seems to have its limitations for Sidney in the New. Dametas and Clinias are the obvious illustrations of this increased irony in the New, comic counterparts to the more serious chivalric heroes. They show unmistakably that Sidney perceived the ludicrous aspects of the chivalric panoply he is said to have admired so unreservedly. Mopsa, too, tells a tale which is a parody of chivalric romance.[9] There is some evidence, as well, that Sidney carried over to the New not only the comic relief which a double plot offers, but the ironic qualification of the "high" plot as well. Zandvoort, appositely enough here, finds "an unmistakable undertone of irony running through these chapters, which is foreign to *Amadis*." [1] Examples of this are not hard to find: Chapter 28 in Book III of the New, where Anaxius and his brethren tangle with Zelmane (Pyrocles, the Cleophila of the Old), is a comic scene which ends with a slaughter falling markedly short of the heroical.[2]

Chivalry's heroism in the New *Arcadia* seems frequently less celebrated than its panoply. Chivalric pageantry, we are told, pleased the sweet tooth of the Elizabethans; Huizinga reminds us that it catered to the medieval need for drama.[3] We ought not to regard all the pageantry as heroical. Some of it—a good deal,

8. *Sidney's Arcadia*, pp. 71–72.
9. *Works, 1*, 241 ff.
1. *Sidney's Arcadia*, p. 107.
2. The comedy is clearly intentional. Pamela, casting off Anaxius' proferred hand in the previous chapter, remarks: "Proud beast (said she) yet thou plaiest worse thy Comedy, then thy Tragedy" (*Works, 1*, 507).
3. *Waning of the Middle Ages*, pp. 68–69.

one would suspect, for most modern readers—is simply long-winded description. The knightly combats adorn a tale whose basic didacticism is far more hard-headedly political. When Sidney remarks aside after the Iberian yearly joust, "But the delight of those pleasing sights have carried me too farre in an unnecessary discourse," [4] we are likely to agree. We can agree, however, without in any way impugning Sidney's devotion to chivalric honor, which ought not to be underestimated.[5]

We should not, then, uncritically accept the New as a serious epic. A comic epic seems a logical outgrowth of the original *Arcadia*, even though the New obviously does not fit into the genre at all points.

Why did Sidney break off his revision? If we dismiss for a moment the fixed idea that death broke it off for him, several possible explanations suggest themselves. He may have become bored. He may have sensed a change of fashion in language, though this is less likely. The revision may have become unmanageably long and offended Sidney's architectonic sense. Moreover, it may have (with the captivity episode, perhaps) so veered away from its original form and direction that Sidney saw no way to return to course without a complete rewriting. To my knowledge, Tucker Brooke is the only scholar who has suggested this possibility: "It is clear, however, that the New *Arcadia* was being carried entirely out of touch with the Old, and it seems doubtful whether Sidney could have brought it to any consistent conclusion." [6] Sidney may well have written himself into a corner. If the protagonists had emerged from the captivity episode with flying colors, it is hard to see how Sidney could have put them on trial as he does in the Old. This is doubly true since in the New as we have it the royal lovers do nothing for which to be tried, and the trial would prob-

4. *Works, 1,* 286.
5. Languet writes revealingly to Sidney: "But you, out of mere love of fame and honour, and to have an opportunity of displaying your courage . . . You and your fellows, I mean men of noble birth, consider that nothing brings you more honour than wholesale slaughter" (*The Correspondence of Sir Philip Sidney and Hubert Languet,* trans. S. A. Pears, London, 1845, p. 154).
6. *A Literary History of England,* p. 476.

ably have been a dramatic anticlimax as well. But without the trial, we are likely to overlook the irony of Sidney's valuation of love or, at the least, be thoroughly confused by the absence of any final moral center in the tale. Sidney could have thought either course—with or without the trial—finally impossible.

We can see, too, a deeper contradiction, one between the comic elements in the Old and the seriousness of the New. Sidney could depend on the restricted aristocratic audience of the Old to know when to laugh, but could he place the same dependence on a wider and more heterogeneous one? The shortcuts of technique, the stylistic and rhetorical maneuver, might well be missed by a less sophisticated audience. And if his intentions were totally heroic in the New, his heroes would have a difficult past to live down in both the public's and the artist's mind. Furthermore, in a wholly serious work, would not a snap ending be far more offensive than it is in the Old?

These questions cannot be answered here, but the problems they pose make very doubtful the wisdom of regarding the composite folio of 1593—the *Arcadia*—as representing Sidney's final intention. I have tried to stress the ways in which the New is a continuation of the Old, but even with such stress the two are clearly very different works. How Sidney completed the first is no guide to how he would have finished the second. It may be objected that the oracle necessitates an ending in the New similar to that in the Old. I do not think this is necessarily true, but if Sidney could not have devised another ending to fit the oracle, one might plausibly guess that he would have chosen to leave his revision unfinished rather than rewrite his tale. In any event, it is clearly unwarranted to use part of the Old as an ending to the New. We must bear with an unsatisfactory state of affairs; two *Arcadias*, one complete and one not, and a respectable bastard third which combines them both. Each has its own uses and virtues, the first two for a study of Sidney, the last for Sidney's place in literary history. But we should keep the differences between Old and New, and the limitations of each, clearly in mind.

8. Conclusion

If Sidney had not been canonized as a kind of plaster saint of chivalry, the *Arcadia* might not now be thought such a plaster romance. A false conception of the *Arcadias*, Old and New, has been created by a false conception of the man. Fulke Greville started it, of course, with a biography which is far more a saint's life than a dispassionate collection of facts. Subsequent biographers have, in the absence of reliable new information about Sidney's life, simply retailed Greville's praise. And, unfortunately, his attitude toward Sidney as well. Our image of Sidney has suffered from the surfeit of his admirers; to this day there is no unalloyed account of the facts of his life. Instead, our meager knowledge is pieced out with such embarrassing rhapsodizing as this:

> Now and then a man transcends the morals and manners of his age and nation, living so honestly and so valiantly that he stands forth as a sea-mark upon the coasts of time. Sidney, as his most devoted friend [Greville] recognized, was such a man.[1]

No one can doubt that Sidney was a remarkable man, possessing a remarkable talent, but he was a man still, not a visitation of

1. Goldman, *Sidney and the Arcadia*, p. 20.

perfection. Few men can have been more quintessentially of their times than Sidney; his fame depends not on his transcendence of the "morals and manners" of his age but on his embodiment of them.

The Sidney legend has obscured both the man and his work. Students under its influence have seen a penetrating and original political philosopher where there was only "an ardent partisan of the status quo." [2] They have seen a skillful diplomat where there was an idealistic but tactless young man. What concerns us here more nearly, they have focused so exclusively on the idealistic devotee of chivalry and chivalrous rhetoric that they have blocked out the extremely clever, humorous parodist and dramatist who lurks behind the devotee. The mixture of Sancho Panza in their knight has passed by undetected.

But it is there. A perceptive reader of the *Arcadia,* New or Old, cannot escape the evidences of Sidney's strong sense of the ludicrous, in both love and war. Even if we ignore the evidence *Astrophil and Stella* presents of a passionate attachment to the world of flesh (as to an extent many critics have done) the humor in the *Arcadia* would dissolve any ethereal portrait of Sidney as the last hope of chivalry. In the Old *Arcadia,* at least, the bravery of his heroes is more Hotspur's than Hal's, his heroines compounded more of Rosalind than Juliet. We should stop making allowances for Sidney's supposed unrelieved idealism and accept the comedy that is its inevitable accompaniment in any balanced conception of human life.

In this investigation I have ignored the Sidney legend largely because I do not believe it, but also because it blurs our view of the Old *Arcadia.* The Sidney who emerges from the Old *Arcadia* read without crippling predispositions is still an idealist and a moralist, but more disillusioned, more tolerant, and readier to laugh than the plaster saint.

The *Arcadia* has been a literary monument for so long, and its style has bored and irritated so many readers, that a student who

2. Fritz Caspari, *Humanism and the Social Order in Tudor England* (Chicago, 1954), p. 171.

thinks the romance still viable is suspected of pedantry or pre-
ciosity or both. But an enjoyable reading of either version need
not be based on these qualities, useful as they often are. If we
approach Sidney's romance without undue solemnity, we can
read it with pleasure.

We should not, of course, commit the opposite error and regard
the Old *Arcadia* as a mere frivolity, but we should not discard our
sense of humor when we read. Especially is this true of the Old
Arcadia. Its didacticism is tempered by a strong element of burlesque. The spirit in which we are to read is a comic spirit.

To call the Old *Arcadia* an epic, Christian, romantic, chivalric,
or other, seems out of the question. It is a romantic comedy, about
what all romantic comedies are about—the triumph of love. And
like others which followed it (early Shakespearean comedy is the
best example), it mocks the language of love as well. No idealization of love takes place, and no total cynical rejection either. A
passage in the New *Arcadia* sums up Sidney's feeling about love
in both romances: "But o Love, it is thou that doost it: thou
changest name upon name; thou disguisest our bodies, and dis-
figurest our mindes. But in deed thou hast reason, for though the
wayes be foule, the journeys end is most faire and honourable." [3]
The reflection is hardly new; few of Sidney's were. His originality
lies in his enormous talent, in the sheer virtuosity with which he
manipulated his rhetorical style, using it to demonstrate the follies,
and the joys, of love. Sidney was doubtless infatuated with words,
and wielded the weapons of rhetoric with unmistakable gusto,
but he was aware of the dangers of a highly rhetorical style—and
of its comic potentialities as well.

The Old *Arcadia*, interesting as it is for what it tells us of the
New or the composite *Arcadia*, stands finally on its own. It needs
no patronization, it does not demand that allowances continually
be made for period, style, and author. We must read it on the
terms of its time, to be sure, but it needs no crutches, historical or
aesthetic. Its didacticism is not shallow or easy, its style not en-
crusted with meaningless ornament. Its chivalric idealism is not

3. *Works, I,* 117.

unmixed with humor. Nothing else quite like it has been left us in English.

"*Arcadia*," writes Muir, "is the first great masterpiece of Elizabethan prose, which might be more generally acknowledged as such if it were more readily accessible to the general reader." [4] But it is the style, not the inaccessibility of the *Arcadia*, which has put readers off. They have disliked it primarily, I feel, because they misunderstood it. It has been dismissed as an unfortunate and transient infatuation with a then relatively unexplored frontier of the English language. A principal purpose of this inquiry has been to make clear in what ways this assessment is, and more importantly is not, true of the first version of Sidney's romance. The second main source of discontent is the facility with which Sidney draws the reader's moral verdicts for him. His world view has seemed to many so complete and so readily applicable that it must have been superficial. This, too, seems a misunderstanding, one I have tried to clarify by pointing out the fundamentally dialectic character of the Old *Arcadia*, and the peculiarly rhetorical quality of its obvious moralizations. The conception of the Old *Arcadia*, and of Sidney, which has emerged from my attempt to meet these two objections differs markedly from the accepted view. The man, with his lusts and frustrations, joins the ranks of humanity again, and the romance, with its ironical qualifications of love and war, becomes finally an attempt not to create an ideal world, but to deal with men as men are.

4. "Sidney," p. 35.

Works Cited

Aristotle, *Rhetorica*, trans. W. Rhys Roberts; *The Works of Aristotle*, 9, ed. W. D. Ross, Oxford, 1924.

Aristotle's Theory of Poetry and Fine Art, trans. S. H. Butcher, 4th ed. London, 1920.

Atkins, J. W. H., "Elizabethan Prose Fiction," *Cambridge History of English Literature*, 3 (1909).

Auerbach, Erich, *Mimesis*, trans. Willard R. Trask, Princeton, New Jersey, 1953.

Boas, Frederick S., *Sir Philip Sidney, Representative Elizabethan: His Life and Writings*, London, 1955.

Booth, Wayne C., *The Rhetoric of Fiction*, Chicago, 1961.

Brie, Friedrich, *Sidneys Arcadia*, Quellen und Forschungen, 124, Strassburg, 1918.

Brooke, Tucker, "The Renaissance," in Albert C. Baugh et al., *A Literary History of England*, New York, 1948.

Burckhardt, Jacob, *The Civilization of the Renaissance in Italy*, trans. S. G. C. Middlemore, ed. L. Goldscheider (from 4th ed. rev. Phaidon Press), New York, 1951.

Caspari, Fritz, *Humanism and the Social Order in Tudor England*, (Fyler), Chicago, 1954.

Castiglione, Baldesar, *The Book of the Courtier*, trans. Charles S. Singleton, Anchor Books, 1959.

Cicero, *Brutus*, English trans. G. L. Hendrickson; *Orator*, English trans. H. M. Hubbell; Loeb Classical Library, 1939.

———, *De Oratore*, English trans. E. W. Sutton and H. Rackham, 2 vols. rev. ed., Loeb Classical Library, 1959.

[Cicero], *Ad C. Herennium: De Ratione Dicendi* (Rhetorica Ad Herennium), English trans. Harry Caplan, Loeb Classical Library, 1954.

Cooke, Paul John, "The Spanish Romances in Sir Philip Sidney's *Arcadia*," abstract of unpublished dissertation, University of Illinois, 1931.

Cooper, Lane, *Theories of Style*, London, 1907.

Crane, W. G., *Wit and Rhetoric in the Renaissance*, New York, 1937.

Danby, John F., *Poets on Fortune's Hill: Studies in Sidney, Shakespeare, Beaumont and Fletcher*, London, 1952.

Davis, Walter R., "Thematic Unity in the *New Arcadia*," *Studies in Philology*, 57 (1960), 123–43.

Dobell, Bertram, "New Light upon Sir Philip Sidney's 'Arcadia,' " *Quarterly Review*, 211 (1909), 74–100.

Duhamel, P. Albert, "Sidney's *Arcadia* and Elizabethan Rhetoric," *Studies in Philology*, 45 (1948), 134–50.

Fisher, George William, *Annals of Shrewsbury School*, London, 1899.

Fraunce, Abraham, *The Arcadian Rhetorike*, ed. Ethel Seaton from edition of 1588, Luttrell Society Reprints, No. 9, Oxford, 1950.

Genouy, Hector, *L' "Arcadia" de Sidney dans ses rapports avec l' "Arcadia" de Sannazaro et la "Diana" de Montemayor*, Montpellier, 1928.

Goldman, Marcus S., *Sir Philip Sidney and the Arcadia*, Reprinted from University of Illinois Studies in Language and Literature, 17, Nos. 1–2, 1934.

Gosson, Stephen, *The School of Abuse*, ed. E. Arber, English Reprints, London, 1868.

Greg, Walter W., *Pastoral Poetry and Pastoral Drama*, New York, 1959.

Greville, Sir Fulke, *Life of Sir Philip Sidney*, ed. Nowell Smith, Oxford, 1907.

Hadas, Moses, trans., *Three Greek Romances*, Anchor Books, 1953.

Harkness, Stanley, *The Prose Style of Sir Philip Sidney*, University of Wisconsin Studies in Language and Literature, 2 (Madison, 1918), 57–76.

Hazlitt, William, "Lectures on the Age of Elizabeth," in *The Collected Works of William Hazlitt*, 12 vols. ed. A. P. Waller and Arnold Glover, 5, London, 1902.

Hill, Herbert Wynford, *Sidney's "Arcadia" and the Elizabethan Drama*, University of Nevada Studies, 1–3 (1908–1911), 1–59.

Howell, Wilbur Samuel, *Logic and Rhetoric in England, 1500–1700*, New York, 1961.

Huizinga, J., *The Waning of the Middle Ages*, London, 1924.

Jones, R. F., *The Triumph of the English Language*, Stanford, 1953.

Joseph, Sister Miriam, C.S.C., *Shakespeare's Use of the Arts of Language*, New York, 1947.

Jusserand, J. J., *The English Novel in the Time of Shakespeare*, trans. Elizabeth Lee, 4th ed. London, 1901.

Krapp, George Phillip, *The Rise of English Literary Prose*, New York, 1915.

Lewis, C. S., *English Literature in the Sixteenth Century; excluding Drama*, Oxford, 1954.

Miller, Peter MacNaughton, Jr., "The Rhetoric of Sidney's *Arcadia*," unpublished dissertation, Princeton University, 1939.

Montgomery, Robert L., Jr., *Symmetry and Sense: The Poetry of Sir Philip Sidney*, Austin, Texas, 1961.

Muir, Kenneth, ed., *Elizabethan and Jacobean Prose: 1500-1620*, Pelican Books, 1956.

———, "Sir Philip Sidney," *Writers and Their Work*, No. 120, London, 1960.

Works Cited

Myrick, Kenneth Orne, *Sir Philip Sidney as a Literary Craftsman*, Harvard Studies in English, 14, Cambridge, Mass., 1935.

Osborn, Albert W., *Sir Philip Sidney en France*, Paris, 1932.

Palmer, John, *Comic Characters of Shakespeare*, London, 1946.

Peacham, Henry, *The Garden of Eloquence (1593)*, ed. William G. Crane, Scholars' Facsimiles and Reprints, Gainesville, Florida, 1954.

Pears, Steuart A., trans., *The Correspondence of Sir Philip Sidney and Hubert Languet*, London, 1845.

Potts, L. C., *Comedy*, London, n.d.

Praz, Mario, "Sidney's Original Arcadia," *London Mercury*, 15 (1926–1927), 507–14.

Prouty, Charles T., "Some Observations on Shakespeare's Sources," *Shakespeare Jahrbuch*, 96 (1960), 64–77.

Ringler, William, *Stephen Gosson: A Biography and Critical Study*, Princeton Studies in English, 25, Princeton, 1942.

Rougemont, Denis de, *Love in the Western World*, trans. Montgomery Belgion, rev. and augmented edition, Anchor Books, 1957.

Rowe, Kenneth Thorpe, *Romantic Love and Parental Authority in Sidney's "Arcadia,"* University of Michigan Contributions in Modern Philology 4, 1947.

Sannazaro, Iacobo, *Opere Volgari*, ed. Alfredo Mauro, Bari, 1961.

Scribner, Brother Simon, *Figures of Word-Repetition in the First Book of Sir Philip Sidney's Arcadia*, Washington, D.C., 1948.

The Prose Works of Sir Philip Sidney, ed. Albert Feuillerat, 4 vols. Cambridge, England, 1962.

The Poems of Sir Philip Sidney, ed. William A. Ringler, Jr., Oxford, 1962.

Smith, G. Gregory, *Elizabethan Critical Essays*, 2 vols. London, 1904.

Tillyard, E. M. W., *The English Epic*, New York, 1954.

———, *Shakespeare's Last Plays*, London, 1954.

Underdowne, Thomas, trans., *Heliodorus' An Æthiopian Historie*, London, 1606.

Waith, Eugene M., *The Pattern of Tragicomedy in Beaumont and Fletcher*, Yale Studies in English, 120. New Haven, 1952.

Wallace, Malcolm W., *The Life of Sir Philip Sidney*, Cambridge, 1915.

Wilson, Mona, *Sir Philip Sidney*, New York, 1932.

Wilson, Thomas, *The Arte of Rhetorique*, ed. G. H. Mair, Oxford, 1909.

Wimsatt, William K., Jr. and Cleanth Brooks, *Literary Criticism: A Short History*, New York, 1957.

Wolff, Samuel Lee, *The Greek Romances in Elizabethan Prose Fiction*, New York, 1912.

Zandvoort, R. W., *Sidney's Arcadia: A Comparison between the Two Versions*, Amsterdam, 1929.

Index

411

Index

Cardan, Jerome, 173

Casella, Mario, 9

Caspari, Fritz, 403 n. 2

Castiglione, Baldassare, *Il Libro del Cortegiano*, 68, 77 n. 5, 84 n. 1, 85 n. 2, 123 n. 4, 128 n. 5, 160 n. 2, 162, 174, 197, 341 n. 6

Catullus, 46

Centorio, Ascanio, 20–21, 22; *L'Aura Soave*, 35, 42

Cervantes, Miguel de, 36; *Don Quixote*, 9, 10; *Galatea*, 26, 35

Chaucer, Geoffrey, 24 n. 1, 49 n. 5, 87 n. 6, 381

Chivalric: tradition, 10; romance, 21–22; sources for *Arcadia*, 45, 47; elements in *Arcadia*, 54, 114, 198, 312, 370, 373–74, 378–81 passim, 390, 391, 397, 399, 400

Chivalry, decay of, 371

Chrétien de Troyes, 9, 10, 389

Christian elements in *Arcadia*, 65, 75–76, 77, 81, 82, 227, 284, 288, 376, 378

Cicero, 142 n. 5, 239, 241, 337, 338, 339

Cinthio, G. B. Giraldi, 9

Cleonarde, 338 n. 8

Colonna, Francesco, *Hypnerotomachia*, 87–88

Commedia dell' Arte, 360

Cooke, P. J., 194

Corral, Don Gabriel de, 26, 38

Counter Reformation, 57 n. 4

Coverdale, Miles, 76

Crane, W. G., 340

Cumont, Franz, 86–87, n. 4

Cythera, Renaissance associations for, 86–88

Danby, J. F., 56 n. 1, 75 n. 9, 285, 370–71, 376

Dante Alighieri, 7, 61, 86 n. 3, 178

Daphnis and Chloe, 8, 32–34, 37

Davis, Walter R., 79 n. 7, 97 n. 7, 200–01, 376

Deloney, Thomas, *Jack of Newbury*, 393 n. 7

Desportes, Philippe, 98 n. 8

Devereux, Penelope, 188, 230, 378

Dickens, Charles, 380

Dobell, Bertram, 49 n. 5, 188, 189, 191, 194 n. 7, 376

Donne, John, 340

Dowland, John, 76

Dowlin, C. M., 49 n. 5

Du Bartas, Guillaume de Salluste, 86 n. 3

Duhamel, P. Albert, 253 n. 8, 355

Dryden, John, 347

Eclogue: classical pastoral, 7; settting of, 8, 28; Renaissance, 11–12; as source of Sannazaro's *Arcadia*, 19; source for Sidney's *Arcadia*, 45. See *also* Sidney, *Arcadia*

Elegies, Renaissance, 45

Elizabeth I, 144, 241, 244

Elyot, Sir Thomas, 75, 76, 86–87 n. 4, 149

Emblem books, 142

England, equated with Arcadia, 389

Epic: and romance plot, 9; Italian cavalleresque, 10; tradition vs. pastoral, 28, 37; elements of in romance, 38; not mode of Old *Arcadia*, 365, 404; New *Arcadia* as, 395, 396, 398

Erasmus, 62 n. 3, 148, 149, 173

Fenton, Sir Geoffrey, 394

Feuillerat, Albert, 2, 192, 194 n. 7

Ficino, Marsilio, 67 n. 2, 68, 69, 70, 71, 86–87, 104 n. 9, 123, 123 n. 4, 130 n. 7, 141, 142, 174

Firenzuola, Agnolo, 20

Fletcher, John, 366

Fowler, Earl B., 88 n. 8

Fraunce, Abraham, 79 n. 7, 86–87 n. 4

Frye, Northrop, 10 n. 5

Fulgentius, 142

Gálvez de Montalvo, Luis, 20, 46–47, 54; elements in *Arcadia* compared with, 47 n. 8

Gascoigne, George, 82, 144, 145; *The Adventures of Master F. J.* as source of *Arcadia*, 392–93

Index

Index

Medieval (*continued*)
  as element of Renaissance pastoral
  romance, 7–8; Boccaccio's *Ameto*
  as, 17; critique of in *Arcadia*,
  165 n. 8 m. romance: *Arcadia's* dis-
  similarities to, 380; and New *Ar-
  cadia*, 390
Melbancke, Brian, 82, 143, 145
Menéndez y Pelayo, Marcelino, 47 n. 8
Menina e Moça, 22, 37
Mercader, Don Gaspar, 20
Meres, Francis, 193
Mérimée, Henri, 24 n. 1
Miller, Peter MacNaughton, 348 n. 9
Milton, John, 65, 67 n. 3, 74, 179
Minturno, Antonio, 9, 26 n. 3, 396
Mirrour for Magistrates, 120, 241, 362
Molyneux, Edmund, 185, 187, 341–42,
  n. 6
Montemayor, Jorge de, *Diana*, 13, 22–
  27, 35, 36, 38, 49, 52, 54, 55, 56, 57, 90,
  122, 143, 145, 168; influence of, 26–27,
  42–43; influence on Sidney, 46, 50
Montgomery, Robert L., 354 n. 4, 372–
  73
Moody, William Vaughn, 46
More, Thomas, 173
Mornay, Philippe de, seigneur du
  Plessis-Marly, 63 n. 4, 140, 163 n. 7
Muir, Kenneth, 192 n. 4, 321, 393, 397,
  405
Myrick, Kenneth Orne, 5 n. 3, 121 n. 1,
  132, 185 n. 1, 192, 194, 194 n. 7, 318,
  319, 342, 356–57, 370, 395–96, 397

Nashe, Thomas, *The Unfortunate
  Traveller*, 383, 393
Nelson, William, 83 n. 9
Nenna, G. B., 142
Neoplatonism. *See entry under* Plato

Obryzius, Robertus, 12 n. 7
Osborn, Albert W., 192 n. 4
Ovid, 13, 31, 35, 79 n. 7, 338 n. 8

Palmer, John, 369
Pandosto, 39

Paradise, Garden of: Arcadia's relation
  to, 60–62, 67
Paris, Judgment of, 142, 143
Pastoral romance: tradition of, 5, 7, 13,
  168; Renaissance p. romances, 4, 7,
  34; and *Arcadia*, 49–52, 59, 89, 168–
  79, 193–94, 325; *Arcadia* distinct
  from, 54; Sidney's innovations in,
  55–56; Sidney's place in, 57; consideration of Old *Arcadia* as antipastoral, 360–61. *See also* Romance
Pastoral tradition: concepts of good
  and evil in, 9; unity in, 10–13; pushed
  toward plot emphasis, 22; prose becomes dominant in, 26; settings used
  in, 27, 28, 36; Renaissance inheritance from classical, 34, 36; and romance, 37; schematic action of, 38–
  39; sources for *Arcadia*, 45; Sidney's
  debt to, 50; Sidney's grasp of philosophical implications, 163; elements
  in Old *Arcadia*, 213, 215
Peacham, Henry, 338
Peele, George, 142
Pembroke, Countess of. *See* Herbert,
  Mary
Perkinson, Richard H., 49 n. 5
Petrarch, 7, 13, 35, 98 n. 8, 348; (-an)
  elements in *Arcadia*, 372, 374; (-an)
  conventions, 377, 389 n. 1, 392
Pico della Mirandola, Giovanni, Conte,
  69, 123 n. 4, 142, 174
Pigna, Giambattista, 9
Plato, and Platonic elements in *Arca-
  dia*, 47, 86, 137–42 passim, 144–57
  passim, 169, 173, 343 n. 9, 372, 378;
  Neoplatonic (Renaissance) thought,
  67 n. 2, 82, 84, 94, 104, 128 n. 5, 173,
  255, 372; Sidney's departures from,
  83
Plotinus, 65, 66, 67 n. 2, 94–95, 163 n. 6
Poirer, Michel, 98 n. 8
Pole, Reginald, 173
Politics, Renaissance theorists' view of,
  137. For political elements in *Arca-
  dia*, see Sidney, *Arcadia*
Ponsonbie (Ponsonby), William, 2, 187

414

Index

415

Index